ALASTAIR SAWDAY'S
SPECIAL PLACES TO STAY

ITALY

Design:	Caroline King
Maps & Mapping:	Bartholomew Mapping, a division of HarperCollins, Glasgow
Printing:	Canale, Italy
UK Distribution:	Portfolio, Greenford, Middlesex
US Distribution:	The Globe Pequot Press, Guilford, Connecticut

Published in 2003

Alastair Sawday Publishing Co. Ltd
The Home Farm Stables, Barrow Gurney, Bristol BS48 3RW
Tel: +44 (0)1275 464891 Fax: +44 (0)1275 464887
E-mail: info@specialplacestostay.com Web: www.specialplacestostay.com

The Globe Pequot Press
P. O. Box 480, Guilford, Connecticut 06437, USA
Tel: +1 203 458 4500 Fax: +1 203 458 4601
E-mail: info@globe-pequot.com Web: www.GlobePequot.com

Third edition

Copyright © 2003 Alastair Sawday Publishing Co. Ltd

ISBN 1-901970-37-X in the UK
ISBN 0-7627-2858-2 in the US

Printed in Italy

A WORD FROM ALASTAIR SAWDAY

Our views on any country are often shaped by an embarrassingly limited range of sources: newspaper articles, conversations and even brief visits, perhaps a book or a work of art. Mention 'Rome' and some of us think of Caesar. Try 'Bologna', and see how we think of pasta sauce. The same with Sicily and the Mafiosi. It is all slightly barmy, but that is how it is for many of us. Now, even if you can tell a dome from a *duomo* and a small canal from a Canaletto, I challenge you to get more under the skin of Italy than you can with this book tucked under your arm.

We are launching this third edition with terrific confidence – for it's the best yet. Our inspectors have penetrated the furthest corners of Italy and have found delights hitherto unimagined. Friendships have been formed, new food enjoyed, new wines uncorked and prejudices tossed aside. People have stayed in the strangest and most entertaining places – from mediaeval castles to glitzy town houses. Rare and wonderful characters have been met, lessons learned and new ideas rolled around the mind.

When I am perusing the draft version of this book I am struck by how many of the owners have opted out of the urban rat-race to pursue radically different careers – supported by their B&B or small hotel. High-strutting Milanese film-producers have turned tail and gone to the hills; business executives have climbed out of their grey trousers and into farming garb. The results are usually happy, and you can be the beneficiaries, for it is good to be in the company of contented people in beautiful places.

We are proud of this edition and of the people and places in it. I hope you will have marvellous tales to tell upon your return.

Alastair Sawday

ACKNOWLEDGEMENTS

We owe the triumphal success of this third edition to the resourcefulness and sheer hard work of Emma Carey and Philippa Rogers. They put a team of inspectors together – who turned out to be superb. They then worked extraordinary charms on Italian owners for there are some 120 new ones in this book. In fact, I don't imagine that the owners had much chance – they were hooked.

But let us not imagine worn-down women shackled irretrievably to their desks: Emma travelled to Sicily to cast an eagle eye over places there; Philippa careered around the Bologna area. They know Italy well and have brought terrific linguistic gifts to the task.

Paul Groom and Rachel Coe, among others, have provided solid and intelligent support on the production side, Jo Boissevain and Vivien Cripps have brought their own creative flair to the writing, while Jenny Purdy has dealt brilliantly with the vagaries of the Italian fiscal system. And lastly, this third edition stands squarely on the shoulders of the second, for which we have Rose Shawe-Taylor to thank.

Alastair Sawday

Series Editor:	Alastair Sawday
Editor:	Emma Carey
Assistant to Editor:	Philippa Rogers
Editorial Director:	Annie Shillito
Production Manager:	Julia Richardson
Web & IT:	Russell Wilkinson, Matt Kenefick
Editorial:	Sarah Bolton, Roanne Finch, Jessica Hughes, Danielle Williams
Copy Editor:	Jo Boissevain
Production Assistants:	Rachel Coe, Paul Groom, Beth Thomas
Accounts:	Bridget Bishop, Sheila Clifton, Jenny Purdy, Sandra Hassell
PR:	Sarah Bolton
Sales & Marketing:	Siobhan Flynn, Julia Forster
Writing:	Jo Boissevain, Vivien Cripps
Inspections:	Richard & Linda Armspach, Fiona Bennie, Emma Carey, Lucinda Carling, Denise Goss, Jill Greetham, Aideen Reid, Philippa Rogers, Juliet Walford.

And special thanks to Maria-Vittoria Addis for all of her help and to those people, not mentioned here, who visited just one or two places for us.

WHAT'S IN THE BOOK?

CONTENTS

CONTENTS

CONTENTS

CONTENTS

INTRODUCTION

Compiling this edition has given me fascinating new insights into the *Bel Paese*. Owners have been charming, relaxed and entertaining. Any problems have been met with good-natured helpfulness and my sometimes rusty Italian with a well-intentioned grammar lesson!

Rumour had it that communicating with Italy was frustrating; certainly the post can be 'erratic'. But, the Italians have wholeheartedly embraced new technology and whether they run a luxury hotel or a tiny *agriturismo* know how to use the web and e-mail. This has made putting a book together, and organising an Italian holiday, far easier than it was before. So, if you're nervous about speaking Italian, just get online and hurdle the language barrier.

This guide is the perfect antidote to all that talk about Europe becoming homogenised. Italians have only lived together as one nation since 1861 and the position and geography of the country have enabled them to hold onto their strong regional identities. The baffling assortment of dialects reflects them, as do the food and architecture. The enormous variety of places to stay in Italy is striking, too. There are huge regional differences, and few set patterns on how places 'should' be run. The result is a very personal and wide range of places to lay your head.

The well-known hot spots, like Tuscany, are well-represented here but we have found special places all over the country: from the heel of Puglia to the mountains of Val d'Aosta via Italy's amazing islands. Hotels, inns and guesthouses all have their place. The *agriturismi* phenomenon, which started with government initiatives to boost the rural economy, is also well represented. Guests get a taste of life on a working farm or estate and owners share their homes with guests keen to learn more about Italy. *Agriturismi* have gone from strength to strength, and are creeping further south. Bed & Breakfasts ('Baydanbrreekfass') have recently appeared on the scene, a very personal alternative to hotels, sometimes simple, sometimes more affordable luxury, and the chance to stay in some gorgeous homes.

INTRODUCTION

What is a Special Place?

We look for owners, homes and hotels that we like – and we are fiercely subjective in our choices. 'Special' for us is not about the number of creature comforts but relates to many different elements that make a place 'work'. Certainly the way guests are treated comes as high on our list as the setting, the architecture and the food.

How do we choose our Special Places?

We have selected the widest range of possibilities for you to choose from – castles, villas, hotels, farmhouses, simple country inns – even a monastery or two. The colourful diversity of Italy is reflected here, and these special places won't all be memorable for the same reason. It might be breakfast under the frescoed ceiling of a Renaissance villa that is special, or a large and boisterously friendly dinner in a farmhouse kitchen, or the view from the window of your monastic cell. We have selected not necessarily the most opulent places to stay, but the most interesting and satisfying.

What to expect

With Italy it's not always easy to distinguish myth from reality. For centuries poets and painters (and everyone else who's ever been there) have fallen in love with it. And because Italy has, to quote Lord Byron, "the fatal gift of beauty" it is easy to forget that it can also be downright ugly. Don't be put off when you discover that there are factories (yes, even in Tuscany), pylons and overhead cables, not to mention great swathes of industrial plant. These things can't be airbrushed out, but acknowledge that they exist and they won't spoil your fun.

Finding the right place for you

It's our job to help you find a place you like. We give honest descriptions of our houses and owners and you should glean from the write-up what the owners, manager or staff are like and how formal or casual the place is. This edition also includes a huge number of self-catering possibilities (see the Quick Reference Indices at the back of the book).

In each write-up there are clues about the mood of the house, and there is an enormous variety within this book. The older ones may seem more immediately appealing, but don't overlook the more modern ones - they often have great personality, too. It's always the owners and their staff who have the biggest influence on the atmosphere you experience.

INTRODUCTION

Each entry is simply labelled (e.g. B&B or hotel) to guide you but these pages reveal many different terms to describe the various hostelries. We include no star ratings in our guides; let our descriptions inform you. This list serves as a rough guide to what you might expect to find behind each name.

Locanda Literally means 'inn' but is sometimes used to describe a restaurant only.

Agriturismo Farm with rooms or apartments.

Azienda Agraria/Agricola Farm company.

Country House A new concept in Italian hospitality, usually family-run and akin to a villa.

Podere Farm or smallholding.

Cascina Originally a farmhouse.

Corte Literally, court.

Albergo The Italian word for 'hotel' but perhaps smaller and more personal than its larger sister.

Palazzo Palace or, more usually, mansion.

Cà/Casa (Cà in Venetian dialect) House.

Villa Privately owned, usually, but not always, a country residence.

Relais An imported French term meaning 'inn'.

Residenza An apartment or house with rooms for guests (not manned 24 hours, but usually 8am-8pm). Guests have a key to come and go as they please and use of communal areas.

How to use
this book

Map

Look at the map at the front of the book to find your area, then the detailed maps to find the places. The numbers correspond to the page numbers of the book. Or choose from the individual entries, then check the map reference at the bottom of the page. Our maps are for guidance only; take a detailed road map to find your way around. Self-catering places are marked in pink on the maps; others are marked in blue.

Rooms

We tell you about the range of accommodation in singles, doubles, twins, family rooms and suites as well as apartments and whole houses. A 'family' room is a loose term because in Italy triples and quadruples can often sleep more than the heading suggests; extra beds can often be added for children, usually with an extra charge. Check when booking.

INTRODUCTION

Where an entry reads 4 + 2 this means 4 rooms and '2' apartments or similar are available for self-catering.

Bathrooms

Assume that bathrooms are en suite unless we say otherwise.

Symbols

There is an explanation of our symbols on the inside of the back cover. These are intended as a guide rather than as an unequivocal statement of fact, and should an owner not have the symbol that you're looking for, it's still worth discussing your needs.

Practical matters

Prices

The prices we quote are the room prices per night unless otherwise stated. In other words, we specify if the price is per person (p.p.) or per week for self-catering. If lunch and dinner are available we try to give you an approximate price and specify if wine is included.

Prices quoted are those given to us for 2003. We publish every two years so they cannot be current throughout the book's life. Treat them as a guideline rather than as infallible.

Phones & Phone Codes

From Italy to another country: dial 00 followed by the country code and then the area code without the first 0. When dialling Alastair Sawday Publishing from Italy, the UK no. 01275 464891 becomes 00 44 1275 464891.

From another country to Italy:
From the UK dial 00 then the full number given
From the USA dial 011 then the full number given.
Within Italy: simply drop the country code (39) and dial the numbers given.
Italian mobile numbers start with 033 but when calling from abroad or a foreign mobile drop the zero eg: 0039 33.....

Telephone cards (*carte telefoniche*) can be bought from tobacconists, post offices and newspaper stands.

Meals

Eating in Italy is one of life's great pleasures. There is plenty of variety, and each region has its own specialities and its surprises. We used to have a symbol to show where food was organically grown, home-grown or locally grown. In Italy this

INTRODUCTION

almost goes without saying as so many owners use locally grown ingredients and more often than not have grown or produced some part of your meal.

Breakfast

What constitutes breakfast varies enormously from place to place. Many hotels don't offer it at all, especially in towns, where it is normal to walk to the nearest bar for your first espresso. Prices double or triple as soon as you sit down, so if you want to save money, join the locals at the bar. On the farms you will probably find homemade jams and cakes as well as home-produced cheeses and fruit.

Dinner

We tell you if the owners offer lunches and dinners, and give an average per person price. Hotels and other places with restaurants usually offer the widest à la carte choice. Smaller places may offer a set dinner (at a set time) and you will need to book in advance. In family-run establishments you will sometimes find yourself eating in a separate dining room, served by a member of the family; in some cases, you will eat with the family. Small farms and inns often offer sumptuous dinners which are excellent value and delicious, so keep an open mind.

Vegetarians

There is so much fresh, seasonal food available that vegetarians should have no difficulty in Italy. Although main courses are often meaty there are plenty of pasta dishes to suit vegetarians, and it is quite common to order a plate of seasonal vegetables as a separate course.

Tipping

Leaving a tip is still the norm in Italy. In bars you are given your change on a small saucer, and it is usual to leave a couple of small coins there.

A cover charge on restaurant meals is standard. A small tip in family-run establishments is also welcome, so leave one if you wish.

INTRODUCTION

Seasons and Public Holidays

On the days before public holidays Italians like to stock up, so be prepared for long queues in the supermarket. *Ferragosto* marks the summer holiday for Italians and, for the week before and the week after, most places totally close down. Most families and even large companies take a holiday and head for the sea so some inland hotels consider August to be low season and prices go down accordingly.

January 1	New Year's Day	*Capo d'Anno*
January 6	Epiphany	*La Befana*
	Easter	*Pasqua*
April 25	Liberation Day	*Venticinque Aprile*
May 1	Labour Day	*Primo Maggio*
August 15	Assumption of the Virgin	*Ferragosto*
November 1	All Saints' Day	*Tutti Santi*
December 8	Feast of the Immaculate Conception	*Festa dell'Immacolata*
December 25	Christmas Day	*Natale*
December 26	Boxing Day	*Santo Stefano*

There are also lots of other pagan holidays all over Italy, and each town has its own patron saint who has his/her holiday too.

Booking

Try to book well ahead if you plan to visit Italy during school holidays. Hotels will usually ask you for a credit card number for confirmation. Remember to let smaller places know if you are likely to be arriving late, and if you want dinner.

There's a bilingual booking form at the back of the book. Hotels often send back a signed or stamped copy as confirmation but don't necessarily expect a speedy reply!

Some of the major cities get very full around the time of trade fairs (e.g. fashion fairs in Milan, the children's book fair in Bologna). Avoid these times if you can, or book well ahead.

Cancellation

Please give as much notice as possible. Cancellation charges will vary, so do check.

INTRODUCTION

Registration

Visitors to Italy are obliged to carry some form of identification at all times. It is a good idea to take some form of ID other than your passport so that if you have handed your passport in at hotel reception on arrival, you can still prove who you are.

Payment

The most commonly accepted credit cards are Visa, Eurocard, MasterCard and Amex. Many places in this book don't take plastic because of high bank charges. It's a good idea to check the symbols at the bottom of each entry before you arrive, in case you are a long way from a cash dispenser.

Consider taking...

- Electrical adaptors: virtually all sockets now have 2-pin plugs that run on 220/240 AC voltage
- A universal bath plug in case yours is missing
- Ear plugs could be useful for a light-sleeper driven mad by late-night Vespas
- A small electric fan for your bedside in high summer

Italian Tourist Offices

UK – 1 Princes Street, London W1R 8AY. Tel: 0207 408 1254

USA – 630 Fifth Avenue, New York 10111. Tel: 212 245 5618

Business Hours

Most shops are closed 10-4pm. Restaurants are often closed on Mondays.

Environment

We try to reduce our impact on the environment by:

- publishing our books on recycled paper
- planting trees. We are officially Carbon Neutral®. The emissions directly related to our office, paper production and printing of this book have been 'neutralised' through the planting of indigenous woodlands with Future Forests
- re-using paper, recycling stationery, tins, bottles, etc
- encouraging staff use of bicycles (they're loaned free) and car sharing
- celebrating the use of organic, home-grown and locally-produced food
- publishing books that support, in however small a way, the rural economy and small-scale businesses

INTRODUCTION

• publishing *The Little Earth Book*, a collection of essays on environmental issues and *The Little Food Book*, a hard-hitting analysis of the food industry. *The Little Money Book* is under way, too. See our web site www.fragile-earth.com for more information on any of these titles

Subscription Owners pay to appear in this guide. Their fee goes towards the costs of inspections and producing an all-colour book. We only include places and owners that we find positively special. It is not possible for anyone to buy his/her way into our guides.

Internet Our web site www.specialplacestostay.com has online pages for all the places featured here and from all our other books – around 3,500 Special Places in Britain, Ireland, France, Italy, Spain and Portugal - soon to be joined by India and Morocco. There's a searchable database, a taster of the write-ups and colour photos. For more details see the back of the book.

Disclaimer We make no claims to pure objectivity in choosing our Special Places to Stay. They are here because we like them. Our opinions and tastes are ours alone and this book is a statement of them; we hope that you will share them.

We have done our utmost to get our facts right but apologise unreservedly for any mistakes that may have crept in. Feedback from you is invaluable and we always act upon comments. With your help and our own inspections we can maintain our reputation for dependability.

You should know that we do not check such things as fire alarms, swimming pool security or any other regulation with which owners of properties receiving paying guests should comply. This is the responsibility of the owners.

And finally We want to hear whether your stay was a triumph or not. If you are unhappy about something then do speak to the owner or the manager while you are there. Many problems are best solved 'on the spot'. Please fill out the report form at the back of the book or e-mail us at italy@sawdays.co.uk. We also value your recommendations – for this, or any other book in the series. Do keep writing. If your recommendation results in the inclusion of a special place in any of our guides we'll send you a free copy.

Buon viaggio!

Emma Carey

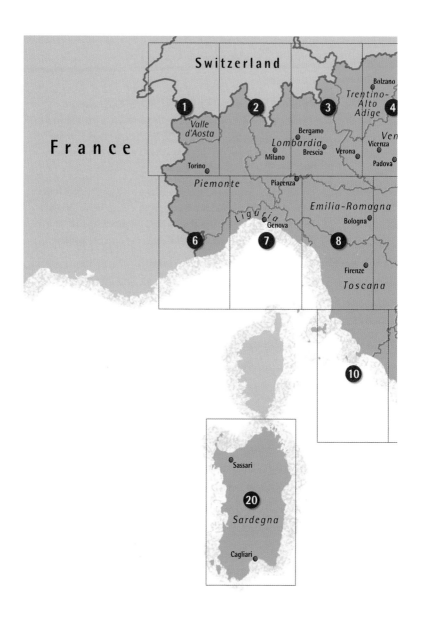

Key to property 'flags' on map pages:

- self-catering accommodation
- catered accommodation
- both self-catering & catered accommodation

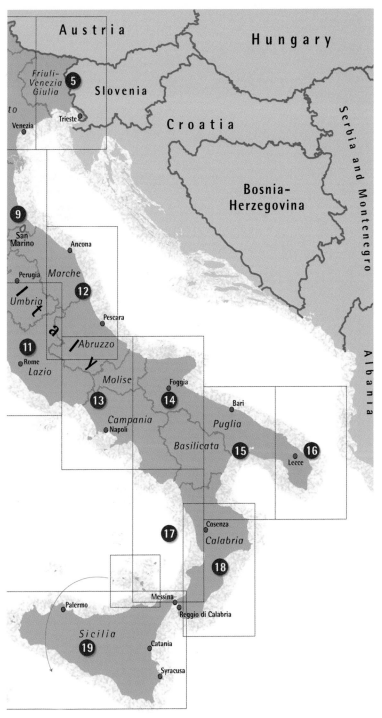

A guide to our map page numbers

© Bartholomew Ltd 2003

CITTÀSLOW - SLOW CITY MOVEMENT

Towns with Cittàslow status at the time of going to press

Asti	Bra
Canale	Castelnuovo Berardenga
Castelnuovo di Garfagnana	Castiglione del Lago
Chiavenna	Città di Castello
Civitella in Val di Chiana	Francavilla al Mare
Greve in Chianti	Loreto
Martinafranca	Massa Marittima
Medea	Orvieto
Palestrina	Penne
Positano	Rivello
San Daniele del Friuli	San Miniato
San Vincenzo	Sangemini
Satriano	Teglio
Todi	Trani
Trevi	Urbino
Verteneglio	Viareggio
Zibello	

www.cittaslow.stratos.it

Major towns

The major towns generally have a different name in English, smaller towns remain the same. To avoid the plight of the visitor who drove around on a fruitless search for Florence, never seeing it once appear on road signs, here is a reminder:

Florence - *Firenze*   Venice - *Venezia*   Naples - *Napoli*
Turin - *Torino*   Milan - *Milano*   Genoa - *Genova*
Leghorn - *Livorno*

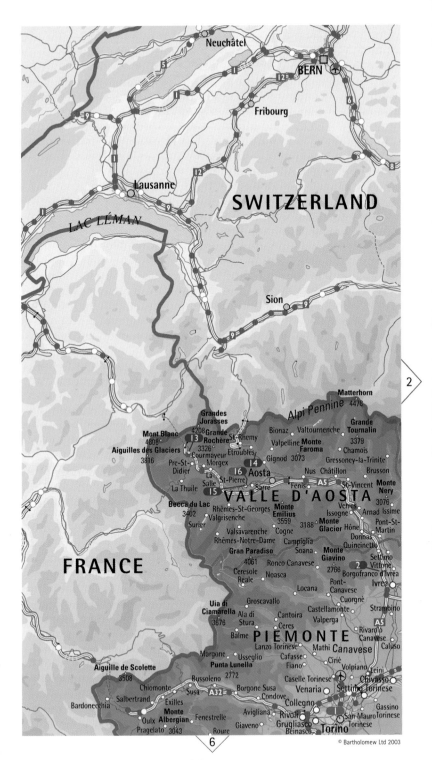

Neuchâtel

BERN

Fribourg

SWITZERLAND

Lausanne

LAC LÉMAN

Sion

Matterhorn
4478
Alpi Pennine

Grandes
Jorasses
4208
Mont Blanc
4809
Aiguilles des Glaciers
3816

Grande
Rochère
3326
Courmayeur
Morgex
Pré-St-
Didier
La Thuile

St-Rhémy
Etroubles

Bionaz   Valtournenche   Grande
Tournalin
Valpelline Monte   3379
Faroma   Chamois
Gignod 3073   Gressoney-la-Trinité
Nus Châtillon   Brusson
Monte
Nery
3076

13

La
Salle
St-Pierre

14

16 Aosta
15

Sarre

Fénis   St-Vincent   A5
Vetres   Arnad Issime
Issogne   Pont-St-
Monte   Hône   Martin
Glacier   Donnas
3188   Quincinetto

VALLE D'AOSTA

Becca du Lac
3402
Surier

Rhêmes-St-Georges Monte
Emilius
Valgrisenche   3559
Valsavarenche   Cogne
Rhêmes-Notre-Dame
Gran Paradiso
4061   Ronco Canavese
Ceresole   Noasca
Reale

Monte
Giavino
2766

Settimo
Vittone
Borgofranco d'Ivrea
Ivrea

FRANCE

Locana

Pont-
Canavese
Cuorgnè   Strambino
Castellamonte
Cantoira   Valperga   A5
Ceres   Rivarolo
Canavese Caluso

Uia di
Ciamarella
3676

Groscavallo
Ala di
Stura
Balme

PIEMONTE

Margone   Lanzo Torinese
Usseglio
Cafasse
Punta Lunella   Fiano
2772   Caselle Torinese

Mathi Canavese
Cirié
Volpiano Leini

Aiguille de Scolette
3508
Bardonecchia Salbertrand
Chiomonte
Oulx
Pragelato Albergian
3043

Bussoleno
Susa   A32
Exilles
Fenestrelle
Roure

Borgone Susa
Condove
Avigliana
Giaveno

Venaria
Collegno
Rivoli
Grugliasco
Beinasco

Chivasso
Settimo Torinese
Gassino
San Mauro Torinese
Torino

© Bartholomew Ltd 2003

6

Map 1

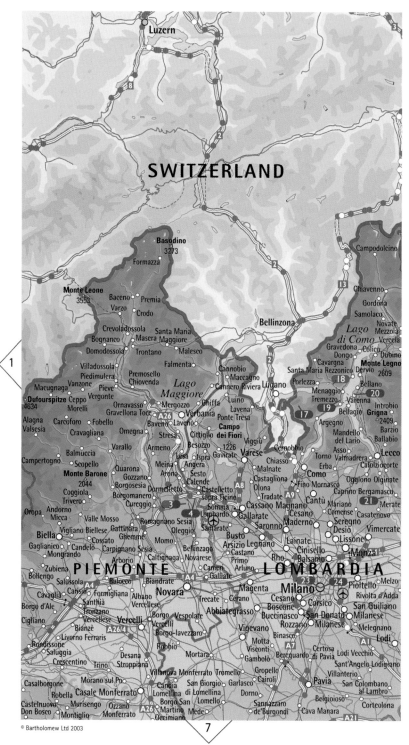

7

Map 2

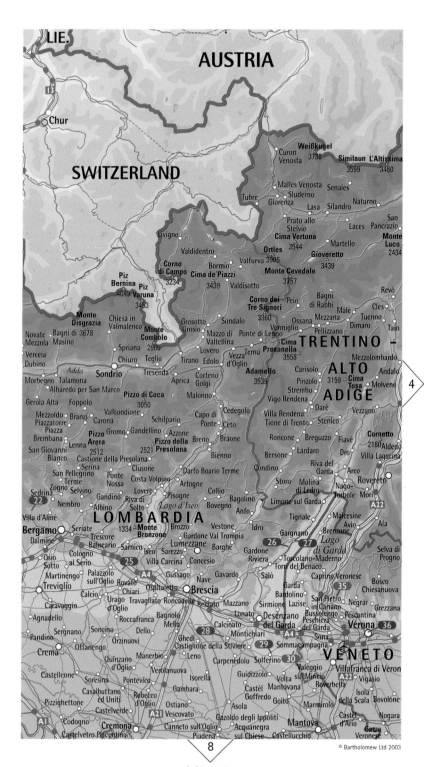

Map 3

© Bartholomew Ltd 2003

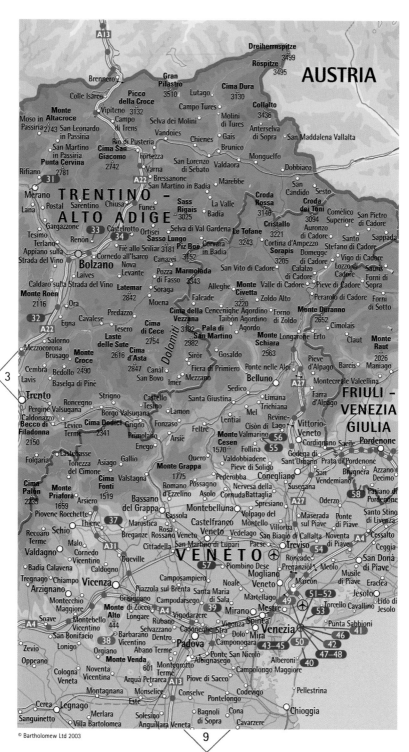

© Bartholomew Ltd 2003

9

Map 4

Map 5

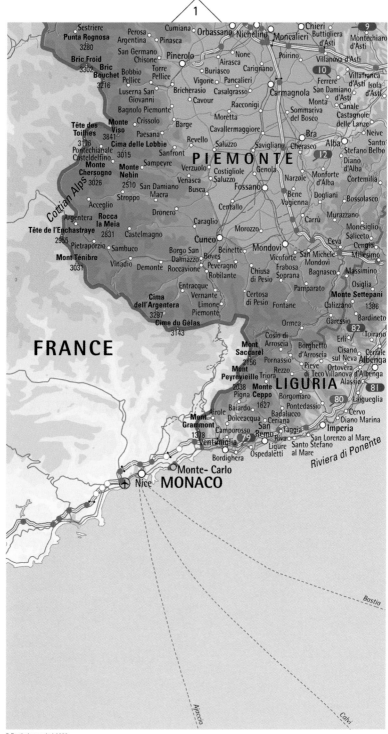

1

9

Sestriere
Punta Rognosa
3280
Bric Froid
3302   Bric
        Bouchet
        3216

Cumiana
Perosa   Orbassano Nichelino
Argentina Pinasca   Moncalieri Buttigliera
San Germano   None   d'Asti   Montechiaro
Chisone   Pinerolo   Poirino   d'Asti
Torre   Airasca   Carignano   Villanova d'Asti
Bobbio   Pellice   Buriasco   10
Pellice   Vigone Pancalieri   Ferrere   Villafranca
Luserna San   Bricherasio Casalgrasso   Carmagnola San Damiano Isola
Giovanni   Cavour   d'Asti   d'Asti
Bagnolo Piemonte   Racconigi   Monta
Crissolo   Sommariva   Canale
Monte   Barge   Moretta   del Bosco   Castagnole
Viso   Cavallermaggiore   delle Lanze
3841   Paesana Revello   Bra   Neive
Cima delle Lobbie Sanfront Saluzzo Savigliano Cherasco Alba Santo
3015   12   Stefano Belbò
Sampeyre Verzuolo   Genola   Narzole Monforte Diano
Monte   Costigliole   d'Alba   d'Alba
Nebin   San Damiano Saluzzo   Cortemilia
2510   Macra   Venasca Fossano   Bene   Dogliani
Busca   Vagienna   Bossolasco
Stroppo Centallo   Murazzano
Dronero   Morozzo   Carrù   Monesiglio
Caraglio   Saliceto
Cuneo   Beinette Mondovì Ceva Cengio
Borgo San   Vicoforte San Michele Millesimo
Dalmazzo Boves Peveragno Frabosa   Mondovi
Roccavione Robilante Chiusa Soprana Bagnasco Massimino
di Pesio   Osiglia
Entracque   Vernante   Pamparato Monte Settepani
Limone   Certosa Fontane   1386
Piemonte di Pesio   Calizzano Bardineto
Ormea   Garessio
82   Toirano
Cosio di   Erli
Arroscia   Borghetto Cisano Cerrale
Mont   Pornassio d'Arroscia sul Neva Albenga
Saccarel   Pieve   Villanova d'Albenga
2156   Rezzo   di Teco Ortovero
Mont   Triora   Alassio   81
Peyrevieille   Borgomaro   Laigueglia
2038   Monte Pigna Ceppo   Pontedassio   80
Baiardo 1627   Badalucco   Cervo
Mont   Airole Dolceacqua Ceriana Riva Diano Marina
Grammont   San   Taggia Imperia
1378   Camporosso Remo 79 Riva   San Lorenzo al Mare
Ventimiglia   Ligure Santo Stefano
Bordighera   Ospedaletti   al Mare   Riviera di Ponente

PIEMONTE

Cottian Alps
Tête des
Toillies
3176
Pontechianale
Casteldelfino
Monte
Chersogno
3026
Accéglio
Rocca
la Meia
Argentera 2831 Castelmagno
Tête de l'Enchastraye
2955   Pietraporzio
Sambuco
Mont Ténibre Vinadio Demonte
3031
Cima
dell'Argentera
3297
Cime du Gélas
3143

FRANCE

LIGURIA

Nice   Monte-Carlo
MONACO

Bastia

Ajaccio   Calvi

© Bartholomew Ltd 2003

Map 6

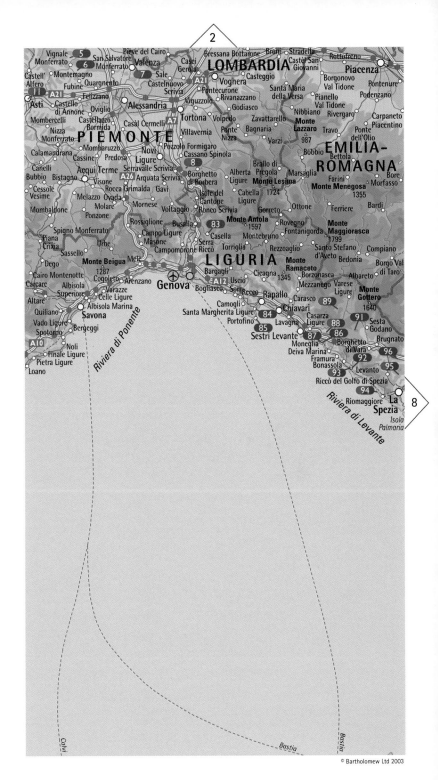

© Bartholomew Ltd 2003

Map 7

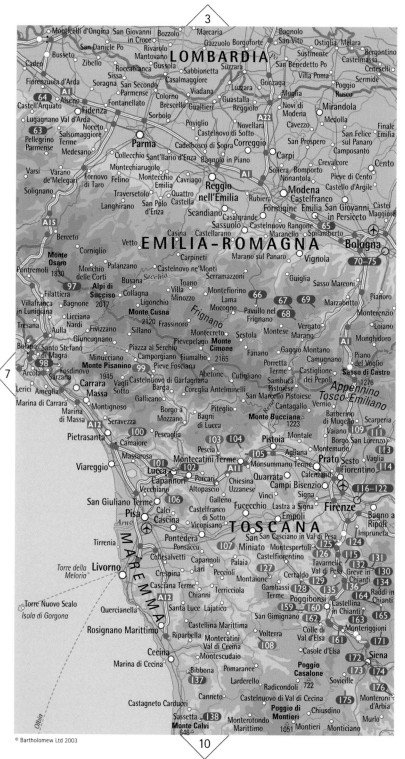

Map 8

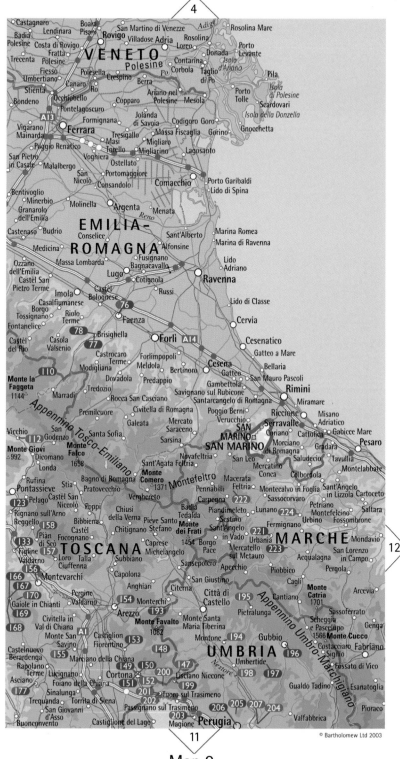

Castagnaro Boara Pisani San Martino di Venezze *Adige* Rosolina Mare
Badì Lendinara Rovigo Villadose Adria Rosolina
Polesine Costa di Rovigo Fratta Loreo
Trecenta Polesine *Polesine* Contarina Donada Porto
Fiesso Polesella Corbola Levante
Umbertiano Canaro Crespino *Po* Taglio *Isola*
Stienta Occhiobello Ro Berra Ariano nel di Po d'Ariano
Bondeno Pontelagoscuro Copparo Polesine Mesola Porto Pila
Tolle *Isola*
VENETO Jolanda Codigoro Goro *di Polesine*
Vigarano Formignana di Savoia Gorino Scardovari
Mainarda **A13** **Ferrara** Massa Fiscaglia *Isola della Donzella*
Poggio Renatico Tresigallo Migliaro Lagosanto Gnocchetta
San Pietro Masi Torello Migliarino
in Casale Malalbergo Voghiera Ostellato
San Portomaggiore Porto Garibaldi
Nicolò Consandolo Lido di Spina
Bentivoglio **Comacchio**
Minerbio Molinella Argenta Menata
Granarolo dell'Emilia
Castenaso Budrio **EMILIA-** Sant'Alberto Marina Romea
Conselice Marina di Ravenna
Medicina **ROMAGNA** Fusignano Lido
Ozzano Massa Lombarda Bagnacavallo Adriano
dell'Emilia Lugo Cotignola **Ravenna**
Castèl San Castel Russi
Pietro Terme Imola Bolognese
Casalfiumanese **76** Lido di Classe
Borgo Riolo
Tossignano Terme Faenza Cervia
Fontanelice
Castèl **78** Brisighella **Forlì** **A14** Cesenatico
del Rio Casola
110 Valsenio Castrocaro Forlimpopoli Gatteo a Mare
Modigliana Terme Meldola Bertinoro Bellaria
Dovadola **Cesena** Gatteo San Mauro Pascoli
Monte la Tredozio Predappio Gambettola
Faggeta Savignano sul Rubicone **Rimini**
1144 Marradi Rocca San Casciano Santarcangelo di Romagna Miramare
Premilcuore Civitella di Romagna Poggio Berni
Vicchio San Galeata Mercato Verucchio Riccione Misano
Godenzo Santa Sofia Saraceno **SAN** Coriano Serravalle Adriatico
Monte Giovi **112** Sarsina **MARINO** Morciano Cattolica Gabicce Mare
992 Dicomano **Monte** **SAN MARINO** di Romagna Gradara
Londa **Falco** Novafeltria Saludecio Tavullia **Pesaro**
1658 Sant'Agata Feltria San Leo Mercatino Colbordolo Montelabbate
Rufina Stia Bagno di Romagna **Monte** Conca
Pontassieve Pratovecchio **Comero** Macerata Montecalvo in Foglia Sant'Angelo
123 Pelago Castèl San Verghereto 1371 Montefeltro Feltria Sassocorvaro in Lizzola Cartoceto
Rignano sull'Arno Niccolò Poppi Pennabilli **222** Petriano
Reggello Bibbiena Chiusi Carpegna Piandimeleto Lunano **224** Montefelcino Saltara
158 Castèl della Verna **Badia** Sestino Urbino Fossombrone
133 Pian Focognano Pieve Santo **Tedalda** Sant'Angelo Fermignano
di Scò Chitignano Stefano **Monte** in Vado **221** **MARCHE**
157 Loro Talla **Caprese** **dei Frati** Urbania Mondavio
Figline Ciuffenna Michelangelo 1454 Borgo Mercatello **223** San Lorenzo
156 Subbiano Pace sul Metauro Acqualagna in Campo
166 Montevarchi Capolona Sansepolcro Apecchio Pergola
167 Anghiari San Giustino Piobbico
170 Pergine Citerna Città di Cagli **Monte**
Gaiole in Chianti Valdarno **154** Monterchi Castello **195** Cantiano **Catria** Arcevia
169 1701
168 Civitella in **193** Pietralunga Sassoferrato
Val di Chiana **Arezzo** Monte Santa Scheggia Genga
Monte San **Monte Favalto** Maria Tiberina e Pascelupo **Monte Cucco**
Castelnuovo Savino **A1** 1082 Montone **194** Gubbio **196** 1566 Costacciaro Fabriano
Berardenga **155** Castiglion **148** Sigillo Fossato di Vico
Rapolano Marciano della Chiana Fiorentino **UMBRIA** Gualdo Tadino Esanatoglia
Terme Lucignano **150** **147** Umbertide **197**
Asciano **151** Foiano della Chiana Cortona **200** Lisciano Niccone **198**
177 Sinalunga **152** **199** Pioraco
Trequanda Torrita di Siena **201** Tuoro sul Trasimeno Valfabbrica
San Giovanni Passignano sul Trasimeno **202** **206** **205** **207** **204**
d'Asso Castiglione del Lago **203** Magione **Perugia**
Buonconvento

Adige *Po* *Reno* *Appennino Tosco-Emiliano* *Montefeltro* *Appennino Umbro-Marchigiano* *Nestore*

Map 9

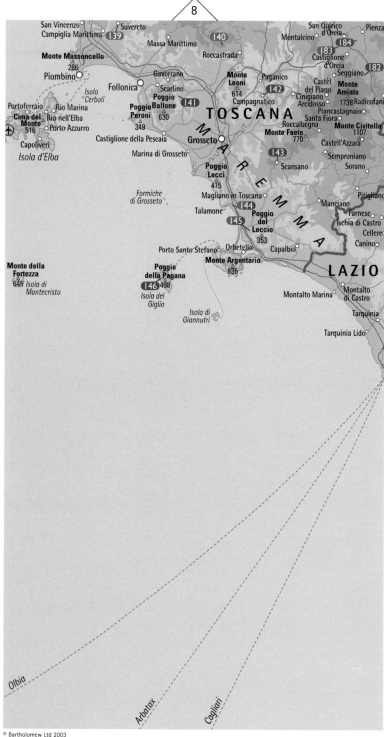

San Vincenzo
Suvereto
Campiglia Marittima 139
140
Massa Marittimo
San Quirico d'Orcia
Pienza
Montalcino
183
184
Castiglione d'Orcia
Seggiano
Monte Massoncello
286
Roccastrada
182
Piombino
Gavorrano
Monte Leoni
614
Paganico
142
Castèl del Piano
Monte Amiata
1738 Radicofani
Follonica
Scarlino
Campagnatico
Cinigiano
Arcidosso
Piancastagnaio
Isola Cerboli
Poggio Ballone
141
TOSCANA
Santa Fiora
Portoferraio
Rio Marina
Poggio Peroni
630
Roccalbegna
Monte Civitella
1107
Cima del Monte
516
Rio nell'Elba
349
Monte Faete
770
Castell'Azzara
Porto Azzurro
Castiglione della Pescaia
Grosseto
Capoliveri
Marina di Grosseto
143
Semproniano
Isola d'Elba
Scansano
Sorano
Poggio Lecci
415
Formiche di Grosseto
Magliano in Toscana
Pitigliano
Manciano
Talamone
144
Farnese
Ischia di Castro
145
Poggio del Leccio
353
Cellere
Canino
Porto Santo Stefano
Orbetello
Capalbio
Monte della Fortezza
645 Isola di Montecristo
Poggio della Pagana
146 498
Monte Argentario
635
LAZIO
Isola del Giglio
Montalto Marina
Montalto di Castro
Isola di Giannutri
Tarquinia
Tarquinia Lido

Olbia

Arbatax

Cagliari

Map 10

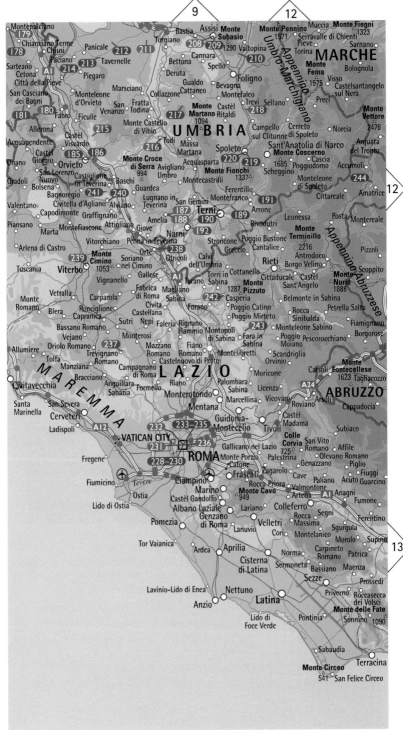

Map 11

DRIVING IN ITALY

Driving in Italy

Don't forget your driving licence; it is an offence to drive without it and, if you hire a car, you must show it. Remember that you don't automatically have right of way on a roundabout in Italy. If the traffic coming from the right does not have a stop sign, you will have to stop on the roundabout, and give way. The following are general guidelines, though the size and condition of each road can vary from region to region.

Autostrada - toll motorway, indicated with green road signs and numbers and preceded by 'A'. Generally shown on maps with bold double black line.

Superstrada - Primary routes usually shown in bold red on maps and marked 'SS'.

Strada Statale - State roads, usually in finer red and also marked 'SS' or 'ss'.

Strada Provincial - Secondary routes, marked in yellow and with numbers preceded by 'prov'. Marked 'SP'.

Strada Bianca - Unpaved roads, often with no number at all.

Public transport

Public transport is good and reliable in Italy but do check times, it's frustrating to arrive somewhere at midday just as everything is shutting down for lunch. This is particularly true the further south you go. Don't forget to validate *"compostare"* your ticket on the bus or on the platform before you get on the train.

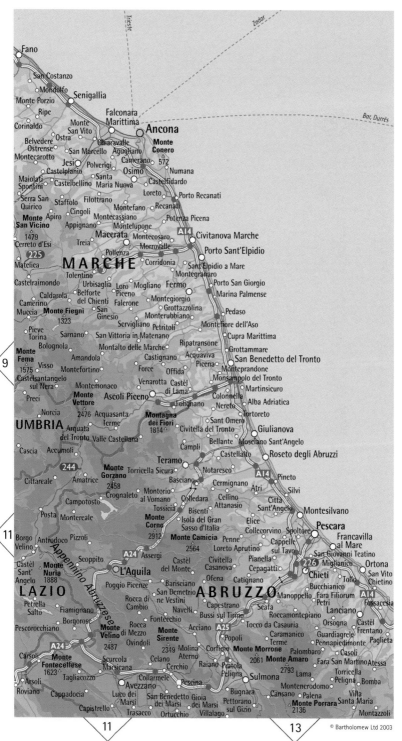

Map 12

© Bartholomew Ltd 2003

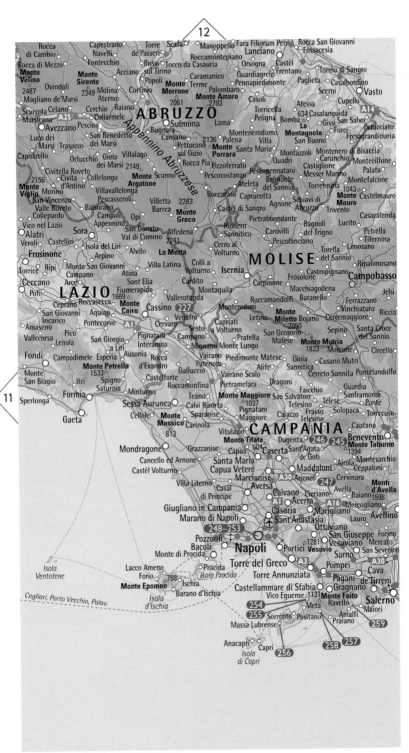

Map 13

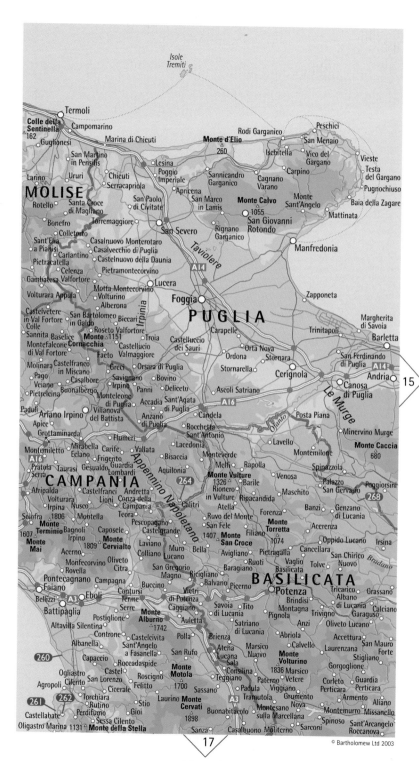

Isole
Tremiti

Termoli
**Colle della
Sentinella** △162
Camporimano
Marina di Chieuti
Rodi Garganico
Peschici
San Menaio
Monte d'Elio 260
Ischitella
Vico del
Gargano
Vieste
Testa
del Gargano
Guglionesi
San Martino
in Pensilis
Ururi
Chieuti
Serracapriola
Lesina
Poggio
Imperiale
Apricena
Sannicandro
Garganico
Cagnano
Varano
Carpino
Monte
Sant'Angelo
Pugnochiuso
Baia della Zagare
Larino
Rotello
Santa Croce
di Magliano
San Paolo
di Civitate
San Marco
in Lamis
Monte Calvo
△1055
San Giovanni
Rotondo
Mattinata

MOLISE
Bonefro
Colletorto
Sant'Elia
a Pianisi
Carlantino
Pietracatella
Torremaggiore
Casalnuovo Monterotaro
Casalvecchio di Puglia
Castelnuovo della Daunia
San Severo
Rignano
Garganico
Manfredonia

Celenza
Valfortore
Gambatesa
Volturara Appula
Volturino
Pietramontecorvino
Motta Montecorvino
Lucera
Taviolere
A14
Zapponeta

Castelvetere
in Val Fortore
Colle
Sannita
Montefalcone
di Val Fortore
San Bartolomeo
in Galdo
Alberona
Biccari
Roseto Valfortore
Monte
Cornacchia △1151
Castellucio
Troia
Faeto
Valmaggiore
Baselice

Foggia

PUGLIA

Carapelle
Margherita
di Savoia
Trinitapoli
Barletta

Molinara
Pago
Veiano
Pietrelcina
Castelfranco
in Miscano
Casalbore
Buonalbergo
Greci
Savignano
Irpino
Panni
Orsara di Puglia
Bovino
Deliceto
Castelluccio
dei Sauri
Ordona
Stornarella
Orta Nova
Stornara
Cerignola
Ascoli Satriano
Sant'Agata
di Puglia
San Ferdinando
di Puglia
Andria
A14
Canosa
di Puglia
15

Paduli
Ariano Irpino
Apice
Grottaminarda
Monteleone
di Puglia
Villanova
del Battista
Accadia
Anzano
di Puglia
Candela
A16
Rocchetta
Sant'Antonio
Posta Piana
Le Murge
Ofanto
Minervino Murge
Monte Caccia
△680

Montemiletto
Eclano
Mirabella
Pratola
Serra
Taurasi
Carife
Frigento
Gesualdo
Guardia
Lombardi
Vallata
Bisaccia
Aquilonia
Lacedonia
Monteverde
Melfi
Rapolla
Lavello
Montemilone
Spinazzola
Palazzo
San Gervasio
Poggiorsini
268
CAMPANIA
A16
264

Atripalda
Volturara
Irpina
Nusco
Castelfranci
Lioni
Andretta
Conza della
Campania
Teora
Calitri
Monte Vulture
△1326
Rionero
in Vulture
Barile
Ripacandida
Atella
Maschito
Venosa
Banzi
Genzano
di Lucania
Irsina
Bradano

Solofra
△1806
Montella
Bagnoli
Irpino
Monte
Terminio
1607△
Monte
Mai
Acerno
Caposele
Monte
Cervialto △1809
Pescopagano
Castelgrande
Laviano
Colliano
Muro
Lucano
Bella
San Fele
Ruvo del Monte
Filiano
Avigliano
Ruoti
Monte
Torretta
Forenza
Acerenza
Monte
San Croce △1407
△1074
Pietragalla
Cancellara
Oppido Lucano
San Chirico
Nuovo

Monfecorvino
Rovella
Pontecagnano
Faiano
Bellizzi
Oliveto
Citra
Campagna
Buccino
San Gregorio
Magno
Ricigliano
Vaglio
Baragiano
Balvano
Tolve
BASILICATA
Picerno
Potenza
Tricarico
Grassano
Albano
di Lucania
Calciano

Battipaglia
Eboli
Contursi
Terme
Serre
Vietri
di Potenza
Caggiano
Savoia
di Lucania
Tito
Montagna
Pignola
Anzi
Brindisi
Trivigno
Garaguso

Altavilla Silentina
Postiglione
Monte
Alburno △1742
Auletta
Polla
Brienza
Satriano
di Lucania
Abriola
Calvello
Oliveto Lucano
Accettura
San Mauro
Forte

Controne
Albanella
Sant'Angelo
a Fasanella
Castelcivita
Capaccio
Roccadaspide
San Rufo
Atena
Lucana
Marsico
Nuovo
Sala
Monte
Volturino △1836
Laurenzana
Stigliano

Ogliastro
Cilento
Agropoli
260
San Lorenzo
Castel
Cilento
Roscigno
Felitto
Monte
Motola △1700
Teggiano
Consilina
Paterno
Marsico
Vetere
Viggiano
Padula
Corleto
Perticara
Gorgoglione
Guardia
Perticara

261
262
Torchiara
Rutino
Perdifumo
Castellabate
Sessa Cilento
Stio
Gioi
Laurino
Monte
Cervati △1898
Sassano
Tramutola
A3
Buonabitacolo
Grumento
Nova
Armento
Aliano
Missanello

Oligastro Marina △1131 **Monte della Stella**
Sanza
Casalbuono
Moliterno
Montesano
sulla Marcellana
Sarconi
Spinoso
Montemurro
Missanello
Sant'Arcangelo
Roccanova

17

© Bartholomew Ltd 2003

Map 14

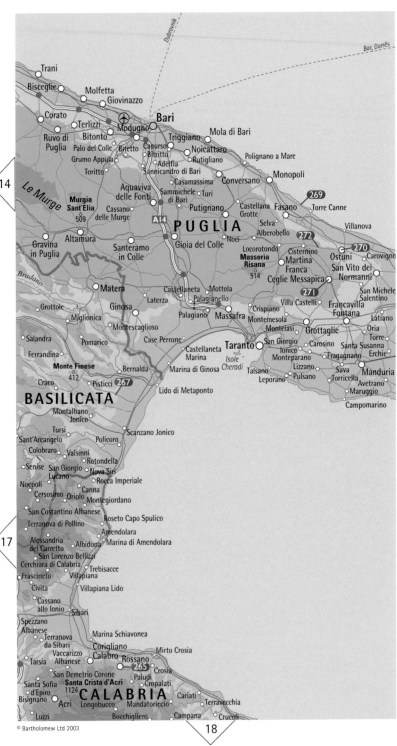

Dubrovnik

Bar, Durrës

Trani
Bisceglie
Molfetta
Corato
Giovinazzo
Ruvo di
Puglia
Terlizzi
Modugno
Bari
Bitonto
Palo del Colle
Biretto
Cagurso
Bitritto
Triggiano
Mola di Bari
Grumo Appula
Adelfia
Noicattaro
Toritto
Sannicandro di Bari
Rutigliano
Polignano a Mare
Casamassima
Conversano
Monopoli
14
Aquaviva
delle Fonti
Sammichele
di Bari
Turi
Castellana
Grotte
Fasano
Le Murge
Putignano
Torre Canne
Murgia
Sant'Elia
509
Cassano
delle Murge
Selva
Alberobello
Villanova
269
PUGLIA
Gravina
in Puglia
Altamura
Santeramo
in Colle
Gioia del Colle
Noci
Locorotondo
272
Cisternino
Ostuni
Carovigno
270
Bradano
Masseria
Risana
Martina
Franca
514
San Vito dei
Normanni
Matera
Castellaneta
Mottola
Palagianello
Ceglie Messapica
271
San Michele
Salentino
Grottole
Ginosa
Laterza
Palagiano
Massafra
Villa Castelli
Francavilla
Fontana
Latiano
Miglionica
Montescaglioso
Crispiano
Montemesola
Monteiasi
Grottaglie
Oria
Torre
Salandra
Pomarico
Case Perrone
Castellaneta
Marina
Taranto
San Giorgio
Ionico
Carosino
Santa Susanna
Erchie
Ferrandina
Monteparano
Sava
Fragagnano
Monte Finese
412
Bernalda
Marina di Ginosa
Isole
Cheradi
Talsano
Lizzano
Pulsano
Leporano
Torricella
Manduria
Avetrano
Craco
Pisticci
267
Lido di Metaponto
Maruggio
Campomarino
BASILICATA
Montalbano
Jonico
Tursi
Sant'Arcangelo
Policoro
Scanzano Jonico
Colobraro
Valsinni
Senise
San Giorgio
Lucano
Rotondella
Nova Siri
Noepoli
Cersosimo
Oriolo
Canna
Rocca Imperiale
San Costantino Albanese
Montegiordano
Terranova di Pollino
Roseto Capo Spulico
17
Alessandria
del Carretto
Albidona
Amendolara
Marina di Amendolara
San Lorenzo Bellizzi
Cerchiara di Calabria
Trebisacce
Frascineto
Villapiana
Civita
Villapiana Lido
Cassano
allo Ionio
Sibari
Spezzano
Albanese
Terranova
da Sibari
Marina Schiavonea
Vaccarizzo
Albanese
Corigliano
Calabro
Rossano
Mirto Crosia
Tarsia
265
Crosia
San Demetrio Corone
Paludi
Santa Sofia
d'Epiro
Santa Crista d'Acri
1124
Cropalati
Cariati
Terravecchia
Bisignano
Acri
CALABRIA
Mandatoriccio
Luzzi
Longobucco
Bocchigliero
Campana
Crucoli

18

© Bartholomew Ltd 2003

Map 15

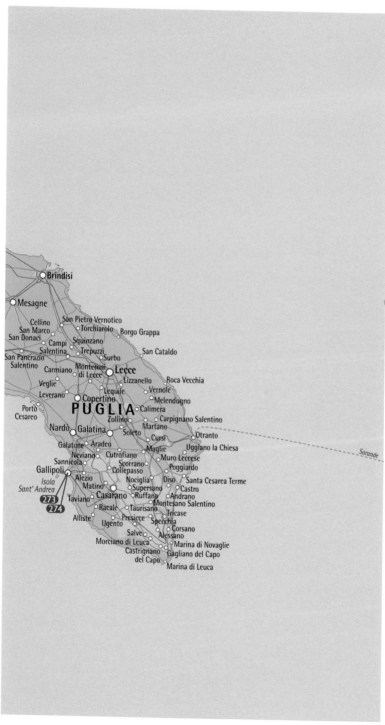

Brindisi
Mesagne
Cellino
San Marco
San Donaci
San Pancrazio
Salentino
Veglie
Leverano
Porto
Cesareo
Nardò
Galatone
Neviano
Sannicola
Gallipoli
Isola
Sant' Andrea
Alezio
Matino
Taviano
Alliste

San Pietro Vernotico
Torchiarolo
Campi Squinzano
Salentina Trepuzzi
Carmiano Surbo
Monteroni
di Lecce
Lequile
Copertino
PUGLIA
Zollino
Galatina Soleto
Aradeo
Cutrofiano
Scorrano
Collepasso
Nociglia
Casarano Supersano
Racale
Presicce
Ugento
Salve
Morciano di Leuca
Castrignano
del Capo

Borgo Grappa
San Cataldo
Lecce
Lizzanello Roca Vecchia
Vernole
Melendugno
Calimera
Carpignano Salentino
Martano
Cursi
Maglie Uggiano la Chiesa
Muro Leccese
Poggiardo
Diso Santa Cesarea Terme
Ruffano Castro
Andrano
Montesano Salentino
Taurisano Tricase
Specchia
Corsano
Alessano
Marina di Novaglie
Gagliano del Capo
Marina di Leuca

Otranto

Sarande

273
274

© Bartholomew Ltd 2003

Map 16

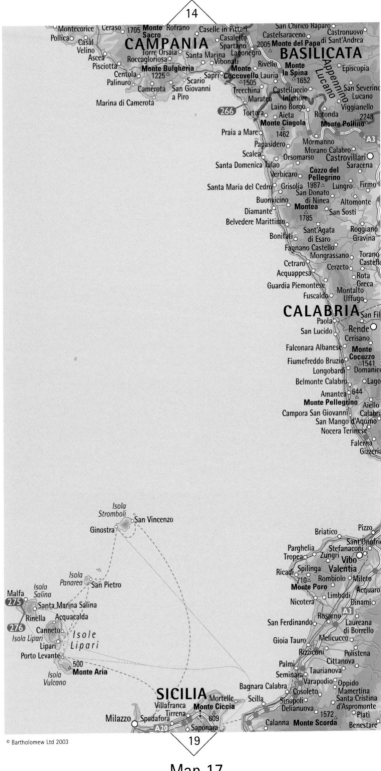

Montecorice Ceraso 1705 **Monte** Rofrano Caselle in Pittari San Chirico Raparo Castronuovo
Pollica Casal   **Sacro**   Casaletto Castelsaraceno di Sant'Andrea
        Velino Torre Orsaia Santa Marina Spartano Lagonegro **BASILICATA**
Ascea Roccagloriosa   Vibonati 2005 **Monte del Papa**
Pisciotta **Monte Bulgheria** Rivello **Monte** Episcopia
Centola 1225 Scario **Monte** Lauria **la Spina**
Palinuro   Camerota San Giovanni **Coccovello** ^1652
                a Piro Trecchina Castelluccio San Severino
Marina di Camerota   Maratea Inferiore Lucano
                        266 Tortora Aieta Laino Borgo Viggianello
                                        Rotonda 2248
                Praia a Mare **Monte Ciagola** **Monte Pollino**
                              1462
                        Papasidero Mormanno A3
                        Scalea Morano Calabro
                Santa Domenica Talao Orsomarso Castrovillari
                        Verbicaro **Cozzo del** Saracena
                Santa Maria del Cedro Grisolia 1987 **Pellegrino** Lungro Firmo
                        Buonvicino San Donato Altomonte
                        Diamante di Ninea **Montea**
                Belvedere Marittimo 1785 San Sosti
                        Bonifati Sant'Agata Roggiano
                        Fagnano Castello di Esaro Gravina
                        Mongrassano Torano
                Cetraro Cerzeto Castello
                Acquappesa Rota
                Guardia Piemontese Montalto Greca
                Fuscaldo Uffugo
                CALABRIA San Fil
                        Paola Rende
                San Lucido Cerisano
                Falconara Albanese **Monte**
                Fiumefreddo Bruzio **Cocuzzo**
                        Longobardi ^1541
                Belmonte Calabro Domanice
                        Lago
                Amantea 644
                Monte Pellegrino Aiello
                Campora San Giovanni Calabro
                San Mango d'Aquino
                Nocera Terinese
                        Falerna
                        Gizzeria

                Isola
                Stromboli San Vincenzo
                Ginostra Briatico Pizzo
                                Parghelia Sant'Onofrio
                                Tropea Stefanaconi
                                Zungri **Vibo**
                Isola Ricadi Spilinga **Valentia**
                Panarea San Pietro 710 Rombiolo Mileto
                Isola **Monte Poro** Acquaro
                Malfa *Salina* Limbadi Dinami
                275 Santa Marina Salina Nicotera
                Rinella Acquacalda Rosarno A3
                276 Canneto *Isole* San Ferdinando Laureana
                Isola Lipari *Lipari* di Borrello
                Lipari Gioia Tauro Melicucco
                Porto Levante Rizziconi Polistena
                500 Palmi Cittanova
                Isola **Monte Aria** Seminara Taurianova
                Vulcano Bagnara Calabria Varapodio Oppido
                                Cosoleto Mamertina
                SICILIA Mortelle Scilla Sinopoli Santa Cristina
                Villafranca **Monte Ciccia** Delianuova d'Aspromonte
                Tirrena 609 1572 Plati
                Milazzo Spadafora Calanna **Monte Scorda** Benestare
                A20 Saponara

© Bartholomew Ltd 2003

Map 17

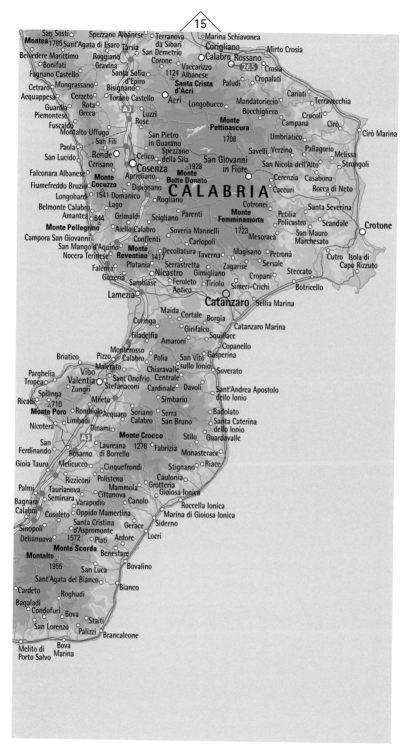

San Sosti • Spezzano Albanese ○ Terranova • Marina Schiavonea
Montea 1785 Sant'Agata di Esaro Tarsia da Sibari
Belvedere Marittimo ○ Roggiano San Demetrio ○ Coriglano
  ○ Bonifati Gravina Corone Calabro Rossano • Mirto Crosia
Fagnano Castello ○ Santa Sofia ○ Vaccarizzo ○ Crosia
Cetraro ○ Mongrassano d'Epiro 1124 Albanese ○ Cropalati
Acquappesa Bisignano **Santa Crista** Paludi ○ Cariati
  ○ Guardia Rota Torano Castello ○ **d'Acri** ○ Terravecchia
Piemontese ○ Cerzeto ○ Greca Acri Longobucco ○ Mandatoriccio ○ Crucoli
  ○ Fuscaldo Luzzi ○ Bocchigliero Campana ○ Cirò
Montalto Uffugo Rose San Pietro **Monte** Umbriatico ○ ○ Cirò Marina
  ○ Paola San Fili in Guarano **Pettinascura** Savelli ○ Verzino Pallagorio ○ Melissa
San Lucido ○ Rende Celico Spezzano 1708 San Nicola dell'Alto ○ Strongoli
  Cerisano della Sila San Giovanni Cerenzia ○ Casabona
Falconara Albanese **Cosenza** in Fiore ○ Rocca di Neto
Fiumefreddo Bruzio **Monte** Aprigliano **Monte** Caccuri ○ Santa Severina
  Cocuzzo ○ Dipignano **Botte Donato** **C A L A B R I A** Cotronei
Longobardi 1541 Domanico ○ Rogliano Petilia ○ Scandale
Belmonte Calabro ○ Lago Grimaldi Scigliano Parenti **Monte** Policastro ○ ○ **Crotone**
  Amantea 644 **Femminamorta** Mesoraca San Mauro
Monte Pellegrino Aiello Calabro Soveria Mannelli 1723 Marchesato
Campora San Giovanni Conflenti Carlopoli Magisano ○ Petronà Cutro Isola di
San Mango d'Aquino **Monte** Decollatura Tavernà ○ Sersale Capo Rizzuto
Nocera Terinese **Reventino** 1417 Serrastretta Zagarise ○ Steccato
  Falerna ○ Platania Nicastro Gimigliano Cropani ○ Botricello
Gizzeria Sambiase Feroleto Tiriolo Simeri-Crichi
  Lamezia Antica **Catanzaro** Sellia Marina
  Maida ○ Cortale Borgia
  Curinga ○ Girifalco Catanzaro Marina
  Filadelfia Amaroni Squillace
  Monterosso Polia Copanello
Briatico Pizzo Calabro ○ San Vito Gasperina
  Majerato Chiaravalle sullo Ionio
Parghelia **Vibo** Sant'Onofrio Centrale Soverato
Tropea **Valentia** Stefanaconi Cardinale ○ Davoli
  Spilinga Zungri Sant'Andrea Apostolo
Ricadi 710 Mileto Simbario dello Ionio
Monte Poro Rombiolo Acquaro Soriano ○ Serra Badolato
Nicotera Limbadi Calabro San Bruno Santa Caterina
  Dinami **Monte Crocco** Stilo dello Ionio
San Laureana 1276 Fabrizia Guardavalle
Ferdinando Rosarno di Borrello Monasterace
Gioia Tauro Melicucco Cinquefrondi Stignano ○ Riace
  Rizziconi Polistena Caulonia
Palmi Taurianova Mammola Grotteria
Bagnara Seminara Cittanova Canolo Gioiosa Ionica
Calabra Cosoleto Varapodio Roccella Ionica
  Sinopoli Oppido Mamertina Marina di Gioiosa Ionica
Delianuova Santa Cristina Gerace Siderno
  1572 d'Aspromonte Plati Ardore Locri
Monte Scorda Benestare
Montalto
  1955 San Luca Bovalino
Sant'Agata del Bianco Bianco
Cardeto Roghudi
Bagaladi
  Condofuri Bova
San Lorenzo Staiti
  Palizzi Brancaleone
Melito di Bova
Porto Salvo Marina

© Bartholomew Ltd 2003

Map 18

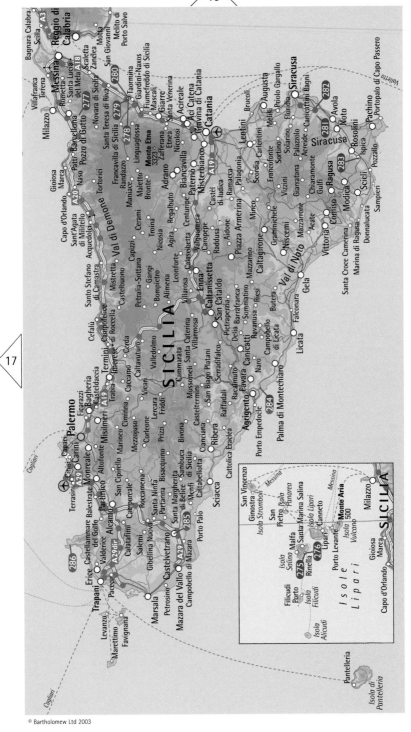

© Bartholomew Ltd 2003

Map 19

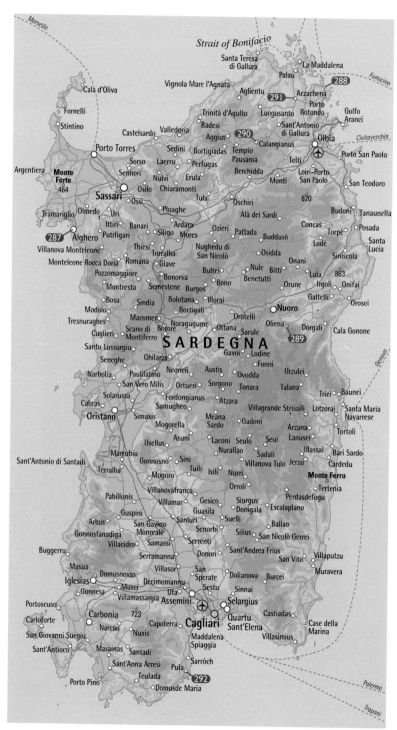

Map 20

Photography by Michael Busselle

piedmont &
valle d'aosta

La Costa

Via Baghetti 16, 10143 Turin

Sparkling white under the burning sun, the house is blessedly cool within. Built in the 1800s as a summer retreat, it stands – as the name suggests – near a ridge amid the vineyards of Liguria. The holiday apartment is on the ground floor, freshly and simply styled in white and blue by the artistic Silvia, who is a whizz at stencilling and *trompe l'oeil*. Serene bedrooms have muslin curtains and mosquito nets, pretty iron bedsteads and bunkbeds; beds are a generous size. The shower room, with heated towel rack and wicker baskets, is perfect, the kitchen small and beautifully equipped, the sitting room charming. There's a Mediterranean garden with lavender, lime trees and a two-headed palm from which magnificent views extend over the olive groves to the sea; a huge terrace leads straight off the master bedroom and the sitting room, wonderful for meals. Silvia is warm-hearted with an outrageous sense of humour and divides her time between the top floor here, and Turin. You are on the edge of the village with its little *osteria*, and a five-minute drive from the Ligurian 'riviera'. A super spot for families.

The local Vermentino grapes produce fruity, dry white wines characteristic of Liguria which is also the home of the now ubiquitous Pesto alla Genovese.

rooms	Sleeps 4: 1 double, 1 room with bunkbeds (large enough for adults).
price	€ 600–€ 700 per week. Heating € 100.
meals	Self-catering.
closed	Rarely.
directions	From motorway exit San Bartolomeo Al Mare; signs for Diano Marina & Diano Castello. Call Silvia for directions.

Silvia di Felice

tel	+39 011 4374192
mobile	+39 339 6394463
e-mail	silviadifelice@virgilio.it

Self-catering

La Miniera

Via Miniere 9, 10010 Calea di Lessolo

There's a large, lush garden which has been established with surprising success on top of the old mine spoil, and Roberta's fabulous, Jewish-Italian cooking: wild fungi and berries picked from the woods above the house find their way into her seasonal menus. Hard to believe these former headquarters of a disused iron-ore mine were once completely derelict. Today Roberta and her husband, and dogs, live in the former mine office. There are also two B&B rooms, and more in the director's house – and, usefully, a kitchen and dishwasher for guests. The bedrooms, which vary in size, are light and airy and simply decorated with old-fashioned "grandmother's furniture". A further, smaller house in the garden, cosy with heating and open fire, is for self-catering. The Anaus are also steadily assembling a museum on the history of the mine – it dates back to Roman times. There are shady terraces with proper deckchairs, ruins to explore and even Napoleonic mule tracks. You may spot local owls in these 40 wooded acres, and wild boar wandering round the garden from time to time – Roberta doesn't mind a bit.

rooms	6 + 1: 1 double, 1 triple, 1 quadruple; 2 doubles sharing bath. 1 cottage for 2-3.
price	€46–€54; triple €99; quadruple €132. Cottage €68 per night, €450 per week.
meals	Breakfast €6. Dinner €22–€28, book ahead.
closed	Rarely.
directions	From Ivrea to Lessolo for 6km. Ignore 1st sign for Lessolo, on for 1.5km, left for Calea. Signed.

Nearby Ivrea, known by the Romans as Eporedia, was founded in 100 BC. It is now the headquarters of Olivetti.

	Signora Roberta Anau
tel	+39 0125 58618
fax	+39 0125 561963
e-mail	roberta@laminiera.it
web	www.laminiera.it

B&B & Self-catering

map 1   entry 2

Cascina Motto

Via Marzabotto 7, 28010 Divignano

There are flowers everywhere, spilling from the balcony, crowding the patio, climbing the walls of the cottage... wisteria, azaleas, roses. It's a delightful garden, with lawns, spreading trees and a discreet, pretty swimming pool. Roberta's lovely, too, and so warm and friendly that you are bound to feel at home. The family came here years ago – Roberta and David, who's American, their daughters and Roberta's parents, Sergio and Lilla. And their four dogs. They clearly adore the house, which they've restored and filled with paintings and beautiful things, creating an attractive and restful place to stay. The bedroom in the main house has windows facing two ways – over the garden and towards Monte Rosa. Whitewashed walls, a wooden floor, blue cotton rugs and beds painted by the family give it an appealing simplicity. There's a comfortable sofa, too, and lots of books, records and family photos. The cottage, once a hayloft, is charming – bright and airy, with stripped wooden floors, country-style furniture and a balcony. It turns its back on the main house and is completely independent of it. *Minimum stay two nights.*

The National Film Museum in Turin is world-famous and well worth a visit.

rooms	1 + 1: 1 twin. 1 cottage for 2-4.
price	€ 65. Cottage € 75 for 2; € 125 for 4.
meals	Restaurants € 20–€ 25, 1km.
closed	December-February.
directions	From Milano A4 (Laghi); after Gallarate A26 for Alessandria exit Castelletto Ticino. Signs for Novara SS32, 3rd exit for Divignano (via Boschi di Sopra). At Divignano, 2nd left Via Marzabotto.

Roberta Plevani

tel	+39 0321 995350
fax	+39 0321 995350
e-mail	david_robi@katamail.com
web	www.casepiemontesi-novara.vze.com/motto.htm

B&B & Self-catering

Cascina Cesarina

Via dei Cesari 32, Frazione Gagnago, 28040 Borgo Ticino

Drying bunches of maize and gourd hang from the balconies which run across the entire length of the farmhouse's pale exterior, poignant reminders of the sights and smells of harvest festival. Other clues that this is a working farm can be found in the kitchen, where Lorraine cooks using home-grown organic produce, and seems happy to provide whatever combination of meals her guests require. You can have lunch and dinner *in famiglia* in the big farmhouse kitchen, or take a packed lunch and disappear for the day. And there is lots to do: good walks in all directions from the doorstep, and Lake Maggiore and Lake Orta to explore. Those who seek urban pleasures go to Milan or Como, or to shop at the designer outlets just across the border into Switzerland. Lorraine, who is English, knows the area thoroughly. Bedrooms have beamed ceilings and country furniture, and look over the farmyard or across the wild garden (with play area for children, pool and barbecue); the bathroom is shared. Only the occasional bark of a deer from the neighbouring nature reserve disturbs the absolute quiet.

rooms	2: 1 double, 1 family.
price	€ 70–€ 80. Family room € 108. Half-board € 50–€ 58 p.p.
meals	Dinner € 15–€ 18.
closed	Christmas & New Year.
directions	Exit A26 at Castelletto Ticino on SS32 for Novara until Borgo Ticino. On to Gagnago. There, at top of hill, right down Via dei Cesari. Follow road to no. 25, left under arch to house.

	Lorraine Buckley
tel	+39 0321 90491
fax	+39 0321 90491
e-mail	cascinacesarinamail@yahoo.com

The gardens at Villa Taranto and Isola Madre are a must. If you prefer man-made objects, the transport museum at Ranco has a sail tram (sic).

B&B

map 2   entry 4

Il Mongetto Dré Castè

Via Piave 2, 15049 Vignale Monferrato

The epitome of a grand Italian country house, Il Mongetto shows you two sides of Italian life. Hidden behind a high wall, through a massive wooden gate… a handsome 18th-century townhouse. The jam at breakfast, however, is from the farm a couple of miles away. Carlo, a moustachoed, eccentric character with a dry sense of humour, is a fantastic host and produces wine, vegetables and fruit on his organic estate. Your rooms are huge, old and regal, and frescoed ceilings and heavy antiques add splendour. The two top-floor apartments are just as original; private, too; wood is left dry and chopped for you to burn in the open fireplaces. You can have breakfast outside on a terrace, as early or as late as you wish, surrounded by rolling hills. Staff will come to cook you dinner on Friday and Saturday nights and Sunday lunchtime, using produce from the farm, and the food is delicious. One warning: as the rice fields of Vercelli are not too far away, you will need to take mosquito cream should the little beasts find you irresistible. *Minimum stay two nights.*

rooms	3 + 2: 1 double, 2 doubles sharing bath. 2 apartments for 2.
price	€60–€70.
meals	Breakfast €6. Sunday lunch €26. Dinner Friday & Saturday, €26.
closed	Christmas, January, 15-31 August.
directions	In Vignale, through Piazza Mezzarda for Camagna. Entrance 200m on right through large archway with (usually closed) wooden doors.

The Romanesque cathedral at Casale Monferrato was consecrated in 1107 and restored in the 19th century. It has a statue of Mary Magdalene by Bernero.

	Signor Carlo Santopietro
tel	+39 0142 933442
fax	+39 0142 920921
e-mail	info@mongetto.it
web	www.mongetto.it

B&B & Self-catering

Cascina Alberta

Loc. Ca' Prano 14, 15049 Vignale Monferrato

People rave about this attractive hilltop farmhouse in this famous wine-producing area. Marked by two stately cypress trees, the house is two kilometres from the town centre and has 360° views of the surrounding vineyards and hills – sensational. The business is run on *agriturismo* lines by smiling, capable Raffaella. Tiled guest bedrooms are extremely pretty: an old marble-topped table here, a country wardrobe there, beds painted duck-egg blue, walls in soft pastel, and many pieces beautifully painted by Raffaella. Both the bedrooms and the frescoed dining room lie across the farmyard from the main house; here you dine at your own table on delicious Piedmontese dishes at very reasonable prices, and wines are from the estate – some of them have been aged in wooden barrels and are hard to find outside the area. Raffaella pours huge amounts of energy and love into her farmhouse-cosy *cascina*; she speaks excellent English and is happy to help guests get the most out of this enchanting area. Just an hour's drive from the coast.

rooms	5 doubles.
price	€ 54.
meals	Dinner € 16.
closed	January & August.
directions	From Vignale, follow signs to Camagna. After 2km left at roadside chapel. Cascina 400m on right.

	Signora Raffaella de Cristofaro
tel	+39 0142 933313
fax	+39 0142 933313
e-mail	cascinalberta@italnet.it

There's an impressive 11th-century church in Lomello, with flying buttresses supporting an open roof truss, and the remains of a crypt beneath the apse.

B&B

map 7   entry 6

Cascina Nuova
Strada per Pavia 2, 15048 Valenza

Cascina Nuova would not suit everyone. It's a real farm, with tractors parked all over the place – don't expect hanging baskets! Hard-working Federico – friendly and sociable when he has time – farms 300 acres of corn, sunflowers and poplar trees, and has almost achieved his goal of becoming fully organic. The rooms are in the farmhouse, the apartments are in an old stable block, and what they lack in rustic charm they make up for in roominess and practicality. Two are on the ground floor and have been specially designed for wheelchair users; the others are reached via a large communal terrace overlooking the farmyard. Breakfast is at the main house: it's good, with plenty of Federico's own produce. His lovely wife, Armanda, is a busy farmer, too, so can only cook breakfast – but, if you are self-catering, you can buy their eggs, vegetables, jam and home-baked bread to use as you will. The region is not big on tourism but worth exploring – a good spot for a break on your way south. Hikers and bikers will find plenty to do, and Federico will show you where to fish or ride.

Pope Pius V, born in Bosco Marenga nearby, was buried with fitting pomp and ceremony in a huge mausoleum in the church of Santa Croce.

rooms	2 + 10: 1 double, 1 triple. 10 apartments for 2-4.
price	€60. Triple €72. Apartments €300-€500 per week.
meals	Self-catering. Breakfast €8, on request.
closed	Rarely.
directions	From Valenza for Milano, Casale & Pavia. Farm on right 1km out of town.

	Signora Armanda Felli
tel	+39 0131 954763
fax	+39 0131 928553
e-mail	cascinanuova@tin.it
web	www.cascinanuova.com

Self-catering & B&B

La Traversina
Cascina La Traversina 109, 15060 Stazzano

With drowsy shutters and walls swathed in roses, the house and outbuildings appear to be in a permanent state of siesta. As do (by day, at least) the ten cats, basking on warm windowsills and shady terraces. There's a touch of the *Secret Garden* about the half-hidden doors, enticing steps and riotous plants around the place... irises, lavender, oregano. A place to drift and dream, eat and sleep, read and swim. And pretend it's your own, without worrying that the shutters need repainting or the geraniums repotting. The house and farm, on a wooded hillside, have belonged to Rosanna's family for nearly 300 years; she gave up a career as an architect to take them over. It's a most attractive place, full of books, pictures and old furniture. Everyone eats together at a long table in the conservatory or outside, where lights glow in the trees at night. Rosanna and Domenico are the friendliest, most delightful hosts and the home-grown, home-cooked food is a revelation. Sit back and enjoy the flow of wine and multilingual conversation. This is what *agriturismo* should be but, alas, seldom is. *Children over 12 welcome.*

rooms	2 + 4: 1 double, 1 family. 4 apartments: 3 for 2, 1 for 4.
price	€ 84–€ 98. Half-board € 60–€ 68 p.p. Apartments € 105–€ 120 per night.
meals	Dinner included in half-board.
closed	Rarely.
directions	A7 Milan-Genova exit Vignole Borbera for Stazzano; 4km; signs for La Traversina.

Rosanna & Domenico Varese
tel	+39 0143 613 77
fax	+39 0143 613 77
e-mail	latraversina@latraversina.com
web	www.latraversina.com

Stazzano has a High Renaissance parish church, S. Giorgio, commissioned by the Bishop of Tortona.

B&B & Self-catering

map 7   entry 8

Cascina Piola

Via Fontana 2, Fraz. Serra, 14014 Capriglio

Raffaella and Piero are former teachers who left Turin many years ago to bring up their children in the country. Their village home is a late 19th-century farmhouse hidden away in a walled garden next to the church. The two guest bedrooms are warm, cheerful and homely, and have a country farmhouse feel; you have your own entrance so feel very private. Meals are served in a small guests' dining room at one table, and the food is good and generous – as are your hosts. Raffaella describes her style as regional home cooking and emphasises vegetarian dishes; ingredients, and wine, are entirely organic. With the produce from their smallholding they also make and sell large quantities of chutneys, preserves and jam. Surrounded by flat farmland you are off the beaten tourist track but you'll find plenty to do: walking, biking, horse-riding... there are also some lovely old churches and castles to visit. It would be a shame to make this house a mere pit-stop – delightful hosts and good cooking mean guests return again and again.

rooms	2 doubles each with separate bath & shower.
price	€ 58. Half-board € 48 p.p.
meals	Lunch/dinner € 25; book ahead.
closed	15 June-5 July; 24 December-10 January.
directions	A21 exit Villanova d'Asti towards Buttigliera d'Asti to Colle Don Bosco Santuario, then towards Montafia for 1km. House in Serra di Capriglio, beside white church.

Asti, primarily famous among the Brits for 'Spumante', has a superb Gothic cathedral, built in alternating colours of bricks and completed in 1354.

Signora Raffaella Firpo
tel +39 0141 997447
fax +39 0141 997447
e-mail cascinapiola@inwind.it

B&B

Cascina Papa Mora
Via Ferrere 16, 14014 Cellarengo

Come for a taste of life as it is lived on a small farm in northern Italy. Maria Teresa runs the *agriturismo* with her sister, speaks fluent English and makes you really welcome. The farm produces wine, vegetables and fruit, so the only animals you're likely to see here are the frogs hopping around the pond. This is one of Italy's top wine regions for Barbera, Dolcetto, the aristocratic Bracchetto, and Spumante, cheap and cheerful champagne. We can't say that the farmhouse has been lovingly restored – more razed to the ground and rebuilt. However, the bedrooms are pretty with their rafters and pink and green chintz, and the bathrooms are immaculate. There is a pleasant veranda and garden, and a brand new pool. Maria Teresa and her sister also run a restaurant here; they are serious about their organic credentials and use only seasonal produce. Dinner is a feast of gnocchi, tagliatelle, pepperoni cream puffs, anchovies in almond sauce… it's huge fun. Breakfast outside on warm days – the blossom is wonderful, the hills surround you, and the bread comes warm from the wood oven.

rooms	6 doubles/twins.
price	€ 52–€ 68.
meals	Lunch/dinner € 18–€ 23.
closed	2 January–28 February.
directions	A21 exit Villanova d'Asti & for Cellarengo. On outskirts of village left into Via Ferrere, past small chapel to farm.

	Adriana & Maria Teresa Bucco
tel	+39 0141 935126
fax	+39 0141 935444
e-mail	papamora@tin.it

In the church of S. Giovanni Battista in nearby Alba, over the first altar on the left, is a fine portrait of the Madonna by Barnaba di Modena (1377).

Inn

map 6   entry 10

Villa Sampaguita

Bricco Cravera, Valleandona 117, 14100 Asti

Laze in the garden and listen to the crickets. Potter in the woods or orchards and look for fossils. Then, when you're thoroughly rested, sally forth to explore the region's vineyards. (Asti, the centre of the Piedmont wine region, is a 10-minute drive.) The Villa is a modernised late-18th-century *cascina* in an 11-hectare farm in the Val de Botto e Valleandona national park. Standing on a ridge, it has fine views of the Monferrato hills – even, on a clear day, of the Alps. Tim and Rina have converted their barn into a pleasant guest wing, furnished with traditional farmhouse pieces. The bedrooms have French windows and a private balcony; the apartments, on the ground floor, open to verandas. There's also a large guest sitting room with a wood-burning stove and big windows overlooking the terrace. The area is full of good restaurants but, if you don't feel like eating out, Tim and Rina are very happy for you to dine in with them. Rina loves cooking and uses home-grown organic produce in her Italian and Asian dishes. She's kind and charming, and Tim, an American, is a well-travelled and friendly host.

Asti's famous Palio, a bareback horse race around the central Piazza, is the oldest such race in Italy.

rooms	4 + 2: 4 doubles. 2 apartments: 1 for 2, 1 for 4.
price	€ 80–€ 100. Apts € 100–€ 150 per night; € 600–€ 900 per week.
meals	Dinner € 20–€ 25, with wine.
closed	B&B closed 15 December–15 March.
directions	From Asti Ovest exit on A21. Travel away from Asti for 2km. Just after Palucco right at sign 'Valcoresa'. Under autostrada to top of hill. Signed left.

Tim Brewer
tel	+39 0141 295802
fax	+39 0141 295970
e-mail	timbrewer@virgilio.it
web	www.villasampaguita.com

B&B & Self-catering

Il Gioco dell'Oca

Via Crosia 46, 12060 Barolo

Raffaella spent much of her childhood here – the farm used to belong to her grandparents. She is happy to be back, and has tampered as little as possible with the pretty, 18th-century farmhouse. The well-worn, welcoming kitchen, still much as it must have been 50 years ago, is there for you to use as and when you like – it is the warm hub of a sociable house. Next door is an attractive breakfast room, though if it's fine you'll prefer to enjoy breakfast – a feast – out in the garden; it's big enough for everyone to find their own secluded corner. The bedrooms are simple and cosy, with family furniture and wooden beds that look as though they've been there forever. Bathrooms are bright and new. One bedroom has a hob, sink and fridge – a bonus if you have little ones with you. The farm, up in the hills near Barolo (a fabulous area for wines and cheeses), produces wine, fruit and hazelnuts. It's a pity the road is so close but you'll forgive that for the pleasure of staying in such a relaxed, hospitable place, with a charming hostess and a lovely atmosphere.

rooms	7: 6 twins/doubles, 1 triple.
price	€ 60–€ 70. Triple € 65–€ 75.
meals	Restaurant 500m in Barolo.
closed	January-February.
directions	From Asti (east) exit autostrada TO-PC. Follow sign for Alba & Barolo. Left 2km before village, 50m on right sign for house.

	Raffaella Pittatore
tel	+39 0173 56206
fax	+39 0173 56206
e-mail	gioco-delloca@piemonte.com
web	www.gioco-delloca.it

In 1250 the town of Barolo was given to the Falletti family who owned it until 1864. The Barolo wine making technique was invented by the last member of the family, Giulia.

B&B & Self-catering

map 6   entry 12

Auberge de la Maison

Fraz. Entrèves, 11013 Courmayeur

Mont Blanc, the Grandes Jorasses and the Courmayeur valley – what a setting! You're in the old part of the village of Val Fenet, three kilometres from Courmayeur. The Auberge is surrounded by gentle terraces, gardens and meadows and has a quietly elegant and exclusive feel. Yet it's not in the least intimidating, thanks to the cheerful, efficient staff and friendly feel. The bedrooms are uncluttered, stylish and comfortable, with mellow colours and lots of space. Many have a third bed disguised as a sofa; nearly all have a balcony, with views that range from good to superb. A Tuscan influence is detectable in the décor (the owner is from Florence); his impressive collection of pictures and prints of Val d'Aosta, from old promotional posters to oil paintings, makes a fascinating display on the walls, and an old, reassembled wooden mountain house is an unusual feature in the reception/sitting area. The inn has a small fitness centre, too, with a sauna and hydromassage. Depending on the season, you can fish for trout or play a round of golf, ski right to the ski lift or don crampons for a winter ascent.

rooms	33: 27 doubles, 3 family rooms, 3 suites.
price	€ 105–€ 160. Half-board € 160–€ 210.
meals	Dinner € 30; wine-list.
closed	40 days after end ski season.
directions	From Courmayeur for Traforo del Monte Bianco, past garage & Entrèves, keep right, signposted.

'It commenced snowing and blowing hard. I sounded a retreat at once and ordered them to make tracks for Courmayeur.' Edward Whymper, from his diary, 21 June, 1865

Leo Garin

tel	+39 0165 869811
fax	+39 0165 869759
e-mail	info@aubergemaison.it
web	www.aubergemaison.it

Hotel

Lo Ratelë

Fraz. Ville 33, 11010 Allein

Paola's cooking and the matchless views are the two major attractions of this entirely unpretentious *pensione*. The simple, bistro-style restaurant – converted from old, arched animal stalls – is a popular eating place, so you'll need to book in advance. Hams, sausages, country soups and home-baked black bread are specialities, as well as *la coppa del'Amicizia* – a mix of hot coffee and liqueur drunk from a many-spouted wooden bowl. Goats, cows and sheep are reared on the small family farm, and Paola grows her own vegetables, too. She's a real countrywoman, with twinkling eyes and feet planted firmly on the ground. If your French or Italian is up to it, you'll glean lots of entertaining information about the valley. She'll also sell you some of her home-produced goodies (her old-fashioned kitchen is packed with gleaming jars). The clean, no-frills bedrooms are fairly basic but, if you get one at the front of the house, you'll have the most wonderful views from a balcony scarlet with geraniums. Lo Ratelë's long, traditional stone front faces out over a wide, lovely valley to snow-capped mountains.

rooms	7 doubles.
price	€72–€78 for 2 half-board.
meals	Dinner €21, book ahead.
closed	10-20 September & February.
directions	From Aosta route 27; after Gignod right. Towards Allein on A2, signposted.

Lo Ratelë *means honey badger.*

	Signora Paola Conchâtre
tel	+39 0165 78265
fax	+39 0165 78265

B&B

map 1   entry 14

Les Écureuils

Fraz. Homené Dessus 8, 11010 Saint Pierre

No designer chic here, but a hard-working farm, specialising in – and known for – superb goat's cheese. Dating back to the 14th century, it's a half-way house between the valley and the high alpine pastures. The bedrooms feel like proper family spare rooms rather than units done up for tourists: homely and cosy. There are old linen window-hangings and photos showing the farm in different seasons. The dining room, just off the kitchen, is bistro-like; crochet-trimmed shelves hold books and miscellaneous collections of ornaments. Excellent food is presented in a stylish, rustic fashion – everything, apart from the local bread and wine, is home-grown or homemade. (There's a little farm shop, too, where you can stock up on goat's cheese if you haven't overdosed already.) Outside, the garden is steep but the odd chair or bench on the small terraces makes a great place to sit and absorb the mountain views across the Val d'Aosta. Three generations of the family live here. They are quiet and friendly and immensely committed to what they do. Given time, they'll talk to you about their way of life.

It was through the Val d'Aosta that Hannibal marched his elephants in the third century BC.

rooms	5: 3 doubles, 1 triple, 1 single.
price	€ 44–€ 50.
meals	Dinner € 13–€ 20.
closed	December–January.
directions	From Aosta SS26 for M. Biano. At Sarre right up hill to Ville-sur-Sarre; left signed to Les Écureuils.

Famiglia Gontier-Ballauri-Moniotto

tel	+39 0165 903831
fax	+39 0165 909849
e-mail	lesecureuils@libero.it
web	www.lesecureuils.it

B&B

Petit Coin de Paradis
Loc. Vetan 19, 11010 Saint Pierre

Wide open meadows and exceptional views, marmots, chamois and glorious flowers. At 1,680m above sea level, this really is a wonderful position, surrounded by high alp and snow-capped mountains, with the splendours of the Gran Paradiso National Park to the south. What was once a tiny hamlet has been turned into a colourful, rustic place to stay. The old, rough-stone houses have pretty wooden balconies with flowers tumbling through the railings. Green lawns with lots of toys make a great place for children to play and there's comfortable garden furniture for the grown-ups. The whole atmosphere is casual, friendly and full of good cheer, and you can self-cater or do B&B. Daniela is a delightful character and has done all the interior decoration herself; it is charmingly rural. Some of the bedrooms are reached by ladder-like stairs; throughout there's a mix of modern pine panelling and white walls, country furniture and wood-burning stoves, bright gingham and Swiss cotton. Just across the track from the houses is a tiny whitewashed church, silhouetted against the mountains and the sky. *French spoken.*

rooms	3 apartments: 1 for 2, 2 for 5.
price	€65. Singles €37.
meals	Self-catering. Agriturismo 50m up hill.
closed	Rarely.
directions	Autostrada A5 exit Aosta ovest for Saint Pierre. Left at 1st traffic lights, right to Saint Nicolas, up hill onto Vetan 8km.

	Signora Daniela Berlier
tel	+39 0165 908970
fax	+39 0165 908970
e-mail	info@bebvetan.it
web	www.bebvetan.it

The first recorded ascent of Gran Paradiso (4,061m) was made in 1860 by J Cowell, W Dundas, M Payot and J Tairraz.

B&B & Self-catering

map 1   entry 16

www.thirdangle.com

lombardy

Villa Simplicitas & Solferino

22028 San Fedele d'Intelvi

The presiding genius behind this quaint, wonderful place is Ulla. Everything about her 19th-century villa is a reflection of her intensely human approach; she's serene, imaginative and unconventional, too. Bedrooms are decorated with murals, soft browns and wrought-iron or brass beds; all draw on the grand old sweet-chestnut trees that survey the garden and seem to be a part of the rooms. There's a warm sense of fun glowing in every corner, whether from a dotty old lamp stand – balefully ugly – or from the antique piano and the billiard table that's as old as the house. The food, served with understated elegance in the handsome conservatory (or on the candlelit terrace at night) is superb. Above all, there is an abiding impression of deep rural tranquillity at San Fedele; it really is worth sacrificing a couple of days of sun-baking on the lake shores to stay here. Strike out from the door on wonderful walks, reach Como in 15 minutes by car. The lakes, with the mountains, are irresistible – and due to the high altitude, you never get too hot at night.

rooms	10 doubles.
price	€94–€120.
	Half-board €60–€75 p.p.
	Full-board €70–€85 p.p.
meals	Dinner included.
closed	10 October–April.
directions	From Como north for Argegno; left through San Fedele. After 1st bus station bear left; follow winding road for 2km.

'One cannot describe the beauty of the Italian Lakes, nor would one try if one could,' wrote Henry James in a mood of uncharacteristic brevity.

Signora Ulla Wagner

tel	+39 031 831132
fax	+39 031 830455
e-mail	ulwagner@tin.it
web	www.villasimplicitas.it

Hotel

Villetta il Ghiro & Villetta la Vigna

Via al Forno 5, Cardano, 22010 Grandola ed Uniti

Wisteria was growing *through* the old convent when Ann and her husband fell in love with it. The roof had fallen in as well but, undeterred, they went ahead and turned it into the lovely place it is today. Though you can't see the lake from here, you do get a glimpse of the magnificent golf course Ann's father-in-law once part-owned – the second oldest in Italy. The apartments are attractive, homely and extremely well-equipped, with large, airy rooms and outside stairs. Il Ghiro is on the first floor of a former hay barn; La Vigna, above the garages, has a second bedroom opening off the first and a little balcony which catches the afternoon sun. Children are welcome but must be supervised in the lovely garden because of the pool, even though it is fenced. (There's tennis, too.) Birdsong is all you hear, yet you are a short drive from the bustle of Menaggio and Como. The position is wonderful, on the isthmus between Lakes Lugano and Como, on the edge of a cobbled village, encircled by mountains, meadows, hamlets and winding country lanes.

rooms	2 apartments: 1 for 2, 1 for 2-8.
price	Apartment for 2 €516–€1,032 per week; for 2-8 €516–€2,364 per week.
meals	Self-catering. 2 restaurants 5-minute walk.
closed	October-April.
directions	From Menaggio Porlezza N340 to Grandola, towards Porlezza & Lugano. Right at bakery; immediately right for Cardano. Right into Via al Forno.

The Villa Carlotta, built for Princess Carlotta by her Prussian mother, has a collection of 18th-century sculpture, including Canova's Cupid and Psyche

	Mrs Ann Dexter
tel	+39 0344 32740
fax	+39 0344 30206
e-mail	ann.dexter@libero.it

Self-catering

map 2   entry 18

Alberghetto La Marianna

Via Regina 57, 22011 Cadenabbia di Griante

Paola understands the needs of the modestly-heeled traveller like no other: she and her family ran one of Italy's best youth hostels for 20 years. Now they've bought this lakeside villa and set it up for B&B. It has been simply modernised and redecorated and has a relaxing, homely feel. Bedrooms are fresh and functional, with cheerfully tiled shower rooms and lakeside views. Some have balconies, one has its own little terrace; a road runs between you and the busy lake, so, if you're a light sleeper, it might be worth giving up those watery views for a room at the back – at least in summer. Paola is a delight and, in her own words, treats guests as friends. Breakfasts include homemade bread, cakes and jams; she's also a good cook and a "mistress of desserts" – try them out in the restaurant for dinner (run by husband Ty and chef Antonio). You won't be short of advice here on things to do: visits to gardens and villas, boat tours to Isola Comacina, day trips to St Moritz and the Engadine. Or simply dream away the hours on the terrace that juts onto the shimmering lake.

The Isola Comacina is one of the major archeological sites in Lombardy and is known as the 'medieval Larian Pompeii'.

rooms	8: 7 doubles, 1 single.
price	€68–€75. Singles €52–€58.
meals	Restaurant €20–€50, with wine.
closed	Mid-November-mid-March.
directions	From Como on lakeside road to Cadenabbia 30km, 300m after ferry port.

Paola Cioccarelli

tel	+39 0344 43095
fax	+39 0344 43095
e-mail	inn@la-marianna.com
web	www.la-marianna.com

B&B

Albergo Milano
Via XX Settembre 29, 23829 Varenna

Colour-washed houses cluster round the church on a little, rocky promontory. The lake laps gently on three sides; on the fourth, tree-covered slopes rear steeply upwards. Wander along a narrow cobbled street, catching glimpses of the lake down every side alley, and you come to Albergo Milano, right on the waterfront. It's pretty, traditional and disarmingly small – just eight bedrooms. Bettina and Egidio are engaging hosts, thrilled to be running their own very personal little hotel after years of working for big companies in the hotel industry. They have just one helper and otherwise do everything themselves. Everywhere is simply and stylishly furnished, with warm colours and country furniture. Each bedroom is individual, with a balcony or terrace and a lake view. The dining room's big French windows open onto a wonderful wide terrace, where you can eat out on fine days, the lake stirring beside you. Bettina is a good source of information about Varenna and its surroundings: this is a great spot from which to explore Lake Como and there's a regular train service into Bergamo and Milan. A little gem.

rooms	8 doubles.
price	€ 110–€ 130. Singles €95–€ 105.
meals	Dinner € 25.
closed	December-February.
directions	From Lecco SS36 for Sondrio; 1st exit for Abbadia Lariana. After 15km, before tunnel, left for Varenna.

The Fiumelatte, only 250m long, has the distinction of being the shortest river in Italy.

Bettina & Egidio Mallone

tel	+39 0341 830298
fax	+39 0341 830061
e-mail	hotelmilano@varenna.net
web	www.varenna.net

Hotel

map 2   entry 20

Il Torchio

Via Ghislanzoni 24, Loc. Vescogna , 23885 Calco

Marcella's happy personality fills the house with good cheer. She and Franco are artists – she an animator, he a painter; if you enjoy the bohemian life you will love it here. Franco also has an antiquarian bookshop in Milan, which explains all the books in the sitting room. Their home began life in 1600 as the stables of the noble Calchi family; now you enter through a fine stone archway into a courtyard. Franco's bold paintings adorn the walls and every corner is crammed with curios that Marcella has picked up on flea market forays. Bedrooms are endearingly old-fashioned – no frills but good, comfortable beds. The big, private suite is entered via French windows; another window has green views down to Calco. There's a huge, comfortable bed, family photos on the walls, and a cabinet filled amusingly with children's old toys. The bathroom is basic with lovely hand-painted tiles. The whole family is a delight, including the cats, and Marcella's cooking is superb. Canoe or ski (a one-hour drive), or visit Verona, Lake Como and the chic shops of Milan.

rooms	3: 1 double, 1 twin, sharing bath, 1 suite.
price	€ 52. Suite € 67.
meals	Dinner € 15; book ahead.
closed	Rarely.
directions	From Calco right at traffic lights after petrol station for Corso Italia. Right via Ghislanzoni. At top drive on right of right-hand turn; 100m 2nd left (signed Vescogna). House on left.

Worth seeing up the road in Pondida is a Benedictine monastery with two cloisters, and the 14th-century church of S. Giacomo.

Signora Marcella Pisacane

tel	+39 039 508724
fax	+39 0286 453229
e-mail	il_torchio@hotmail.com

B&B

Casa Clelia

Via Corna 1/3, 24039 Sotto il Monte Giovanni XXIII

The hotel has been sculpted out of the 11th-century convent, using the principles of eco-bio architecture. Cows peer from sheds as you arrive, chickens, geese and sheep bustle – this is a working farm. The main house stands proud against wooded hills and beyond are convent, outhouses, orchards and barns. Rosanna is a dear and looks after you as well as she looks after her young family. She is a talented cook and one of her treats is her taster menu, whereby you can nibble, guilt-free, at several delicacies at once. The bedrooms, all a good size, are stunning, and original, warm with wood, stone and bold colours; bathroom are modern, lighting subtle. Heat comes from a woodburner integrated with solar panels; cork and coconut ensure the sound-proofing of walls. There are three resident children, so your own will be welcome, free to run wild in the gardens, orchards and 80,000 square metres of woods. There's horse-riding nearby, too. Hard to imagine a more wonderful place for families... or for a get-away-from-it-all weekend.

rooms	10: 8 doubles, 2 triples.
price	€80–€95.
meals	Lunch/dinner €15–€28 with wine.
closed	Rarely.
directions	Exit A4 at Capriate to Sotto il Monte. Follow yellow signs.

	Signora Rosanna Minonzio
tel	+39 035 799133
fax	+39 035 791788
e-mail	info@casaclelia.com
web	www.casaclelia.com

At Almenno S. Bartolomeo, the circular church of S. Tomé dates from around 1,000 AD, the best example of early Romanesque architecture in Lombardy.

B&B

map 3   entry 22

B&B Vecchia Milano

Via Ruggero Bonghi 12, 20141 Milan

This really is different. As you arrive at no. 12 of this block of flats, you'll wonder what you've let yourself in for – a hundred names on the buzzer! Once inside, be prepared for a labyrinth of courtyards and passageways before arrival on the fourth floor. But it's worth it – you couldn't be staying with nicer people. Edy, the mother, is a wonderful cook; her mother, Anselma Ferrari, is an artist who gives lessons nearby. And the accommodation is a delight: the apartment's polished wooden floors and white walls are a perfect foil for beautiful old rugs and Anselma's unexpected, vibrant paintings and sculptures. Brass pots and pans gleam in the kitchen and one bedroom is stuffed with exciting reminders of the family's travels round the world. The bedroom in the house (it and the apartment have their own private entrances) belonged to son Davide before he left home. It shares a clean, bright bathroom with the household's youngest son and is a cosy and interesting room, with an old rocking horse, bookshelves spilling over with travel guides, and a map of the world over the bed.

Leonardo da Vinci's The Last Supper *is on the walls of the refectory of Santa Maria Delle Grazie in Milan.*

rooms	1 + 1: 1 single + sofabed, sharing bath. 1 apartment for 2-4.
price	€ 72–€ 90. Singles € 45–€ 60.
meals	Dinner € 20, book ahead.
closed	June-August.
directions	In Milan, ringroad south, exit Viale Liguria for Assago to Piazza Maggi. Right over Cavalcavia bridge, left at lights; Via Ruggero Bonghi 2nd right.

Edy Lurani
tel +39 02 45494348
e-mail edylurani@hotmail.com

Antica Locanda dei Mercanti

Via San Tomaso 6, 20123 Milan

A special find in a city of charmless hotels, though on arrival you may wonder whether you've come to the right place. Press on – one of those bells is the right one. Up to the second floor, where the tiny reception area does little to announce itself, and you've arrived: no public spaces, just a brilliantly designed collection of beautiful bedrooms. Four of them have private terraces edged with lush bamboo which, together with the white elegance and simplicity of the bedrooms, give a Japanese feel. The master bedrooms are large with double windows draped in rich damask, deep carpets and soft sofas; there's air-conditioning or ceiling fans, bathrooms are impeccable, and books and magazines replace TV. The standard rooms, too, have charm, with beamed ceilings and bedspreads and curtains *all'antica*. The brains behind this novel concept is Paola, as efficient as she is friendly and engaging. All this is a short stroll from the Duomo, the Castello Sforzesca and the lovely restaurants of the Brera district.

rooms	14 doubles, 4 with private roof terrace.
price	€ 129–€ 155, with roof terrace € 250.
meals	Breakfast € 9, served in your room. Lovely restaurants nearby.
closed	Rarely.
directions	Via San Tomaso is small street off Via Rovello, near Piazza Castello. No sign, just a brass plate.

Signora Paola Ora

tel	+39 02 8054080
fax	+39 02 8054090
e-mail	locanda@locanda.it
web	www.locanda.it

The Piazza dei Mercanti was the commercial centre of medieval Milan, and its palaces the seats of the various city guilds.

Hotel

 map 2   entry 24

Cappuccini
Via Cappuccini 54, 25033 Cologne Franciacorta

It must have been a formidable task to restore this old monastery, perched amid olive groves on the slopes of Mount Orfano, but it has been done with such sympathy and ingenuity that many would willingly be cloistered here forever. Happily much remains unchanged; the cloister is simply graced with lemon trees and in the corner a small door leads to a spiral stone staircase and up to a narrow corridor with six small doors. The rooms beyond these are, however, beyond the dreams of any monk. Immaculate cream-washed walls, white linen on big beds, rugs on stone floors, the odd antique, exquisite lighting. The bathroom basins are old marble on antique stands, mirrors are large, towels snowy white. Camouflaged in each room are a fridge, television, phone and CD player, and music to play (Gregorian chants, perhaps?). Downstairs is a labyrinth of rooms including a small sitting room with an open fireplace and a huge, illuminated, stained-glass panel. The dining room is elegant, the menu mouthwatering. Monastic peace for sophisticates.

rooms	7: 6 doubles, 1 suite.
price	€ 190. Suite € 220.
meals	Breakfast € 15. Restaurant à la carte.
closed	Rarely.
directions	A4 exit Palazzolo sull'Oglio towards Brescia. Before Cologne left for Erbusco, right in village. Cappuccini on left.

Don't miss the lovely old centre of Bergamo, and the Accademia Carrara museum has works by Botticelli, Giovanni Bellini, Carpaccio and many more...

Massimo & Rosalba Pelizzari

tel	+39 030 7157254
fax	+39 030 7157257
e-mail	info@cappuccini.it
web	www.cappuccini.it

B&B

Hotel du Lac
Via P. Colletta 21, 25084 Villa di Gargnano

The hotel oozes old-fashioned charm. A 1900s townhouse, it shares the same street as the villa from where DH Lawrence eulogised about the "milky lake" – Lake Garda. The ox-blood façade with white relief and green shutters is as striking as the view from the patio that overhangs the water... and you can swim from here. Valerio's grandparents lived in the house until 1959 and much of their furniture remains. The family is charming, and could not be more helpful. Roomy bedrooms are wonderfully old-fashioned with big beds and wardrobes, Thirties' lights and polished terrazzo floors; beds are deeply comfortable, dressed in crisp cotton. Six of the rooms look onto the lake and have small balconies; others have terraces. The dining room, around a central courtyard with a palm that disappears into the clouds, looks directly onto the lake. You can also dine upstairs on the open terrace, where metal tables and chairs are shaded by an arbour of kiwi – a magical spot at night, the water lapping below, the lights twinkling in the distance. There's even a small music room with a piano to play – guests often do.

rooms	12 doubles.
price	€84–€114.
meals	Restaurant à la carte, from €35.
closed	First week of November–week before Easter.
directions	Bus: N.45 to Villa (di Gargnano) & slip road down to lake; left into Via P. Colletta. Parking 100m from hotel at Hotel Gardenia.

	Signor Valerio Arosio
tel	+39 0365 71107
fax	+39 0365 71055
e-mail	info@hotel-dulac.it
web	www.hotel-dulac.it

Just beyond Gardone Riviera is the Vittoriale estate which belonged to the poet Gabriele D'Annunzion, with a museum dedicated to his turbulent life.

Hotel

map 3   entry 26

Hotel Gardenia al Lago
Via Colletta 53, 25084 Villa di Gargnano

Jasmine-scented gardens and green lawns reach to the lake's edge; a wide terrace makes the most of the fabulous views. The hotel stands cream and white and dignified against the steep, wooded foothills of Mount Baldo. It was bought by the Arosio family as a summer home in 1925. They were piano-makers from Milan (note the name of the piano in the lounge) and in the 1950s turned the house first into a guesthouse, then, in the early 1960s, into a hotel. The bedrooms have just been completely renovated – some attractive frescoes were uncovered in the process – and are now very beautiful, decorated and furnished in creams and beige, with wonderfully restored terrazzo floors and exquisite new bathrooms. Some have French windows onto a private terrace, others a small balcony. The rest of the hotel has kept a rather charming 1950s/60s flavour, comfortable and friendly. Many guests return again and again, some to paint – the walls are adorned with their watercolours. All around the hotel are lemon and olive trees: the family produce their own olive oil and the Lake Garda variety is reputed to be the best!

rooms	25: 17 doubles, 8 singles.
price	€94–€120. Singles €40–€50.
meals	Dinner €30.
closed	First week of November-week before Easter.
directions	Take 45 bis to Villa di Gargnano & slip road down to lake. Left into Via Colletta. Parking at hotel.

In 1440 Lake Garda was the scene of a major battle between Venice and the Viscontis, rulers of Milan.

Giorgio & Andrea Arosio
tel	+39 0365 71195
fax	+39 0365 72594
e-mail	info@hotel-gardenia.it
web	www.hotel-gardenia.it

Hotel

Villa San Pietro
Via San Pietro 25, 25018 Montichiari

A splendid 17th-century home. Annamaria, warm, vivacious, multi-lingual, is married to a Jacques, French and charming; they have a young child, and Anna's parents live in self-contained splendour at the far end. A rather grand name for a house that is one of a terrace, but once inside you realise why we have included it here. No expense has been spared; it is an immaculate home. There are oak beams, ancient brick floors, fine family antiques, floral fabrics, not a speck of dust. Guests have their own sitting room with a frescoed ceiling, and bedrooms (air-conditioned) are delightful. Perhaps the most exceptional thing about the house are the large garden and terrace, and there is also a pretty ground-floor *loggia* for memorable meals (Annamaria's dinners are sophisticated regional affairs, we are told.) You are close to the town centre yet in a quiet road, and Montichiari is perfectly sited for forays into Garda, Brescia, Verona and Venice. Your hosts, who own a cosmetic company, can even arrange massages and facials. *Minimum stay two nights.*

rooms	3 doubles.
price	€90. Singles €50.
meals	Dinner with wine €25–€30, on request.
closed	Rarely.
directions	From Milan motorway A4 exit Brescia east towards Montichiari, city centre & Duomo. Via S. Pietro leads off corner of central piazza.

	Jacques & Annamaria Ducroz
tel	+39 030 961232
fax	+39 030 9981098
e-mail	villa-san-pietro@art-with-attitude.com
web	www.art-with-attitude.com/villa/san_pietro.html

The facade of the 18th-century parish church in Montichiari, and the frescoes by Scalvini, are worth seeing — as is the 12th-century church S. Pancrazio.

B&B

map 3   entry 28

Tenuta Le Sorgive - Le Volpi

Via Piridello 6, 46040 Solferino

Although one cannot deny the beauty of Lake Garda, it's a relief to escape to the open land of Lombardy. This 19th-century *cascina* with ochre-washed façade and green shutters has been in the Serenelli family for two generations. The exterior, crowned with pierced dovecote and flanked by a carriage house and stables with wide open arches, remains impressive, even if a little of its character has been lost during restoration. Le Sorgive is still a working 28-hectare family farm with vines, cereal crops and livestock; the eight big rooms, with wooden rafters, are a mix of old and new. Some have attractive, metalwork beds, others a balcony; two have a mezzanine with beds for the children. All are crisp and clean. This is a great place for families to visit as there's so much to do: horse-riding and mountain biking from the farm, go-karting and archery nearby, watersports at Garda. There's also a large gym and a pool. Vittorio's sister has a *cascina* down the road where you can sample delicious gnocchi, Mantovan sausages and mouthwatering fruit tarts.

rooms	8 + 2: 8 twins/doubles. 2 apartments for 4.
price	€82–€102. Apartments €516–€845 per week.
meals	Dinner with wine €15–€23. Restaurant closed January & Monday-Tuesday.
closed	Rarely.
directions	Exit A4 Milano-Venezia at Desenzano for Castiglione & then Mantova. Solferino signed to left. House on left before town.

The 1859 Battle of Solferino, when Piedmontese and French troops beat the Austrians to achieve Italian independence, is marked by a museum and a monument.

	Signor Vittorio Serenelli
tel	+39 0376 854252
fax	+39 0376 855256
e-mail	info@lesorgive.it
web	www.lesorgive.it

B&B & Self-catering

Trebisonda

Via Tononi 100, Loc. Trebisonda, 46040 Monzambano

Enrico and Valeria have exchanged the rat race for the country life amid olive and peach groves and three hectares of prairie. They are the loveliest people, full of enthusiasm for this place and keen to share its beauty. The farmhouse, which dates back to the 15th century, has been renovated and decorated with understated good taste. Apartments are big, with white walls and original floors, fabrics and towels are cream and white, the furniture a mix of antique, Conran and flea-market finds. Shower rooms are gorgeous, old railway sleepers set against white walls make a perfect stair to beds upstairs, kitchens are simple but well-equipped. Enrico and Valeria breed horses, and will take you to meet the foals. Breakfast is a dizzy array of organic honeys and homemade jams, served in the main house. Cycle along the Mincio river, visit Lake Garda, Mantova or Venice, play golf… or stay here and glory in the views, the peace punctuated only by distant bells. *Minimum stay two nights.*

rooms	3 apartments: 2 for 2 + 2 children, 1 for 4.
price	€ 75 for 2; € 95 for 3; € 120 for 4.
meals	Pizzeria nearby, € 15.
closed	Rarely.
directions	From autostrada Milano-Venezia exit Peschiera del Garda & Valeggio. Head for Borghetto & Solferino. After 3km, signs for Trebisonda.

	Signora Valeria Moretti
tel	+39 0376 809381
fax	+39 0376 809381
e-mail	trebisonda@libero.it

The Veneto 'risotti' tend to be more liquid than those to the west and often contain seafood and vegetables such as peas, spinach and asparagus.

B&B & Self-catering

map 3   entry 30

Photography by Michael Busselle

trentino-alto adige

Hotel Castel Fragsburg

Via Fragsburger Strasse 3, 39012 Merano

Stay in May and you'll experience the glory and the scent of the wisteria that drapes itself the length the *loggia* where meals are served. The Fragsburg, built as a shooting lodge for the local gentry, perches on the side of a hill with a crystal-clear view across the valley to spectacular mountains; perhaps the most magnificent spot from which to enjoy the view is the pool. Sun yourself on the screened deck on a hot day; wander the grounds, beautiful with huge, sub-tropical trees, and surrounded by vineyards. Big bedrooms have been redecorated and the combination of rugs, wood and some old painted headboards softens any stark newness. Beds are deeply inviting with piles of pillows; white bathrooms are stunning, full of bathrobes and yellow and white striped towels. The whole feel of the place is wonderfully Austrian, food and meal times included. The fairytale castles and scenery of this northern region are not to be missed, and the Ortner family ensure you get the most out of your stay.

'Mountains are to the rest of the body of the earth, what violent muscular action is to the body of man.' John Ruskin, *Modern Painters*

rooms	18: 6 doubles, 2 singles, 10 suites.
price	€150–€190.
	Half-board €95–€145 p.p.
meals	Dinner à la carte from €25.
closed	9 November–25 March.
directions	Exit A22 Bolzano Sud; Merano Sud. Right to Merano. After 1.5km right at Shell station to Scenna. After 2.5km, bridge on right, signed to Labers. Over bridge for 5km.

Signor Alexander Ortner

tel	+39 0473 244071
fax	+39 0473 244493
e-mail	info@fragsburg.com
web	www.fragsburg.com

Hotel

Schwarz Adler Turm Hotel

Kirchgasse 2, 39040 Kurtatsch/Cortaccia

All around are the soaring, craggy Dolomites – there's nothing like them to give a sobering perspective on man's place in nature's scheme. But if you do feel overawed, you'll be soothed on arrival – Manfred, Sonja and their staff are so delighted to see you, so eager to do all they can to help. Though the hotel is only 11 years old, it's a faithful reproduction of a traditional manor house, and blends in well with the 16th-century houses in the village. The roomy, light bedrooms are carpeted, comfortable and quiet, with glorious views. Each has a loggia, balcony or direct access to the garden. Cortaccia (or Kurtasch, as the locals still call it) stands at 300m, looking down over a wide valley floor green with orchards. The area, originally in Austria, has only been part of Italy since 1919 and the hotel's cuisine reflects this – an imaginative tour de force of Italian and South Tyrolean dishes. There's a terrific wine list, too. You could complete the soothing process by a visit to the Verona Opera Festival; the town is just an hour's drive away and the hotel will arrange tickets and a bus service.

rooms	24 doubles.
price	€ 120–€ 160. Half-board € 138–€ 178 (5 March-15 November).
meals	Restaurants within walking distance.
closed	22-27 December, 2 weeks January.
directions	From A22 exit Egna/Ora. On for 8km for Termeno; left for Cortaccia; signs.

Bolzano's Museum of Archaeology is the home of Ötzi, the 5,000 year-old Ice Man found in the glacier by two climbers.

	Famiglia Pomella
tel	+39 0471 880600
fax	+39 0471 880601
e-mail	info@turmhotel.it
web	www.turmhotel.it

Hotel

map 4   entry 32

Ploerr

Oberinn 45, 39050 Renon

Heidi country – and if gentle walks with heavenly views, healthy home cooking and the only entertainment a pack of cards are what make your perfect holiday, then you'll love it here. The Vigl family run the guesthouse and nine-hectare farm with quiet efficiency. Franz milks the cows, sitting on a one-legged stool, and serves at table. Maria Luisa does the cooking and son Herbert does a bit of everything. Rooms are simple with spotless white duvets on new pine beds and all but one have a balcony (south-facing, in most cases) and a view. Take your own big fluffy towel if you can't live without one! For breakfast there are their own cheese and eggs, served outside in the fresh mountain air; this is also a popular lunch stop for walkers. Pretty alpine tables and cushioned benches are yours for the evening. Children will be in their element, with the endless fields, the cows and two wooden swings in the garden. Gentle Franz was anxious to emphasize that the family still think of themselves as farmers, and they open their house to guests in the best tradition of hospitality. You will be made very welcome. *Minimum stay three nights.*

Titian, born at Pieve di Cadore, often recalled the strange limestone spires and peaks of the Dolomites in the backgrounds of his paintings.

rooms	11: 10 doubles, 1 single.
price	€45. Half-board €32.50 p.p.
meals	Breakfast €7. Lunch/dinner €10.
closed	10 January–20 February.
directions	Exit A22 at Bolzano Nord; to Renon. At Colalbo left before petrol station & left to Anna di Sopra. After 4km signs.

Signor Herbert Vigl
tel	+39 0471 602118
fax	+39 0471 602251
e-mail	berggasthof@ploerr.com
web	www.ploerr.com

B&B

Hotel Cavallino D'Oro

Piazza Kraus 1, 39040 Castelrotto

The village is postcard Tyrolean, and the Little Gold Horse has been welcoming travellers for 600 years. The market still runs every Friday in the summer months: local farmers set up their stalls at the foot of the beautiful 18th-century bell tower. This was Austria once, not so very long ago: the local customs, and dress, are still alive, and regular concerts take place at the inn over dinner. Bedrooms, though not large, are delightful; some look onto the medieval square, others have balconies with glorious hill and mountain views. There's a fascinating mix of antique country beds, some hand-decorated, some four-poster, some both. Many of the doors are painted, too, as are the beams in the muted green and peach sitting room. Dine in the smart, wooden-ceilinged dining room; breakfast in the rustic *stube*, a wood-panelled room with geraniums at the window and cheery check tablecloths. Susanna and Stefan are as friendly as they are efficient. There's swimming, walking and biking in summer; sleigh rides, skiing and alpine magic in winter. Alpe di Siusi is a free bus ride away.

rooms	18: 5 doubles, 2 twins, 4 triples, 4 singles, 3 suites.
price	€80. Singles €50. Suites €100. Half-board €49–€75 p.p.
meals	Full board & half-board available.
closed	November.
directions	A22 motorway, exit Bolzano Nord. Castelrotto signed at exit. Hotel in market square in town centre.

	Susanna & Stefan Urthaler
tel	+39 0471 706337
fax	+39 0471 707172
e-mail	cavallino@cavallino.it
web	www.cavallino.it

The men in these parts traditionally wear blue aprons jauntily tucked up into their belts. Why? Answers on a postcard, please.

Hotel

map 4   entry 34

Photography by John Coe

veneto &
fruili-venezia giulia

La Foresteria Serego Alighieri
Via Stazione 2, 37020 Gargagnago di Valpolicella

Feel immersed in history on this vast, magnificent 650-year-old estate. It lies in the very heart of the Valpolicella wine-producing region, so wine is the thing: apartments are named after local grapes and the wine shop is open six days a week. They also produce olive oil, balsamic vinegar, grappa, honey and jam and if you're serious about cooking you can do a course (pre-arranged, for a minimum of 12). Learn how the ingredients are grown, how the locals would prepare and eat them, and with which wine; then have a go in the professionally equipped kitchen. The apartments are roomy, with a soft green, white and creamy-yellow colour scheme and are in a separate, carefully restored wing. Oseleta, for two, is on three floors of an old tower, with rooms linked by a narrow spiral stair. All of them have kitchens – though it's hard to imagine guests here lugging plastic bags from the car to self-cater; nor is there anything so brash as a swimming pool! The gardens and orchards are dreamy, and the all-pervading peace a balm – even the staff, Italian and delightful, speak in soft voices.

'Wine brings to light the hidden secrets of the soul.' Horace

rooms	8 apartments: 4 for 2, 2 for 3, 2 for 4.
price	Apartment for 2 € 125–€ 190; for 3 € 180–€ 252; for 4 € 200–€ 307.
meals	Breakfast included, otherwise self-catering.
closed	January.
directions	A22 exit Verona Nord for Valpolicella & Trento. At end left for S. Ambrogio for La Foresteria.

Conte Pieralvise di Serego Alighieri

tel	+39 045 7703622
fax	+39 045 7703523
e-mail	serego@easyasp.it
web	www.seregoalighieri.it

Self-catering

Cà del Rocolo

Via Gaspari 3, località Quinto, 37034 Verona

Such an undemanding, delightful place to be and such a warm, enthusiastic young family to be with. Maurizio used to run a vegetarian restaurant in Verona, Ilaria was a journalist, and they gave it all up to find a better life for their children. Their 19th-century farmhouse is on the side of a hill overlooking green forested hills and the vast Lessinia National Park. Maurizio has done much of the renovation himself, using traditional materials, and the result is attractive and unfussy. Simple cotton rugs cover stripped bedroom floors, rough plaster walls are whitewashed and the rooms are big and airy, with solid country furniture and excellent beds and bathrooms. Family meals are at the long farmhouse kitchen table or out on the terrace, making the most of the views. Delicious fresh food, local organic wines and great conversation make dinner a memorable occasion. (The food is mostly vegetarian, so if you want fish or chicken you'll have to ask.) It's a seven-hectare farm, with olives, fruit trees and vines, chickens and horses; there are local walks and nature trails galore and always something going on.

rooms	3: 2 doubles, 1 family room.
price	€61; €380 per week.
meals	Restaurant 4km.
closed	Rarely.
directions	Detailed directions sent by email or fax.

Local specialities include 'gnocchi de malga', Monte Veronese cheese and the Valpolicella, Soave and Lessini Durello wines.

	Ilaria & Maurizio Corazza
tel	+39 045 8700879
fax	+39 045 8700879
e-mail	info@cadelrocolo.com
web	www.cadelrocolo.com

B&B

map 3 entry 36

Casa Belmonte

Via Belmonte 2, 36030 Sarcedo

From the moment the gates swing open you are in for a treat. Up the long, statuette-lined drive… step onto the gravel and your luggage is whisked off you. Bedrooms have elegance, seduction and style: soft colours, rich fabrics, antiques, monogrammed sheets and towels; bathrooms are big and mosaic-tiled. Once her children had flown the nest Mariarosa turned her full attention to creating these six gorgeous retreats. She is the most delightful hostess and genuinely loves having guests to stay. The house sits on the top of Belmonte hill overlooking the small town of Sarcedo in seven hectares of vineyards, olive groves and manicured gardens – the azaleas in May are stunning, and the pool divine. Views are panoramic, and delicious breakfasts of yogurt, fruit, cheese and ham are served in the summer house. Roberto is proud of his small wine cellar, and selects some of the best wines from Italy for his most important guests. Casa Belmonte is an easy launch pad for forays to Venice, Padua, Verona and Piacenza, and, considering that luxury doesn't come much better than this, is very good value.

rooms	6: 2 doubles, 1 twin, 2 suites, 1 single.
price	€ 129–€ 181. Singles € 103–€ 129. Suites € 181–€ 258.
meals	Breakfast € 15–€ 23. Restaurants 2km–7km (Michelin starred).
closed	Rarely.
directions	A31 exit for Dueville. Left & left again for Bassano. After 2km left for Sarcedo. There, entrance 600m after traffic lights to right of junction. Ring bell at gate.

The church at Marostica has a masterpiece by Jacopo and Francesco Bassano – 'St Paul in Athens' (1574).

Signora Mariarosa Arcaro
tel	+39 0445 884833
fax	+39 0445 884134
e-mail	info@casabelmonte.com
web	www.casabelmonte.com

B&B

Il Castello

Via Castello 6, 36021 Barbarano Vicentino

A narrow, winding road leads up to the *castello* at the foot of the Berici hills. Also known as the Villa Godi-Marinoni, the castle was built by Count Godi in the 15th century, on the ruins of an old feudal castle. Massive hewn walls enclose the compound, with its terraced vines, orchard and Italian garden; you enter via an arched entrance, ancient cobbles beneath your feet. The villa itself is still lived in by the family: Signora Marinoni and her son, courteous and attentive, run this vast estate together. Guest apartments are in a separate building with curious Gothic details in the plastered façade and furnishings are a mix of dark antique and contemporary. Hidden below the castle walls is the garden and fish pond; in spring and summer, hundreds of lemon trees are wheeled out to stand grandly on pedestals. The climate is mild and the hillside a mass of olive groves. Olive oil, honey and five DOC wines are produced on the 10-hectare estate – there's a wine cellar in the bowels of the castle, and a *cantina* where you can buy. *Minimum stay one week.*

rooms	4 apartments for 2-4.
price	€50–€56 for two per night.
meals	Self-catering. Good choice of restaurants nearby.
closed	Rarely.
directions	A4 exit Vicenza Est; immed. left to Noventa; T-junc. left; small r'bout right; cross bridge; T-junc. left to Noventa; traffic lights right Ponte Il Barbarano. In piazza at Barbarano left for Villaga; villa 500m on left.

	Signor Lorenzo Marinoni
tel	+39 0444 886055
fax	+39 0444 777140
e-mail	castellomarinoni@tin.it
web	www.castellomarinoni.it

'... for I have Pisa left And am to Padua come,
as he that leaves A shallow plash to plunge him
in the deep And with satiety seeks to quench his
thirst'. Shakespeare, *The Taming of the Shrew*

Self-catering

map 4   entry 38

Villa Rizzi Albarea

Via Albarea 53, 30030 Pianiga di Venezia

Hidden behind the house is the most lovely wild garden. Exciting pathways thread their way past statues and trees; there are bridges and even a small lake with a Rapunzel tower and a pair of swans. The house is intriguing, too, with its long history and imposing exterior partly screened by roses. Once a convent for the Giudecca nuns, its origins go back 10 centuries. Though wars and fire have meant much restoration work, it's a beautiful place, deep in the country but not isolated – nor badly affected by the nearby motorway. The bedrooms are fresh and colour co-ordinated – a mix of traditional and flounced – with delectable antiques and comfortable beds. Those on the first floor have old frescoes, those at the top of the house stunning ceilings with original beams. Persian rugs glow on stone or wooden floors. On each floor, too, is an inviting sitting area with paintings and fine old desks. The atmosphere is serene and civilised; sometimes the delightful sound of your hostess's piano-playing fills the air. She and her husband are both charming and will do all they can to make sure your stay is a happy one. *Minimum stay two nights*.

rooms	7 + 1: 7 suites. 1 apartment for 2-4.
price	€180-€280. Apt €200-€280.
meals	Wide choice of restaurants.
closed	Rarely.
directions	From Autostrada A4 Milano-Venezia, exit Dolo, over lights, 1.5km. Right at Albarea sign, 1km, signs for Villa.

'At the turn of the road the Postillion pointed with his whip & cried, "Venice" and there it was just above a low horizon shining in the sun … an image of extreme beauty.' Samuel Rogers

Aida & Pierluigi Rizzi

tel	+39 041 5100933
fax	+39 041 5100933
e-mail	info@villa-albarea.com
web	www.villa-albarea.com

B&B & Self-catering

Le Garzette
Lungomare Alberoni 32, 30010 Malamocco

Once it was the vegetable garden of Venice; now the Lido has few agricultural areas left. Le Garzette, near the foot of this long, thin island, is one of them. A lush, two-hectare market garden produces quantities of organic vegetables and soft fruit – asparagus, aubergines, raspberries, strawberries... Along with fresh fish, sea food and home-reared poultry, all find their way onto the plates of the farmhouse restaurant. It's pleasant and bistro-like, with an open fireplace and covered patio, and very popular with the locals. The house had been abandoned for 20 years when Renza and Salvatore bought it and restored it in the 1990s, creating simple, rustic rooms. Bedrooms have whitewashed walls, dark old furniture, lamps and mirrors; some of the clean, reasonably modern bathrooms are shared. At the bottom of the garden is a beach – and a sea wall to walk or cycle on. It's a friendly, peaceful place to stay, well away from the seaside-resort atmosphere of Lido town, and a good, rural spot to explore Venice from. A bus will take you to the ferry at Lido (both bus and boat fares are covered by Tourist Tickets).

rooms	4: 2 doubles sharing bath, 1 twin, 1 triple.
price	€90, triple €110, half-board €70p.p.
meals	€40-€45.
closed	Last 2 weeks of December.
directions	Car ferry from Tronchetto. Water taxi or bus, line B from Lido to Malamocco-Alberoni.

Effie Ruskin used to go bathing on the Lido while her husband concentrated on writing The Stones of Venice in 1851.

Renza di Orazia & Salvatore Manzi

tel	+39 041 731078
fax	+39 041 2428798
e-mail	legarzette@libero.it
web	www.legarzette.on.to

B&B

map 4   entry 40

Madonna

Campiello Piave, Cannaregio, Venice

What bliss to escape the Venetian crowds and return to this friendly little ground-floor apartment with its own entrancing walled garden. Passionflowers climb the warm brick walls; there are chairs and a table, roses and hydrangeas. Close by is the Madonna dell' Orte Church (known as Tintoretto's church) and the area is pretty and quiet, with – for Venice – a rare feeling of space. Susan is an American and comes to Italy whenever she can but is happy to let her apartment at other times. It has all the attraction of a real home. Though the rooms aren't very large, they are furnished with style and individuality. Interesting pictures hang on the white walls and the terracotta floor tiles are covered with rugs. The bedroom is cool and airy with muslin curtains; the living room has two large day sofas which turn into single beds. A big gilt mirror, a stereo, cushions and plenty of books make it a charming, restful room. At one end is the long, galley-style kitchen. It's well equipped, with a hob, microwave and fridge (no oven but there are lots of restaurants nearby) and a door opening into that lovely garden.

rooms	Sleeps 2-4: 1 double, 2 sofabeds.
price	£500 for 2-4 per week.
meals	Restaurants nearby.
closed	Rarely.
directions	Nearest water bus stop: Madonna dell'Orta n.42 & n.52.

'Of all the dreamy delights, that of floating in a gondola among the canals and out of the Lagoon is surely the greatest.' George Eliot, 1880.

Susan Schiavon
tel +44 (0)20 7348 3800
fax +44 (0)870 134 2820
e-mail susan.venice@iol.it

Self-catering

entry 41   map 4

Pensione La Calcina - Apartments

Fondamenta Zattere ai Gesuati, Dorsoduro 780, 30123 Venice

Two minutes' walk from the hotel of the same name, a clutch of beautiful apartments on the fashionable Zattere. Though they vary in size and in feel, each has a sitting room, a double bedroom and a bathroom; two have kitchens, all are named after flowers. Giglio is large and lovely, with a white-walled sitting room, exposed beams in a vaulted ceiling and a view onto a garden. Rosa is deliciously rustic, with lovely old pieces of furniture and colourful rugs, and a fabulous kitchen. Marble-floored Viola feels Venetian, with its white drapes, fragments of Istrian stone and glimpse of church and small square; Iris looks onto an elegant well with a little fountain and has a contemporary air. Dalia, the smallest, is designed by the famous Italian architect, Carlo Scarpa. Inspired by views that sail over the boat-busy lagoon he has created a nautical den of wooden panelling, padded seating, latticed windows, a boatish door; views skim the water and the sunlight dances on the ceiling. All apartments have fridges, and you breakfast at La Piscina (see entry 43). Deep comfort is yours in one of the greenest corners of Venice.

rooms	5 apartments for 2.
price	€161–€239 with breakfast.
meals	Lunch or dinner €10–€40.
closed	Rarely.
directions	Water bus line 51 or 61 from Piazzale Roma or Railway Station. Line 82 from Tronchetto.

	Signor Alessandro Szemere
tel	+39 041 5206466
fax	+39 041 5227045
e-mail	la.calcina@libero.it
web	www.lacalcina.com

Scarpa ended up designing works meant to elude time, favouring the vivid colours of the past above the dull grey of the future.

Self-catering & B&B

map 4   entry 42

Pensione La Calcina

Fondamenta Zattere ai Gesuati, Dorsoduro 780, 30123 Venice

Catch the sea breezes of early evening from the terrace butting out over the water as you watch the beautiful people stroll the Zattere. Or look across the lagoon to the Rendentore. Ruskin stayed here in 1876, and for many people this corner of Venice, facing the Guidecca and with old Venice just behind you, beats the crowds of San Marco any day. The hotel has been discretely modernised by its charming young owners, and comfortable bedrooms have air-conditioning, antiques and parquet floors. Those at the front, with views, are dearer; best of all are the corner rooms. A small roof terrace can be booked for romantic evenings and you can breakfast, lunch or dinner at the delightful floating café, La Piscina, open to all – simple dishes are available all day and the fruit juices and milkshakes are delicious. Pause for a moment and remember Ruskin's words on the city he loved: "a ghost upon the sands of the sea, so weak, so quiet, so bereft of all but her loveliness, that we might well doubt, as we watched her faint reflection on the mirage of the lagoon, which was the City and which the shadow."

rooms	29: 9 singles, 20 doubles.
price	€ 130–€ 182. Suites € 161–€ 239. Singles € 96–€ 106.
meals	Lunch/dinner € 10–€ 40.
closed	Rarely.
directions	Water bus line 51 or 61 from Piazzale Roma or Railway Station; Line 82 from Tronchetto.

The Gesuati on the Zattere, unremarkable from the outside, has a ceiling by Giovanni Battista Tiepolo depicting the Virgin handing the rosary to S. Dominic.

Signor Alessandro Szemere
tel +39 041 5206466
fax +39 041 5227045
e-mail la.calcina@libero.it
web www.lacalcina.com

Hotel

Club Cristal

Calle Zanardi 4133, Cannaregio, 30100 Venice

The concept of the wrong 'location' has little meaning in Venice: every area is a discovery. Near the Campo dei Gesuiti, on the northern edge, this is wonderfully quiet and as beautiful as anywhere. A canal skirts one side of the house, a large garden much of its length. Via a fine marble stair you enter a huge living room, cluttered yet welcoming with its books, magazines and two friendly dogs. The floors are of marble, there are two columns, some landscapes on the walls, vast potted plants, a piano and, best of all, big doors onto a roof terrace. The green, silk-hung dining room is equally unexpected; bedrooms, too. One has a pink, extremely comfortable queen-size bed, a 17th-century fireplace, hand-painted double doors, an endearingly old-fashioned bathroom and views to garden and canal (note, the canal bustle gets going around 7.30am). Much charm and character here, thanks to Susan, a fascinating lady who is passionate about Venice and its ongoing restoration. *Children over 12 welcome. Daylight arrival recommended.*

rooms	5: 4 twins/doubles, 1 small double all sharing 3 baths & 1 shower.
price	£80–£130. Singles £50–£85.
meals	Dinner with wine, £25–£30; book ahead.
closed	Rarely.
directions	From airport take water bus to Fondamente Nuova or line 1 to Ca'd'Oro.

	Susan Schiavon
tel	+44 (0)20 7722 5060
fax	+44 (0)20 7586 3004
e-mail	info@club-cristal-venice.com
web	www.club-cristal-venice.com

'When I went to Venice, my dream became my address.' Marcel Proust, *letter to Madame Strauss, c. 1906.*

B&B

map 4   entry 44

Ai due fanali

Campo San Simeon Grande, Santa Croce 946, 30135 Venice

Venetian sophistication without San Marco prices. Hidden away near the church of San Simeon Grande this quiet little hotel is a short walk from the station. It was originally a religious school and there are still reminders of its former life: a beautiful relief of the saint on the portico, ceiling frescoes by Palma il Giovane. Not so long ago the hotel had a complete makeover and is in pristine condition. Bedrooms come with the usual modern conveniences such as air-conditioning, telephone and mini-bar and are quietly elegant with carpeted floors, delicately sponged walls, darkly beamed ceilings, good beds and fabrics and the odd special touch – a marble fireplace, a Venetian-painted chest of drawers. Public rooms have polished floors, marquetry tables, big ornate mirrors, fresh flowers; the dining room has wonderful rooftop views. Best of all is the roof terrace, brimming with roses and oleander, stylish with white-and-blue-dressed chairs. Room prices vary according to season but this place is worth every penny. *Apartments to rent nearby.*

rooms	16: 12 double/twins, 4 singles.
price	€ 93–€ 200. Singles € 83–€ 160.
meals	Restaurants within walking distance.
closed	Rarely.
directions	Take water bus line 1 & stop at Riva di Biasio. Or 5-minute walk from train station.

On the way to the Frari, don't miss the 'Scuola Grande' of San Giovanni Evangelista which has a superb staircase by Mauro Codussi.

Signora Marina Ferron

tel	+39 041 718490
fax	+39 041 718344
e-mail	request@aiduefanali.com
web	www.aiduefanali.com

B&B

Hotel Locanda Fiorita

Campiello Nuovo, San Marco 3457/A, 30124 Venice

A low-budget option for those who have neither boundless wealth nor the inclination to spend their time lounging around a grand Venetian hotel. The Locanda Fiorita is tucked away behind the Campo Santo Stefano, close to the Accademia Bridge – a good base from which to stroll in all directions. It is a dark russet palazzo hung with vines, in a tiny square which somehow contrives to look green in an area without gardens. The terrace at the front is a charmingly ramshackle affair, from which people spill out onto the *piazzetta* for cappuccini and newspapers. Bedrooms vary in size but have pleasant Venetian-style painted tables and chests and some antique mirrors; ask for rooms in the main building rather than the annexe – we prefer them. There's no restaurant, but there are plenty of places to eat nearby for dinner; cross the Accademia Bridge and dive into the network of alleyways on the far side, trailing a thread like Ariadne so that you can find your way back again.

rooms	19 + 1: 8 doubles; 1 double, 1 single both with separate bath. Annexe: 8 doubles; 1 double with separate bathroom. 1 apt for 3.
price	€93–€140. Singles €62–€78. Apartment €93–€135.
meals	Wide choice of restaurants nearby.
closed	Rarely.
directions	From train station vaporetto no. 1 or 82; get off at S. Angelo. 5-minute walk to Piazza Santo Stefano. On right before piazza.

	Renato Colombera
tel	+39 041 5234754
fax	+39 041 5228043
e-mail	info@locandafiorita.com
web	www.locandafiorita.com

Nearby Campo S. Stefano has a statue of Nicolò Tommaseo, a leading figure in the 'Risorgimento'.

Hotel & Self-catering

map 4   entry 46

Locanda ai Santi Apostoli
Strada Nova 4391, 30131 Venice

You could walk straight past without even noticing that there is a hotel within this palazzo – and miss one of the best surprises in Venice. The Locanda is on the third floor of the 15th-century Bianchi Michiel, known locally as the Palazzo Michiel Brusà on account of its having burnt down two centuries ago. Nor does the courtyard through which you pass gives any clue as to what's in store. The next thing you know, you are walking into a Henry James novel... in a Venetian palace on the Grand Canal. Public rooms, opening off a central salon, are still hung with the fabrics and papers of grander days, and antique beds and chests, patterned damasks and touches of chinoiserie are further reminders of the buildings's earlier status. Ask for a room with a view: the two at the front, with views across the Grand Canal to the fish markets, are truly wonderful. Stefano is the most courteous of hosts and could not be kinder; his family has owned the palazzo since it was built. There is some noise, but this is Venice. A marvellous little find.

The Church of S. Giovanni Crisostomo nearby contains the last and one of the greatest altarpieces of Giovanni Bellini.

rooms	10: 9 doubles, 1 suite for 4.
price	€ 185-€ 330. Suite € 320-€ 420.
meals	Good restaurants 5-minute walk.
closed	Mid-December-February; 2nd & 3rd weeks of August.
directions	Water bus stop: Ca'd'Oro (line 1). Private dock for water taxis.

Conte Stefano Bianchi-Michiel

tel	+39 041 5212612
fax	+39 041 5212611
e-mail	aisantia@tin.it
web	www.locandasantiapostoli.com

Hotel

Casa Martini

Rio Terà San Leonardo 1314, Cannaregio, 30121 Venice

An old Venetian townhouse and stylish B&B — you'd never guess such a fabulous place existed, tucked as it is down a side alley off one of the liveliest streets. Smiling Orietta loves Venice and the house in which her husband grew up; she couldn't be nicer and wants you to leave with happy memories. During the winter months she brings you breakfast in the elegant little *salotto* with its balcony overlooking the Ponte di Guglie; in summer, you start the day on the terrace under the huge parasol, surrounded by flowers and overlooking the colourful facades. Bedrooms (air-conditioned) are furnished in 18th-century Venetian style, with damask wallpaper and ornate bedheads; bathrooms have walk-in showers and fluffy white towels. Discover the open-air markets, restaurants, bars and shops that jostle outside the door, take a tour of the Ghetto, walk to St Mark's Square (it takes 15 minutes). At the beginning of the *sottoportico* are signs of the gate which used to close the entrance at night, and a long list of the rules for the inhabitants, inscribed in stone in 1541.

rooms	9: 6 doubles, 2 family, 1 single.
price	€100–€145. Family €175. Singles €60–€90.
meals	Restaurants walking distance.
closed	Rarely.
directions	Few minutes' walk from Ponte delle Guglie, & short walk from S. Lucia railway station. Water bus line 52 (stop: 'Guglie') & line 82 (stop: 'S. Marcuola').

Nearby is the Ghetto, from the Venetian 'Geto', a place where metal is cast, the area where the Jews were confined.

Orietta & Luigi Martini

tel	+39 041 717512
fax	+39 041 2758329
e-mail	locandamartini@libero.it
web	www.casamartini.it

B&B

map 4   entry 48

Martinengo Apartment
Calle Martinengo dalle Palle, Castello, Venice

Recline languorously on one of many lovely rugs, bring your own CDs, revel in the sensation of staying in a 17th-century Venetian home: this first-floor apartment is as far from a 'serviced apartment' as you can get. The furniture is deliciously antique, the walls drip with paintings ancient and modern, there are stacks of records and books, intriguing wooden statues and carvings abound, rooms stretch on and on. The double bedroom has high ceilings, terrazzo floors, stunning mirrors, a four-poster, a Venetian chandelier: almost outrageously luxurious, with a bathroom to match. The little study (which doubles as a single room) invites idleness or scholarship, the street is so narrow you could exchange cooking ingredients with your neighbour, and there is a delightful little terrace with a long view down the narrow side canal. The kitchen — slightly old-fashioned — is bright and pretty, with great marble slabs and everything you need. An unusual and wonderfully central Venetian retreat, worth every penny. *Maid service mid-week. Ask about prices in low season.*

A short walk to the Campo S. Maria Formosa which has a bell tower with a grotesque face carved on it, which epitomised for Ruskin the decline of Venice.

rooms	1 apartment for 4–5.
price	£1120 per week. Prices for 2 on request.
meals	Self-catering.
closed	Never.
directions	Nearest water bus stop: Rialto n.82 - San Marco n.82.

	Susan Schiavon
tel	+44 (0)20 7348 3800
fax	+44 (0)870 134 2820
e-mail	susan.venice@iol.it

Self-catering

Riva degli Schiavoni Apartments

Calle del Cagnoletto 4084, 30135 Venice

If you're looking for a room with a view, then look no further: from your apartment you can see the island of San Giorgio and the whole sweeping basin of San Marco. The Riva degli Schiavoni is a wide and bustling quay, with landing stages for vaporetti and moorings for gondolas. Further along is the Palazzo Dandolo, better known as The Danieli; around the corner is the Church of San Giovanni in Bragora, with its altarpiece by Cima de Conegliano, *The Baptism of Christ* (its realistic landscape a watershed in Renaissance art). Such is the setting. As for the apartments, what freedom! And what comfort. Every day a maid arrives to clean, every day the provisions for a continental breakfast are provided. The furniture is a mix of repro 18th-century Venetian and contempoary, with antique scones for lighting and everything spotlessly presented. Modern extras include air conditioning, a security box and a direct phone line to the owners' offices, so you can get everything you need in the twinkle of an eye, including advice. *Minimum stay three nights.*

rooms	4 apartments for 2-4.
price	€206-€380 per night.
meals	Self-catering. Wide choice of restaurants in Venice.
closed	Rarely.
directions	Water bus line 1 or 41, stop at Arsenale.

The Riva degli Schiavoni means 'the waterfront of the Slavs', who were colonised by Venice through its Dalmation territories.

	Signora Marina Ferron
tel	+39 041 718490
fax	+39 041 718344
e-mail	request@aiduefanali.com
web	www.aiduefanali.com

Self-catering

map 4   entry 50

Locanda al Leon

Campo Santi Filippo e Giacamo 4270, Castello, 30122 Venice

Such friendly people, such a perfect spot: three minutes' walk from the Basilica end of St Mark's Square, and the same from the airport Alilaguna and the vaporetto stops. This small, unpretentious, family-run hotel, its characterful old entrance off a narrow side street, is an excellent choice if you're visiting Venice on a tightish budget but still want to be at the centre of it all. It's been recently, modestly modernised: all is spotless, everything works, and there's heating for winter stays. Compact, carpeted bedrooms (the biggest are on the corner of the building, looking onto the Campo San Filippo e Giacome and the Calle degli Albanesi) have Venetian-style bedheads with scrolled edges and floral motifs; there are matching striped counterpanes and curtains, modern Murano glass chandeliers and neat shower rooms. Breakfast is taken at little tables on the big, first-floor landing, buffet-style: breads and croissants, yogurts and fruit juice – what you'd expect for the price. And there's no shortage of advice – one or two members of the delightful Dall' Agnola family are always around.

rooms	6: 4 doubles, 1 triple, 1 single.
price	€80–€160. Triple €100–€180. Singles €60–€130.
meals	Restaurant Chinellato, €40.
closed	Rarely.
directions	Water boat Line 1 or Line 82 direct to San Zaccaria. Calle degli Albanesi until last door on left; signs.

'Dear old Venice has lost her complexion, her figure, her reputation, her self-respect; and yet, with it all, has so puzzlingly not lost a shred of her distinction.' Henry James

Marcella & Giuliano Dall' Agnola

tel	+39 041 2770393
fax	+39 041 5210348
e-mail	leon@hotelalleon.com
web	www.hotelalleon.com

Hotel

Locanda Casa alla Fenice

Rio terrà degli Assassini 3701, San Marco, 30124 Venice

A great little spot, just off the beaten track; hire a water taxi from the station and you will be ferried almost to the door. The Battistini family – parents and student son – are full of friendly enthusiasm, love their city, and know as much about its restaurants and nightlife as its history and culture. Your rooms are on the upper floors of this small townhouse in a quiet quarter – a red light district in the 1700s… utterly quiet, apart from the evening serenade of the gondolier. High-ceilinged, light and airy and with air-conditioning, bedrooms have mottled marble floors and individual touches – a decorated door, a chandelier, an ornate mirror. White curtains billow at windows that open to alley views. Bedheads are newly gilded, fabrics are fancy and some rooms carry a beautiful mural of a 17th-century Venetian scene painted by a young local artist. Breakfasts are basic and taken in your room; it's more fun to visit the local bar. With your own keys you come and go as you please. Signor has a boat and may be persuaded in summer to take you on a jaunt around the lagoon. *Minimum stay two nights.*

rooms	6: 4 doubles/twins, 2 singles.
price	€75–€230. Singles €60–€180.
meals	Breakfast €6.
closed	Rarely.
directions	5 minutes from San Marco or water taxi to Rio Terrà Assassini.

	Adriana Lucchesi & Alvise Battistini
tel	+39 041 5280105
fax	+39 041 5220896
e-mail	info@casaallafenice.com
web	www.casaallafenice.com

Napoleon once called the Piazza San Marco, which was laid out in the 17th century, "the finest drawing room in Europe".

B&B

map 4   entry 52

Locanda Conterie

Calle Conterie 21, Murano, 30141 Venice

A rare chance to stay on the island of Murano, the glass-blowing centre of Venice. Originally converted to accommodate buyers visiting the workshops, the Tosi brothers' villa has nothing remotely touristy about it. Instead, it is – rather charmingly – exactly what Italians produce for other Italians. Its 16th-century origins have largely disappeared in the renovation; smart, adequately-sized rooms have repro/traditional furniture, fabric-lined walls, satin-striped covers and, of course, lots of Venetian glass. (The brothers' own firm, a family business since the 16th century, specialises in mirrors.) Don't be put off by outside appearances. Just think how smug you'll feel watching the hoards of day trippers arrive on the vaporetti every morning while you take your breakfast in a bar. (Because of the room-only deal you go out, Italian-style, for meals.) Staying on the island also means you can visit the workshops out of tourist hours – a big plus if you're serious about buying glass. Visit the museum, too, and the church of Saints Maria and Donato.

rooms	9 doubles.
price	€ 60–€ 90. Singles € 40–€ 60.
meals	Bars & restaurants nearby.
closed	Rarely.
directions	From train station line 42 to Murano Museo.

'What, they lived once thus at Venice where the merchants were the kings/Where Saint Mark's is, where the Doges used to wed the sea with rings?'
Robert Browning, *A Toccata of Galuppi's*

Signor Massimo Tosi
tel +39 041 5275003
fax +39 041 5274245
e-mail info@locandaconterie.com
web www.locandaconterie.com

Inn

Castello di Roncade

via Roma 14, 31056 Roncade

Don't be misled: the grandeur of the imposing entrance, splendid gardens and lovely 16th-century villa do not mean impossible prices. Three beautiful double rooms, furnished with antiques, are available in the villa and – ideal for families – three vast and simply furnished apartments in the corner towers. All have central heating in winter, while in summer, thick walls keep you cool. Surrounding the castle and the village are the estate vineyards, which produce some excellent wines; try the Villa Giustinian Rosso della Casa or the Pinot Grigio, and you'll be tempted to take a case home. Or sample them at dinner in the villa, an occasional rather than a regular event but a fabulous experience, with everyone seated at one table in a magnificent family dining room. The food is superb and the Baron and Baroness are lovely, hospitable hosts. You don't need to take a car onto Venice; take the train from Treviso, 15km away – itself an ancient place of cloisters and canals, frescoes and churches.

rooms	3 + 3: 3 doubles. 3 apartments for 4–6.
price	€83–€93. Apartments €31–€36 p.p.
meals	Self-catering in apartments; occasional dinner.
closed	Rarely.
directions	Exit A4 for Trieste at Quarto d'Altino towards Altino & then Roncade. Castello 7km from A4 exit.

Barone Vincenzo Ciani Bassetti

tel	+39 0422 708736
fax	+39 0422 840964
e-mail	vcianib@tin.it
web	www.castellodironcade.com

The Castello is attributed to an architect in the circle of Mauro Codussi, and is an important prototype for Palladio's villa style.

Self-catering & B&B

map 4   entry 54

Il Giardino Segreto

Piazza della Vittoria 22, 31020 Cison di Valmarino

For years it was Janine's dream to do up a farmhouse. Six years ago she found one – and a partner to share the dream. Janine is Belgian, Angelo Italian and the house they bought is in a hamlet surrounded by mountains, its little garden hidden behind green gates. A great deal of work has gone into restoring the place and keeping as much of the old 18th-century feel as possible; the stairs still creak charmingly and the chestnut floorboards show the cracks of age. One big bedroom is in the attic; the other, painted sunflower yellow, is over the barn. There's also the *cantina* (where once grappa was made) which has a living area opening onto the garden and a bedroom above. Furnishings are frugal but interesting – no TV but hundreds of books. Janine and Angelo have a small daughter, so the house is well geared up for children, and the food is healthy and good, with superb homemade bread. Janine sometimes gives one-to-one Italian conversation courses and the village is a great starting point for walks and mountain bike rides; the Passo San Boldo with its 18 hairpin bends is quite a challenge.

There's an Annual International Exhibition of Children's Illustrations every December in Sarmede.

rooms	3: 2 doubles sharing bath; 1 suite.
price	€ 60. Suite € 75.
meals	Dinner with wine, € 15; book ahead.
closed	Rarely.
directions	From A27 exit Vittorio Veneto Nord for centre, right for Cison, 10km. Green gate set back from main square by side of Locanda Bar Al Bàkarò.

Janine Raedts & Angelo Vettorello

tel	+39 0438 85953
mobile	+39 320 0525289
e-mail	giardinosegreto@tiscali.it

B&B

B&B Toffolatti

Via Amedeo di Savoia 2, 31030 Cison di Valmarino

Behind the peeling stucco façade and faded green shutters you might expect to find cobwebs and a few rickety antiques. Maybe even an Italian Miss Havisham. Instead, you're confronted with a refreshing, almost stark modernity and a delightful mother-and-son partnership. The B&B is a new venture for Marco and Teresa but they're enthusiastic and deserve to succeed. It's on the upper two floors (the ground floor remains neglected) and is reached via two flights of outside steps. The house is in the middle of a large, sleepy village, looking out to the valley and hills beyond. This is an area popular with walkers and cyclists and there are plenty of CAI marked paths. You can breakfast simply on the prettily-planted roof terrace and watch village life go by or, if the weather's bad, stay in the breakfast room where small white-and-chrome round tables give the feel of a 1950s coffee bar. There's plenty more chrome, too, in the sparkling white bathrooms. The bedrooms are uncluttered and airy, with painted floorboards, pale, translucent curtains and low beds covered with plain or striped linen. Not a cobweb in sight.

rooms	3: 2 doubles, 1 triple.
price	€60–€80. Triples €70–€95.
meals	Restaurants €20–€25, 500m.
closed	Rarely.
directions	From A27 exit Vittorio Veneto Nord towards centre, right for Cison. B&B in centre, over bridge, left; second door down on right.

Not surprisingly in this Prosecco region, Conegliano has a School of Viticulture and Enology, founded in 1876.

	Marco Toffolatti
tel	+39 0438 975117
fax	+39 0438 975117
e-mail	info@toffolatti.net
web	www.toffolatti.net

B&B

map 4   entry 56

Gargan L'Agriturismo

Via Marco Polo 2, 35017 Levada di Piombino Dese

Such a surprise: behind the slightly forbidding exterior lie a sophisticated interior and mouthwatering food. Elegant rooms, delightful antiques, pale-green-painted beams, tables laid with linen and silver... such are the rewards for those who cross the uneventful landscape of the Veneto to get here. Bedrooms stand in a class of their own, with iron bedheads and cotton quilts, mellow brick floors strewn with rugs, armchairs to sink into. The several rooms on the ground floor given over to dining indicate the importance attached to food here – Sunday lunch is not to be missed. Tables are immaculately set, and the food is delicious; it is Signora Calzavara's passion. She is aided by a team of chefs, and has been known to pass on her "secret recipes" to her guests. Children will love the gardens (source of the freshest fruits and vegetables) with resident donkey. Venice, Padua, Vicenza and Treviso are all a gentle drive away, so this would be a wonderful base for those who like to explore the city, then retreat to the countryside and the *agriturismo*'s delights.

rooms	6: 4 doubles, 2 suites.
price	€ 65. Suite € 85.
meals	Lunch/dinner € 22, book ahead.
closed	December-February; August.
directions	A4 exit Padova Est, SS515 for Treviso. After Noale & level crossing for Badoere, Montebelluna. After S. Ambrogio left at traffic lights. In Levadi di Piombino, right at church; farm 100m, park behind house.

Don't miss Palladio's Villa Cornaro, hidden away in Piombino Dese. Open on Saturdays only, 3.30-6.00, from May-Sept and to groups of 10+ by appointment.

Signor Alessandro Calzavara

tel	+39 049 9350308
fax	+39 049 9350016
e-mail	gargan@gargan.it
web	www.gargan.it

B&B

Hotel Villa Luppis

Via San Martino 34, 33080 Rivarotta di Pasiano

There is a sense of time warp. This is still the grand country mansion it became in the early 1800s, when Napoleon secularised the monastery that had been here for centuries; the present owner's ancestors later made it a base for their diplomatic and industrial activities. Geographically, it feels in limbo, too − on the border between Veneto and Friuli and surrounded by acres of flat farmland. The hotel, all creamy peeling stucco and terracotta roof tiles, is reached via an imposing gateway. Twelve acres of grounds include lawns, massive trees, gravel paths and a fountain. Inside, the various formal reception and dining areas are graced with antiques, presided over by dignified staff. Bedrooms are elegantly old-fashioned, with comfortable beds and excellent bathrooms. You can go for walks along the river bank but really this place acts as a centre for day excursions. There's a daily shuttle bus into Venice and the staff will organise trips to other towns and cities, as well as to the Venetian and Palladian villas along the river Brenta. Cookery courses are an option, too − and wine-tasting in what was once the monks' ice-cellar.

rooms	39: 31 doubles, 2 singles, 6 suites.
price	€ 191–€ 235. Single € 102–€ 112. Suite € 265–€ 298.
meals	Dinner from € 50.
closed	Rarely.
directions	From Oderzo towards Pordenone. Right at Mansue, signed.

The ancient winery of the Doges of Venice is in a Venetian villa nearby.

	Signor Giorgio Ricci Luppis
tel	+39 0434 626969
fax	+39 0434 626228
e-mail	hotel@villaluppis.it
web	www.villaluppis.it

Hotel

map 4   entry 58

Casa del Grivò

Borgo Canal del Ferro 19, 33040 Faédis

This is the house that Toni built – or, rather, lovingly revived from ruin. Their smallholding sits in a hamlet on the edge of a plain; behind, wonderful, high-wooded hills extend to the Slovenian border, sometimes crossed to gather wild berries and mushrooms. Your most welcoming hosts have three young children. Simplicity, rusticity and a 'green' environment are the keynotes here; be prepared for traditional wool-and-vegetable-fibre-filled mattresses! Your children will adore all the open spaces, the animals and the little pool that's been created by diverting a stream. Adults can relax with a book on a bedroom balcony, or in a distant corner of the garden. Maps are laid out at breakfast, and there's a small library of guidebooks, too; the walking is wonderful, there's a castle to visit and a river to picnic by. Paola cooks dinner using old recipes and their own produce from the beautifully tended, organic vegetable garden. There's a lovely open fire for cooking, and you dine by candlelight, sometimes to the gentle accompaniment of country songs – Paula was a professional singer. *Minimum stay two nights, five in summer.*

Udine was captured in 1420 by the Venetians, who set about creating the beautiful Renaissance 'Piazza della Libertà' – a sort of Venice in miniature.

rooms	4: 1 double, 2 family; 1 family with separate bath.
price	€ 55. Half-board € 41 p.p.
meals	Lunches in summer only; picnics on request. Dinner from € 25, good wine list, book ahead.
closed	December.
directions	From Faédis, Via dei Castelli for Canébola. After 1.5km right, over bridge; 2nd house on left.

Toni & Paola Costalunga

tel	+39 0432 728638
fax	+39 0432 728638
e-mail	casadelgrivo@libero.it
web	www.grivo.has.it

B&B

Agriturismo La Faula

Via Faula 5, Ravosa di Povoletto, 33040 Udine

An exuberant miscellany of dogs, donkeys and peacocks on a modern, working farm where rural laissez-faire and modern commerce happily mingle. La Faula has been in Luca's family for years; she and Paul, young and dynamic, abandoned the city to find themselves working harder than ever! Yet they put as much thought and energy into their guests as into the wine business and farm. The house stands in gentle countryside at the base of the Julian Alps; it is a big and comfortable home, and each bedroom is delightful: furniture is old, bathrooms new. There is a bistro-style restaurant where wonderful home-produced produce is served (free-range veal, beef, chicken, lamb, and vegetables and fruits); on summer nights dinner may take the form of a barbecue. An enormous old pergola provides dappled shade during the day; sit here and dream with a glass of the estate wine or acquavita. Or wander round the vineyard and *cantina*, watch the wine-making in progress, cool off in the river, visit the beaches of the Adriatic. *Discounts for longer stays. Meals not provided during grape harvest (approx. 10 Sept-25 Oct). Min. stay three nights.*

rooms	9 + 4: 9 doubles/twins. 4 mini-apartments for 2-4.
price	€40-€49. Singles €30. Apartments from €57.
meals	Breakfast €5-€7. Dinner €15-€18.
closed	Rarely.
directions	SS54 from Udine for Cividale. After 3km, left for Salt, then Magredis; from Ravosa for Attimis; right by shrine, La Faula over bridge.

	Paul Mackay & Luca Colautti
tel	+39 0432 666394
fax	+39 0432 666032
e-mail	info@faula.com
web	www.faula.com

Drive to San Danieli dei Fruili where you can feast on the famous and succulent 'Prosciutto Prolongo', delicious both cooked and cured.

B&B & Self-catering

map 5   entry 60

Golf Hotel Castello Formentini

Via Oslavia 2, 34070 San Floriano del Collio

A wild boar prances on a weathervane above a creeper-covered tower. You've arrived at a medieval, hilltop castle near the Slovenian border, surrounded by rolling hills and vineyards. It's a comfortable, stylish place to stay – whether in the castle itself (specify when booking) or in the mellow, friendly little inn across the way. The Formentini have been here since 1520 and the wild boar motif, in triplicate on the family coat of arms, recurs throughout the hotel – on fine porcelain, damask linen, crisp sheets. A note from the Contessa welcomes you to a pleasant, roomy bedroom, inviting with amoretti biscuits, candles and a bottle of Prosecco. Enjoy a drink by candlelight in a delicious bathroom. You won't oversleep the next morning: the church clock begins its routine at 7am and continues until 10 at night. Breakfast is on a stone terrace looking down over the village rooftops – a lavish, excellent affair which will fuel you through even the most energetic day. There are a couple of tennis courts and a swimming pool, as well as a nine-hole golf course and arrangements for discounts at four more in the area.

rooms	15: 6 doubles, 6 twins, 2 singles, 1 suite.
price	€ 195. Single € 115–€ 158. Suite € 305.
meals	Choice of restaurants nearby.
closed	Mid–November-March
directions	From Goriza signs for hotel, 6km.

Collio is one of Italy's finest wine regions; the Counts of Formentini have been vintners since the 15th century.

	Contessa Isabella Formentini
tel	+39 0481 884051
fax	+39 0481 884052
e-mail	isabellaformentini@tiscalinet.it
web	www.golfhotelcastelloformentini.it

Hotel

Casa Mattiroli

Locanda Scedina I, 34070 San Floriano del Collio

You feel very much part of the household here, surrounded by signs of domestic routine – gardening gloves, books, baskets of ironing... It's a rare insight into ordinary Italian life; and a rare chance to be taught Italian cookery in a real home kitchen. Francesca is a highly trained chef who has worked in Brussels and London and her classes are hands-on and great fun. She and her mother are delightful hosts, unassuming, down-to-earth and comfortable to be with. Their quiet, modern house is similarly unpretentious and attractive. The double bedroom has some fine old family pieces; white walls, light fabrics and a pale wooden floor add a sense of light and space. Since Francesca only takes one set of guests at a time, the twin room is normally just used when there's a family with children. The house stands among cherry trees in a meadow-like garden, surrounded by vineyards with views down to the plain. Come at blossom or jam-making time (and maybe take some pots away with you). Guests are allowed to use the pool, tennis courts and hilly golf course of the neighbouring Golf Hotel Castello Formentini. *Minimum stay two nights.*

rooms	2: 1double; 1 twin sharing bath.
price	€ 50–€ 60.
meals	Dinner € 25–€ 31. Restaurant nearby.
closed	December–February.
directions	From Gorizia to San Floriano (follow signs to Golf Hotel Castello Formentini) facing church take road to right of hotel signed Gorizia 6km; house on left.

	Serena & Francesca Mattiroli
tel	+39 0481 884260
fax	+39 0481 519707
e-mail	serenatomadin@tiscalinet.it

'...A sea / Of glory streams along the Alpine height / Of blue Friuli's mountains...' Lord Byron, *Childe Harold's Pilgrimage.*

B&B

map 5   entry 62

www.thirdangle.com

emilia-romagna

Antica Torre

Case Bussandri 197, Loc. Cangelasio, 43039 Salsomaggiore Terme

Vanda and Francesco speak better French or Spanish than English, but don't let that put you off; they are gentle, congenial hosts. The Antica Torre is a venerable place, built in 1350; before this there was a salt store on the site for local monks. The tower itself has three bedrooms, each with a bathroom and small sitting area with wooden benches and cushions. There's also a fridge – handy for the summer months – and a billiard room with an open fire. The spiral stair in the tower might be too much of a challenge for the very young; indeed, children are not encouraged – this is more the sort of place for those wanting to escape the patter of tiny feet! The other five guest bedrooms are in the house, their white walls a simple foil for well-polished old pieces of furniture. Vanda does most of the cooking and will make up a picnic for lunch. Meals are served in the converted barn and breakfast is continental with a few extras. Yet another barn has been turned into a dayroom for guests but is a touch bleak; there's also an apartment. The pool is a great distraction, as are the mountain bikes. A gentle, quiet place. *Minimum stay two nights.*

Nearby, Fidenza has a remarkable 11th-century cathedral. The lovely carved decoration of the central portal is by the Parma sculptor Benedetto Antelami.

rooms	9: 8 doubles/twins, 1 suite for 4.
price	€ 100. Half-board € 70 p.p.
meals	Dinner € 20.
closed	December–February.
directions	From Salsomaggiore centre SP27 for Cangelasio & Piacenza. Fork left (signed Cangelasio); after 1.5km left for Antica Torre. Driveway left after 1.5km.

Signor Francesco Pavesi
tel +39 0524 575425
fax +39 0524 575425
e-mail info@anticatorre.it
web www.anticatorre.it

Hotel

Villa Bellaria

Via dei Gasperini 6, 29010 Cortina di Alseno

A delightful place to relax in a hammock slung on the veranda, or to breakfast *al fresco* on Marina's delectable homemade plum tart (in season). Inside, the rooms are cool and refreshing. White, silky bedspreads cover beds with delicately-crafted, wrought-iron bedsteads, the pale walls are hung with prints and there is some fine 18th-century furniture. The large living room extends to a wide paved area, roofed over like a veranda. Beyond is the garden; beyond that, rolling hills, shaded country lanes, woods and vineyards. There are medieval villages, spa towns and a Cistercian abbey to visit; riding, golf (bring your own club membership card if you plan to play) and swimming are nearby. Villa Bellaria was once the summer home of a Piacenza family, then Marina and her husband bought and renovated it, creating the ideal place to escape to from the heat of the plain. You must book in advance and you do need your own transport. Small pets are welcome, but a word of warning: the two resident cats do not like dogs!

rooms	3 doubles.
price	€ 52–€ 62. Singles € 32–€ 42.
meals	Choice of restaurants nearby.
closed	Rarely.
directions	After Alseno right for Vernasca. On for 5km, right into small street; house 2km with green gate on left.

Busseto is the birthplace of Giuseppe Verdi and has a museum dedicated to him.

	Sig.ra Marina Cazzaniga Calderoni
tel	+39 0523 947537
e-mail	info@villabellariabb.it
web	www.villabellariabb.it

B&B

map 8   entry 64

Villa Gaidello

Via Gaidello 18, 41013 Castelfranco Emilia

A neat, pretty pattern of vineyards and fields edged with cypresses, two infant canals and a lake with swans. This is an unexpected find just off the main Modena-Bologna road and it gets better. The Osteria, Paola's restaurant in a stone barn, serves the most wonderful organic dishes and looks like an old oil painting – a long table bright with flowers, expectant rows of chairs, shadowy, arched ceilings, shelves of gleaming jars... There are three old farmhouses to stay in on the estate. The first, the *casa patronale*, is Gaidello, overlooking the garden and the lake. Further along the winding, tree-lined road are green-shuttered Gaianello and San Giacomo. The apartments range from old, thick-walled rooms with dark, period furniture to slightly more modern spaces with lighter furnishing and pale floor tiles. Bathrooms and kitchens are basic and functional. San Giacomo also has two independent double rooms with wrought-iron beds, fresh colours, matching friezes and wooden stable doors. Paola is the hard-working genius behind this peaceful place, a relaxed and friendly hostess. *Ask about gastronomic visits and courses.*

rooms	2 + 7: 2 doubles. 7 apartments for 1–6.
price	€68–€97. Apartments €90–€238.
meals	Dinner with local wine, €45. Restaurant closed on Mondays.
closed	August.
directions	From Modena Via Emilia to Castelfranco Emilia. Left at hospital lights for Nonantola. Under bridge, immediate right; 3rd left onto Via Gaidello, 500m, signs.

'But still the Vine her ancient Ruby yields / And still a Garden by the Water blows.' Edward Fitzgerald The Rubaiyat of Omar Khayyam.

Signora Paola Bini

tel	+39 059 926 806
fax	+39 059 926 620
e-mail	gaidello@tin.it
web	www.gaidello.com

B&B & Self-catering

entry 65   map 8

Beneverchio

Via Niviano 18, 41026 Pavullo nel Frignano

Come for the views – they are amazing. Across the gentle, wooded hills to the valley below and up again to the Abetone mountains…The walking, of course, is superb. Beneverchio was originally built as a lodging for pilgrims; a simple *agriturismo*, it remains as unadorned today – and the lodging probably as cheap. Claudia is the driving force, helped by her mother and her partner Ornello who looks after the farm. There are four simple rooms in the main house; given the size of the building they are unexpectedly small, and not particularly light, but they do have good mattresses to ensure a restful night. There is also a sitting room with various relics, such as a framed group of old keys and an old sewing table, a courtyard where dogs roam and Claudia's great pride – the kitchen and dining room. The food is diverse and delicious and fit for Gargantua: homemade breads, antipasti, a trio of pastas, two main courses – leave room if you can for the home-made puddings – all washed down with local wine and a *digestivo*.

rooms	4 doubles.
price	€40.
meals	Dinner €20.
closed	Mondays.
directions	From Pavullo, SS12 south to Abetone; left for Niviano/Montorso. Up hill past house with mural. Beneverchio is on right.

	Claudia Ori & Ornello Giusti
tel	+39 0536 325290
fax	+39 0536 308961
e-mail	agriturismo@beneverchio.com
web	www.beneverchio.it

Take a look at Pieve Trébbio, an 11th-century Romanesque church with separate poly-gonal bapistery and bell tower, the oldest church in the Modenese Appenines.

B&B

map 8   entry 66

Azienda Agrituristica Tizzano

Via Lamizze no. 1197, 41050 Monteombraro

There are animals everywhere. Ducks pick their way through scattered straw across the yard, goats and ponies wander free, a tabby cat basks on ancient stone steps, a peacock screeches. Tizzano is a proper, organic farm, which Stefano hopes to make completely self-sufficient one day. His mother, Leonilde, uses home-grown produce – cherries and chestnuts, meat and cheese – in her cooking; the results are superb and justify a detour. But there are many other reasons for coming here, especially if you seek an authentic taste of rural life. The farmhouse is medieval, set among fields on a hillside (be warned, not the easiest place to find). Roses and vines climb its rough, peeling walls, small, shuttered windows keep the inside cool and an old archway leads to the kitchen, bright with postcards. The simple dining room is reminiscent of a village school 50 years ago. Big, clean, basic bedrooms (two in the 19th-century barn) have shared bathrooms and lovely views. Their furniture dates back to the time of Stefano's grandparents. Stefano knows the area inside out and can tell you all about walks and places to visit. Excellent value.

rooms	7: 2 doubles, 3 family for 4, 2 triples, sharing bath. In barn: 1 family for 3, 1 family for 5.
price	€44. Half-board €35 p.p. Apt for 2 €70, for 4 €90.
meals	Dinner €20.
closed	Rarely.
directions	From Modena A1 for Bologna exit Spilamberto; left for Bazzano, right for Monteveglio & Monteombraro. Before village right on Via Lamizze for 3km, left at no. 1197.

'Wherein were all manner of four-footed beasts of the earth...' Acts of the Apostles

Stefano & Leonilde Fogacci

tel	+39 059 989581
fax	+39 059 989581
e-mail	agriturismo.tizzano@libero.it

B&B

La Piana dei Castagni

Via Lusignano 11, 40040 Rocca di Roffeno

Write, paint, read or idle to your heart's content: here, deep in the woods, there's nothing to disturb or distract you. This is a secret little Hansel and Gretel house with demure shutters and lace-trimmed curtains. It stands isolated among chestnut trees, reached via a long, wriggling track; below are bucolic meadows, falling to a farm or two, and a further distant descent along the yawning valley. An old stone farmhouse newly converted and adapted for B&B, La Piana is a modest place to stay. The bedrooms, named after local berries, are a good size and painted in clean, pastel colours; tiny pictures hang above beds and little windows set in thick walls look out over the glorious valley. The bathrooms – one of them once an old chicken shed! – are tiled, with showers. Valeria lives 10 minutes away at La Civetta. She is gentle, kind and accommodating; she's also very knowledgeable about the region and will help organise trekking to truffle-hunting. Rocca di Roffeno is a pretty medieval village, with 14th-century buildings and towers, a smattering of Roman ruins and lots of restaurants with Bolognese specialities to try.

rooms	5: 2 doubles, 2 triples, 1 single.
price	€60–€72. Singles €35. Triple €80.
meals	Dinner, set menu, €15.
closed	December–March.
directions	From Tolè, follow signs for S. Lucia, Bocca Ravari & after "Torre Jussi" follow signs.

	Signora Valeria Vitali
tel	+39 051 912985
fax	+39 051 912985
e-mail	info@pianadeicastagni.it
web	www.pianadeicastagni.it

Civetta means little 'owl', and also 'flirt'. In Mozart's Marriage of Figaro, Figaro *sings that women are 'owls that entice us to pluck all our feathers'!*

B&B

map 8   entry 68

La Fenice

Via S. Lucia 29, Ca' de Gatti, 40040 Rocca di Roffeno

It's a spectacular spot for riding – trek off on your Anglo-Arab horse into the Natural Park of Samone, visit the stones of Rocca Malatina, the waterfalls of Labante. A qualified instructor is on hand in the summer. Remo and Paolo are brothers, were born here, and have taken the farm in an unusual direction, growing seed potatoes for export, so the land is officially 'closed' to other crops; they've done much of the renovation themselves and you'll probably find them in overalls working on the latest project. Guest bedrooms feel like the spare rooms of a big house – they have a hotchpotch of furniture that hangs together well, a masculine touch here and there, and lovely big rafters, some very low. They are a bit dark, as the windows are small, but most have their own outside door, and some an open fireplace and a supply of logs – you'll be cosy in winter. Breakfast is the usual: coffee, with hot chocolate for the children, bread and brioche, but do stay for dinner: the region is known for the best cooking in the country. All that fresh air – you are 800m above sea level – and outdoor living will build up an appetite.

rooms	9: 6 doubles, 2 triples, 1 family.
price	€ 67. Half-board € 83–€ 93 for two.
meals	Dinner from € 25.
closed	7 January–6 February.
directions	From Bologna SS64 south 30km, right to Tole, then towards Cereglio. After 1.5km, right. La Fenice 5km from Tole on right.

The area is famous for cherries; the April blossom is beautiful. Montese, nearby, has a wild black cherry festival around the third weekend in July.

	Remo & Paolo Giarandoni
tel	+39 051 919272
fax	+39 051 919024
e-mail	lafenice@lafeniceagritur.it
web	www.lafeniceagritur.it

B&B

Hotel Orologio
Via IV Novembre 10, 40123 Bologna

Just off the main part of the Piazza Maggiore, one of the most beautiful medieval squares in Italy, is the Albergo Orologio, a tall, narrow slice of building that is wedged between a bank and a bookshop. It would be easy to miss. Its discreetly smart glass and brass entrance is guarded on either side by a small shrub in a terracotta pot. Immediately above the door, plants trail through a pretty, latticed railing in front of a green-shuttered window. Step into the yellow reception hall, hung with clocks and big mirrors, and make your first acquaintance with the friendly, multi-national staff. Above are the sitting and dining rooms; above them, the simple, comfortably furnished bedrooms, with walls in bold yellow, green or orange, dark carpets and heavy curtains. The generously-sized suites come complete with sitting area, sofabed... and statue. Most of the rooms look over an intriguing maze of terracotta rooftops, or across to the Piazza itself and the Duomo. Outside the hotel entrance are some benches so you can sit and watch the comings and goings in the square before throwing yourself into the glorious fray.

rooms	34 doubles.
price	€ 173–€ 326. Suite € 260–€ 434.
meals	Wide choice of restaurants in Bologna.
closed	Rarely.
directions	Take a taxi from the station or buses 25 or 37 stopping in piazza Maggiore, 70m from hotel.

Bologna's Teatro Communale was inaugurated in May 1763 with a performance of Gluck's Il Trionfo di Clelia.

	Signora Cristina Orsi
tel	+39 051 231253
fax	+39 051 260552
e-mail	orologio@inbo.it
web	www.bolognahotel.net

Hotel

map 8   entry 70

Hotel Commercianti
Via de' Pignattari 11, 40124 Bologna

The Basilica of San Petronio, one of the greatest churches of the Catholic world, is on the other side of the street; opposite its west front is the Piazza Maggiore, Bologna's main square. You really are in the heart of things, yet there is little noise and barely any traffic. The Commercianti is, astonishingly, a restored 12th-century building, whose conversion has – fortunately – managed to avoid the errors of many. Bedrooms are magnificent, many with their massive old beams exposed; six have little terraces overlooking the Gothic Basilica (whose nave is higher than that even of Amiens). The suites are particularly impressive, with lovely sloping beamed ceilings. One room has the exposed remnants of an early fresco; all have a slightly medieval feel, with white, rough-plaster walls, some wrought-iron furniture, wooden floors with Persian rugs. The marble, blue-carpeted staircase leads down past a fine marble bust to the breakfast room, where the first meal of the day does full justice to its impressive setting.

rooms	34: 22 doubles, 7 singles, 3 suites for 3, 2 suites for 4.
price	€ 196–€ 214. Singles € 139. Suites € 284–€ 258.
meals	Great choice of restaurants within walking distance.
closed	Rarely.
directions	Hotel in Old City Centre *Centro Storico*, in pedestrian area.

Bologna is known as 'La grassa' (the fat one). The first tortellini are said to have been made by a Bolognese trying to recreate the beauty of Venus's navel.

	Signor Mauro Orsi
tel	+39 051 233052
fax	+39 051 224733
e-mail	commercianti@inbo.it
web	www.bolognahotel.net

Hotel

entry 71   map 8

Agriturismo Cavaioni
Via Cavaioni 4, 40136 Bologna

A tranquil, undemanding place to return to after coping with urban bustle. Look down over the vineyards and get a different perspective on the roofs and towers of Bologna. Or turn your back on the city and rest your eyes on meadows full of wild flowers. For the house is on a hill and the views are a delight in both directions. Reached by a tree-lined drive, it is 15-minute journey from the centre of Bologna and very peaceful. The family bought it in the 1950s and it has been a B&B for about 10 years – one of the first in the city. It's an unpretentious farmhouse with thick walls, a red-tiled roof, brown blinds and a balcony. The rooms inside, dark and cool, are simply and pleasantly decorated, functional not luxurious. The bedrooms are painted in light colours and plainly furnished with dark wood country furniture. Two have access to the balcony (recline in bed and look across the valley to the rolling hills); two share a bathroom. Davide is helpful and very informative about the city and the area. If you tire of cultural pleasures, there are some lovely walks in the hills close by.

rooms	5 doubles, 2 sharing bathroom.
price	€ 65–€ 110.
meals	Choice of restaurants nearby or in Bologna centre, 15 minutes.
closed	January.
directions	From Bologna Porta San Mamolo follow via San Mamolo; via dei colli. Continue but keep to your right; right at sign for Casaglia. House opposite Parco Cavaioni.

	Davide de Lucca
tel	+39 051 589371 (& fax)
mobile	+39 328 3161357
e-mail	tcavaione@iol.it

The University of Bologna was founded at the end of the 11th century and quickly attracted students from all over medieval Europe.

B&B

map 8   entry 72

B&B a Bologna

Via Cairoli 3, 40121 Bologna

Before it became a B&B, nuns lived here – but if you have in mind cloisters and statues, put those to one side! This is a typical, modern, Italian city apartment block with a central lift and a winding stair. Davide, who also runs Agriturismo Cavaioni, opened for business in March 2003, offering a pleasant, no-frills place to stay in the centre of the city. A long, narrow, white-painted corridor, enlivened with the occasional picture, leads to clean, light bedrooms, cool with tiled floors and blinds. The furniture is fairly minimal but comfortable, beds are floral and there's lots of space. Two of the bedrooms share a huge bathroom (with washing machine), so would be excellent for a family. The Irish pub down the road has a weekly jazz night but otherwise the street is fairly quiet. Breakfast is in your room or in the dining area but, if you want it earlier or later than the norm, Davide will give you vouchers for the bar round the corner. It's all very flexible and friendly, and you have your own keys to come and go as you please. There are plenty of good restaurants to choose from and the Piazza Maggiore is 10 minutes away.

During the 14th century 180 wealthy families left their mark on Bologna's sky-line by erecting towers, 15 of which are still standing.

rooms	4: 1 double, 1 triple; 2 doubles, sharing bath.
price	€ 65–€ 110. Triple € 95–€ 120.
meals	Wide choice of restaurants nearby.
closed	January.
directions	Right out of train station. 1st left onto Via Amendola. 2nd right onto Via Milazzo; 100m, left onto Via Cairoli. Apartment on 2nd floor; ring bell.

Davide de Lucca

tel	+39 051 4210897 (& fax)
mobile	+39 328 3161357
e-mail	takakina@hotmail.com
web	www.traveleurope.it/bolognabb

B&B

Hotel Corona d'Oro 1890

Via Oberdan 12, 40126 Bologna

The palazzo, with its wonderful 14th-century wooden portico, is loaded with history. And the Liberty-style interiors are special. A lavish plastered frieze runs right round the glass-roofed central hall, on one side of which are two mighty columns sheltering floral-patterned wall-seating. Elsewhere: old-fashioned gold-striped sofas and armchairs, slightly formal, entirely fitting. Huge potted plants stand on a fine marble floor, there are Venetian wall lights and some gorgeous Art Nouveau glass; the effect is wonderful, opulent, and is what makes the Corono d'Oro so special. Just off the hall is the charming little bar-cum-breakfast-room, with a mirror reflecting light off the whole of one wall. Bedrooms are solidly comfortable, adhering more closely to a traditional 'hotel' manner, with institutional carpets, brass-edged sockets and light fittings, heavy curtains and built-in desks. Some have tiny terraces or balconies overlooking the glass roof of the central hall; bathrooms are impeccable. And you are as central as you can get – just off a pedestrian street 200m from the two towers.

rooms	40: 30 doubles, 8 singles, 2 suites.
price	€ 191–€ 326. Singles € 135–€ 211. Suite € 278–€ 434.
meals	Restaurant next door.
closed	August.
directions	In *centro storico*, in little street off Via Rizzoli.

For hidden treasures try the Palazzo Magnani (frescoes by the Caracci) and Palazzo Poggi (frescoes by Pellegrino Tibaldi) at nos. 20 and 31 Via Zamboni.

	Signor Mauro Orsi
tel	+39 051 236456
fax	+39 051 262679
e-mail	corona@inbo.it
web	www.bolognahotel.net

Hotel

map 8   entry 74

Hotel Novecento

Piazza Galileo 3/4, 40123 Bologna

Another hotel owned by Cristina and Mauro Orsi, another lovely old townhouse in the centre of Bologna. But this one promises to be radically different. It has been gutted and is being completely refitted in a style that has echoes of 1930s Viennese Secession. The bedrooms will be black and cream, slick, smart and minimalist, with black wrought-iron beds, black wooden furniture and serried ranks of lamps. A central staircase with wrought-iron railings climbs up the different floors to the very top; here is a grand suite with an arched, triple window and a balcony overlooking the quiet street below. Like Albergo Orologio round the corner, the hotel is in a great position, with the Palazzo Communale immediately behind. If you crave something lush and splendid after the hotel's 1930s minimalism, visit the Palazzo: a far cry from British town halls, it's made up of ancient buildings grouped round a beautiful central courtyard. Two lovely 16th-century doorways are attributed to Alessi and there's a fine collection of miniatures and paintings from the Bolognese School on the second floor.

rooms	25: 15 doubles, 9 singles, 1 suite.
price	€ 191–€ 326. Singles € 135–€ 211. Suite € 278–€ 434.
meals	Wide choice of restaurants in Bologna.
closed	August.
directions	Hotel in old part of city, 300m from Piazza Maggiore.

Bologna has not one but two leaning towers, Garisenda and Asinelli, 11th and 12th century respectively.

Mauro Orsi
tel +39 051 236456
fax +39 051 262679
e-mail corona@inbo.it
web www.bolognahotel.net

Hotel

Azienda Vitivinicola e Agrituristica Trerè

Via Casale 19, 48018 Faenza

Stripey vineyards stretch as far as the eye can see. And in the middle of this flat, green Romagna patchwork is a compact grouping of rosy buildings, with a clump of tall trees in one corner. The farmhouse, pink and entertainingly angular, is surrounded by converted barns and stables: today's apartments and conference room. This is a serious, wine-producing estate; around the house are certificates and awards, there's a shop, and a fabulous little rose-and-gold wine museum. Despite all this, the place has a family feel; there are toys scattered about and the atmosphere is easy. The bedrooms in the house have a light and pretty elegance, with beamed ceilings, pastel walls, lovely old family furniture and memorable touches – the deep lace trim of a white sheet folded over a jade bedcover, a wall full of books... The apartments, in the old stables, are also attractive but more modern and functional. Each has French windows opening on a private patio, and a mezzanine with an extra bed tucked under a skylight that children love. Though the restaurant is only open on weekend evenings, there are other places to eat nearby. *Air-conditioning in apartments.*

rooms	4 + 4: 2 doubles, 1 twin, 1 triple. 4 apartments: 3 for 4, 1 for 6.
price	€70. Singles €42–€52. Family €150. Apartment for 2-3 €76–€106; for 4 €150.
meals	Breakfast €5. Dinner in restaurant from €20, closed Jan–Feb & Mon–Thurs. Restaurants, 2km.
closed	Rarely.
directions	From Faenza Via Emilia SS9 for Imola/Bologna. After 3km left after Volvo garage on Via Casale; signed.

	Morena Trerè & Massimiliano Fabbri
tel	+39 0546 47034
fax	+39 0546 47012
e-mail	trere@trere.com
web	www.trere.com

'The luscious clusters of the vine / Upon my mouth do crush their wine...'
Andrew Marvell, *The Garden*

Self-catering & B&B

map 9   entry 76

Torre Pratesi

Via Cavina 11, Cavina, 48013 Brisighella

Sadly for this beautiful, squat and angular 16th-century tower – but luckily for us – the invention of gun powder rendered it defunct. It was roofed and turned into a hunting lodge, and a farmhouse was added in 1800. The two buildings are an impressive sight, and the renovation is immaculate. Inside is a gentle mix of antique and contemporary, with wrought-iron furniture, red leather armchairs, kilim rugs... and, in every room, a brand-new coffee machine! Each floor of the tower – reached via a lift and spiral stair – has a big, tile-floored room with small windows and gorgeous, great big rafters. The suites in the old farmhouse have small sitting areas, some with an open fireplace, and are named after the surrounding mountains. Torre Pratesi is still a working farm and the olive oil, wine, fruit, vegetables and cheese are put to good use in the kitchen by Nerio; Letty is a gentle soul who loves to share the place with guests. A path leads down from the well-kept orchard and garden to the pool and outdoor jacuzzi. This is good walking country, with marked trails stretching away from the ridge behind the house, and the views are lovely.

rooms	9: 3 doubles, 6 suites.
price	€129–€155. Suites €155–€181.
meals	Dinner €39–€44.
closed	10-25 January.
directions	From Brisighella through Fognano. Right just after village. On SP63, 3km to Torre Pratesi.

Brisighella has been inhabited since prehistoric times. There's an archaeological museum in the Palazzo Municipale, with interesting Roman finds.

Nerio & Letty Raccagni

tel	+39 0546 84545
fax	+39 0546 84558
e-mail	torrep@tin.it
web	www.torrepratesi.it

Hotel

Relais Varnello

Via Rontana 34, 48013 Brisighella

A rural address for those who don't want to get their feet muddy! There are electric gates and you're given a remote control for your stay, so no need to stray from tarmac. In young gardens the buildings stand sparklingly clean and heavily restored. Nicely-furnished rooms have views across the valley or garden; the suites are in a separate building, with a sauna. The farm produces Sangiovese DOC wine and olive oil, which you can buy along with Faenza pottery showing the family crest. It is an area famous for its herbs and Liana, the friendly, vivacious wife of the owner Giovanni, uses them in profusion when she cooks for guests. However, the service here is mostly B&B, with the breakfast cakes and pastries coming from a bakery run by Liana's sprightly mother. There are wide views over the Padana and to the Adriatic, and you have a private wild park, Giovanni's pride and joy, just a stroll away – a lovely place for a picnic and a book. Higher up the hill is the Pacro Carné, with CAI-marked walking routes. *Minimum stay two nights.*

rooms	6: 4 doubles/twins, 2 suites.
price	€ 130. Suites € 180.
meals	Dinner from € 20, book ahead.
closed	January–15 March.
directions	From Brisighella on SP23 Montecino & Limisano road, signed to Riolo Terme. After 3km, left after Ristorante È Manicômi, signed to Rontana. Relais 1st building on right.

	Signor Giovanni Liverzani
tel	+39 0546 85493
fax	+39 0546 83124
e-mail	info@varnello.it
web	www.varnello.it

'A meal without wine is like a day without sunshine.' Louis Pasteur *(1822-1895)*

B&B

map 9   entry 78

Photography by Michael Busselle

liguria

Villa Elisa

Via Romana 70, 18012 Bordighera

The climate is kind: visit at any time of the year. The hotel was built in the 20s when Bordighera, a pretty town with sloping tree-lined roads and pastel houses, became a winter retreat. Maurizio's father, who ran it for many years, was a keen painter and had artists to stay – bedroom walls are still hung with the paintings they left him. Some still come, following in the steps of Monet. Maurizio and Rita are the nicest hosts you could wish to meet. Maurizio takes groups off into the Maritime Alps in his minibus and guides them back on three-hour walks, Rita loves to spoil – she has even provided a playroom for younger guests, with special activities for the summer. Bedrooms have parquet floors and are dressed in blue; bathrooms are white-tiled with floral friezes and heated towel rails; larger rooms have terraces with views to the hills. There's a flowery courtyard garden scented with oranges and lemons, and a wonderful pool area with plenty of quiet corners. The pebbled beach is a 10-minute scamper down the hill and the restaurant is absolutely charming; fresh fish is on the menu and the wine list is long.

From San Remo you can take the funicular railway up to Monte Bignoe for wonderful views over the Riviera.

rooms	34 + 1: 30 doubles, 3 singles, 1 suite. 1 apartment for 4.
price	€ 110–€ 170. Singles € 75–€ 105. Half or full-board available for weekly stays.
meals	Lunch/dinner € 40.
closed	5 November–22 December.
directions	Via Romana parallel to main road through town (Via Aurelia), reachable by any crossroad that links the two. Villa Elisa at western end of Via Romana.

Signor Maurizio Oggero

tel	+39 0184 261313
fax	+39 0184 261942
e-mail	info@villaelisa.com
web	www.villaelisa.com

Hotel & & Self-catering

Casa Forcheri

Via Scala Santa 6, 18010 Diano Castello

You're greeted in the entrance *salotto* by framed daguerreotypes of Uncle Raffaele and Aunt Santina (having already passed the arms of the Bishop of Turin on the stairs). This big, gracious apartment is part of a townhouse which once belonged to Maura's forebears. High, beautifully frescoed ceilings, ornate floor tiles and lovingly maintained family antiques give a charmingly dynastic air and the whole apartment is characterised by coolness and space – a pleasant antidote to the searing heat outside. The dining room leads to a large, modern, glazed terrace-cum-drawing room which can be opened right up to bring in the evening breeze. Recline on one of the sofas and browse through Maura's collection of books on the region. Though the big kitchen with its antique dresser has a pre-war feel, it is well equipped with all mod cons. You are right in the middle of Diano Castello, where styles veer delightfully from medieval and baroque to Genoese-Romanesque. Either side, the views are wonderful – in one direction, the ancient hilltop village; in the other, hills, olive groves and sea. *Minimum stay one week.*

rooms	Sleeps 4: 1 double, 1 twin.
price	€ 600–€ 700 per week.
meals	Self-catering. Osteria in the village.
closed	Rarely.
directions	Exit motorway at San Bartolomeo Al Mare towards Diano Marina & then to Diano Castello; park in car park near church.

	Maura Muratorio
tel	+39 0183 498226 (& fax)
mobile	+39 335 45 66 17
e-mail	mauram@libero.it
web	casaforcheri.it

Maura Muratorio is the author of two books on the legendary Hanbury family, whose famous gardens at the Villa Hanbury are now considered an Italian national treasure.

Self-catering

map 6   entry 80

Villa della Pergola
Via privata Montagù 9/1, 17021 Alassio

Above the pretty town of Alassio hang vast, spellbindingly lovely gardens. It's nearly 20 years since the last Hanbury left but the family's legacy remains. Hidden among the glorious trees and shrubs planted by Sir Daniel is this lovely, 19th-century house. Built in Italian colonial style, with colonnades, balustrades and loggias, Villa della Pergola is a chance to see how the English aristocracy once lived on the Riviera. Supreme elegance *all'inglese* combines with the best Italy has to offer: wonderful marble, the yellow, blue and ochre tones of Liguria, columns, Moorish fountains, astonishing views. Though Marcella's family bought the house in 1985, they have kept its English country-house flavour. Luxurious bedrooms in soft, restful colours are each named after a member of the Hanbury family – Daniel, Ruth, Cecile; they still feel part of a long-cherished family home and you almost expect Sir Daniel to knock on your door and invite you down to breakfast when you're ready. Indeed, the breakfast will include marmalade made to the recipe of a former Hanbury family cook. *Minimum two nights.*

Sir Daniel Hanbury exchanged plants and shrubs with that other famous Hanbury establishment at Mortola, near Ventimiglia.

rooms	6: 3 doubles, 1 triple, 1 suite for 2-3, 1 family room.
price	€ 190-€ 220.
meals	Restaurants within walking distance.
closed	Rarely.
directions	Highway A10 Genova-Ventimiglia, exit Albenga 5 km, exit Andora 10km. By train to Alassio station.

Marcella de Martini
tel	+39 3332 789305
fax	+39 0182 554969
e-mail	info@villadellapergola.it
web	www.villadellapergola.it

B&B

Casa Cambi

Via Roma 42, 17024 Castelvecchio di Rocca Barbena

You can hardly believe that such a village has survived unspoilt into the 21st century. It's a fairytale tangle of winding cobbled streets and medieval stone houses on a green and rocky hilltop. All around are dramatic mountains and stupendous views. A square, uncompromising castle dominates the hill; immediately below is Anna's entrancing house. A tiny front door (the house is 700 years old, after all) takes you straight into a delightful, vaulted room – a soothing mix of creams and whites, ochres and umbers. Pale walls contrast with a gleaming wooden floor and old polished furniture; its subtle, restrained country charm sets the tone for the rest of the house. All the rooms are a delight, all full of unexpected touches – jugs of fresh wild flowers, hessian curtains on wrought-iron poles, a rack of old black kitchen implements stark against a white wall... Anna adores her house and has lavished huge care on it. She's bubbly and friendly and loves cooking; her kitchen is a joy to be in. Breakfast out in the pretty terraced garden among olive and fig trees and revel in those mountain views.

rooms	4: 2 doubles, 1 twin, 1 family.
price	€90.
meals	Dinner €25; wine €10 a bottle. Book ahead.
closed	5 November–March.
directions	A10 exit Albenga. S582 for Garessio for Castelvecchio do Rocca Barbena, 12km. Park near church & walk 100m to Casa Cambi.

	Anna Bozano
tel	+39 0182 78009
fax	+39 0182 78009
e-mail	casacambi@casacambi.it
web	www.casacambi.it

'And now they change – a paler shadow strews / Its mantle o'er the mountains...'
Lord Byron, *Childe Harold's Pilgrimage*

B&B

map 6   entry 82

Palazzo Fieschi

Piazza della Chiesa 14, 16010 Savignone

The name of this elegant townhouse near Genoa commemorates former owners, the distinguished Fieschi family, once a significant power in the land. Now it belongs to Simonetta and Aldo Caprile, who left the world of commerce in Genoa for a life of hotel-keeping. They have carefully renovated the old palazzo, adding every modern comfort to its *cinquecento* grandeur. The oldest working hotel in Liguria, it overlooks a square and is a short walk to the centre; there's also a shuttle service for guests. The surrounding countryside is steep and wooded, away from the autostradas and with plenty of walking nearby. Bedrooms are white-walled and spotless, many with fabulous carved or painted bedheads. The rooms vary, but those on the mezzanine floor in the oldest section of the house have the most character, with beautiful tiles, grand doorways and low ceilings. The dining room, with its chandeliers and sweeping red drapes, is perfect for weddings. The Capriles are courteous hosts, and you may encounter the odd musical evening in winter. *Minimum stay two nights.*

rooms	24: 13 doubles, 2 triples, 1 family, 8 singles.
price	€ 118–€ 130. Triples € 156–€ 162. Family room € 170. Singles € 73–€ 98.
meals	Lunch/dinner € 26–€ 41.
closed	25 December–February.
directions	From A7 exit to Busalla. In Busalla for Casella; 3.5km, left for Savignone. Hotel in village centre.

In 1860 Garibaldi, whose family came from nearby, set sail for Sicily with his 'thousand' volunteers from Genoa's harbour.

Aldo & Simonetta Caprile

tel	+39 010 9360063
fax	+39 010 936821
e-mail	fieschi@split.it
web	www.palazzofieschi.it

Hotel

Villa Gnocchi

Via Romana 53, San Lorenzo della Costa, 16038 Santa Margherita Ligure

Why bother with Portofino, wondered our inspector, after a visit full of magic to Roberto's villa? It is an idyllic spot, quiet but close to the action. Roberto, a farmer, trained at Pisa University and inherited the house from his grandfather in a run-down state – what you now see is the result of years of hard work. They love farming here, deep in the country but within sight of the sea; sip a glass of chilled wine from the terrace and gaze down the coast. Bedrooms are individual: some white, some ochre, all simple and charming. Grandfather's old furniture graces parquet floors, muslin curtains flutter at open windows. The check-clothed dining room, too, is friendly and inviting. The only sound to break the peace is birdsong – and the faintest hoot from the streets below. Santa Margherita – a 15-minute walk downhill, a taxi ride up – is a charming little town: a beach, fishing boats, good shops, lively bars. Old framed prints on the walls, delicious meals on the table, paths to most of the villages and buses from the gate to the others: a wonderful spot, and Roberto and Simona so generous and friendly.

rooms	9: 5 doubles, 2 twins, 2 family.
price	€94. Half-board €65 p.p.
meals	Half-board only.
closed	Mid-October-Easter.
directions	From Santa Margherita for S. Lorenzo, 4km. Pass big sign 'Genova & S. Lorenzo' on left & A12 on right, 50m ahead, left down narrow road. At red & white barrier ring bell as another gate further on.

	Signor Roberto Gnocchi
tel	+39 0185 283431
fax	+39 0185 283431
e-mail	roberto.gnocchi@tin.it

Pesto alla Genovese – the name of the local speciality derives from the Italian pestare to grind or crush.

B&B

map 7   entry 84

Hotel Piccolo

Via Duca degli Abruzzi 31, 16034 Portofino

Only God could have arranged such a spot. Once the summer home of a wealthy Genoese family, the Piccolo – not as little as its name suggests – has the only beach around here: cross a small road to the terraced garden and a path leads you down onto an immaculate sheltered-cove pebble beach with loungers. The bedrooms vary in size but are otherwise identical: smart, traditional, decorated in restful shades of salmon pink, with chestnut fitted wardrobes and beautiful soft lighting. All look over the sea and many have a terrace or balcony. Bathrooms have superb walk-in showers and fluffy white towels. Roberto, the helpful manager, will send you off to the market in Santa Margherita or to see the statue of Jesus under the sea off tiny San Fruttuoso. The fascinating village, Italy's very own St Tropez, is a five-minute walk through olives and pines – it may be full of cars in high summer, but you can easily get around by bus or by boat. If you just want to potter, the hotel provides a set lunch and dinner, and the regional cooking is delicious.

From Portofino you can walk across the peninsular to the beautiful Abbey of San Fruttuoso, set among pines and olive groves.

rooms	22: 15 doubles, 4 family, 3 singles.
price	€ 175–€ 310. Singles € 126–€ 192.
meals	Dinner € 31.
closed	November–March.
directions	Exit A12 at Rapallo. Follow signs to Santa Margherita Ligure & Portofino. Enter Portofino on Via Provinciale; hotel 300m before town centre.

Signor Roberto Tiraboschi

tel	+39 0185 269015
fax	+39 0185 269621
e-mail	dopiccol@tin.it
web	www.dominapiccolo.it

Hotel

Hotel Villa Edera

Via Venino 12, 16030 Moneglia

The villa is perched above the village of Moneglia and reached through five low, narrow tunnels: thrilling for some, daunting for others! Regulars often come by train and walk, but staff are perfectly happy to pick you up. This is a true family hotel run by the Schiaffino family who have been in Moneglia for 300 years. Orietta, the elder daughter, is manageress – businesslike yet approachable, she sings in the local choir and loves meeting people who share her interest in music. Her husband and her sister's husband are waiters; her mother, Ida, is a brilliant cook, preparing Ligurian dishes with the freshest organic produce (some vegetarian). Her father, Lino, ensures that it all runs like clockwork. Orietta is a keen walker who may take guests out for some proper hikes, though you may prefer to catch a boat to Portofino or explore the Cinque Terre by sea. You are fairly close to the railway here – such a significant part of the landscape, threading the Cinque Terre villages together – but you would never know. A super hotel and very near the beach, too. *Minimum stay two days.*

rooms	27: 21 doubles, 2 family, 2 singles, 2 suites.
price	€ 120–€ 170. Singles € 80–€ 110. Suites € 160–€ 250. Half-board € 60–€ 95p.p.
meals	Lunch/dinner € 20–€ 28. Restaurant à la carte.
closed	10 November–15 March.
directions	Exit A12 at Sestri Levante, follow signs for Moneglia tunnel. Immediately after 5th tunnel right (at sports field); signs.

Signora Orietta Schiaffino

tel	+39 0185 49291
fax	+39 0185 49470
e-mail	info@villaedera.com
web	www.villaedera.com

The elegant resort of Rapallo, where The Barefoot Contessa *was filmed in 1954, has a 16th-century castle that sometimes hosts exhibitions.*

Hotel

map 7　entry 86

Castello di Monleone
Via Venino 3, 16030 Moneglia

Grandly perched on a rock overlooking Moneglia and the sea, this little castle was built as a summer home by the Marquis de' Fornari in 1905. Despite the neo-Renaissance grandeur and the quietly aristocratic air, the atmosphere is intimate and homely. The bedrooms, furnished with some 17th-and 18th-century pieces, have big beds, majestic mirrors, painted ceilings; all have bathrooms (though some are small) and the suite a jacuzzi. Each bedroom is named after a locally built 19th-century boat: Peodomea, Feluche, José Maria... Ask for one of the quieter ones: a railway runs in the valley below. The small sitting room has a TV (the only one!) and lots of books and a terrace studded with a circular mosaic has a spectacular view over the bay — an idyllic spot for breakfasts in summer. Swim in the pool, visit Portofino and San Fruttuoso, hike in the hills — in the spring, friendly Orietta takes walking groups into the Cinque Terre, an area she loves. *Minimum stay three nights.*

rooms	5: 4 doubles, 1 suite.
price	€ 100–€ 190. Suites € 180–€ 250.
meals	Dinner € 25 at restaurant next door.
closed	Mid-November–mid-December.
directions	Exit A12 at Sestri Levante for Moneglia tunnel. Immediately after 5th tunnel right (at sports field) for Villa Edera & Castello.

The statues here are copies of some that adorned a bridge in Florence; the originals were destroyed by bombing.

Signora Orietta Schiaffino

tel	+39 0185 49291
fax	+39 0185 49470
e-mail	info@castellodimonleone.com
web	www.castellodimonleone.com

Hotel & B&B

Monte Pù

Loc. Monte Pù, 16030 Castiglione Chiavarese

The farm stands, remote and blissfully silent, on the site of a ninth-century Benedictine monastery whose tiny chapel still survives; the cherry and pear orchards and trout ponds are surrounded by woods. Pù (from the Latin *purus*) means pure, referring to the quality of the air and natural spring water and harking back to the importance of purification in monastic life. Organic produce is served in the restaurant here; rabbits, goats, hens, cows all contribute in their various ways. Aurora sometimes finds time to sit with guests on summer evenings – to gaze at the stars, the fireflies and the lights of fishing vessels on the sea far below. It is a magical setting. One of the bedrooms has an optional kitchen, well-equipped but, understandably, seldom used. Provided you can face negotiating the steep, rugged road, this makes a good base – and a minibus to Genoa can be arranged, which can also call at Sestri Levante station. Archery, flower-arranging and cookery lessons are offered, and there's a huge sitting/recreation room. The chapel can even be used for weddings, provided the reception is held here too.

rooms	10 + 1: 5 doubles, 3 triples, 2 family rooms. 1 apartment for 6.
price	€72. Half-board €53 p.p. Apartment €115.
meals	Dinner, €20–€28, on request.
closed	November–Easter.
directions	From Sestri Levante for Casarza. Approx. 1km beyond Casarza, left to Massasco & Campegli. Monte Pù on left just before Campegli, up 4km of private mountain road.

Signora Aurora Giani

tel	+39 0185 408027
fax	+39 0185 408027
e-mail	montepu@libero.it
web	www.montepu.it

If you crave culture in this remote spot, the Pinacoteca Rizzi in Sestri Levante has a good collection of treasures with some Tiepolo, Raphael, Rubens, El Greco.

Hotel & Self-catering

map 7   entry 88

Agriturismo Giandriale

Loc. Giandriale 5, 19010 Tavarone di Maissana

Once city dwellers in Milan, Giani and Lucia have made the restoration of what was a very run-down property their life's work. The surroundings are heavenly: high pastures dotted with trees, dense woods beyond, long alpine views. The Val di Vara is a completely protected environmental zone, where hunting is forbidden and only organic farming is allowed. Lucia and Nereo are happy for you to do absolutely nothing, but you may join in with farm activities if you wish, and Nereo can help you identify flowers, trees and wildlife. Simple bedrooms (no hanging space) are in the house and outbuildings: thick stone walls, wooden furniture, colourful rugs, cane and bamboo. Old farm furniture, much of it chestnut, stands alongside the modern. Your hosts have young children and will be happy to meet yours – there's so much space to run around in. Breakfasts are sociable affairs, held round the big table: a feast of home-grown, organic produce. Beware the rough and narrow track, and good luck to you if your car is low-slung! But tranquillity is your reward: no wonder the locals love it, too.

rooms	6 + 2: 3 doubles, 3 triples. 1 apartment for 4, 1 for 5.
price	€ 30 p.p. Half-board € 45 p.p. Apartment € 37 p.p. with breakfast.
meals	Dinner € 15, book ahead.
closed	Rarely.
directions	From Sestri Levante N523 for Varese Ligure. On for 14km through tunnel & immediately right before 'Torza' for Tavarone then Giandriale. Rough, steep track to top.

Varese Ligure produces a special kind of grappa. And Varese's Augustinian nuns have traditionally made an income from 'scivette' – marzipan flowers.

Giani & Lucia Nereo

tel	+39 0187 840279
fax	+39 0187 840156
e-mail	info@giandriale.it
web	www.giandriale.it

B&B & Self-catering

entry 89   map 7

Osteria Comedi

Numero 0, Via Veriuntidi, 101010 Palestra

Bravo! A decent, primitive little *osteria* in an area that has smartened up a lot recently – too much for the owners of this place. Their commitment to their garden is in no doubt, though their slavish adherence to the 'no tillage' theories of the Japanese gardener-farmer Fukuoka has yet to be rewarded. Note the permanently open door – a charming gesture in this inhospitable age. The original wall colour has been kept, with a noble refusal to subscribe to the ochre-and-terracotta-on-everything design theories so prevalent elsewhere in Italy. They keep, too, their transport system "out the back", ready for use by any visitor caught short. Note, too, the splendidly generous wicker chair kept for special occasions, and the old white bicycle left over from the anarchist days when bikes were freely available to all. (The white plastic chair has, of course, been discarded as being in bad taste.)

rooms	Several, though difficult to tell where one ends and the next begins.
price	A mere Euro or two.
meals	Outside facilities (bits of furniture that survived the fire) supplied for DIY, *al fresco* flame-grilling.
closed	Not even if they really wanted to be.
directions	Arriving at Palestra, do some simple aerobics and at point of sheer exhaustion, tumble onto road and stagger until feet smarting. Osteria will loom on left.

	Padre Pilof Junk
tel	0987654321
e-mail	osteria@someone-please-rebuild.it
web	www.whyis.it/still_standing/?

This was once a real gem of hospitalità, frequently frequented by the likes of Federico Fellini while researching his unfinished follow-up to La Dolce Vita, La Vita Puzza.

Agriturismo Ca' du Chittu

Via Camporione 25, 19012 Carro

A white house stands out against the rounded shoulder of a wooded hill. Beehives colonise one slope, and all around are orchards, vegetable plots and vines. It's rural, genuine, satisfying. The farm belongs to Ennio and Donatella, who work immensely hard and are proud of their 'five-daisy' award for organic produce, much of which can be sampled in Donatella's cooking. Wonderful smells emanate from the kitchen as you pass; meals are at long tables in the plain, uncluttered dining room. There's a lived-in, comfortable sitting room, too, full of games and books. You have plenty to do: explore the surrounding hills on horseback or mountain bike, or spend the day on a cookery or painting course. Then retreat to your simple, immaculate, white-walled bedroom with old country furniture and wooden bedstead. The rooms on the first floor open onto a terracotta-tiled terrace with lovely views. All the bedrooms are named after someone who has worked for Ennio and Donatella over the last 20 years – Livia, Francesca, Orietta… It's a nice touch and typical of this couple's warmth and generosity.

rooms	7 doubles.
price	€ 58. Half-board € 44 p.p.
meals	Dinner € 20.
closed	Rarely.
directions	On outskirts of Carro for Velva; left for Pavareto. Continue, 1st house on left.

'Tom meets us at Genoa – scolds us because 4 hours behind time…We post to Pisa via Sestra, Spezza, Petro Santo – row with the driver when we start.' Rose Trollope, *writing to her husband Anthony, 1853*

B&B

Donatella & Ennio Nardi
tel +39 0187 861205 (& fax)
mobile +39 335 8037376
e-mail caduchittu@virgilio.it
web www.mangiareinliguria.it/caduchittu

Hotel Stella Maris
Via Marconi 4, 19015 Levanto

A grand villa of 1870, oozing character and largesse. The frescoed ceiling in the entrance is a dream, a mere hint of what is to come. Bedrooms have frescoed or stuccoed ceilings, some of which depict the activities carried out in each when the place was a private villa. Every room is tall and splendid; antiques and chandeliers are de rigeur, décor is wine-red and cream. White bathrooms are perfectly proportioned and planned, with delicious linen; rooms in the annexe navy and modern. Renza is adorable; she has an eye for comfort and has thought of everything, even a washing-machine for long-stay guests. She genuinely loves looking after people (she wants you to feel part of one happy family) and does the cooking herself, including occasional dinners served *al fresco* with music. The restaurant is classically elegant and, though tables are separate, Renza is happiest when guests link up. Breakfast is a generous buffet. Ask for a room at the back if you mind being on an animated street... but the town is lovely, full of activity and character. *Minimum stay two nights.*

rooms	8: 3 doubles, 1 twin, 3 family, 1 single.
price	Half-board only. Double €210–€220; Triple €315–€330; Single €115–€120.
meals	Half-board only.
closed	November.
directions	Via Marconi lane off Via Jacopo da Levanto. Hotel above Banco Chiavari bank. Entrance around corner, use 1st-floor doorbell.

Signora Renza Pagnini

tel	+39 0187 808258
fax	+39 0187 807351
e-mail	renza@hotelstellamaris.it
web	www.hotelstellamaris.it

Up the coast at Sestri Levante, Marconi conducted his first experiments with short-wave radio, sending radio waves out to warships off La Spezia.

Hotel

map 7   entry 92

Agriturismo Villanova

Loc. Villanova, 19015 Levanto

Villanova is where Barone Giancarlo Massola's ancestors spent their summers in the 18th century; it has barely changed since. The villa is a mile from Levanto, yet modern life is left far behind, once you've reached the top of the hills. The red and cream villa stands in a small, sunny clearing. Giancarlo is quiet and much-travelled and has a bouncy golden retriever by his side. Guest bedrooms are in both the main house and in a small stone farmhouse behind; they have an elegant, country-house feel, and are large, airy and terracotta-tiled. Furniture is of wood and wrought iron, beautiful fabrics yellow and blue. All have private entrances and terraces with pretty views. Two of the self catering apartments are separate, the third is in the farmhouse. Giancarlo grows organic apricots, figs and vegetables and makes his own wine and olive oil, and breakfasts are delicious. This is a great place to bring children: swings and table tennis in the garden, masses of space to run around in, the coast nearby. There's internet access, too. *Minimum stay two days; one week August.*

Levanto is a charming and ancient town. The parish church (S. Andrea) has a fine Pisan-Gothic façade. And look also at the 13th-century Casa Restani.

rooms	8 + 3: 3 doubles, 3 triples, 2 suites for 3. 3 apartments for 3-6.
price	€ 100–€ 130. Triples € 120–€ 170. Suites € 140–€ 180. Apartments € 600–€ 800 for 4 per week.
meals	Restaurants 2km. Self-catering in apartments.
closed	November-February.
directions	Exit A12 at Carrodano Levanto towards Levanto. Signs from junction before town (direction Monterosso & Cinque Terre).

Barone Giancarlo Massola

tel	+39 0187 802517
fax	+39 0187 803519
e-mail	massola@iol.it
web	www.agrivillanova.com

B&B & Self-catering

Ca' dei Duxi

Via C. Colombo 36, 19017 Riomaggiore

The moment you step in, you will be greeted by a beaming Giorgio – a larger-than-life character who loves to talk. This once dilapidated, 18th-century house stands in the quiet main street of one of the lovely Cinque Terre villages, and has been fully modernised. Biggish rooms are ordinary but comfortable, and have air-conditioning; the best have ancient ceiling beams like ships' masts, and odd quirks have been kept: one bathroom is built into the rock, visible through a perspex screen. The sea views get better the higher up you are – there are a *lot* of stairs – and those at the top have balconies. Giorgio is active on the local council and really cares about tourists getting the best possible impression of Italy. You can enjoy regular tastings of local produce here, but lovely Riomaggiore is the place to eat (though its hills are as steep as Ca' dei Duxi's stairs!). Another steep road takes you down to the little harbour, where you can go diving or hire a boat and explore. And don't miss the market in La Spezia – a 10-minute journey by train. *Private parking €10 a day: book in advance.*

rooms	6 + 3: 3 doubles, 3 family. 3 apartments: 1 for 2-4, 1 for 4, 1 for 6.
price	€70–€120. Family €90-140. Apartments €350–€800 per week.
meals	Self-catering in apartments. Restaurants in walking distance.
closed	Rarely.
directions	From La Spezia for Postovenere, then to Riomaggiore. There, main road to car park; park down main street. Hotel on right.

Giorgio & Samuele Germano

tel	+39 018 7920036
fax	+39 018 7920036
e-mail	info@duxi.it
web	www.duxi.it

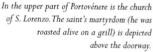

In the upper part of Portovénere is the church of S. Lorenzo. The saint's martyrdom (he was roasted alive on a grill) is depicted above the doorway.

B&B & Self-catering & Hotel

map 7   entry 94

Cascina dei Peri

Via Montefrancio 71, 19030 Castelnuovo Magra

The road rises through beautiful scenery to 100m above the sea. Ring at the gate and wait a moment to be admitted: a charming garden welcomes you, wrapped around a farmhouse that looks like a country villa. In spite of appearances this is indeed a working farm with fields, vineyards, olive groves and hens, and Signor Marcoli will be delighted to show you around (commentary in Italian only). Indoors the accent is on cool efficiency, echoed in the rather functional décor. In low season two of the rooms can be joined to form an apartment, perfect for families; babysitting is available too. Rooms are a decent size and almost all have a sea view from their terraces. A big plus is that Maria Angiola is happy to combine B&B and half-board, so you can be flexible with meals. The Cascina is a splendid setting in every way, and there are masses of delightful walks that you can plan from perusing the maps on the dining room walls. The beach and the promontory of Montemarcello are a short and pleasant drive. *Minimum stay three nights.*

rooms	7: 3 doubles, 4 family; or can be 2 apartments for 4.
price	€ 35–€ 49. Half-board: € 50–€ 65 p.p.
meals	Half-board only.
closed	Rarely.
directions	Exit A12 at Sarzana; SS1 for Pisa, 5km. Left for Castelnuovo Magra. Before road begins to climb; left into Via Montefrancio. Agriturismo signed after 1km.

Shelley spent some months at Lerici before setting off to meet Leigh Hunt at Livorno. His boat, 'Ariel', went down and Shelley drowned.

Signora Maria Angiola Marcoli

tel	+39 0187 674085
fax	+39 0187 674085
e-mail	box@cascinadeiperi.com
web	www.cascinadeiperi.com

B&B & Self-catering

La Carnea
Via San Rocco 10, Carnea, 19020 Follo

Laura and Beppe have been here one year, happy in their new-found haven: an old stone farmhouse deep in the wooded hills overlooking the Ligurian coast. Young, relaxed, full of smiles, they have taken on B&B for the love of it, glad for you to share the good life. On the terraces are vines and olives; vegetables and fruit are organically grown. The bedrooms, in converted outhouses, are simple and small and the bathrooms (some shared) are rudimentary, but you have your own entrance and an incomparable view. Donata cooks, Beppe plays guitar; join in a sing-song after supper. Delicious meals with a vegetarian slant are served in an IKEA-look dining room with views to the sea; breakfasts last until 11am. La Carnea is a wonderful way to enjoy life's simple pleasures and if you do so to excess you can walk it off by taking the coastal route between the cliff towns along the Cinque Terre, or trek in the nearby woods. There are no signs indicating La Carnea so have faith in the directions; there is a hint along the route – *Siete quasi arrivati!* – to reassure you. *Not suitable for children. Minimum stay 2-7 nights.*

rooms	6: 2 doubles; 4 doubles with separate bath.
price	€62–€70. Half-board €50 p.p.
meals	Half-board available.
closed	Rarely.
directions	From Genova A12 exit La Spezia, Vezzano Ligure for Bottagna & Follo. Over bridge & immed. left; right for Carnea. At foot of village sharp left Via S. Rocco. At chapel right on dirt road, 1.5km.

South of Lerici, the comparatively untouched coastal villages of Fiascherino and Tellaro can be reached on foot. Start at the Via DH Lawrence.

	Laura & Beppe Castiglioni
tel	+39 0187 947070
fax	+39 0187 947070
e-mail	agriturismocarnea@hotmail.com

B&B

map 7   entry 96

www.thirdangle.com

tuscany

Villa Mimosa

Corlaga Bagnone, 54021 Bagnone

These are the Apennines, steep chestnut-covered hills that rise to 6,000 feet, topped with snow in winter. Bagnone is a surprise to anyone for whom Tuscany is synonymous with Chianti: a medieval village of huge charm, it has a wilder countryside than its southern counterpart. The Villa Mimosa is a warm and open-hearted retreat run by people for whom hospitality is second nature. Their revamping of the old flour mill has produced a gaily individual house, full of colour and light as well as comfort. You have a bright sitting room with a small grand piano, views over the richly wooded hills, a little reading room stuffed with good books, bedrooms that are wickedly comfortable, food from the Aga worth climbing the hills for (Aga cooking courses, too). English Jennie and Alan are well-rooted in Bagnone and will be hugely helpful. Safe, sandy beaches are a half-hour drive, you are near Lerici with its castle and lovely bay, Parma, Lucca and Pisa are an hour away, Florence 90 minutes. Or just stay put and enjoy the villa and the hills in this fascinating area, dotted with ancient villages.

rooms	4 doubles/twins.
price	€80–€110.
meals	Dinner with wine, €35; book ahead.
closed	November–mid-February.
directions	Exit A15 at Aulla/Pontremoli. SS62 for Bagnone. Through archway, left into V. Niccolo Quatiere (signed Carabinieri). Left at 1st fork. At r'bout to Corlaga. Park opp. church; walk back 50m to 2nd house on left.

The Apuan Alps have for 2,000 years been the marble capital of Italy. It's said that Michelangelo spent seven years at Pietrasanta choosing one marble block.

	Jennie & Alan Pratt
tel	+39 0187 427022
fax	+39 0187 427022
e-mail	mimosa@col.it

B&B

Fosdinovo Bed & Breakfast

Via Montecarboli 12, 54035 Fosdinovo

You really are on top of the hill here and the views are wonderful. From the terrace you look down over Castle Fosdinovo (one of over 100 castles in the area, flood-lit at night) to the Bocca di Magra estuary and Monte Marcello. On a clear day you can see Elba and Corsica – but don't count on it! The house was built in the early 1960s and is open plan. Slate steps lead up to a pleasant sitting area, with a teak-decking floor (from an old boat), a rough-cut stone fireplace and big leather sofas. Masses of videos and books provide entertainment should you get snowed in. The bedrooms are white-walled, comfortable and practical; new beds have lovely embroidered linen sheets which belonged to Lidia's mother. Lidia and Andreas have only recently taken the place over and are friendly, enthusiastic and speak excellent English. You're given your own key and can come and go as you please. There's an excellent restaurant a five minute-drive away but you're welcome to bring your own drinks and snacks to eat on the terrace in the evening; you're also encouraged to help yourself to fruit from the little orchard in front of the house.

rooms	2: 1 double, 1 twin.
price	€ 70.
meals	Good restaurant 5 minutes by car.
closed	November.
directions	From A12 exit Sarzana; SS1 for 3km for Carrara-Massa; left SS446 for Fosdinovo. Pass village & castle. Right at x-roads for Carrara. After 150m, left on V. Montecarboli. After 400m track right. On left.

Luni — the largest Roman ruin in Northern Italy — was a town founded near the mouth of the river Magra in 177BC. It gives its name to modern Lunigiana.

	Lidia & Andrea Fabbretti
tel	+39 0187 684 65
fax	+39 0187 684 65
e-mail	fabb.al@tin.it
web	www.fosdinovo-bb.it

B&B

map 8   entry 98

La Cerreta

Castelnuovo di Garfagnana

Be different and head for the hills of northern Tuscany and the Garfagnana. The chestnut-covered slopes are resplendent in autumn when the smell of woodsmoke hangs in the air, lush in spring and summer, and perfect in winter – after a snowfall – for a day's skiing or sledging at Abetone. You dip down through the vines to La Cerreta, standing sentinel over the valley. Many views are described as breathtaking and here's another – across to the ancient walled town of Castiglione, encircled by snowy peaks. Inside: whitewashed walls, old beams, open fireplaces (there's stacks of wood from your own trees) and central heating to keep you snug in winter. The local restaurant is within walking distance, the shop not much further. Take a lazy lunch on the terrace, skinny-dip in the pool: there's no-one to see you! If it's too relaxing you could always pop down the road to the six-hole golf course with its dinky clubhouse, or pack a picnic and follow one of the many trails along the valley. Jazz and opera fans can head for arty Barga – an irresistibly cobbled, medieval-walled hilltop town – where there always seems to be a festival in the offing.

Seventy per cent of all Italy's species of wildflowers can be found in the Serchio Valley.

rooms	Sleeps 6 + 2: 2 doubles, 1 twin, sofabed & cot.
price	€ 500–€ 1,200.
meals	Restaurants 2-3km.
closed	Rarely.
directions	From Lucca SS12 for Abetone; at Castelnuovo for Modena; left to Pontecosi; sharp right signed to Golf Club after Shell garage. 1km after club, right opp. white house down lane to house.

Sarah Bolton

tel	+44 (0)117 9260867
fax	+44 (0)117 9260867
e-mail	sarah@lacerreta.co.uk
web	www.lacerreta.co.uk

Self-catering

Peralta

Pieve di Camaiore, 55043 Camaiore

Peralta is precariously perched on the foothills of Mount Prana. Sculptress Fiore de Henriquez took it on 30 years ago, a labyrinth of ancient dwellings connected by steep steps and sun-dappled terraces. Lemon trees, jasmine and bougainvillea romp on every corner, a sculpture peeps from every cranny, the chestnut-groved valley swoops to the sea. The whole place hums with creativity. Apartments and rooms are properly rustic and full of charm, some light, some less so; all have vibrant walls, breathtaking views, perhaps an old red sofa, a simple bed covered in a striped cover, a rag rug on a terracotta floor. Four of the apartments have dishwashers, a concession to modernity; shower rooms are new. Dinah and her helpers draw you together like one big family: there's a panoramic terrace where guests gather to swap stories, a light-filled studio for courses (art, writing, Tuscan cookery), a log-fuelled sitting room, a dining table for 14, a small pool. It is an adventure to get here – the approach road will thrill – and an adventure to stay. *You may leave car at bottom of track and they will collect you. Children over 10 welcome.*

rooms	6 + 6: 4 doubles, 1 twin, 1 family. 6 apts for: 2, 4, 5, 7 or 8.
price	€ 60–€ 110. Self-catering apartments € 200–€ 2,120 per week.
meals	Breakfast € 6 for self-catering. Dinner with wine € 25.
closed	December-28 February. (S/c never.)
directions	From A12 Livorno/Genoa, exit Camaiore. Left after Camaiore for Pieve, uphill, signs for Peralta. Left at fork for Peralta, pass blue sign & onto Agliano. Signed.

Peralta lies near to the marble quarries of Carrara. Carrara marble has been used by some of the most famous sculptors in the world, including Michaelangelo.

Kate Simova & Dinah Voisin

tel	+39 0584 951230
fax	+39 0584 951230
e-mail	peraltusc@aol.com
web	www.peraltatuscany.com

Self-catering & B&B

map 8   entry 100

Villa Alessandra

Via Arsina 1100b, 55100 Lucca

They ask that you stay for at least three nights, so do – it is worth every penny. You will be a privileged guest in a beautiful country house close to one of Italy's most perfect towns. Despite an initial touch of formality you will soon find that you can treat the place as home; come and go as you please, take your own picnic into one of the gardens, cool off in the pool. The road to the house is a country lane; you are in the sweetest, gentlest countryside and within distant sight of medieval Lucca. The house is full of interest and there are fascinating *objets* and old furniture in the two sitting rooms, good and homely with their big, floral sofas, CD player and books. All but one of the bedrooms has a view, and all are attractive, with white walls and open stonework, wicker armchairs, generous drapes, splendid bathrooms. One has a four-poster. There are three bikes for you to borrow, walks into the hills, Lucca to explore and the immaculate seaside resort of Forte dei Marmi to discover. Breakfasts are quite a spread. *Minimum stay three nights.*

'It will be quite worthwhile…to come to Lucca next year to see the cyclamens.' John Ruskin in a letter to Mrs La Touche, 1882.

rooms	6: 5 doubles, 1 twin.
price	€125-€155. Villa as a whole €8,000 per week.
meals	Breakfast included - it's quite something!
closed	Christmas.
directions	From Lucca north on Camaiore road; cross River Serchio right to Monte S.Quirico; 1,5km right; left to Arsina (Via Billona) until Via Arsina on right; after 1.1km drive on right; gate 60m.

Signora Enrica Tosca

tel	+39 0583 395171
fax	+39 0583 395828
e-mail	villa.ale@mailcity.com
web	www.villa-alessandra.it

Self-catering & B&B

Albergo San Martino

Via della Dogana 9, 55100 Lucca

There's a fresh-faced enthusiasm about the San Martino. Opened three years ago, it still shines and there's none of the tired cynicism that has overtaken so many central hotels in tourist towns. It is a pretty little three-storey building, painted yellow, and only a brief stroll from the mighty Cathedral. There are no architectural flourishes, no rushes to the head – this is just a simple, comfortable little three-star in one of Italy's loveliest towns. The tiny lobby has a small sofa and armchair of soft blue leather, and original paintings above a Tuscan-style tiled marble floor. The staircase and landings are brightly lit, the bedrooms have impeccably comfortable beds and furniture a touch more personal than that of a chain hotel; bathrooms are spot on. It is satisfying to throw open the shutters and gaze down on a quiet Tuscan street – you feel very much part of Lucca yet you are on a quiet corner. There are some jolly pink and orange bikes to hire for jaunts around town – a fun touch. Excellent value for such a central spot. *Minimum two nights in high season.*

rooms	8: 6 doubles, 2 suites for 3-4.
price	€ 104. Suites € 155 for 3.
meals	Full breakfast extra; restaurants nearby.
closed	Rarely.
directions	In the Old Town next to the Cathedral.

	Signor Andrea Martinelli
tel	+39 0583 469181
fax	+39 0583 991940
e-mail	albergosanmartino@albergosanmartino.it
web	www.albergosanmartino.it

At Puccini's birthplace, Corte San Lorenzo 8, Via di Poggio, you can see the piano he used while composing his final opera, 'Turandot'.

Hotel

map 8   entry 102

Fattoria di Pietrabuona

Via per Medicina 2, Pietrabuona, 51010 Péscia

Hide yourself away in the foothills of the Svizzera Pescintina – Tuscany's own Little Switzerland. Home to a beguiling brood of ancient breed Cinta Senese pigs, this huge estate with 13 separate apartments is presided over by the elegant Signora – a most unlikely-looking pig farmer! The various farmhouses and buildings have been cleverly divided into units which fit together like a jigsaw; we liked the oldest best, particularly those with outside seating and views. The exteriors retain the original character of the various *podere*; the interiors are simple, some of the newer ones have steep stairs, and all are blissfully free of TVs and phones. Do pack your Tuscan cookbook: the kitchens, some with old sinks but all with new cookers, fridges, pots and pans, ask to be used. There's a small shop next to the office that sells estate produce. Some of the roads, though well-maintained, are precipitous in parts – not for the faint-hearted, nor those worried about heavily-laden hire cars – but the views are fabulous, particularly from the swimming pool, and the villages are worth a good wander. *Minimum stay one week.*

This ancient breed of pig is depicted in Ambroglio Lorenzetti's Good and Bad Government. *Doting owners list among their virtues a ' temperamento vivace'.*

Self-catering

rooms	13: 5 apartments for 2, 1 for 3, 5 for 4, 2 for 6.
price	€ 400–€ 1,000 per week.
meals	Restaurants & pizzerias nearby.
closed	November-February, but open Christmas.
directions	Exit A11 at Chiesina Uzzanese towards Péscia & then Abetone & Pietrabuona. After Pietrabuona towards Medicina. After 500m road becomes a long avenue of cypresses Villa & Fattoria at end.

Signora Maristella Galeotti Flori

tel	+39 0572 408115
fax	+39 0572 408150
e-mail	info@pietrabuona.com
web	www.pietrabuona.com

Poderino Lero

Via in Campo 42, 51010 Massa e Cozzile

An old farmhouse up in the hills with beautiful views over olive groves and Montecatini – a perfect place to unwind. There's a homely atmosphere here, with family, cats, dogs and Luisa, who loves having people to stay. Built against a hill in the late 19th century, a lemon tree over the door, the house is cool in summer and warm in winter. The attic room is a haven for meditation and yoga; no courses are being run at present, but you may use the room whenever you wish. Big bedrooms have stone floors, white walls and are furnished with country antiques, many of which Luisa has restored herself. There's good, homemade produce for breakfast, while dinner, up in the hills, is an adventurous, 10-minute drive. Downstairs is a large room with an open fire and sofas, one bright pink, which opens to the large garden. Relax on sunloungers and drink in the views; you are surrounded by tumbling olive groves and vines. Chimes and mosaics in the garden, pot-pourri in the house, Luisa's serene sculptures dotted around: a deeply relaxing place.

rooms	3 doubles.
price	€65. Singles €42.
meals	Choice of restaurants nearby, 2km.
closed	Rarely.
directions	From Montecatini towards Lucca; right for Massa e Cozzile. Pass Massa to end of Cozzile. Left for Confine di Cozzile, right opposite shrine; follow yellow signs.

Signora Maria Luisa Nesti

tel	+39 0572 60218
fax	+39 0572 60218
e-mail	poderinolero@yahoo.it

Montecatini Terme is the most fashionable thermal spa in Italy. There is a funicular railway up to Monte Alto; and a gourmet restaurant in the Via Amendola.

B&B

map 8   entry 104

Antica Casa "Le Rondini"

Via M Pierucci 21, Colle di Buggiano

Imagine a room above an archway in an ancient hilltop village, within ancient castle walls. You lean from the window and watch the swallows dart to and fro – and there are *rondini* inside the room, too, captured in an enchanting 200-year-old fresco. The way through the arch – the Via del Vento (where the wind blows) – and the front door to this captivating house wait just the other side. Step into a lovely room, a study in white – fresh lilies, pure-white walls and sofas – dotted with family antiques and paintings. Fulvia and Carlo are warm, interesting hosts who immediately make you feel at home. The delightfully different bedrooms have wrought-iron bedheads, big mirrors and some original stencilling. Several, like the Swallow Room, have pale frescoes; all have good views. The little apartment, too, is simple, charming, peaceful. Just across the cobbled street is a pretty garden with lemon trees and plenty of shade – an idyllic place for breakfast on sunny mornings. A short walk brings you to the square where elderly village ladies sit playing cards, children scamper and the church bell rings every hour, on the hour.

rooms	5 + 1: 5 doubles.
	1 apartment for 2-4.
price	€75-€110. Apartment €65 for 2.
meals	Restaurant 200m.
closed	November-February.
directions	A11 Firenze-Pisa Nord. Exit Montecatini Terme. Follow signs to Pescia. Left after 4th set of traffic lights. Right after petrol station. Follow sign "Malocchio Colle Buggiano". Up hill to parking area on right.

Giuseppe Verdi spent much time in the nearby spa town of Montecatini Terme and composed some of his operas there.

	Fulvia Musso
tel	+39 0572 33313
fax	+39 0572 905361
e-mail	info@anticacasa.it
web	www.anticacasa.it

B&B & Self-catering

Villa Anna Maria

Strada Statale dell'Abetone 146, 56010 Molina di Quosa

The wrought-iron gates swing open to reveal a tropical paradise. You feel protected here from the outside world, and miles from the heat and bustle of Pisa. It is an intriguing place, laid-back and easy – even bizarre; some bedrooms have been virtually untouched since the 17th century. They are all different, themed and with high ceilings, the most curious being the Persian and the Egyptian. The entrance hall is splendidly marble, graced with columns and chandelier; the library – a touch over the top, maybe – is very much in tune with the ornate house and its entertaining owner. Claudio collects anything and everything and rooms are crammed with antiques and silverware. He is hugely hospitable and kind – your hosts really do care more about people than they do about money – and there are no rules: treat this as your home. There's a game room with billiards and videos (3,000 of them!), table-tennis for the children, woodland paths, a pool with piped music among the bamboo, and a lovely barbecue area for those who've chosen to self-cater. *Minimum stay two nights.*

rooms	6 + 1: 6 doubles/triples (or can be 2 apartments for 2-8). 1 cottage for 3.
price	€120–€150. Singles €90. Apartments €800–€2,000 per week. Ask for price of cottage.
meals	Dinner €40, on request.
closed	Rarely.
directions	From Pisa SS12 for Lucca. At S.Giuliano Terme, SS12 left down hill; after Rigoli to Molina di Quosa. Villa on right opposite pharmacy.

	Signor Claudio Zeppi
tel	+39 050 850139
fax	+39 050 850139
e-mail	zeppi@villaannamaria.com
web	www.villaannamaria.com

The ecclesiastical centre of nearby Pisa, known as the 'Campo dei Miracoli', is still as stunning a sight as it was for medieval travellers.

B&B & Self-catering

map 8   entry 106

Fattoria Varramista

Via Ricavo Varramista, 56020 Montopoli Val d'Arno

Once this area was regularly fought over by the Pisans and the Florentines; now it's blissfully peaceful. The castles have fallen into disrepair; woods, olive groves and vineyards blend serenely into green, rolling hills. The great Varramista estate, too, has beaten its swords into plough shares and settled quietly down to produce fine wines. Its owners have converted two traditional farmsteads, La Lecceta and Il Monsonaccio, into a number of apartments, each on a separate floor. A long, tree-lined avenue brings you from the main road to reception, a wonderful building with big vaulted ceilings and a table piled with interesting books about wine. You'll be met by one of the team, they are all friendly and helpful. The apartments are sparklingly new, a smart mix of old beams and every mod con to keep you in touch with the outside world. They are decorated in soft Tuscan colours and superbly equipped; each farmstead has its own swimming pool and La Frasca a private gym in a converted barn. There are attractive grounds and lovely views in every direction. *Minimum stay two nights.*

rooms	9 apartments + 1 villa: 1 for 4, 1 for 5, 3 for 6, 3 for 8. Villa for 16.
price	€ 750–€ 7,000 per week.
meals	Self-catering.
closed	Rarely.
directions	From Superstrada FI-PI-LI exit Montopoli Val d'Arno; follow road to r'bout. Sign on left for Varramista, right to house.

According to tradition, the Varramista property was given to Gino di Neri Capponi (1350-1421) by the Republic of Florence as a reward for his military victory against Pisa in 1406.

	Matilde Palma
tel	+39 0571 447244
fax	+39 0571 447216
e-mail	info@varramista.it
web	www.varramista.it

Self-catering

Venzano

Mazzolla, 56048 Volterra

A little secret garden, far from the madding crowd. This enchanting place was granted to the Augustinian order in the 10th century and remained in their tender hands for over 900 years. Venzano is now privately owned, and although the main thrust is still agricultural, gardening is the focus. For 14 years Donald and friends have been creating a green enclave in a series of terraces moving outwards from a Roman spring. Their inspiration has been the legacy of the monks' love of plants, for their beauty and their usefulness... you may help yourself to the results. There is, of course, a long tradition of Italian garden design, tempered here by a sense of humility when contemplating the beauty of the surroundings. Parts of the rambling building have been converted into big, lofty apartments; all have terraces, some with views of the rolling hills. Facilities are simple – bathrooms functional, a washing machine to share, firewood and heating provided in cold weather – but the décor of the living spaces is as attractive as it is sparse. Come for the perfectly simple life in a less-known corner of Tuscany. *Minimum stay one week.*

rooms	3 apartments: 2 for 2-3, 1 for 4.
price	€630–€980 per week.
meals	Self-catering. Trattoria 2km.
closed	November-March.
directions	From Volterra SS68 for Colle Val d'Elsa for 10km. Right for Mazzolla. After 3km right for Venzano.

	Donald Leevers
tel	+39 0588 39095
fax	+39 0588 39095
e-mail	venzano@sirt.pisa.it
web	www.venzanogardens.com

The Museo Guarnacci in Volterra contains the best collection of Etruscan artefacts in the country, including over 600 cinerary urns.

Self-catering

map 8   entry 108

Azienda Agricola Il Palazzaccio

Via Rezzano 9, 50031 Galliano di Mugello

Olives and honey. Asparagus, too. This is real *agriturismo*, just 20 minutes from the motorway – a working farm on a hilltop near the little town of Galliano. A long track brings you to a big, white-painted farmhouse, surrounded by trees and looking over Lake Bilancino. Mara and Maurizio are hospitable and hardworking hosts; they love Il Palazzaccio and are keen to share it. Though they don't speak much English, their son Samuele can be called in to interpret. The house, which dates back to the 13th century, still has many original features. It once belonged to the Ubaldini family and Dante is said to have stayed here. The apartments – not lavish but excellent value – are to one side. The décor is simple, rustic and traditional. Oil paintings add a splash of colour to white walls; terracotta floors, beams and fireplaces give a casual, homely look and fresh flowers make you feel very welcome. Outside, the courtyard full of lemon trees is a delightful place to sit with coffee or a glass of wine. It all feels deliciously rural and peaceful though Florence is only half an hour's drive away.

rooms	5 apartments: 2 for 2, 1 for 3, 1 for 4, 1 for 5.
price	€360–€614 per week.
meals	Self-catering.
closed	Never.
directions	From motorway, signs to Scarperia & Borgo San Lorenzo. Left for Galliano until Shell garage on right; left track at junction with sign for Strada Vicinale di Rezzano. Pass olive trees, villa on right.

'It was all clear, overwhelming sunshine, a platform hung in the light. Just below were the confused, tiled roofs of the village...' D. H. Lawrence, *The Spinner and the Monks*

Mara Pasquini
tel	+39 055 8428110
fax	+39 055 8428110
e-mail	ilpalazzaccio@inwind.it
web	www.villailpalazzaccio.com

Self-catering

Locanda Senio

Via Borgo dell'Ore 1, 50035 Palazuolo sul Senio

Food is king here: genuine home cooking from Roberta, and, in the restaurant, much gastronomic enthusiasm from Ercole. Echoing a growing movement to bring lost medieval traditions back to life, they are passionate about wild herbs and lost fruits like wild cherries. The prosciutto from *il porcaro medievale* (ancient breeds of pork) is particularly delicious. Breakfast is a feast of homemade breads, cakes, fruits and jams; dinner a leisurely treat served in the restaurant with nine tables and cosy log fire. The little inn occupies a stunning spot, in a quiet town in the Mugello valley surrounded by rolling hills... there are guided walks through the woods, gastronomic meanders through the valley and cookery courses from time to time. Bedrooms are comfortable and cosy, but it is worth paying extra for the suites if you can; they're in the 17th-century building nearby. And there's a new relaxation centre of which Roberta and Ercole are very proud – the jacuzzi, sauna and Turkish bath have a delicious aroma and a Swedish feel. Steps lead up to an outdoor pool, body and soul will be nurtured. Perfect.

rooms	8: 6 doubles/twins, 2 suites for 2-3.
price	€145-€215. Suites €165-€245. Half-board €95-€150 p.p.
meals	Dinner from €35.
closed	6 January-14 February.
directions	From Bologna A14, exit Imola for Rimini; 50m; for Palazuolo (approx. 40 mins). House in village centre right of fountain & Oratorio dei Santi Carlo e Antonio.

Nearby Sambuca gives its name to a soft, aniseed-scented liqueur.

	Ercole & Roberta Lega
tel	+39 055 8046019
fax	+39 055 8043949
e-mail	info@locandasenio.it
web	www.locandasenio.it

Inn

map 9   entry 110

Villa Torricelli Ciamponi
Via San Clemente 83, 50038 Scarperia

Live as Italians among the Italians. The Mugello – a glorious mix of landscapes and pretty towns straddling the Apennine watershed – is still something of a secret. Jill has lived in Scarperia for over a year without meeting another Brit. Her apartments are in a lovely, recently converted 16th-century palazzo. The smaller, first-floor one looks towards the main square; the larger, on the second floor, faces the hills. Both have little gardens and parking spaces; both are attractively and comfortably furnished, with soft colours and good fabrics. Watercolours and a collection of musical instruments add a charmingly individual touch. Downstairs, the main hall (once the palazzo's grand hall) has a magnificent stone fireplace and a door opening into the historic part of town. Jill is generous and friendly and loves sharing her knowledge of this part of Italy. Her sons used to run a restaurant in England so cooking is in the family; Jill is happy to offer lunch or dinner at her home just up the hill. Public transport in the area is good, so you can dispense with a car if you like, and explore without the headache of parking. *Minimum stay one week.*

rooms	2 apartments: 1 for 2, 1 for 4.
price	€430–€950 per week.
meals	Lunch by the pool or dinner on request €20–€35, with wine.
closed	Rarely.
directions	Exit autostrada at Barberino, signs for Scarperia; at fork follow road for Firenzuola. Villa on left after tennis courts, big gates.

'Lorenzo Il Magnifico… heard the call of the land and here he played, celebrated and rediscovered the joy, beauty and life.'
The Mugello

	Jill Greetham
tel	+39 055 8492091
fax	+39 055 8492091
e-mail	info@atuscanplace.com
web	www.atuscanplace.com

Self-catering

Il Pozzo

Via Casole 48, 50039 Vicchio di Mugello

A white road winds up the hill to a small, creeper-covered stone farmhouse. It is all yours, in green, heavenly countryside; though the track continues, it merely leads to an abandoned house. Il Pozzo (the name means a well and, of course, there is one) is typical of old Tuscan farmhouses: living quarters on the upper floor, animal stalls below. The Stevensons have turned it into a delectable place to stay, without spoiling its essence. Bunches of herbs hang in the big kitchen, which has a sit-in fireplace, a wood-burning brick oven and a plentiful supply of logs. Steps lead down to a little library and sitting room, with a small single bedroom off. All the rooms feel lived-in and comfortable; interesting prints hang on plain walls, there's a good selection of books and an intriguing collection of horse and mule shoes and old agricultural tools... Bath and shower rooms are basic but perfectly adequate. Modern conveniences in the form of washing machine, TV or swimming pool do not exist – but who needs them when there's a lovely terrace, three acres of wonderful, part-wild garden, and vast oak and chestnut woods to explore?

rooms	Sleeps 5: 2 twins, 1 single.
price	€650–€950 per week.
meals	Self-catering.
closed	Rarely.
directions	From Vicchio for Dicomano. Left for Rupecanina & Casole. On for 5km until barrier on right. On right.

Hew & Leslie Stevenson
tel +44 (0)20 7359 2017
e-mail dovebooks@aol.com

'And summer's lease hath all too short a date.'
Shakespeare, Sonnet XVIII

Self-catering

map 9   entry 112

Monsignor della Casa Country Resort

Via di Mucciano 16, 50030 Borgo San Lorenzo

It could be a Giotto landscape: the view of the surrounding countryside and Monte Senario has not changed for 500 years. But the old buildings in the hamlet where estate workers once lived have become a series of attractive apartments. The restoration has been delightfully done, using many materials found on the 200-hectare estate. Run by a charming family, the complex has a warm, inviting feel. Bay hedges and big terracotta pots of herbs scent the courtyards and there are cherry and olive trees everywhere. The apartments are stylish, uncluttered and supremely elegant, with fireplaces, stonework and beams, and each its own piece of garden. Light, airy bedrooms are painted in soft colours; some have four-posters with fine linen drapes, others wrought-iron beds. You can eat in the restaurant where hams hang from the beams: the menu is Tuscan, the wine list extensive. Then burn off the calories in the Wellness Center, splendid with sauna, Turkish bath, jacuzzi and gym. Close by is the Renaissance villa where Monsignor Giovanni Della Casa, a descendant of the Medicis, was born in 1503. *Minimum stay 2-7 nights for B&B.*

Monsignor Giovanni della Casa was famous for writing the 'Galateo' treatise on etiquette, which was used at the court of Queen Elizabeth I.

rooms	26 + 16: 11 doubles, 9 suites, 6 villas. 16 self-catering properties: 9 apartments, 2 villas, 5 suites.
price	€ 160–€ 600. Apts € 700–€ 1,500; villas € 1,550–€ 5,000; suites € 500–€ 1,400. Prices per week.
meals	Dinner, € 25–€ 35.
closed	6 January-15 March.
directions	From motorway exit A1 Barberino di Mugello. Follow signs for Borgo; left on No.302 for Ronta & Mucciano.

Alessio Marzi

tel	+39 055 840821
fax	+39 055 840840
e-mail	booking@monsignore.com
web	www.monsignore.com

B&B & Self-catering

Casa Palmira

Via Faentina 4/1, Loc. Feriolo, 50030 Borgo S. Lorenzo

A medieval farm expertly restored by charming Assunta and Stefano who, being Italian, have a flair for this sort of thing. You are immersed in greenery yet only half an hour from Florentine bustle. The views on the road to Fiesole are so stunning it's hard to keep ones eyes on the road… Stefano will take you round neighbouring villages in his mini-van, or you can hire a mountain bike, tucking one of Assunta's packed picnic baskets on the back. (They run cookery courses here, too.) The log-fired sitting room sets the tone: the *casa* has a warm, Tuscan feel, and bedrooms open off a landing with a brick walled 'garden' in the centre – all Stefano's work. They are a good size and beautifully turned out with a clean, contemporary feel: beds dressed in Florentine fabric, polished wooden floors. You look onto gardens where Assunta grows herbs and vegetables, or onto vines and olive trees. You are 500m above sea level so there's no need for air-conditioning and no mosquitoes! Breakfast on apricots and home-produced yogurt, dine on Tuscan food. There are also many restaurants nearby. *Check-in before 7pm. Minimum stay three nights.*

rooms	7 + 1: 4 twins/doubles, 1 twin, 1 triple, 1 family. 1 apt for 2-3.
price	€65–€85. Triple €105. Family €125. Apartment €500 per week.
meals	Dinner with wine, €25; book ahead. Ristorante Feriolo 700m.
closed	10 January–10 March.
directions	From North A1 exit Barberino del Mugello towards Borgo S. Lorenzo; then SS302 Firenze. After Polcanto, sign on left for Ristorante Feriolo, house on left.

Assunta & Stefano Fiorini-Mattioli

tel	+39 055 8409749
fax	+39 055 8409749
e-mail	info@casapalmira.it
web	www.casapalmira.it

Just outside Fiesole is the hamlet of S. Francesco, whose church contains Fra Angelico's Madonna with Angels and Saints (c. 1430).

B&B & Self-catering

map 8   entry 114

Fonte de' Medici

Via S. Maria a Macerata 31, 50020 Montefiridolfi

A huge and impressive wine estate with breathtaking views on top of a hill, 20 apartments connected by gardens and two pools, a restaurant, a wellness centre and, driving it all, a bevvy of multi-lingual staff and the ever-smiling Gilberto. It's a fabulous set-up, and the renovated apartments, in three clusters of farmhouses set fairly far apart, have all you might expect for the price. Most have a dishwasher, microwave and phone, others air conditioning and internet access too. Furniture and fittings are spanking new, bedrooms have wooden rafters, tiled floors, matching valances and drapes and huge beds, there are private terraces and gardens and splendid valley views. The feel is not rustic but pristine, and if the beautifully equipped kitchens do not appeal, you can always hire a private chef. Or eat in the restaurant on site, or at another Antinori eaterie down the road. Five gardeners dance attendance upon formal gardens fragrant with roses and jasmine, there's a big meeting room for events, wine-tastings for the asking and simply masses of space. *Laundry facilities available.*

The name goes back to 1400 when travellers between Florence and Siena would rest and drink from the spring that still passes through the village of Santa Maria a Macerata.

rooms	8 + 20: 8 doubles. 20 apartments for 2-6.
price	€ 100-€180. Apartments €120-€390.
meals	À la carte restaurant, closed Thursdays.
closed	Rarely.
directions	Superstrada Firenze-Siena exit 'Tavarnelle V P' for Sambuca, continue onto Fabbrica, Montefiridolfi & Antinori Estates, signed.

Signor Gilberto Nori
tel	+39 055 8244700
fax	+39 055 8244701
e-mail	mail@fontedemedici.com
web	www.fontedemedici.com

Self-catering & Hotel

Palazzo Niccolini al Duomo

Via dei Servi 2, 50122 Florence

One minute you're battling with tourists in the Piazza del Duomo, the next you're standing inside this extraordinarily lovely palazzo. The *residenza* is on the second floor (there's a lift); two small trees, a brace of antique chairs and a brass plaque announce that you've arrived at reception – a stylish introduction to a gorgeous place. Ever since it was first built by the Naldini family in the 16th century, on the site of the sculptor Donatello's workshop, the buildings's grandeur has been steadily added to. And the recent restoration hasn't detracted from its beauty, merely added some superb facilities. It's all you hope staying in such a place will be – fabulously elegant and luxurious, with 18th-century frescoes, *trompe-l'oeil* effects, fine antiques and magnificent beds... but in no way awesome, thanks to many personal touches. Relax in the lovely drawing room and look at family portraits, books and photos. Two signed photos are from the King of Italy, sent in 1895 to Contessa Cristina Niccolini, the last of the Naldini. She married into the current owner's family, bringing the palazzo as part of her dowry.

rooms	7: 2 doubles, 2 twins/doubles, 3 suites.
price	€250–€280. Singles €150–€200. Suites €300–€500.
meals	Plenty of restaurants nearby.
closed	Rarely.
directions	Exit Firenze south; head for town centre & Il Duomo. Via dei Servi is off Piazza del Duomo. Park, unload & car will be collected & put in garage €25–€30.

Maura Pedroni

tel	+39 055 282412
fax	+39 055 290979
e-mail	info@niccolinidomepalace.com
web	www.niccolinidomepalace.com

'Donatello's death plunged into mourning the citizens and artists of Florence and all who had known him ... they buried him honourably in San Lorenzo.' Giorgio Vasari, 1550

B&B

map 8   entry 116

Torre di Bellosguardo
Via Roti Michelozzi 2, 50124 Florence

Breathtaking in its beauty and ancient dignity. If luxury is a matter of aesthetics, then this is the purest. The entrance hall is cavernous, beautiful, with a painted ceiling and an ocean of floor; the view reaches through a vast, plaster-crumbling sun room to the garden. Imposing, mellow buildings, glorious gardens, inspirational views of Florence. A water feature meanders along a stone terrace, twisted wisteria shades the walkway to a kitchen garden. An indoor swimming pool and gym occupy the old orangery while another pool settles into a perfect lawn. Most of the bedrooms can be reached by lift but the tower suite, with windows on all sides, demands a long climb. The comfortable bedrooms defy modern convention; they are magnificent in their simplicity, the furniture is richly authentic and there are surprises – such as the glass-walled bathroom looking over the garden. Signor Franchetti is often here, and his manners and his English are impeccable – unlike those of the irrepressible Australian parrot. All this, and Florence a mere 30-minute stroll down the hill.

rooms	16: 8 doubles, 7 suites, 1 single.
price	€ 280. Singles € 160. Suites € 330–€ 430.
meals	Breakfast € 20–€ 25. Dinner, 1 course, € 12. Trattoria close by.
closed	Rarely.
directions	A1 exit Firenze Certosa for Porta Romana or Centre. Left at Porta Romana on Via Ugo Foscolo. Keep right & take Via Piana to end; right into Via Roti Michelozzi.

'Magnificently stern and sombre are the streets of beautiful Florence…' Charles Dickens Pictures *from Italy*

Signor Amerigo Franchetti

tel	+39 055 2298145
fax	+39 055 229008
e-mail	info@torrebellosguardo.com
web	www.torrebellosguardo.com

Hotel

Classic Hotel

Viale Machiavelli 25, 50125 Florence

The hubbub of the city is so overwhelming at times that it is sheer heaven to enter the shaded, gravelled driveway of the Classic. It lies just beyond the old town gate, the Porta Romana, where Florence seems to begin and end. The road by the hotel is leafy and suburban, yet the river Arno is a mere 10-minute walk. The Classic is cool, friendly, peaceful – and elegant in a low-key way. Much of the furniture has come from the owner's parents' house in town (once a famous old hotel): interesting paintings and handsome Tuscan pieces. Its greatest charm, though, is the shaded courtyard garden with trees, shrubs and little corners where you may sit peacefully with a cappuccino – a lovely spot for summer breakfast. In winter there's a breakfast room in the basement. Bedrooms are parquet-floored and modestly attractive; some are lovely, especially those in the attic, with their heavily-beamed, sloping ceilings. Altogether an easy-going and comfortable place to stay for anyone visiting Florence – the feel is more villa than hotel and you're in the countryside in minutes.

rooms	20: 17 doubles, 1 suite, 2 singles.
price	€150–€200. Singles €110.
meals	Breakfast €8.
closed	Occasionally.
directions	15-minute walk from Florence in leafy suburb of Arno. Details on booking.

Ice cream fans should visit the 'Bar Vivoli Gelateria' in the Santa Croce district (Via Isole delle Stinche 7), for 'the best ice cream in the world'.

	Dottoressa Corinne Kraft
tel	+39 055 229351/2
fax	+39 055 229353
e-mail	info@classichotel.it
web	www.classichotel.it

Hotel

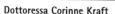
map 8   entry 118

Villa La Sosta

Via Bolognese 83, 50139 Florence

Here is an imposing house built in 1892 as part of a large estate on the Montughi hill; it is a 10-minute walk to Florence's centre, yet the villa stands just off the Via Bolognese in large landscaped gardens – a soothing antidote to city fatigue. The mansard-tower sitting room with sofas, books and views is a lofty place in which to relax, and there's a billiard room, too. Bedrooms, with large windows and wooden shutters, are equally stylish with striking *toile de Jouy* or checks, and dark Tuscan pieces. Interesting, too, are artefacts gathered from the Fantonis' days in Africa – the family ran a banana plantation – including ivory carvings and wooden statues. Breakfast is served outside under an ivy-covered pergola in summer or in the dining room, just off the family's bright sitting room; over excellent coffee Antonio and Giusy – a brother-and-sister team – will help you plan your itinerary. If the city's treasures start to pall they will organise a day in the vineyards or local pottery villages. There's parking off the main road and the number 25 bus, which stops outside the gates, can whisk you into the city or up into the hills.

rooms	5: 3 doubles, 1 triple, 1 quadruple.
price	€ 100–€ 120. Singles € 75–€ 95. Triple € 130–€ 150. Quadruples € 160–€ 180.
meals	Choice of restaurants in Florence.
closed	Rarely.
directions	Follow signs for Centre & Piazza della Libertà, for Via Bolognese. Villa La Sosta on left. Or no. 25 bus from railway station; get off about 800m after Via Bolognese begins, just before Total Petrol Station.

'Florence is the most enchanting place I know in the world.' Matthew Arnold *in a letter to his sister, 1879.*

	Antonio & Giuseppina Fantoni
tel	+39 055 495073
fax	+39 055 495073
e-mail	info@villalasosta.com
web	www.villalasosta.com

B&B

Residenza Hannah & Johanna

Via Bonifacio Lupi 14, 50129 Florence

Astonishingly good value right in the historic centre of Florence – and what an attractive, friendly place to be! You really feel as though you have your own pad in town, away from the tourist bustle. Lea's other *residenze* have been such a success that she and Johanna have opened this one in a lovely 19th-century palazzo, shared with notaries and an embassy. Up the lift or marble stairs to a big welcome from Lea and Evelyne on the second floor. Both are charming, and keen to make your stay a happy one. Graceful arches, polished floors and soft colours give a feeling of light and space to the two parallel corridors; there are comfortable sofas there, too, so you can browse through the books and guides. The bedrooms off are big, airy and cool, with excellent, stylish bathrooms. A small table holds a basket of biscuits, brioches, jam, etc, and tea- and coffee-making things, and you breakfast in your room (there's no dining room). Or you could slip out to a bar for a cappuccino and a panino before wandering happily off to the Duomo, the San Lorenzo leather market and the Piazza della Signoria.

rooms	11: 9 doubles, 2 singles.
price	€ 75. Singles € 50.
meals	Florence is on your doorstep.
closed	Rarely.
directions	From Milan A1 exit Firenze Nord towards Fortezza da Basso & Piazza Libertà. Take Via Cavour (if police present explain going to Johanna); 1st right via S. Anna.

Evelyne Arrighi & Lea Gulmanelli

tel	+39 055 481896
fax	+39 055 482 721
e-mail	lupi@johanna.it
web	www.johanna.it

"Why not finish the apprenticeship?" asked Ghirlandaio. "I'll double the contract money. If you need more later, we can discuss it as friends." Michelangelo stood numb... He left the studio...'
Irving Stone *The Agony & the Ecstasy*.

B&B

map 8   entry 120

Le Residenze Johlea
Via San Gallo 76 & 80, 50129 Florence

Experience living in a real Florentine *residenza*... a particularly delightful and luxurious home, where thoughtful touches make you feel a cherished guest. The restored, late 19th-century building is in the centre of the city, with easy access to train and bus stations. Nos. 76 and 80 have separate entrances and Alexandra or Laura will always be there to greet you. Big, elegant bedrooms have long, shuttered windows, subtle colours and lovely fabrics. All are different and all are immensely comfortable, with settees, polished floors and rugs. Antiques and air conditioning, wooden jigsaw puzzles and books add to the pleasure, and the bathrooms are superb. But perhaps the nicest surprise of all is on up the rooftop: weave your way past little reading corners, old wooden settles and chests tucked under sloping ceilings, then up a stair to a glazed-in balcony... up again to a room where you can make drinks, and, finally, up a short flight of wooden steps to a wide, sun-flooded terrace. Be dazzled by a glorious, all-round panorama of Florence – superb!

rooms	12: 10 doubles, 2 singles.
price	€ 90–€ 100. Singles € 70.
meals	Wide choice of restaurants nearby.
closed	Rarely.
directions	From Milan A1 exit Firenze Nord for Fortezza da Basso & then Piazza Libertà. Via Cavour (if police present explain going to Johlea/Johanna); 1st right via S. Anna.

'One cannot become an angel in this world, but one can become a Florentine. This is possible because Florence is a mood, a will, a conquest.'
Carlo Coccioli, *The Florence I Love*

Lea Gulmanelli
tel	+39 055 4633292
fax	+39 055 4634552
e-mail	johlea@johanna.it
web	www.johanna.it

B&B

Palazzo Magnani Feroni

Borgo San Frediano 5, 50124 Florence

A palace built to impress; it still does. Once the home of an important French dignitary, a place for the grandest and most opulent of receptions, it was bought by the family two centuries ago and was, until recently, one of Europe's great antiques galleries. You step off a busy street, a block away from the Arno, into a cool entrance... flanked by long wooden pews, marble busts and seated lions, with great iron gates at the end. Through the gates, you enter a long and magnificent corridor that runs, cloister-like, along one side of a courtyard. The whole place is lush, elegant, a brilliant and sparkling conversion that gives you every modern spoiling extra, from swish gym to internet office in the rooms. These are vast with high-ceilings, comfortable with armchairs, king-size beds and Afghan rugs on polished *cotto* floors. Ask for one that looks onto the street rather than the inner courtyard. Most delightful of all is the rooftop terrace – studded with wrought-iron tables and cushioned chairs – whence you may gaze in a superior manner over the famous rooftop jumble of Florence. You will be lavishly spoiled.

rooms	12 suites for 2, extra beds available.
price	€ 210–€ 590, extra bed € 52.
meals	Room service à la carte available. Good choice of restaurants in Florence.
closed	Rarely.
directions	On Borgo San Frediano, 50m from corner of Via de'Serragli (1 block from Arno).

	Alberto & Claudia Giannotti
tel	+39 055 2399544
fax	+39 055 2608908
e-mail	info@florencepalace.it
web	www.florencepalace.it

Ideally situated for the church of Santa Maria del Carmine, with the recently restored frescoes by Masaccio in the Brancacci chapel.

Hotel

map 8   entry 122

Relais Chiara e Lorenzo

Via Casolari 74, Torri, 50067 Rignano sull'Arno

An easy place where you can immerse yourself in local culture. Alberto, a retired chef, sometimes takes guests on wine tastings and tours of Florence; he gives occasional cookery classes, too. The 14th-century villa stands a mile from a country road at the end of an extremely rough track (soon to be repaired, we are told), with views across vineyards and olives to the hills of Vallombrosa and the glittering sea. The rooms are a mix of old and new. Big bedrooms are beamy and shuttered, with simple white walls and rugs on tiled floors; in the twin is a vast antique bed bought from a local Marquis on the edge of bankruptcy! A Victorian-style bath with huge brass taps sits in splendour in a spotless bathroom. The dining room has a vaulted ceiling; in the garden a clutch of ubiquitous white plastic garden furniture sits under the pergola, and there's a little pool. Some readers have felt that a slight air of neglect is creeping in: please let us know. *Minimum stay two nights.*

Take a look at the monastery at Torri, which has a superb cloister — well worth a visit.

rooms	4: 2 twins/doubles, both with separate bath; 1 triple, 1 family, sharing bath.
price	€75–€90. Triple €80–€105. Family €105–€130.
meals	Lunch €20–€25. Dinner €26–€35, book ahead.
closed	Rarely.
directions	From Bagno a Ripoli or Pontassieve to Rosano; for Volognano. After approx. 1km left at sign. House over brow of hill after 1km towards river.

Signor Alberto Tozzi

tel	+39 055 8305956
fax	+39 055 8305240
e-mail	altox@centroin.it
web	www.relais-chiaraelorenzo.com

B&B

Relais Villa l'Olmo

Via Imprunetana per Tav 19, 50023 Impruneta

With a bit of luck you will be greeted by Claudia, a lovely German lady of considerable charm, married to a Florentine whose family have owned the property since 1700 (he also owns the sumptuous Palazzo Magnani Feroni in Florence). The Relais is really a clutch of beautifully converted apartments, all looking down over the valley and all shamelessly comfortable – definitely *di lusso*. You will find such things as softly-lit yellow walls beneath chunky Tuscan beamed ceilings, a cloth draped over a table and down to the floor, flowers, brilliantly designed kitchenettes, white china on yellow tablecloths, blue-and-white checked sofas – even a swimming pool for your apartment if you can't face splashing about with others in the big pool. Claudia runs a warmly efficient reception where she provides an e-mail service and rents mountain bikes and mobile phones; she can organise babysitting, cookery classes and wine-tastings, too. There's a restaurant and pizzeria, and own farm products for sale. Florence is 20 minutes away by car or bus – so you can have your cake, and eat it, too.

rooms	7 + 3: 7 apartments for 2-5; 3 villas for 2-6.
price	Villas € 185-€ 344 per night; € 1,245-€ 1,880 per week. Apartments € 95-€ 200 per night; € 580-€ 1,280 per week.
meals	Breakfast € 10. Dinner € 20-€ 40.
closed	Rarely.
directions	A1 exit Firenze Certosa. At r'bout for Tavarnuzze. There, left to Impruneta. Track on right, signed to villa. 200m past sign for Impruneta.

The fair at Impruneta is the subject of one of the most beautiful crowd scenes in art – a print by Jaques Callot of 1620.

	Claudia Jerger
tel	+39 055 2311311
fax	+39 055 2311313
e-mail	florence.chianti@dada.it
web	www.relaisfarmholiday.it

Self-catering & B&B

map 8   entry 124

Villa Il Poggiale Dimora Storica

Via Empolese 69, 50026 San Casciano

This 16th-century villa is so lovely that it's hard to know where to start! Breathe in the scent of old-fashioned roses as you sit in the Renaissance loggia and consider the garden. Wander through the olive trees to the pool and watch the sunset. Or retreat into the house to enjoy the sheer, 1800s elegance of its décor. Obviously much loved and full of memories, it's the childhood home of two brothers, Johanan and Nathanel Vitta, who have devoted two years to its restoration. The rooms are big, beautiful and full of light, and everything is kept as it was. An oil painting of the Vittas's grandmother as a young woman greets you as you enter, and another, Machiavelli by Gilardi, hangs in the *salone*. Upstairs, the rooms still have their old names: the Professor's Room, the Lady's Room, the Owl's Room… all are different, all are striking. Some have frescoes and silk curtains, others fabrics specially produced in a small Tuscan workshop. Everywhere the attention to detail is superb but in no way overpowering. And your hosts really make you feel like wanted guests. A glorious place gloriously set in the Chianti hills.

rooms	20 + 3: 18 doubles, 2 suites. 3 apartments for 2+2.
price	€ 130–€ 190. Suites € 190–€ 240. Apartments € 250–€ 270.
meals	Good choice of restaurants nearby.
closed	February.
directions	From A1 for Rome exit Firenze-Certosa; superstrada Firenze-Siena exit San Casciano; signs for Cerbaia-Empoli. After 3km, signs on left.

'During several years of looking, sometimes
casually, sometimes to the point of exhaustion,
I never heard a house say yes so completely.'
Frances Mayes, *Under the Tuscan Sun*

Catarina Piccolomini

tel	+39 055 828311
fax	+39 055 8294296
e-mail	villailpoggiale@villailpoggiale.it
web	www.villailpoggiale.it

Hotel & Self-catering

    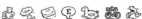

Il Poggetto
Via del Poggetto 14, 50025 Montespertoli

A deliciously green and sunny Tuscan hilltop, surrounded by vineyards and olive groves. Once inside the electronic gates, you'll be captivated by the all-round views. The gardens are delightful, too: three hectares of lawns, fruit trees, azaleas, heathers and roses (there's always something in flower), with pines and cypresses for shade and a terrace dotted with lemon and mandarin trees. Ivana and her family moved to the 400 year-old *casa colonica* in 1974 and have renovated beautifully, using original and traditional materials. The apartments are attractive, uncluttered and full of light. All have big, comfortable beds, antique furniture and private patios. La Loggia was once a hay barn; the huge, raftered living/dining area is superb and the old triangular air bricks are still in place. La Cipressaia, characteristically Tuscan in style and very private, is a conversion of the stable block, and sleeps five. Il Gelsomino, named after the jasmine outside the door, and La Pergola join each other. Everyone has use of the pool, which is set apart in a stunning position: you can watch the sun rise and set from your lounger.

rooms	4 apartments for 2-5.
price	€ 75; € 415-€ 1,175 per week.
meals	Wide choice of restaurants nearby.
closed	Rarely.
directions	From A1 Milano-Roma exit Firenze Signa. Right for Pisa-Livorno exit Ginestra. Right for Montespertoli. 1st left into Via Montegufoni. In Baccaiano left uphill; left for Montagnana. Signposted after 1km.

	Andrea Boretti & Ivana Pieri
tel	+39 339 3784383
fax	+39 02 70035890
e-mail	info@poggetto.it
web	www.poggetto.it

'Here are gardens and meadows where you may divert yourselves till three o'clock, when I shall expect you back, that we may dine in the cool of the day.' Boccaccio, The Decameron

Self-catering

map 8   entry 126

Fattoria di Barbialla Nuova

Via Castastrada 49, 50050 Montaione

By the time you come to the end of the long, cool drive through the woods, you really feel you have escaped modern life. The farm is a magical, exciting place – 500 hectares, specialising in Chianina cattle, olive oil and white truffles. (October and November are the best times if you want to go truffle-hunting – you will be accompanied by an expert and his dog.) Guido, Gianluca and Marco have worked hard to provide somewhere beautiful in this glorious nature reserve. Doderi has three apartments, simple and minimalist with clean lines, fine linen, books, music and the occasional black and white photo; bedcovers designed by Gianluca, stable doors, Roman blinds and 60s-style furniture in Tuscan colours add style, originality and colour. Outside: pergola, patio and pool – cheerful with deckchairs and decking – and orchard and hens. The three apartments in Brentina, deeper in the woods, are a little more primitive; perhaps too much so for some, but others will love the simplicity of their whitewashed walls and handmade staircase; all six have delicious bathrooms. Guido is always around to help if you need anything.

rooms	6 apartments: 1 for 2, 2 for 4, 1 for 4-6, 2 for 6-8.
price	€52–€78 for 2.
meals	Dinner with wine, €25–€40; book ahead.
closed	10 January-10 March.
directions	From Florence S.G.C. FI-PI-LI at Firenze Signa for Pisa, exit San Miniato for Montaione; 1km after Corazzano, signs on right.

Truffles have continued to fascinate Europeans, who between the 16th and 17th centuries formulated the science of mycology to study how various mushrooms grow.

	Guido Rasponi
tel	+39 0571 677227
fax	+39 0571 677227
e-mail	info@barbiallanuova.it
web	www.barbiallanuova.it

Self-catering

entry 127   map 8

Fattoria del Bassetto
Via Avanella 42, 50052 Certaldo

The Benedictine monks who lived here used to open their doors to weary pilgrims passing through Tuscany. That tradition of hospitality is kept alive by Dafne and her three sons today – in such spirit that most guests find themselves, like Pozzo in *Waiting for Godot*, unable to leave. As well as the villa with its genuinely old-fashioned bedrooms there's a hostel in the old *convento* beloved by backpackers. The pool and hammocks are shared. The feel of the place is house-party rather than hotel: there's a key for the front door but the bedrooms don't have keys (though they can be locked from the inside), and the kitchen is for communal use, with breakfast ingredients supplied; cook all your meals here if you like. Two terraces and a library with sofas are also available for villa guests to use. This is Tuscan countryside at its least rose-tinted – the presence of a factory or two and the proximity of road and rail cannot be disguised – but there are plenty of hidden and visible rewards, and the glories of Florence, Siena and San Gimignano are a train ride away. *Minimum stay two nights.*

rooms	11: Villa: 2 doubles, 2 twins, 2 family; bathrooms shared. Hostel: 5 dormitories for 3-6.
price	€80. Singles €52.
meals	Choice of trattorias 10-minute walk.
closed	Rarely.
directions	From Florence-Siena motorway, exit Poggibonsi Nord for Poggibonsi. SS429 for Certaldo. After 5.2km Fattoria signed on right.

	Duchessa Dafne Canevaro Guicciardini di Zoagli
tel	+39 0571 668342
fax	+39 0571 664945
e-mail	info@bassettoguesthouse.com
web	www.bassettoguesthouse.com

Walk up to Certaldo Alto, the birthplace of Boccaccio, from here. An underground passage is said to link it to the Fattoria Bassetto… as yet undiscovered.

B&B & Self-catering

map 8   entry 128

Sovigliano

Strada Magliano 9, 50028 Tavarnelle Val di Pesa

Walking distance from Tavarnelle, down a country lane, stands this ancient farmhouse among vineyards, olives, cypresses and pines. Though the setting is secluded, you are in the middle of some of the most popular touring country in Italy, within sight – on a clear day – of the towers of San Gimignano. Every view is breathtaking. Sovigliano has been renovated by the family with deep respect for the architecture and materials, and you stay in self-catering apartments – one palatial, with a glorious stone fireplace. All are very attractive, with white walls, ancient rafters, good beds, country antiques. Or you may have one of the charming double rooms, with breakfast (or dinner) laid on as well. A big, delightfully rustic kitchen, with a private fridge for each guest, makes a perfect place for you to meet others. Relax under the pines in the garden, take a dip in the pool, work out in the outdoor exercise area (where children must be supervised), sip a pre-dinner drink. Vin Santo, olive oil and grappa are for sale, Signora is most helpful and visitors can scarcely tear themselves away. *Minimum three nights.*

rooms	4 + 4: 2 doubles, 2 twins. 4 apartments for 2-4.
price	€93–€110. Apartments €110–€235.
meals	Dinner €31, on request.
closed	Rarely.
directions	Exit SS2 Firenze-Siena at Tavarnelle. On entering town right & follow Marcialla. Sovigliano just out of town: left at 4th r'bout down lane signed Magliano; follow signs.

San Casciano in Val di Pesa is a lovely hill village. The church, the 'Chiesa della Misericordia', has a fine carved pulpit by Giovanni di Balduccio.

Signora Patrizia Bicego

tel	+39 055 8076217
fax	+39 055 8050770
e-mail	info@sovigliano.com
web	www.sovigliano.com

Self-catering & B&B

Corte di Valle

Via Chiantigiana, Loc. Le Bolle, 50022 Greve in Chianti

The British ambassador in the 1920s, Sir Ronald Graham (a reputed pro-fascist) lived here, and what was good enough for him… But it did go downhill, and Marco, who left banking after 35 years to pursue this dream, has had to pour money as well as affection into it. He has succeeded brilliantly: the old villa is a handsome, even stylish, place to stay and has kept all of its dignity and character. Bedrooms are de-luxe size even if the decoration is a little sparse, the shower rooms are immaculate and the beds very comfortable. Downstairs is a huge sitting room where you can gather with your friends, and an old kitchen with lovely vaulted brick ceiling that is used as a second living room – there is generous sitting space, as well as a cavernous hall and upstairs corridor. Meals are served in their cosy and attractive restaurant across the yard. Marco loves food and wine and enjoys offering tastings, not least of his own wine; Irene is gentle and friendly. All around you lies lush Chianti countryside, and the idyllic little town of Greve is five kilometres away.

rooms	8: 7 doubles, 1 twin.
price	€124.
meals	Dinner €26.
closed	Rarely.
directions	5km north of Greve in Chianti, on west side of the S222, north of turning to Passo dei Paccorai. House visible from road.

	Irene Mazzoni
tel	+39 055 853939
fax	+39 055 8544163
e-mail	cortedivalle@cortedivalle.it
web	www.cortedivalle.it

A 'belvedere' is an open-sided room or tower on the roof of a house – a distinctive feature of Italian architecture and there is a good example here.

B&B

map 8   entry 130

Poggio all'Olmo

Via Petriolo 30, 50022 Greve in Chianti

A small, 10-hectare Tuscan farm, six kilometres from Greve, where wine and olive oil are produced in the traditional way. Three generations of Vannis still toil, grandfather tending fat tomatoes in the kitchen garden and pruning the vines. Francesca enjoys having people to stay and looks after you well. The farmhouse, which dates back to the 17th century, has two guest bedrooms, each with a kitchenette – basic, no frills – while the old hay barn has been converted into a couple of simple but comfortable apartments with beams and terracotta. The lower of the two has an extra bed and its own patio; the views, across vineyards and olive groves to the undulating hills beyond, are superb. The landscape is typical Chianti, the air as pure as can be, and the swimming pool, fragrant with the scent of herbs and roses, a delight. Witness the day-to-day activities of a working farm without stirring from your chair – though there is a guide in nearby Lamole who will take you for walks. Utter peace and tranquillity, genuine family life, home-produced wine and olive oil. *Minimum stay in apartment three nights.*

The word 'olmo' means elm, and often crops up in place names in this part of Italy.

rooms	2 + 2: 2 doubles. 2 apartments: 1 for 2-3, 1 for 2-4.
price	€ 75. Apartments € 90 per night.
meals	Breakfast on request. Dinner 2–3 times weekly at Villa Vignamaggio with Chianti & grappa tastings, 1km.
closed	Rarely.
directions	From Greve in Chianti SS222 for Panzano. After 2km left for Lamole & on for 5km. House between Vignamaggio & Lamole, signed.

Francesca Vanni

tel	+39 055 8549056
fax	+39 055 853755
e-mail	olmo@greve-in-chianti.com
web	www.greve-in-chianti.com/olmo.htm

Self-catering

Podere Torre

Via di San Cresci 29, 50022 Greve in Chianti

This place exudes contentment; no wonder the antique roses do so well. They are coaxed and charmed by Cecilia, who has the same effect upon her guests. Hers is no ordinary B&B: everything is intuitively and thoughtfully presented. Next to the main house is La Stalla, a cool, ground-floor bedroom in the watchtower. Concimaia (the name refers to its unpoetical origins as a manure store) is reached across a flowery terrace with table and chairs for two; you may interconnect with Fienile, the studio apartment in the small barn, if you are a party of four. Cecilia gives you fluffy towels, cotton bed linen, blocks of Marsiglia soap, lavender bags, even candles and matches for evening relaxation. Swallows nest in the laundry room – where you can wash and iron – and Cecilia provides the basics, including bottle openers and candles, to enable you to rustle up a picnic supper and dine here *al fresco*. She and Paolo run a small vineyard producing good-quality wine and olive oil. There is a taverna within walking distance if you prefer to eat out, but at breakfast-time we advise you stay and be pampered.

rooms	2 + 1: 2 doubles. 1 apartment for 2.
price	€ 70; € 450 per week. Apartment € 85; € 550 per week.
meals	Breakfast € 7.50.
closed	Rarely.
directions	From Greve in Chianti for Pieve di San Cresci; signs for 3km on minor road.

	Signora Cecilia Torrigiani
tel	+39 055 8544714
fax	+39 055 8544714
e-mail	poderetorre@greve-in-chianti.com
web	www.greve-in-chianti.com/poderetorre.htm

'The Plant of Roses, though it be a shrub full of prickles, yet it has been fit and convenient to have placed it with the most glorious flowers of the world.' John Gerard's, *Herball*, 1636.

Self-catering & B&B

map 8   entry 132

Podere La Casellina

Via Poggio alla Croce 60, 50063 Figline Valdarno

Come here for life's slow rhythm – and for the family. The Bensi grandparents moved here in 1936 (see below), when the local church put the *podere* into their careful hands; the family and Michelangelo have worked the land ever since. Anyone wishing to experience the 'real' side of peasant life – and learn something of its history – should come here; so little has changed at La Casellina, inside or out, and there are few concessions to modernity. Guest bedrooms are in the old hayloft and stables, simple but comfortable, with views of the little San Pietro al Terreno church. The landscape, between Chianti and Valdarno, is exquisite; you have the chestnut woods of the Chianti mountains to one side, and oaks, cypresses and olives to the other. Learn to prune vines and pick olives on the farm; gather chestnuts and wild mushrooms in the woods. Go riding or biking, then come back to sample Grandma's recipes – the grape flan is delicious. There's passion fruit for breakfast, and Michelangelo is a dear who speaks brilliant English. *Minimum stay two nights.*

'In sweet Val d'Arno it is permissable enough to dream among the orange blossoms, and forget the day in twilight of ilex.' John Ruskin *Modern Painters*

rooms	3 doubles.
price	From € 76.
meals	Lunch € 18. Dinner € 23.
closed	10 January-28 February.
directions	Leave A1 at Incisa; take Figline road. Just before Figline, right to Brollo & Poggio alla Croce. After 4km Podere on right.

Signor Michelangelo Bensi
tel +39 055 9500070
e-mail poderelacasellina@tin.it
web www.poderelacasellina.it

B&B

Villa Le Barone

Via San Leolino 19, 50020 Panzano in Chianti

You can immediately tell that the house still belongs to the Della Robbia family. (The Marchesa has written a delightful book about her passion for the countryside and her beautiful old home.) It's a gorgeous place, with every modern indulgence, yet feels unspoiled, and staff bustle about with an easy-going friendliness under the supervision of the charming Catarina. Bedrooms vary; some are in the villa, others in outbuildings around the estate; some are on a grand scale, others have an authentic Tuscan style and some unusual pieces of furniture. The sitting room has a deep, lush comfort – irresistible; vast coffee table books are guaranteed to whet your appetite for Italy. The restaurant – once the wine cellar – serves traditional, delicious, Tuscan food, and wine-tastings in local Chianti Classico vineyards can be arranged. The gardens are no less appealing, with flowers, views, tennis for the energetic, a terrace with bright yellow parasols for the idle, and a pool that is far too seductive for anyone set on a cultural holiday. That said, do visit the exquisite church of San Leolino, on the doorstep.

rooms	30: 29 doubles/twins, 1 single.
price	€ 105–€ 135.
	Half-board € 101–€ 129 p.p.
meals	Lunch/dinner € 34.
closed	November–March.
directions	Well signed from Greve in Chianti.

	Marchesa Viviani Della Robbia
tel	+39 055 852621
fax	+39 055 852277
e-mail	info@villalebarone.it
web	www.villalebarone.it

The exquisite church of San Leolino is only yards away.

Hotel

map 8   entry 134

Fattoria Casa Sola

Via Cortine 88, 50021 Barberino Val d'Elsa

Count Giuseppe Gambaro and his wife Claudia tend the wine and olive oil production as the family has done for generations. The estate grows a variety of grapes, and gates are shut at night to prevent wild boar from snaffling them! The two-storey apartments, 700m from the main house and pool, are cool, fresh and comfortable with whitewashed walls, tiled floors, traditional country bedspreads and vineyard views. They are named – Red, White, Yellow – and each garden has roses to match. Your hosts are charming and courteous and passionate about their wine, and give you a bottle on arrival. Once a week they take guests round the vineyards and wine-making facilities, rounding off the visit with a glass of *Vin Santo* and *cantucci* biscuits. Claudia is very fond of children and organises weekly races and games. There are cookery and watercolour classes for grown-ups, and you can also play tennis and ride. Order a takeaway meal for your supper, or eat out in Barberino and San Donato. Or drive the 30 minutes to Florence or Siena. *Minimum stay one week in high season.*

Poggibonsi was destroyed by Guy de Montfort in 1270 and rebuilt in 1478. It contains the wonderful Gothic battlemented 'Palazzo Pretorio'.

Self-catering

rooms	6 apartments: 1 for 2-4, 2 for 4, 2 for 4-6, 1 for 8.
price	€ 500–€ 1799 per week.
meals	Self-catering.
closed	Rarely.
directions	From Firenze-Siena superstrada exit at S. Donato in Poggio; SS101 past S. Donato church. After 1.5km, right to Cortine & Casa Sola.

Conte Giuseppe Gambaro

tel	+39 055 8075028
fax	+39 055 8059194
e-mail	casasola@chianticlassico.com
web	www.fattoriacasasola.com

Fattoria Viticcio

Via San Cresci 12/a, 50022 Greve in Chianti

You're on a hill above Greve in beautiful Chianti Classico country. Alessandro's father, Lucio, bought the farm in the 1960s and set about producing fine wines for export. It was a brave move at a time when people were moving away from the countryside. Now managed by Alessandro, the vineyard has an international reputation; visit the vaults and taste for yourself. Nicoletta runs the *agriturismo*, helped by their daughters – though the youngest is only four! The apartments, each named after a daughter – Beatrice, Arianna, Camilla – are at the heart of the estate and much thought has gone into them. Plain-coloured walls, brick arches, beams and terracotta floor tiles give an attractively simple air; the rooms have well-made furniture and some carefully selected antiques; kitchens are delightful. The pool is in a walled garden, with a small play area for children, and a second pool and tennis court in the olive groves are planned for 2004. You may hear the occasional tractor – this is a working estate – but the farmyard is tidy and well-kept, with tubs of flowers everywhere. There's a lovely family atmosphere, too, and wonderful views.

rooms	3 apartments: 1 for 3, 1 for 4, 1 for 6.
price	€90–€155; €515–€775 per week.
meals	Restaurants in Greve, 15-minute walk.
closed	Rarely.
directions	From A1 exit Firenze Sud; Via Chiantigiana SS222. In Greve follow signs for pool (piscina) over small bridge past pool on right, take track for Viticcio, signposted.

	Alessandro Landini &
	Nicoletta Florio Deleuze
tel	+39 055 854210
fax	+39 055 8544866
e-mail	info@fattoriaviticcio.com
web	www.fattoriaviticcio.com

'The vineyards are echoing with laughter and sprinkled with happy people ... come to help the ingathering, not for pay or wages but in expectation of similar assistance.'
Edward Hutton
Self-catering

map 8   entry 136

Podere Le Mezzelune

Via Mezzelune 126, 57020 Bibbona

What a treat it is to find this house in the north Maremma. After a long, winding track, big wooden gates; ring the bell and they swing open to reveal a tree-lined drive... Miele the labrador will be the first to greet you. The Chiesas have turned their home into a delightful B&B where you feel as though you are visiting friends. Downstairs, a huge dining table for breakfasts of fresh, home-baked pastries and seasonal fruits, and open fire for winter. Upstairs: bedrooms, each at a corner of the house with a wisteria-clad terrace (two look out to sea). Painted white and cream, they have linen curtains, wooden floors, furniture made to Luisa's design... charming with candles, fresh fruit and old wooden pegs hung with an antique shawl. Bathrooms, too, are perfect. For longer stays you have two little cottages in the garden, comfortable with open fires, dishwashers and beams. You are surrounded by cypresses, vines, flowers, herbs and 2,000 olive trees. A magical place, five minutes from the historic centre, not far from the sea and blissfully free of newspapers and TV. *Minimum stay two nights; three nights in cottages.*

rooms	4 + 2: 4 doubles/twins. 2 cottages for 2.
price	€146–€176. Cottages €156–€176 per night; €980–€1,162 per week.
meals	Breakfast in cottages €13–€15, on request. Good restaurants 3-7km.
closed	Rarely.
directions	Exit SS1 at La California towards Bibbona. Just before village, signs for Il Mezzelune on left. Follow for approx 2km till farm gate.

The town of Massa Marittima has a beautiful medieval central square, a majestic cathedral and an interesting archaeological museum.

	Luisa & Sergio Chiesa
tel	+39 0586 670266
fax	+39 0586 671814
e-mail	relais@lemezzelune.it
web	www.lemezzelune.it

B&B & Self-catering

Villa la Bandita

Tenuta la Bandita, Via Campagiva Nord 30, 57020 Sassetta

There's still a magical, undiscovered feel about the high Maremma — sunny hills, spectacular views and ancient forest with deer, porcupine and wild boar. The sense of space is wonderful. Villa la Bandita was once Daniella's family's summer retreat. As a teenager she had a vision of turning the house into a small hotel or guest house; now she and her husband live on the 85-hectare estate and her vision has been realised. Staying in the elegant, 17th-century, two-storeyed villa is like being a guest in a private country house, with an approachable, humorous and charming hostess. It's all very quiet, relaxing and civilised. The dining room walls are hung with huge tapestries and there are masses of fresh flowers, collections of jugs and interesting antiques. Dino and Daniella usually join guests for meals at the great glass table supported by two lions. Gracious bedrooms look out over open countryside: the estate has cedar and pine woods, olive groves, vineyards, vegetable gardens, orchards and two small lakes. From some places you can catch a distant, tantalising glimpse of the Tyrrhenian Sea.

rooms	11: 10 doubles, 1 suite.
price	€90–€140. Suite €135–€165.
meals	Dinner à la carte. Restaurant 3-6km.
closed	November-March.
directions	SS1 Aurelia South - exit Donoratico. Follow signs for Castagneto Carducci then Monteverdi. Before Sassetta, left for Monteverdi. After 2km, La Tenuta on right.

A jetty was built at Livorno (Leghorn) in 1571 by Cosimo I. Today it is the largest commercial harbour in Tuscany.

	Dino & Daniella Filippi
tel	+39 0565 794350
fax	+39 0565 794350
e-mail	bandita@tin.it
web	www.labandita.com

Le Foreste

Le Foreste 135, 57028 Suvereto

No dense dark forest this – more a gentle landscape of chestnut woodland, cork oak and Mediterranean scrub... and views across to a delicious stretch of Tuscan coast with Elba sparkling in the distance. Nervous drivers might find the approach road something of a challenge – don't be put off. This mini medieval *borgo*, now a private home with self-catering apartments, sits in harmony with its setting and is perfect for nature and wildlife enthusiasts – fall asleep to the hoot of the owl. Dogs and cats laze on stone walls amid cascades of flowers – a colourful reminder of the Swiss window boxes of Edith's homeland. Inside, each unit is cool and cosy with a mix of confident colour in the fabrics and on the walls, mostly rough-washed in ochre or ox-blood-red. Chunky rafters, twirly wrought-iron beds, mosquito nets, yet somehow different from the rustic-by-numbers Tuscan interiors so often found. The living spaces have sofabeds for squeezing in extras; there are tiled cooking areas, and private patios for sitting out. Smiling, friendly Edith ensures everything is perfect for guests.

rooms	6+2: 2 apartments for 2, 1 for 2-3, 1 for 3-4, 1 for 3-5, 1 for 4-5. 1 cottage for 2, 1 for 6-8.
price	Apartments € 200–€ 890. Cottage for 2-8 € 290–€ 1,360.
meals	Self-catering.
closed	Mid–January–mid-February.
directions	Exit m'way at Venturina for Suvereto; pass Cafaggio after approx 3km cont. to ostrich farm, sign on left. After 150m left for Il Falcone. Le Foreste then signed.

The popular eating house Antica Osteria dei Tre Briganti in Suvereto is owned by Edith and her husband. A must when staying here.

	Edith Keller
tel	+39 0565 854105
fax	+39 0565 854105
e-mail	info@leforeste.it
web	www.leforeste.it

Self-catering

Pieve di Caminino

Via Prov. di Peruzzo, 58028 Roccatederighi

A fallen column lying deep in the grass, woods, a quiet lake... It's all so tranquil that it's hard to believe what a lively history this settlement has had since it was first recorded in 1075. Set in a huge natural amphitheatre, ringed by hills and medieval fortresses, it has seen battles rage and monks and hermits come and go. There's even a magic spring. Once you've driven through the big, rusty gates and down the tree-lined drive, you'll be greeted by your hosts in an 11th-century church – part of the owners' private quarters. It's the most lovely, airy space, with battered columns, soaring arches, and elegant furniture – a subtle study in cream, gold and brown. The apartments, too, are beautiful. Each has its own terrace or balcony and is simply furnished with family antiques and fine old paintings. Enchanting windows look over the grounds; the massive walls are rough stone or plaster, the ceilings beamed or vaulted. The 500-hectare estate produces its own olive oil and wine and has distant views to the sea and the isle of Elba. *Minimum stay three nights in peak season.*

rooms	7 apts: 2 for 3, 3 for 4, 2 for 5.
price	€90–€210; €455–€1099 per week.
meals	Restaurant La Rose Blu, 7km.
closed	Rarely.
directions	From Milan m'way Bologna – Firenze exit Firenze Certosa, for Siena-Grosseto, exit Civitella Marittima for Follonica. 5km before Montemassi right for Sassofortino. On right 1km.

Piero Marrucchi & Daniela Locatelli

tel	+39 0564 569737
fax	+39 0564 568756
e-mail	caminino@caminino.com
web	www.caminino.com

The famous fresco by Simone Martini (1328) shows the soldier Guidoriccio da Fogliani on horseback after the battle between the fortresses of Montemassi and Roccatederighi.

Self-catering

map 10   entry 140

Azienda Agricola Montebelli

Loc. Molinetto, 58023 Caldana Bivio

Step outside and breathe in the scents of myrtle and juniper. Wander up to the ancient oak at the top of the hill and watch the sun set. Best of all, explore this whole lovely area on horseback: Montebelli has nine horses and three ponies... and there are mountain bikes if horses aren't your thing. Little tracks lead you past gnarled oaks to vineyards, olive groves and a small lake. The farm is run by Carla, her husband and their son Alessandro, who came back to Italy after many years in South Africa. Jars of the farm's produce – honey, jam, olive oil, grappa and wine – are displayed in the reception area, alongside a blackboard giving the day's dinner menu of regional cuisine with home-grown organic ingredients. If you'd like to learn how to concoct some local dishes, cookery courses are available on request. Breakfast is out on the big, covered terrace, also used for concerts and barbecues in the summer. The bedrooms are cool, clean and welcoming – and excellent value. Their white walls, wooden floors, understated furnishing and interesting pictures strike the perfect note of simplicity in this lovely, unspoiled place.

Castiglione della Pescaia's medieval citadel is dominated by an Aragonese castle.

rooms	21: 11 doubles, 2 suites, 8 triples.
price	Half-board only, € 79–€ 105 p.p.
meals	Half-board.
closed	January–March.
directions	From SS1 exit Gavorrano Scalo for Ravi-Caldana; 5km, turn for Caldana. After 2.5 km, signed.

Carla Filotico Tosi

tel	+39 0566 887100
fax	+39 0566 81439
e-mail	info@montebelli.it
web	www.montebelli.com

B&B

Azienda Agrituristica Santa Caterina
Loc. Granaione, Campagnatico

Sit under a fig tree in the garden, and chisel your first flint spearhead. Or learn to make bows and arrows, light fires with fungus and flints, create clay pots using ancient techniques. Or just contemplate the countryside and the sea. Santa Caterina is a family farm set in the hills, with the rare bonus of a prehistoric village, Gli Albori, right by. The 6,000-year-old archaeological site is run by Ricardo, in collaboration with the University of Ferrara, and his parents run the *agriturismo*. No TV, no pool, no frills – but such a rewarding place to be, with friendly, endearing hosts, real farmhouse accommodation and lots of food for thought. There's plenty of nourishment for the body, too with delicious, organically-grown Tuscan fare: pecorino cheese and ricotta from Santa Caterina's sheep and salami and ham from the Cinta Senese pigs. Meals are eaten round the big table in the dining room of the 19th-century house. The bedrooms are minimalist and comfortable, with big windows and exposed stone or colour-washed walls. Each has steps up to a mezzanine for an extra bed or a study area. A great place for a family holiday.

rooms	8: 6 doubles, 2 family rooms.
price	€60.
meals	Dinner with wine, €20.
closed	Rarely.
directions	From Siena Superstrada, exit Campagnatico (after Paganico), towards Arcille. Left in Sant Antonio for Granaione. Santa Caterina is signposted on right (1km before Granaione).

Adriana Demo & Pietro Chessa

tel	+39 0564 998364
fax	+39 0564 998364
e-mail	adriana.demo@tin.it
web	www.gruppostudionet.com/ereditaperduta/ santacaterina/ita/agriturismo/default.htm

Man has been able to hunt here since ancient times owing to the great mammals which have always been a characteristic feature of the Maremma region.

B&B

map 10   entry 142

Antico Casale di Scansano

Loc. Castagneta, 58054 Scansano

The food is good here; breakfasts are way above average, and the restaurant gets full marks for not overwhelming you with a long menu. Be idle, if you choose – what are holidays for? – but when you see the eager faces of your fellow guests as they scurry off to various parts of this friendly place to cook, ride or walk the day away, you might wish to join them. There are courses in Tuscan cookery led by Mariella Pellegrini, while down at the stables nonchalance and bravado go hand-in-hand under the watchful and twinkling eye of Athos; you can choose a day's trekking, or take a lesson in the riding school. The bedrooms in the old hotel vary in size; those in the new building have balconies with good views and some open fires. All are plainly furnished, with air conditioning; the cheaper ones lie closest to the road. There's an open plan feel to the sitting area, with big sofas, open fire and children's games on the tables. The Pellegrini family create a relaxed and friendly atmosphere: this is a cheerful place, and wonderful for children.

rooms	32: 21 doubles, 5 suites, 6 singles.
price	€ 108–€ 150. Suites € 150–€ 180. Singles € 70–€ 86.
meals	Hotel restaurant (closed Jan-March).
closed	Rarely.
directions	From Scansano towards Manciano (SS322). House 2.5km east of Scansano.

Wine was considered so important in this area that anyone who allowed their farm animals to damage vines was liable to a fine of two carline.

Signor Massimo Pellegrini

tel	+39 0564 507219
fax	+39 0564 507805
e-mail	info@anticocasalediscansano.com
web	www.anticocasalediscansano.com

Hotel

Villa Bengodi

Via Bengodi 2, Loc. Bengodi, 58010 Fonteblanda

A house that matches its owners: gentle, unpretentious, full of old-fashioned charm. Great-aunt Zia Ernesta lived in the room with the angel frescoes for most of her life; now Caterina, who lives in Florence, shares the running of the B&B with her brother and his wife. The villa and its gardens are their pride and joy. Bedrooms are generous, light and spotless with a hotchpotch of furniture from past decades; one has a ceiling painted in 1940, another a terrace; all have original floor tiles in varying patterns. Modern bathrooms are excellent, vistas are to the garden or sea. While away the days in the enchanting palm-fringed garden, or on the terrace where views reach to Corsica on a clear day. Beaches and mile upon mile of surf are a sprint away – or you could walk the full mile to Talamone, where a family friend takes you out on his boat to fish and to swim (you eat on board what you catch). The apartment is newly done up and has its own garden. Dine in summer on the terrace, in winter under a chandelier made of antlers and pine cones. A very personal home in a magical setting. *Minimum stay three nights.*

rooms	6 + 1: 6 doubles. 1 apartment for 5.
price	€100–€150. Apartment €500–€1,400 per week.
meals	Dinner €30.
closed	Rarely.
directions	From Grosseró/Roma superstrada, towards Talamone. First left & where road ends near station right into Via Bengodi. First right again.

Famiglia Orlandi

tel	+39 335 420334
fax	+39 0564 885515
e-mail	villabengodi@toskana.net

The hill rising above Talamone is said to be the burial mound of Telamon, who took part in the Argonauts' expedition to Colchis in search of the Golden Fleece.

B&B & Self-catering

map 10   entry 144

Tenuta La Parrina

KM.146 via Aurelia, 58010 Albinia

For all its relaxed and agreeable air, this is a serious working estate – 450 acres producing the famous Parrina wines and a whole range of fabulous foods, stocked by the estate shop. Wonderful if you're self-catering and if you're not, you'll find them all on the dining room menu. The estate was formed around 1800 and has been in the same family ever since. At its centre, standing among trees in an attractive garden, is a long, creamy, three-storeyed house with green shutters and a shady veranda. It is a friendly place, full of family paintings and possessions and lots of wine references – even the lights are shaped like bunches of grapes. The pretty, softly-coloured bedrooms are comfortably furnished and the reception areas are elegant and welcoming. Breakfast is on the veranda, overlooking green lawns, bay hedges and terracotta urns. Just across from the main house are the apartments, which have a lovely courtyard and lots of space. The estate stretches along the aromatic Mediterranean scrubland at the foot of the Maremma hills, close to the sea. A great place for food and wine lovers. *Min. stay 3 nights in winter, 7 in summer.*

The name Parrina most probably derives from the Castilian word Parra, meaning vine or pergola.

rooms	11 + 8: 9 doubles, 2 family. 8 apartments.
price	€ 120–€ 180. Apartments € 900.
meals	Dinner € 24, book ahead. Restaurants 3-10km.
closed	Rarely.
directions	From SS Aurelia, at 146km take fork for Parrina. After 2km right, opposite Mediterranean Plant Nursery.

Franca Spinola

tel	+39 0564 865586
fax	+39 0564 862626
e-mail	parrina@dada.it
web	www.parrina.it

B&B & Self-catering

Il Pardini's Hermitage
Loc. Cala degli Alberi, 58013 Isola del Giglio

You arrive by sea; the trip around the coast from Giglio Porto takes 20 minutes. Once on the island, your only mode of transport is on foot or by donkey! It's quite a hike up to the villa, but there are plenty of little areas to sit and catch your breath along the way. The island is a wonder of flora and fauna – peregrine falcons, kestrels and buzzards if you're lucky, gorgeous wild flowers.... This once-hermitage, now a private villa, is far from any village or coastal resort – perfect seclusion. Bedrooms are simple, pale-walled, delicious; the doubles have stunning sea views. Find a quiet spot in the well-kept gardens, colourful with cacti and flowers, or indulge in a bout of sea-water therapy – there's a beautiful platform to dive from and the water is crystal clear. Paint or pot, play an instrument or a game, ride a donkey, visit a beach on the other side. And dress up for dinner, a formal affair of stiff white napery and hushed conversation. *Minimum stay three nights. Watercolour, ceramics and raku (pottery) courses available; also health and beauty weeks.*

rooms	13: 10 doubles, 2 singles, 1 suite.
price	Full-board € 108–€ 155 p.p. Half-board €92–€ 142.
meals	Included. Drinks (wine, coffee, etc) not included.
closed	October–March, but open as a retreat.
directions	Accessible by boat from Giglio Porto; takes about 20 minutes along coast. If seas are high or rough, travel on foot or by mule. Full details at time of booking.

Federigo & Barbara Pardini

tel	+39 0564 809034
fax	+39 0564 809177
e-mail	hermitage@hfs.it
web	www.finalserv.it/hermitage/

The theme of exile is common to all the islands of the Tuscan archipelago, most memorably in the case of Elba's famous prisoner.

Hotel

map 10   entry 146

La Palazzina

Sant'Andrea di Sorbello, 52040 Mercatale di Cortona

There is an English inflection to La Palazzina, with its quirky 14th-century watch tower planted inexplicably beside the main house. It makes a most unusual self-contained retreat with luscious views across the wooded valley. You have a well-equipped kitchen, a woodburner for cosy nights, a winding stair to a half-moon double, and, at the top, a twin with a stunning, brick-beehive ceiling. The honeysuckle-strewn terrace is just as you would wish, with cypress trees marching sedately up the hill and only birdsong to disturb the peace. There's a second apartment at one end of the farmhouse, with its own private entrance under a *loggia*. The grounds, including a swimming pool with views, are for you to explore and lead to some of the loveliest walks in the valley. David and Salina are great company and will cook dinner for you on your first evening. Hannibal defeated the Roman army at nearby Lake Trasimeno and there is little that David doesn't know about the historical importance of this area – his enthusiasm is contagious. *Minimum stay one week in tower, three nights in farmhouse.*

rooms	Farmhouse apartment for 2. Tower apartment for 4.
price	Tower €802–€1,200 (£520–£795) per week. Farmhouse €80–€130 (£56–£85) per night.
meals	Self-catering. Dinner with wine on request for first evening, €20.
closed	Rarely.
directions	Details will be given at time of booking.

Roman legions, Charlemagne, St Francis, and medieval armies have all travelled down this magical valley on the Tuscany-Umbria border.

	David & Salina Lloyd–Edwards
tel	+39 0575 638111
fax	+39 0575 638111
e-mail	italianencounters@technet.it
web	www.italianencounters.com/lapal.htm

Self-catering

Stoppiacce

San Pietro A Dame, 52044 Cortona

Thirty minutes of scenic driving from the Etruscan town of Cortona brings you to this ancient stone farmhouse at the end of a one-kilometre drive. It has been sensitively restored and beautifully furnished with antiques, family portraits and interesting paintings (some by Scarlett's grandfathers, both painters). She and Colin love meeting people and give guests three charming double bedrooms with bathrooms en suite. Below the main house, down a fairly steep incline, is a tiny stone dwelling where chestnuts were once dried, hence its name, Il Castagno. It is as intimate and cosy a self-catering retreat as any couple could wish for, and has its own terrace with views over the lushly wooded valley. The garden is a magical little oasis of terraces, flowers and lawns, impressively green; the pool higher up the hill has the sort of views that make it doubly hard to leave. Guests have been full of praise – but note, this is an isolated spot! Don't imagine you can nip off to the shops in a hurry, or take in a church or two before breakfast. *Minimum stay three nights.*

rooms	3 + 1: 3 doubles. 1 apartment for 2.
price	€ 130. Apartments € 155 per night B&B, min. stay 3 nights; € 670 per week self-catering.
meals	Lunch € 23. Dinner € 44, on request.
closed	November-April.
directions	From Cortona follow Citta di Castello for approx. 7km to Portole. Left fork to San Pietro A Dame. Through village, right at Stoppiacce sign; on down stone road.

Don't miss Fra Angelico's 'Annunciation' in the Diocesan Museum in Cortona.

	Colin & Scarlett Campbell
tel	+39 0575 690058
fax	+39 0575 690058
e-mail	stoppiacce@technet.it
web	www.stoppiacce.com

Self-catering & B&B

map 9   entry 148

Villa Marsili

Viale Cesare Battisti 13, 52044 Cortona

Throughout its turbulent career the building has re-emerged in various different guises before finally settling down in its dotage as an elegant hotel. The site is steeped in history: in the 14th century the church of the Madonna degli Alemanni stood here, built to house the miraculous image of the Virgin and Child known as the *Madonna della Manna*. Beneath, an Oratory was linked by a flight of stairs (which can still be seen in the breakfast room); in 1786 the church was demolished and an elegant mansion built on the site. The owners have carefully preserved many of the original architectural features lost or hidden over the centuries, and hall and bedrooms are immaculately and individually decorated with *trompe l'œils* and hand-painted borders. Colours are gentle yellows and all the bedrooms have lovely views. The front of the house looks onto a garden with a pergola where you can breakfast to a view of the Valdichiana and Lake Trasimeno. On the northern side is a winter garden, with the Borgo San Domenico a mesmerising backdrop.

The Celle, about 4km beyond Cortona where St Frances founded a monastery in the 12th century, are quite extraordinary, and well worth a visit.

rooms	27: 19 doubles, 3 suites, 5 singles.
price	€ 132–€ 217. Suites € 260-€ 310. Singles € 110-€ 130.
meals	À la carte dinner generally available, € 36-€ 41. Restaurant 10-minute walk uphill.
closed	9 January–1 March.
directions	Leave A1 at Val di Chiana, take Siena/Perugia motorway; 2nd exit for Cortona. Follow signs for Cortona Centro.

tel	+39 0575 605252
fax	+39 0575 605618
e-mail	info@villamarsili.net
web	www.villamarsili.net

Hotel

Casa Bellavista
Loc. Creti C.S. 40, 52044 Cortona

A glass of wine at a table in the orchard. Birdsong for background music – or occasionally foreground, if the family rooster is feeling conversational. And a panorama of Tuscan landscape. Bellavista deserves its name: its all-round views take in Monte Arniata, Foiano della Chiana and the old Abbey of Farneta. Next door is a field of sunflowers. There was a farm here for 200 years but the house was extensively restored about 30 years ago. It still has the original brick exterior, now softened by creepers, and a welcoming, family atmosphere (Simonetta and her husband have two young children). There's an assured, uncluttered country elegance to the rooms. Pretty, airy bedrooms – one rose, one blue and one green – are furnished with family antiques and interesting engravings. Simonetta's kitchen has a huge marble table top for kneading bread and she cooks traditional farmhouse food for her guests. She also gives cookery lessons for a maximum of four, so if you want to learn how to make gnocchi, fresh pasta, focaccia… Her husband, who's in the restaurant business, sees to the wines. It's a real Italian family B&B.

rooms	3: 1 double, 2 doubles/twins.
price	€ 115–€ 130.
meals	Dinner € 30; good wine list.
closed	January–March.
directions	Autostrada Valdichiana exit Perugia; exit Foiano. After 400m, right for Fratta-S.Caterina. On for 2.8km, right next to ruined building. After 1km, right at junc.; keep to left-hand road. After 600m, right onto a dirt road.

	Simonetta Demarchi
tel	+39 0575 610311
fax	+39 0575 610311
e-mail	info@casabellavista.it
web	www.casabellavista.it

Flat breads, referred to generically in Italy as 'focaccia', need only a topping such as cheese, herbs or oil to become a sort of pizza. Burton Anderson, Pleasures of the Italian table

B&B

map 9   entry 150

Hotel San Michele

Via Guelfa 15, 52044 Cortona

A door set in a grey stone arch and flanked by simple brass plates makes a sober entrance to this refreshing, unexpected hotel. Back in 1980 the Alunnos took on the challenge of restoring not one but *three* Renaissance palazzos, grouped round a courtyard in the centre of Cortona. It was an enormous risk and for the first few years Dottor Alunno virtually locked himself in and worked non-stop on the buildings. The result is an unusually lovely place to stay, with an intimate, relaxed feel that owes much to the approachable, friendly owners and their staff. So, in spite of its size, elegance and weight of history, it is not at all intimidating. (A fresco by Masaccio of Mary and the Four Apostles has recently been uncovered in one room and the splendid, first-floor breakfast room was once a study for 18th-century members of the Etruscan Academy – and still has a Latin inscription over the door.) The big, beautiful, comfortable bedrooms are decorated and furnished with subtlety and restraint. Some look across the Tuscan/Umbrian border, others have views to Lake Trasimeno. Outside the windows, swifts swoop and soar.

Cortona was annexed to Florence in 1411 and has hardly changed since the Renaissance period.

rooms	43: 39 doubles, 4 suites.
price	€ 134–€ 150. Suites € 200.
meals	Restaurants nearby.
closed	January–March.
directions	Given at time of booking.

Dottor Paolo Alunno

tel	+39 0575 604348
fax	+39 0575 630147
e-mail	info@hotelsanmichele.net
web	www.hotelsanmichele.net

Hotel & B&B

Residence Borgo San Pietro

Loc. San Pietro a Cegliolo, 52044 Cortona

Timeless style on the hillsides of San Pietro a Cegliolo. Dottor Paolo and his wife have poured affection and simple good taste – as Italians do so well – into this young complex of apartments and pool. The whole place breathes an air of well-being, especially *al fresco*. The big grassy garden is dotted with proper loungers and white parasols (no ubiquitous plastic here!), there are clumps of roses and lavender, well-tended paths and the serenest of pools. All feels settled, there's no one to rush you, and breakfast is served on a table fresh with flowers and white china. The beautifully converted apartments are a real treat, with their whitewashed walls, lovely rafters, wooden shutters and immaculate floors. Furniture is a successful combination of designer-modern and country antique, with the odd dash of yellow or sea-green from bedcover and sofa. There is much attention to detail here, and staff are warm and kind. You are surrounded by olive groves, and are a five-minute drive from the walled Etruscan town of Cortona – worth a visit as much for its panoramic terraces as its ancient treasures.

rooms	13 apartments for 2-4.
price	€575–€1,262 per week.
meals	Self-catering. Restaurants nearby.
closed	Rarely.
directions	From A1 exit Valdichiana onto Superstrada for Perugia; exit Cortona; SS71 for Arezzo. Right in Tavernelle for Borgo San Pietro.

	Dottor Paolo Alunno
tel	+39 0575 604348
fax	+39 0575 630147
e-mail	info@borgosanpietro.com
web	www.borgosanpietro.com

'Many of the historical reasons for coming to Italy are entirely imaginary.'
Luigi Barzini, *The Italians*

Self-catering

map 9   entry 152

Relais San Pietro in Polvano

Loc. Polvano 3, 52043 Castiglion Fiorentino

Paradise high in the hills. Signor Protti and his wife run this little hotel with their son and daughter-in-law and the thought and care which they lavish on the place is apparent at every turn. Bedrooms have white walls and gorgeous old rafters, delightful, wide wrought-iron beds, elegant painted wardrobes and doors, a single rug on a tiled floor. In winter, relax on cream sofas in front of a log fire. The pool, on a terrace just below, must have one of the best views in Tuscany: keep your head above water while doing a leisurely breaststroke and you will be rewarded with the blue-tinted panorama for which Italy is famous. There is a restaurant for guests serving delicious, local food and their own olive oil; bread comes fresh from the bread oven. In summer you dine at beautifully dressed tables on a terrace overlooking the valley – the 18th-century estate is surrounded by olive groves. An atmosphere of luxurious calm and seclusion prevails, and your hosts are a delight. For those who choose to venture forth from this heavenly place, note that gates close at midnight. *Children over 12 welcome. Minimum stay two nights.*

rooms	11: 5 doubles, 1 single, 5 suites.
price	€ 170–€ 200. Single € 130–€ 150. Suites € 250–€ 300.
meals	Restaurant à la carte, € 30–€ 45.
closed	November–March.
directions	From A1 Rome-Milan exit Monte San Savino for Castiglion Fiorentino. At 3rd traffic lights left for Polvano. After 7km left for Relais San Pietro.

In the church of San Francesco in Castiglion Fiorentino is a depiction of the saint by Margaritone d'Arezzo, the oldest known painter of the Italian Renaissance.

	Signor Luigi Protti
tel	+39 0575 650100
fax	+39 0575 650255
e-mail	info@polvano.com
web	www.polvano.com

Hotel

Villa i Bossi
Gragnone 44-46, 52100 Arezzo

Fifty people once lived on the ground floor of the old house and everything is still as it was – the great box which held the bread for 50 hungry mouths, the carpenter's room crammed with tools, the rich robes hanging in the Sacristy, the old oven for making charcoal… Francesca loves showing people round. Her husband's family have lived here since 1240 and the house is full of their treasures. There's even a wonderful fireplace sculpted by Benedetto da Maiano in the 1300s – his thank-you-for-having-me present to the family. You can sleep in high, ornate beds in the ancient splendour of the main villa – a bit like sleeping in a grand museum – or opt for the modern comforts of the attractive rooms in the Orangery. This really is a magical place, full of character and memories, with lively, friendly hosts. The gardens, set among gentle green hills, are a delight: Italian box hedges and avenues, grassy banks and shady trees, a pond and enticing seats under arching shrubs – and olives. The Tosco delgi Albergotti olive oil is one of the family's riches – as is their Chianti Gragnon Nero.

rooms	10 + 1: 2 doubles, 2 twins in main villa; 2 doubles, 2 triples, 2 quadruples in Orangery. 1 self-catering apartment for 3 in main villa.
price	From € 110.
meals	Lots of restaurants in the area.
closed	Rarely.
directions	In Arezzo follow signs to stadium. Pass Esso garage & on to Bagnoro. Then to Gragnone. 2km to villa.

	Francesca Viguali Albergotti
tel	+39 0575 365642
fax	+39 0575 964900
e-mail	franvig@ats.it
web	www.villaibossi.com

'There were advantages in living in the country which contained the most beauty. There were certain impressions that one could get only in Italy.' Henry James, *Portrait of a Lady*

B&B & Self-catering

map 9   entry 154

Castello di Gargonza

Loc. Gargonza, 52048 Monte San Savino

A fortified Romanesque village in the beauty of the Tuscan hills, whose 800-year-old steps, stones, rafters and tiles remain virtually intact. Today it is a private, uniquely Italian marriage of exquisitely ancient and exemplary modern. Seen from the air it is perfect, as if shaped by the gods to inspire Man to greater works: a magical maze of paths, nooks and crannies, castellated tower, great octagonal well, a heavy gate that lets the road slip out and tumble down, breathtaking views. No cars, no shops, but a chapel, gardens, pool and old olive press for meetings, concerts or breakfasts, cosy with big fireplace and comfy chairs. An excellent restaurant sits just outside the walls. The count and countess and their staff are passionate about the place, and look after you well. Choose between self-catering and B&B – bedrooms and apartments are 'rustic deluxe' with smart modern furnishings, white-rendered walls, superb rafters, open fireplaces, tiny old doors. Intriguing, delightful, and sociable too: a perfect place for families. *Minimum stay two nights; apartments one week.*

Monte San Savino is where the Renaissance architect Andrea Sansovino was born. The 'Loggia dei Mercanti' is attributed to him.

rooms	24 + 8: 21 doubles, 3 suites. 8 apartments for 2-10.
price	€ 101–€ 171. Suites € 163–€ 181. Apartments € 672–€ 1715 per week.
meals	Restaurant 'La Torre di Gargonza', à la carte.
closed	10-31 January; November-2 December.
directions	Exit A1 at Monte S. Savino; SS73 for Siena. Approx 7km after Monte S. Savino right for Gargonza; follow signs.

Conte Roberto Guicciardini
tel	+39 0575 847021
fax	+39 0575 847054
e-mail	gargonza@gargonza.it
web	www.gargonza.it

B&B & Self-catering

Rendola Riding

Rendola 66, Montevarchi , 52025 Arezzo

One of the forerunners of *agriturismo* in Tuscany, Jenny started Rendola back in the 70s and gives you the best possible way of seeing Chianti – on horseback. Of course, you *do* need to be able to ride. Equestrians will appreciate the beautiful conditions and the English – as opposed to the Western – style of riding. There are lessons with set timetables, and a more relaxed atmosphere prevails on the rides and the treks. (Non-riders will appreciate Jenny's expert advice on what to see and do in the area.) After a long, hot day in the saddle it is wonderful to return to showers and welcoming rooms. You may relax, too, in the sitting room with its big fireplace, books and music library. At the rustic ring of a cow bell, guests, family and stable workers gather in the dining room for dinner, where Pietro – in his seventies – serves wholesome, mostly organic Tuscan fare washed down with Chianti, and regales the assembled company with many a tale. *Minimum age for riders 10. Minimum stay two nights. Guests can be collected from Montevarchi train station.*

rooms	7 + 2: 4 doubles/twins, 2 family, 1 single. 2 apartments for 2.
price	€ 74–€ 82. Half-board € 52–€ 57 p.p. Full-board € 67–€ 72 p.p. Singles € 37. Apartment € 82 inc. breakfast.
meals	Lunch/dinner with wine, € 15–€ 20.
closed	Rarely.
directions	From autostrada del Sole exit 25 for Montevarchi & Mercatale Valdarno. After 5km right for Rendola; house 200m from village.

'England is a paradise for women and hell for horses; Italy a paradise for horses, hell for women, as the proverb goes.' Robert Burton (1577-1640)

	Jenny Bawtree
tel	+39 055 9707045
fax	+39 055 9707045
e-mail	bawtree@ats.it
web	www.rendolariding.freeweb.org

Inn & Self-catering

map 9   entry 156

Odina Agriturismo

Loc. Odina, 52024 Loro Ciuffenna

You are 650m above sea level and feel on top of the world – the Arno valley reaches out before you and the air is pure oxygen. Antonella takes great pride in this solid, pale-blue-shuttered house and its surrounding gardens. Each bush, tree and herb has been chosen with care, and the interiors of house and apartments are delightfully rustic and contemporary. Each is different: some kitchen surfaces are of granite, others of local *pietra serena*; bathroom walls are softly ragged in varying shades; all have French windows to a patio with wooden outdoor furniture. Oil, vinegar, sugar, coffee, salt and washing-up liquid are provided, and if you ask in advance they will lay on more for which you would pay. The reception is in a beautifully restored, deconsecrated chapel, with an old bread-making chest and a 'shop' selling Odina olive oil and beans. Take a dip in the pool, go for long, lazy walks in the olive groves and chestnut woods, prepare a barbecue. Garden courses and visits – highly recommended – are held here in May. *Minimum stay seven days.*

The monastery at Vallombrosa (mentioned in Milton's Paradise Lost) is worth visiting, not least because the town is charming and the views spectacular.

rooms	4 apartments for 2, 5, 6, 7. Also 1 farmhouse for 8-10.
price	€400-€750 for 2. €650-€110 for 4. €750-€1,350 for 5. €1,600-€2,700 for 8-10 per week.
meals	Self-catering.
closed	Rarely.
directions	From Florence A1 for Rome. Exit Valdarno. In Terranuova, follow Loro Ciuffenna. Before town, left for Querceto & Odina.

Signor Paolo Trenti

tel	+39 055 969304
fax	+39 055 969305
e-mail	info@odina.it
web	www.odina.it

Self-catering

entry 157   map 9

San Rocco

Fattoria Casamora, Loc. Campiana Di Sotto, 80, 52026 Pian di Scò

Forget the Tuscany of swimming pools and chic restaurants – here is a gentler place. The old farmhouse sits in a magical spot, surrounded by vineyards and at the end of a *strada bianca*. Gail comes here whenever she can, children in tow; she brims with kindness and good humour and enjoys having people to stay. These old houses were built to be cool in summer, cosy in winter... especially in front of a crackling log fire. The renovated house has plain white walls, tiled floors, dark-varnished beams, shutters inside and out; there's a comfortable hotchpotch of country furniture and a big dining table for meals. Bedrooms are simple and in keeping: twin beds with carved headboards, a four-poster with muslin drapes, a double with a homely patchwork quilt. Bathrooms are shiny and new. There are the wooded slopes of Pratamagno to conquer (see eagles soar), mountain streams in which to bathe, and a loggia to sit on so you can savour a glass of wine along with the view. English hospitality, Italian cooking, comfortable beds, deep peace – who could ask for more? *Minimum stay three nights.*

rooms	3: 2 doubles, 1 twin, sharing 2 separate bathrooms.
price	€ 100–€ 110. Ask about prices for renting the whole house.
meals	Dinner € 15 with wine.
closed	Rarely.
directions	Directions on booking.

According to some, Pian di Sco is derived from Pian di Resco – a torrent that runs close to the village.

	Gail Alexander
tel	+44 (0)1373 834609
fax	+44 (0)1373 834005
e-mail	alexander_gail@hotmail.com

Il Casale del Cotone

Loc. Cellole 59 , 53037 San Gimignano

It is a relief to escape the heaving crowds of San Gimignano and to look back from Il Casale del Cotone over the vineyards and ancient olive groves to that towering Manhattan of Tuscany. The house is 17th century, and it was in this parish that Puccini composed *Suore Angelica*. Inspiration may strike here in other ways and certainly the landscape is such to tempt many an amateur painter. Alessandro is proud of the old family house, so carefully restored, dotted with Grandfather's furniture and the occasional restoration 'find'. Big double rooms are furnished in local style, with tiled floors and generous wrought-iron beds; those on the ground floor have patios where pots of jasmine scent the air, those above, views of the hills. The apartments, too, are delightful. Breakfast is served in the courtyard opposite the little chapel or in the hunting room. Across the road is the old coach house which has also been restored to its former glory and once again hosts weary travellers on the well-trodden route between San Gimignano and Certaldo.

rooms	11 + 2: 9 doubles, 2 triples. 2 apartments: 1 for 2, 1 for 3.
price	€92–€105. Triples €120–€135.
meals	Dinner with wine, from €30.
closed	Rarely.
directions	From S. Gimignano for Certaldo. Casale del Cotone 3km on left.

It is said that if you walk thrice around the well in the Piazza della Cisterna you will ensure your safe return to San Gimignano.

Signor Alessandro Martelli

tel	+39 0577 943236
fax	+39 0577 943236
e-mail	info@casaledelcotone.com
web	www.casaledelcotone.com

B&B & Self-catering

Fattoria Guicciardini

Viale Garibaldi 2/A, Piazza S. Agostino 2, 53037 San Gimignano

A visit to San Gimignano is a must; a stay here is even better. These simple but comfortable self-catering apartments in the centre have been immaculately converted from a 15th-century complex of farm buildings. Two were granaries in a former life (their snug bedrooms on a mezzanine floor), another was the farm cook's house. Some have huge raftered ceilings, others arched windows or original fireplaces and tiles; all have been furnished in a contemporary style with new sofas, kilim-style rugs, white curtains and the occasional antique. There are entrances from both outside the city walls and from the Piazza S. Agostino (and do sneak a look at the church's altar frescoes by Benozzo Gozzoli.) Get up early and watch the mists fall away to reveal the vineyards all around, then drink in the astonishing art of San Gimignano before the army of tourists descends. Evening in the city is magical, too, when the city's fairytale towers are floodlit. This is the time of day at which San Gimignano – honey pot of Tuscan tourism – is at its most lovely.

rooms	8 apartments: 5 for 2-4, 3 for 4-6.
price	€ 114-€ 140; € 684-€ 840 per week.
meals	Self-catering.
closed	Rarely.
directions	Leave Florence-Siena m'way at S. Gimignano & Poggibonsi Nord exit. Fattoria in centre of S.Gimignano.

	Signor Tuccio Guicciardini
tel	+39 0577 907185
fax	+39 0577 907185
e-mail	info@guicciardini.com
web	www.guicciardini.com

'The man that wishes to have a tranquil mind, must learn to endure Fortune in both her aspects, that is, both when she frowns and when she smiles.' Francesco Guicciardini

Self-catering

map 8   entry 160

Antico Borgo Poggiarello

Strada di San Monti 12, Monteriggioni

The 17th-century farm buildings in the woods – the *borgo* – have been transformed into holiday homes and linked by a circuit of well-considered paths. Poggiarello is a family set-up: Signora Giove does the cooking, and is happy, son Roberto does front of house and is even happier – he once worked in a tax office and has no regrets! Nino, Paolo and Duke – the perfectly behaved English setter – are there when you need them. You can self-cater or do B&B here: arrangements are flexible. Most apartments are for two; some interconnect and are ideal for eight. Rooms are big and comfortable with brand-new wrought-iron beds, cream curtains and covers, new tiles; all have private patios and great views. Two are excellent for wheelchair-users. Days are spent lolling by the pool, evenings sunset-gazing on the terrace. Though the treasures of Siena, Monteriggioni, Volterra lie a short drive away, it's hard to leave... there's a beautifully-lit bath housed in a cave that's heated all year to 38 degrees, and a dear little restaurant where you can sample the best of Tuscan home cooking.

rooms	2 + 12: 2 suites. 12 apartments: 8 for 2-4, 3 for 4-6, 1 for 6-8.
price	€98–€147. Self-catering €682–€1,727 per week.
meals	Dinner, 6 courses, €23.
closed	November.
directions	From Florence-Siena m'way exit Monteriggioni. Right after stop sign, 1.4km, left for Abbadia a Isola & Stove. After 6km, left for Scorgiano. On for 4km, left at 'Fattoria di Scorgiano'. Left on track after 2km.

Dante in his Divine Comedy describes the nearby fortress at Monteriggioni. It was formerly a Ghibelline outpost built by the Sienese in the early 13th century.

Roberto Giove

tel	+39 0577 301003
fax	+39 0577 301003
e-mail	info@poggiarello.com
web	www.poggiarello.com

B&B & Self-catering

Podere il Sasso - Rosae Villa

Loc. Fabbricciano 50, 53034 Colle di Val d'Elsa

A real Tuscan kitchen, with dried herbs hanging from the beams and dressers painted with fruit and flowers. Anna makes much of her guests, spoiling them with silver cutlery, crystal and fine linen. She's energetic, full of fun and a great cook; though she doesn't speak English, she has a daughter close by who does. This is a real family home, full of photos and ornaments, surrounded by olive trees, orchards and garden. There are lemon trees in big terracotta pots, patios to sit out on and plenty of trees for shade. A black cockerel and his harem peck contentedly around. The house is 16th century in origin, with attractive, flexible accommodation, full of the scent of fresh flowers and lavender. The smaller apartment, in a separate little building, has a tiny kitchen with an exposed rock wall and a woodburning stove; the larger one – in the house but with its own entrance – has a living area with wide brick arches, terracotta floor and an open fireplace. (The bedrooms in either can also be let on their own.) From the bedroom in the house you can glimpse the extraordinary towers of San Gimignano. *Minimum two nights.*

rooms	4 doubles (can be 2 apartments).
price	€ 88; € 700 per week.
meals	Choice of restaurants nearby.
closed	November.
directions	A1 exit Firenze & Certosa; superstrada Firenze/Siena, exit Colle di Val d'Elsa. Follow signs for centre; go to Piazza Arnolfo & call, Anna will come & meet you in 5 minutes.

Colle di val d'Elsa is famous as Italy's most important area for crystal production.

	Anna Piccolo
tel	+39 0577 920377
fax	+39 0577 920674
e-mail	info@rosaevilla.it
web	www.rosaevilla.it

B&B & Self-catering

map 8   entry 162

Locanda 'Le Piazze'

Loc. Le Piazze, 53032 Castellina in Chianti

The road appears to descend into vast and empty space, taking you perilously far from certainty... but you are rewarded with an oasis of luxury, and vast views. Here are an old farmhouse and outbuildings impeccably restored. Bedrooms are all different, each with something special: beautifully raftered ceilings, spotless terracotta floors, furnishings by Ralph Lauren. Most are of average size and some are huge, with their own terraces and jacuzzi baths; all the bathrooms encourage pampering. If you are a work junkie, there are fax and secretarial services available, too. Big Tuscan fireplaces, lavender-fringed terraces, a fine swimming pool with uninterrupted views, books to devour, quiet corners and, everywhere, much unselfconscious good taste. The restaurant is in a beautiful, modern conservatory. It is the best kind of hotel, and is overseen with crisp efficiency by Signora Maureen Skelly Bonini. Not for those looking for chaotic family fun, maybe, but perfect if you seek a dash of luxury far from the tanning crowds.

Look out for the lovely vaulted street in Castellina in Chianti called, appropriately, the 'Via delle Volte'.

rooms	20 doubles.
price	€ 155–€ 280.
meals	Dinner € 37.
closed	November–Easter.
directions	South on Firenze-Siena m'way take exit Poggibonsi south. Under bridge, left at r'bout, right over bridge to 2nd r'bout. Follow SP130 Strada di Castagnoli to Locanda, sign on right.

Signora Maureen Skelly Bonini

tel	+39 0577 743190
fax	+39 0577 743191
e-mail	lepiazze@chiantinet.it
web	www.chiantinet.it/lepiazze

Hotel

Palazzo Leopoldo

Via Roma 33, Radda, 53017 Radda in Chianti

In one corner of the hall there's a stone carving of a swaddled baby — evidence of a hospital here in the 1300s. For the last few centuries, though, this has been a manor house, standing bang in the middle of the medieval town of Radda. It's surprisingly peaceful (handy, too — you can walk to all the *enotecas* to taste the finest vintages of Chianti without having to worry about driving back!). The whole house has a delightful atmosphere. The hall is light, with white-painted arches, an old tiled floor, the occasional bright rug, lots of fresh flowers. Walk onto the terrace, where Vittorio offers welcoming drinks, and gaze over the rolling Chianti hills. The bedrooms range from suites to apartments in the eaves but all are generously-sized and equipped. Some once housed royal guests and many still have the old bell-pulls for service. There are original stoves and frescoes, too, and even the old, pitted glass in some windows. The owner has tried to preserve as much as possible. Breakfast is in the remarkable 18th-century kitchen, which still has its old range, and there are a number of good restaurants in town.

rooms	17: 12 doubles, 5 suites.
price	€160–€220. Suites €220–€490.
meals	Restaurant next door; choice in Radda.
closed	January & February.
directions	Signs in centre of Radda in Chianti.

	Vittorio Trevisan
tel	+39 0577 735605
fax	+39 0577 738031
e-mail	leopoldo@chiantinet.it
web	www.palazzoleopoldo.it

It may dream a little less, it may be less rumbustious now. But were the old ghosts to return, they would not feel out of place.'
Raymond Flower, *Chianti, 1978*

Hotel

map 8   entry 164

La Locanda

Loc. Montanino, 53017 Radda in Chianti

Admire the view from the pool – both are stunning. This is a magical place – a soft green lawn edged with Mediterranean shrubs slopes down to the pool, a covered terrace overlooks medieval Volpaia. (Some of the best Chianti is produced here, and the village is a 20-minute walk.) The house vibrates with bold colours and lively fabrics. The beautiful raftered living room, with open fireplace, big, stylish sofas and pale terracotta floor, reveals photos of Guido and Martina, he from the South, she from the North. They scoured Tuscany before they found their perfect inn, renovated these two houses and filled them with fine antiques, delightful prints, candles and fun touches, like the straw hats in the entrance hall. There's a library/bar where you can choose books from many languages and where Guido is generous with the grappa. The bedrooms are in a separate building and have big beds, great bathrooms and whitewashed rafters, as was the custom here. Martina cooks and gardens while Guido acts as host – they are a charming pair. Once settled in you'll find it hard to stir.

Visit the Castello Brolio, down the S484 towards Siena; owned by the Ricasoli family since the 11th century – the view from the walls is breathtaking.

rooms	7: 3 doubles, 3 twins, 1 suite.
price	€180–€235. Suite €250. Singles €165–€215.
meals	Dinner €30, book ahead.
closed	Mid-November–mid-March.
directions	From Volpaia village square take narrow road to right which becomes track. On for 2km past small sign for La Locanda to left; 1km further to group of houses.

Guido & Martina Bevilacqua

tel	+39 0577 738833
fax	+39 0577 739263
e-mail	info@lalocanda.it
web	www.lalocanda.it

Inn

Locanda del Mulino

Loc. Mulino delle Bagnaie, 53013 Gaiole in Chianti

A comfortable bed in the Tuscan hills, where only bird ballad disturbs the peace. Il Mulino is in such a prime position that even the nuns at nearby San Giusto were once involved in a wrangle about the place. You are in a beautiful, lush valley with tracks down to the river, and a five-minute walk to waterfalls and little pools: sheer delight for children, provided you watch little ones as the water in parts is quite deep. Hospitable Giorgio and gentle Grazia share a passion for good food and wine, and both are excellent cooks. They originally ran Il Mulino as a restaurant, and its popularity made the addition of rooms merely a matter of time. The old waterwheel and granite millstone are still in place in the cosy room where you breakfast, and the sensitive restoration of the guest rooms in an outbuilding (less ancient than the mill) follows a simple Tuscan style. Dinner is served on the terrace in warm months, and there is a large, shaded and slightly unkempt garden, onto which some of the bedrooms have a little door. Delicious food, delightful hosts and a big welcome for your dog.

rooms	5 doubles.
price	€ 67. Singles € 41.
meals	Dinner in restaurant from € 18, book ahead.
closed	November-February.
directions	On SS408 halfway between Gaiole & Siena, 1km from Pianella. Sign for Locanda at milestone 11.

Badia a Coltibuono once contained a prosperous abbey, the buildings of which are still there, though mostly used as a farm.

	Signor Giorgio Ceccarelli
tel	+39 0577 747103
fax	+39 0577 747614
e-mail	locandamulino@tin.it
web	www.locandadelmulino.it

B&B

map 9   entry 166

L'Ultimo Mulino

Loc. La Ripresa di Vistarenni, 53013 Gaiole in Chianti

The sense of space is stunning – the vast, medieval hall, lofty ceilings, stone walls, flights of stairs... Original arches give glimpses of passageways beyond and many of the rooms are connected by little 'bridges' from which you can see the millstream far below. Outside there's a big terrace and, next to it, a small, restored amphitheatre where concerts are held from time to time. But it all feels friendly and relaxed, too. You're surrounded by trees and it's immensely quiet – just the sound of water and birds. Everywhere smells fresh and clean, welcoming and lived in – and nothing is too much trouble for the staff. The mill was in ruins when the owners started to rebuild and they've done a terrific job. Sparsely, elegantly and comfortably furnished, the great hall makes a cool, beautiful centrepiece to the building; there's a snug with a fireplace, too, where you can roast chestnuts in season. Excellently equipped bedrooms have terracotta tiled floors and good, generously sized beds. You dine in the conservatory, overlooking the stream, on mainly Tuscan dishes, tempted by truffles and local delicacies.

rooms	13: 12 doubles, 1 suite.
price	€ 175–€ 232. Suite € 230–€ 284.
meals	Dinner € 35.
closed	November-March.
directions	From Gaiole in Chianti 1st right on road to Radda. Mill on right after bend.

'Truffles are... treasures to unearth with ritual respect and to cherish... like fine gems.' Burton Anderson Pleasures of the Italian Table

Lorenza Padoan

tel	+39 0577 738520
fax	+39 0577 7386590
e-mail	hotelmulino@chiantinet.it
web	www.ultimomulino.it

Hotel

Hotel Villa la Grotta

Brolio, 53013 Gaiole in Chianti

There are plenty of treats in store. The first, glimpsed on your way in, is the marvellous Castello di Brolio. The second is Villa la Grotta, part of the castle's 4000-acre estate. Originally a ninth-century manor house and later a nunnery, it has been restored and converted into a delightful small hotel by its Swiss owner, Philipp. (He also plays the clarinet and is part of a quartet which often meets at the Villa.) A bottle of wine will be waiting to welcome you to a cool, inviting bedroom, with pastel walls, soft lighting and colourful kilim rugs on terracotta-tiled floors. Most have a four-poster bed. Doogie runs the hotel with great panache; her sense of fun and dynamism give it a friendly, lively atmosphere. You're pampered, too: there's a Turkish bath, a small spa for therapeutic treatment and two pools – the outdoor one with pillars sculpted by a local artist. But, if you're a foodie, perhaps the biggest treat of all is chef Giovanni Mariani's exquisite food, cooked to perfection and served with superb wines in the stylish dining room. Giovanni has a huge following and people flock from as far as Florence.

rooms	12: 10 doubles, 2 suites.
price	€ 230–€ 270. Suite € 310–€ 325.
meals	Dinner € 30–€ 35.
closed	January-February.
directions	From Gaiole to Castello di Brolio; left of castle for Castelnuovo Berardenga, signs 1km, hotel on right.

	Doogie Morley–Bodle
tel	+39 0577 747125
fax	+39 0577 747145
e-mail	info@hotelvillalagrotta.it
web	www.hotelvillalagrotta.it

'In the midst of a thick forest, there was a castle
that gave shelter to all travellers
overtaken by night on their journey.'
Italo Calvino, *The Castle.*

Hotel

map 9   entry 168

Borgo Argenina

Loc. Argenina, S.M. Monti, 53013 Gaiole in Chianti

Weeds smothered the stone walls and there was no running water or electricity: the tiny hamlet had been abandoned for 20 years when Elena bought it. Much hard labour has gone into restoration and the results show all the creativity you'd expect from a former fashion designer. Elena's artistry is apparent everywhere, from patchwork tablecloths to delicately stencilled arches and ceilings – exquisite. Rooms are scented with lavender, sage and roses, bedrooms have quilts and cushions made from fabrics found in antique markets, furniture is hand-painted by Elena in soft Tuscan colours. In the pretty breakfast room, old grilled doors open on to a bright garden. The house and villa, set slightly apart, are equally refreshing, full of imaginative detail, and have plenty of privacy; you may prepare your own meals if you wish. Elena is a most engaging hostess and she and her daughter Fiorenza look after you wonderfully well; if you're a castle enthusiast, she'll draw you a map of all the castles in the area (and there are many!). An enchanting place, hidden well away from the rest of Chianti. *Minimum three nights.*

rooms	6 + 3: 4 doubles, 2 suites. 2 houses for 2-3, 1 villa for 4.
price	€ 130. Suites € 160. House € 180-€ 200. Villa € 400-€ 450.
meals	Osteria del Castello is nearby.
closed	October-March.
directions	From Gaiole towards Siena follow signs for San Marcellino Monte. Left to Argenina.

There are many castles in this area – the nearby privately owned Meleto Castle is a fine example of a quadrangular medieval castle, with round towers at the corners.

Elena Nappa
tel	+39 0577 747117
fax	+39 0577 747228
e-mail	borgoargenina@libero.it
web	www.borgoargenina.it

B&B

Borgo Casa Al Vento

Loc. Casa al Vento, 53013 Gaiole in Chianti

Comfortable *agriturismo* in green Chianti; the approach to the hamlet down the long, sandy track is stunning. Proceed to your airy rooms and prepare to unwind in this marvellously peaceful rural retreat, surrounded by wooded hills, tree-fringed lake, olives and vineyards. The property is made up of a clutch of ancient buildings, medieval in origin, that were given a complete makeover some years ago. Exposed beams, stone walls and red-tiled floors create a rustic mood, while the décor, though not the most stylish we have ever seen – dralon and velour are not in short supply – is as neat as a new pin and as comfortable as can be. Each apartment is different, some have patios and all are a short walk from the lake with geese and ducks. The B&B rooms are in two separate houses and share a beamy lounge. The cellar restaurant is jolly with red tablecloths; pizzas are baked in a wood-fired oven. Come for the gardens and terraces, mini-playground and pretty pool – and Giuseppe, ever helpful and charming. A grand spot for families.

rooms	4 + 9: 3 doubles, 1 suite, 9 apartments.
price	€ 135. Suite € 150. Apartments € 542–€ 1,600 per week.
meals	Breakfast € 8. Dinner € 25, book ahead.
closed	Rarely.
directions	Exit A1 at Valdarno. Follow signs for Siena & Gaiole in Chianti, about 20km. At Gaiole, signs to Casa al Vento, about 3km.

	Signor Giuseppe Gioffreda
tel	+39 0577 749068
fax	+39 0226 40754
e-mail	info@borgocasaalvento.com
web	www.borgocasaalvento.com

The village of Montevarchi has a lively market, selling Arno valley chickens and Arentino wine.

B&B & Self-catering

map 9   entry 170

Casali della Aiola

53010 Vagliagli

Around you are the vineyards of Aiola; across the road, a house that pulsates with history. The Florentines battered it into submission in the 1550s and a Renaissance villa arose from the ashes, still with the moat (now empty) and drawbridge. One day, perhaps, Enrico will let you sleep in the great villa; meanwhile you will have to content yourself – and this is not difficult – with Tuscan-style bedrooms in a converted farm building across the road. Dark beams and stone and whitewashed walls offset lovely wrought-iron beds and elegant antiques, softly lit. There is an unusual sitting/reading room in another barn, and a breakfast room with separate tables and white tablecloths. This is a refined, exceptionally tranquil retreat, and the peace is as deep as the countryside. An evening glass of wine (there's an honesty bar) by the sitting room window-with-views is something to remember. Come in early October and help with the wine harvest; return in mid-November and you can whack the olive trees to help produce the extra virgin olive oil. If that's not enough, there's smiling Enrico to take you on guided minibus tours of the area.

rooms	8: 6 doubles, 1 twin, 1 suite for 4.
price	€93. Singles €83. Suite €119 for 2, €139 for 4.
meals	Good restaurant & wine bar, 1km.
closed	Rarely.
directions	Leave Siena S222 for Castellina, just outside Siena right SP102 to Vagliagli. Aiola estate 1km past Vagliagli.

Autumn is the season of the 'vendemmia', the grape harvest, and the best time to appreciate that quality of light for which Tuscany is so praised.

	Enrico & Federica Campelli
tel	+39 0577 322797
fax	+39 0577 322509
e-mail	casali_aiola@hotmail.com
web	www.aiola.net

B&B

Frances' Lodge

Strada di Valdipugna 2, 53100 Siena

You stay in a hilltop orangery, minutes from the centre of the city – catch your breath at views that soar across olive, lemon and quince groves to the Torre del Mangia of Siena. The old farmhouse was bought by Franca's family as a summer retreat. Now she and Franco – warm, charming, intelligent – have filled the lofty, light-filled *limonaia* with beautiful things: an oriental carpet, a butter-yellow leather sofa, vibrant art by Franca. Guests may use this lovely room until 8.30pm. A glass partition traced with a lemon tree leads to the kitchen, Franca's domain, and breakfasts at the long table – or on the loggia in summer – are to linger over: Tuscan salami and pecorino, fresh figs, delicious coffee. Bedrooms burst with personality and colour – one, warm, cosy and Moroccan, another huge, white and cream, with terrace. There's chic coloured linen on the beds, murals on the walls, a fridge stocked with juice and water, towels for the pool. And what a pool – it lies in the listed rose- and lemon-fragrant gardens, filled with views. A special place with a big heart. *Minimum two nights.*

rooms	4: 3 doubles; 1 suite with living/dining room & kitchenette.
price	€ 150–€ 180. Suite € 200.
meals	Wide choice of restaurants nearby, 2km.
closed	10 January–10 February.
directions	From Tangenziale Firenze-Siena towards Arezzo until exit Siena 'Est' until 'Due Ponti'; take road to S. Regina, 1st right Strada di ValdiPugna; signs on right.

tel	+39 0577 281061
fax	+39 0577 222224
e-mail	info@franceslodge.it
web	www.franceslodge.it

'There is a subtle, exquisite scent of lemon flowers. Then I notice a citron. He hangs heavy and bloated upon so small a tree, that he seems a dark green enormity,'
D.H. Lawrence, *The Lemon Gardens*

B&B

map 8   entry 172

La Grotta di Montecchino

Via Grossetana 87, S. Andrea a Montecchino, 53010 Costalpino

A fantastic position, high on a hill five kilometres above Siena, with views over olive groves, cornfields and sunflowers. You can see Siena in the distance – but why base yourself in the city when you can escape here? La Grotta is a 25-acre organic farm producing wine, olive oil and corn. The owners, both dentists, are frustrated farmers and stay here as often as they can, in their own quarters 400m away. Guests have a lovely old farm building converted into holiday lets. Each one, although simple, is roomy with some special touches: stencil decorations, woodburning stoves for the colder months, the odd antique. Some of the furniture is makeshift and the lighting barely enough to read by, but this is a superb place for families: there's a big pool surrounded by jolly parasols and plastic loungers, a football pitch and masses of open space. There's also a new and characterful little restaurant in the old cellar; Simonetta loves baking and makes spectacularly good tarts. You won't be short of things to do: cookery classes here, wine-tastings nearby, and history and culture in Siena, a bus ride away.

Go into Siena if only to see one thing: the carved marble pulpit in the Duomo, made in 1265-8 by Nicola Pisano, depicting scenes from the life of Christ.

rooms	6 apartments for 2-4.
price	€ 300-€ 450 for 2, per week; € 400-€ 620 for 4, per week.
meals	Self-catering or restaurant in hotel.
closed	15-30 November.
directions	From Siena, SS73 to Roccastrada. At Costalpino towards S. Rocco a Pilli & Grosseto. At S. Andrea, 'Montecchio' signposted right. Follow farm track, 1km to farmhouse.

Dottor Agostino Pecciarini

tel	+39 0577 394250
fax	+39 0577 394256
e-mail	info@montecchino.it
web	www.montecchino.it

Self-catering

Villa Fiorita
Viale Cavour 75, 53100 Siena

Wafts of nostalgia drift elegantly through this roomy villa on the northern side of Siena (Palio fans may note it's in the district of the porcupine). Furnished in the Liberty style, all the rage in Italy during the early 20th century, it has enough distinction to attract the attention of Florence's architecture students. Time stands still: very little has been added to or altered over the years. Enter via the elegant, marble-floored hall, waft up the wide wooden stair to the rooms. Antiques and conversation pieces (an old washstand here, a sewing machine there) grace polished parquet floors; big chandeliers add a touch of class. Each room is named after flowers and marked with a prettily painted ceramic tile. There's plenty of public space for relaxing, reminding you of a more leisured era. It is very much a period piece, with bags of atmosphere and a lovely feel – a truly relaxing place to stay. Breakfast is served either in your bedroom or in the pretty little town garden.

rooms	7 doubles/twins.
price	€55–€80, single occ. €45–€65.
meals	Breakfast €6. Restaurants nearby.
closed	Christmas.
directions	Exit Firenze–Siena motorway at Siena Nord; right for 'Centro'. At r'about, far left exit on V. Florentina. At 3rd traffic lights right; right again for rear entrance. Metered parking.

	Mario Fontani
tel	+39 0577 44877
fax	+39 0577 237392
e-mail	info@miniresidencevillafiorita.it
web	www.miniresidencevillafiorita.it

In Rumer Godden's, The battle of the Villa Fiorita, *persistent English children persuade their mother against starting a new life with her Italian lover.*

B&B

map 8   entry 174

Il Colombaio

Podere Il Colombaio 12 , Torri, 53010 Sovicille

As soon as you walk in you see that creative minds have been at work. Barbara is Venetian and a ceramicist and her work is everywhere, though she spends more time these days looking after her young son and their guests. Daniele – his 'art name' is Antar – painted and made the furniture. The whole place is a sort of live-in art gallery, and the old bones of the house, the knotted timbers, pitted stone steps and well-trodden tiles, seem to take a tolerant view. Bedrooms are named after the pictures which adorn them: the Lover's Room is perhaps the nicest, with its old tiled floor and rafters, four-poster bed, figurative canvas on the wall and leafy views through ancient glass. Walls are distressed orange or yellow, ceramic figures dot the garden, one stair is red. Though somewhat frayed around the edges, the old house is perfectly clean and tidy. The land around is forested, terraced and olive-groved to the hilt, and belonged once to the monastery at Torri. A good base for sociable, arty types, with some great walks and bike trails. Barbara holds pottery classes here, too.

To the west are the Metallifere hills, strange countryside full of hot jet streams and copper mines. The monastery at Torri has a superb cloister.

rooms	6 doubles/triples, all with separate bath.
price	€ 87–€ 92, triples € 107–€ 115, single occ. € 77–€ 82.
meals	Local restaurant & pizzeria 1–3km.
closed	Rarely.
directions	From Siena SS223 for Grosseto. 12km on, right for Rosia. Left for Torri at junction with 2 tall cypresses. Follow avenue, just before end take 1st left unpaved road. Il Colombaio signed after 20m.

Daniele Buraggi & Barbara Viale

tel	+39 0577 344027
fax	+39 0577 344027
e-mail	ilcolombaio@tin.it
web	www.toscanaholiday.com

B&B

Podere Belcaro

Tenuta di San Fabiano, 53014 Monteroni d'Arbia

A simple Tuscan farmhouse, beautifully faded, Belcaro is on the Fiorentini estate, a working farm of some 1,500 acres. Simon, who lives in the restored barn, will take care of you – you could not have a nicer host. This is a wonderful, big, generous house that has barely changed over the years. The open-plan kitchen leads into a living room dominated by a fireplace; a narrow stone stair winds up to bedrooms on the first floor. All are big – as are the five bathrooms (one en suite). Artistic touches include the lightly colour-washed walls and a number of old wall hangings and fabrics – the work of Count Fiorentini's daughter and her husband, Simon's brother. The lovely big garden has plenty of places in which to wine and dine, including a covered *loggia*; there's a barbecue, too, and a pool from which you can spot the medieval towers of Siena. A restored stable block provides another double bedroom, bathroom and kitchen/living area – put the two together and you have a house party of 14. There's masses to see and do, including art classes, in English, right next door.

rooms	1 apartment for 2. 1 house for 14.
price	Apartment € 150 per night. House € 3000–€ 3750 per week, excl. heating.
meals	Self-catering. Breakfast, lunch or dinner on request, book ahead.
closed	Rarely.
directions	From SS2 left at Monteroni d'Arbia for Asciano; 400m, under bypass & over bridge. Entrance at sharp bend. Left 200m after wire fence, before trees. Follow drive to end.

The road from Siena to Asciano passes through the strange landscape of the 'Crete Senese', sometimes called the Tuscan desert.

	Simon Mennell
tel	+39 0577 373206
fax	+39 0577 373206
e-mail	popsanoodle@hotmail.com

Self-catering & B&B

map 8   entry 176

Azienda Agricola Casabianca Srl
Loc. Casabianca, 53041 Asciano

A medieval hamlet on top of a hill, meticulously restored. Although in theory this is a farm, it has really more the feel of a country estate. Signora Alba Ines Calusi has seen to all the detail. The padronal villa with its tiny chapel standing alongside now contains a four-star hotel, where terracotta-tiled bedrooms are grand with elaborate ceilings, rich drapes and chandeliers. Some even carry the original 18th-century wall decoration. The surrounding stables and barns have been made into 20 self-contained, individually furnished apartments, nicely rustic with white walls, old beams and chunky terracotta. This is a perfect set-up for families and for those who like to mix. Each has its own little garden, many have balconies or terraces and stupendous views that reach over the forested estate to the Atlantic. There are wonderful walks in the surrounding countryside, bikes to explore further afield, and you can meander down to the lake to fish, relax at the pool-side bar or hide away in the secluded cloister garden. The restaurant in the old wine cellars still has the original vats and press.

The abbey of Monte Oliveto Maggiore, nestling among cypress trees, has a cloister decorated with frescoes depicting the life of St Benedict.

rooms	9 + 20: 3 doubles, 6 suites. 20 apartments: 15 apartments for 2; 5 apartments for 4-6.
price	€ 163. Suites € 293-€ 353. Apartments € 922 for 2 per week, € 1356 for 4-6 per week.
meals	Breakfast € 12 for apartments. Dinner € 25-€ 55.
closed	7 January-April.
directions	From A1 exit 28 for Valdichiana towards Sinalunga & Asciano. After Asciano Casabianca 6km on left.

Signora Alba Ines Calusi

tel	+39 0577 704362
fax	+39 0577 704622
e-mail	casabianca@casabianca.it
web	www.casabianca.it

Hotel & Self-catering

Villa Poggiano
Via di Poggiano 7, 53045 Montepulciano

It's the gardens that capture the imagination here – six enchanting hectares of them. Two-hundred-year-old cypresses line the paths, a stone table in a secluded alcove overlooks a breathtaking view, flowers tumble out of stately pots on the terrace. The house and gardens once belonged to a German general and it was he who imported the larger-than-life stone statues, dating back to the 1900s, and built the memorable pool. Austerely beautiful, it is made of travertine stone, with more statues presiding over the patio and surrounding walls. There's a fountain, too, in what was once the children's pool. Stefania's family bought the place three years ago and it has taken them two years to restore it. Now immaculate, the villa is elegantly and traditionally furnished with antiques and old paintings. The suites are luxurious and the bathrooms sumptuous – they have space and marble in plenty, and pretty tiles from Capri. Two of the suites, just across from the villa, are independent. One has a terrace, the other a garden, and both have wonderful views to Monte Amiata and the Torre di Montichiello. *Minimum stay two nights.*

rooms	9: Villa: 1 double, 5 suites; Guesthouse: 2 doubles, 1 suite.
price	€ 180–€ 200. Suites € 230–€ 285.
meals	Good choice of restaurants nearby.
closed	December–March.
directions	From A1 exit Valdichiana for Montepulciano & Chiusi. After 5km left at lights in Torre di Siena for Montepulciano. On for 8km SS146 for Pienza. 2km further left at Relais Villa Poggiano. Left to Villa after 800m.

Montepulciano is the highest of the Tuscan hill towns (nearly 2,000 feet) and has an unusual array of Renaissance churches and palaces.

	Stefania Savini
tel	+39 0578 758292
fax	+39 0578 715635
e-mail	info@villapoggiano.com
web	www.villapoggiano.com

B&B

map 11   entry 178

Montorio

Strada per Pienza 2, 53045 Montepulciano

As you come up the drive, you will be stunned by the Temple of San Biagio. A Renaissance masterpiece designed by Antonio Sangallo the Elder, it makes an unforgettable backdrop to Montorio – the icing on the cake of the villa's superb position. It stands on top of its own little hill, 600m above sea level, overlooking a vast green swathe of Tuscany. The house, all warm stone walls and roofs on different levels, was once a *casa colonica*. It is now divided into five attractive apartments, each named after someone important (one being Sangallo), each with a well-equipped kitchen and an open fire. White walls, beams and terracotta floors set a tone of rural simplicity; antiques, paintings and wrought-iron lights made by Florentine craftsmen add a touch of style; leather chesterfields and big beds ensure comfort. The big terraced garden – full of ancient cypress trees, pots of flowers and alluring places to sit – drops gently down to olive groves and vineyards. Stefania's other villa, Poggiano, is 10 minutes away and historic Montepulciano, full of shops and eating places, is close enough to walk. *Minimum stay three nights.*

"They were among olives again, and the wood with its beauty and wildness had passed away.' E M Forster, *Where Angels Fear To Tread*

rooms	5 apartments: 3 for 2, 2 for 4.
price	For 2 €120–€180; €500–€1200 per week. For 4 €180–€250, €1,100–€1,700 per week.
meals	Self-catering.
closed	December-January.
directions	A1 exit Valdichiana for Montepulciano & Chiusi. In Torrita di Siena, left at lights to M. There, signs to Chianciano. Right at x-roads bilvio di S. Biagio.

Stefania Savini
tel +39 0578 717442
fax +39 0578 715456
e-mail info@montorio.com
web www.montorio.com

Self-catering

Le Radici Natura & Benessere

Loc. Palazzone, 53040 San Casciano dei Bagni

The densely wooded, unmade road that leads to Le Radici gives little away. It twists and curves and, just when you think you'll never make it, opens into a little oasis. Alfredo and Marcello's conversion of this solitary 15th-century stone farmhouse has been a labour of love; Alfredo scoured the antique markets and raided his stock of family heirlooms to furnish the rooms, and the decoration is 'elegant country'. Rooms are a good size, with delicately toned, hand-finished walls and colour from armchairs and kilims. Alfredo has been able to indulge his passion for cooking with the small restaurant they have created in the vaulted former pigsty, and makes good use of the rich array of ingredients which Tuscany can offer. The geraniums thrive in this microclimate and bloom even in November, tumbling down from large urns, window sills and balconies. A beautiful pool blends into the landscape, and a little winding footpath takes you up to the wooded crown of the hill where you can sit and enjoy the glorious views. *Minimum two nights.*

rooms	10 + 1: 7 doubles, 3 suites. 1 apartment for 2.
price	€ 120–€ 184. Suites € 172–€ 204.
meals	Lunch/dinner € 33, available on request.
closed	9 December-March.
directions	Exit A1 at Chiusi for S. Casciano & Palazzone. Left for Palazzone. Through village; track uphill past small church on right. Le Radici signed down narrow track to right.

The church of S. Maria Vecchia in Ficulle, just east of the A1, has a fine Gothic portal and some 15th-century frescoes.

	Alfredo Ferrari & Marcello Mancini
tel	+39 0578 56038
fax	+39 0578 56033
e-mail	leradici@leradici.it
web	www.leradici.it

B&B & Self-catering

map 11   entry 180

La Crocetta

Loc. La Crocetta, 53040 San Casciano dei Bagni

Inauspiciously sited in the middle of a housing estate, the 900 farmed acres nevertheless spill over with good things: cereals, wine, olive oil... the food here is fabulous. The large stone building dates from 1835, and was completely restored in 1993. Though next to a main road, it is shielded by oak trees and a large garden and feels wonderfully secluded. The interior is furnished with attractively colour-washed or stencilled walls and rush-seated chairs. Open fires add warmth in winter. Bedrooms are simple but cosy, with good modern shower rooms; some are country-Italian in style, others traditional-English, with floral fabrics and chintz. Cooking is a strong point – mouthwatering aromas drift in from the kitchen towards mealtimes and there's always a choice, including vegetarian. Cristina and Andrea are engaging hosts and conversation is easy; he's the cook, she does the interiors. There's a brand new pool, and it's no more than a five-minute walk to the spa in town. Note: anyone allergic to cats should be aware that there were 10 around at the last count! *Minimum stay three nights.*

Nearby, Castel Viscardo, as the name implies, has a grand 15th-century castle.

rooms	8: 4 doubles, 3 twins, 1 single.
price	€ 100. Singles € 54. Half-board € 75 p.p.
meals	Dinner available.
closed	Mid-November–March.
directions	Exit A1 motorway at Chiusi towards S. Casciano dei Bagni. In S. Casciano signs for La Crocetta.

Andrea & Cristina Leotti

tel	+39 0578 58360
fax	+39 0578 58353
e-mail	lacrocetta@ftbcc.it
web	www.agriturismolacrocetta.it

B&B

Hotel Terme San Filippo

Via San Filippo 23, 53020 Bagni San Filippo

Pope Pio II, who suffered from arthritis, came here in 1462. The Italians still adore hot thermal springs, and this place is one of the best, sited in the gorgeous Orcia valley. Slap on some mud, too – one of many beauty treatments. People come from all over to test for themselves the healing properties of what many believe to be miraculous minerals – don't be alarmed by the occasional wafts of sulphur. There's a pool heated to 40 degrees (phew!), a superb waterfall, cold showers, a garden with an avenue of trees and a second thermal pool, and the chance of a workout in the woods. And you are a five-minute walk to the extraordinary, calcareous Fosso Bianco. Bedrooms are comfortable, nothing fancy. Well-presented regional dishes are served in the yellow dining room; hand-written menus can be perused each morning. Walls have been faux-marbled "for fun", says Gabriella – she's a mine of information and as delightful as her team. The atmosphere is bustling yet relaxed, with everyone wandering around in towelled robes. A great place for a healthy, pampering weekend break. *Minimum stay two nights.*

rooms	27: 23 doubles, 4 singles.
price	€88–€108. Singles €52–€62. Half-board €57–€67 p.p. Full-board €64–€74 p.p.
meals	Lunch/dinner €18.
closed	January-Easter.
directions	From Siena SS2 for Rome, then to Bagni S. Filippo. Via S. Filippo is main road through village.

	Gabriella Contorni
tel	+39 0577 872982
fax	+39 0577 872684
e-mail	info@termesanfilippo.it
web	www.termesanfilippo.it

If you follow the Fosso Bianco through the woods you come to the extraordinary forms of calcifications, symptoms of this strange thermal landscape.

Hotel

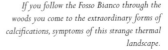

map 10   entry 182

Castello di Ripa d'Orcia

Via della Contea 1/16, 53027 Ripa d'Orcia

As you drive up the long, white road, the castle comes into view: a thrilling sight. Ripa d'Orcia dates from the 13th century, one of Siena's most important strongholds. The battlemented fortress (closed to the public) dominates the *borgo* encircled by small medieval dwellings. The family are descendants of the Piccolomini's who acquired the estate in 1484 and are hugely proud of their heritage; Signor Rossi runs it all with efficiency and charm. Let your mind wander – grand banquets and knights in shining armour will come to mind... children would love staying here. Rooms and apartments have huge raftered ceilings and are furnished simply and well; many have breathtaking views. There's also a day room, filled with lovely furniture and stacks of books for you to browse. You breakfast in a small annexe off the main restaurant, and there's a cellar that opened this year for wine-tastings. The area is a paradise for walkers and there is enough on the spot to keep lovers of history and architecture happy for hours – before the 'official' sightseeing begins. *Minimum stay two nights; one week in apartments.*

rooms	6 + 8: 6 twins/doubles. 8 apartments: 5 for 2, 3 for 4.
price	€ 110–€ 135. Singles € 89–€ 110. Apartments € 490–€ 575 for 2, € 649–€ 750 for 4, per week.
meals	Dinner à la carte. Closed Mondays.
closed	November–February.
directions	From SS2 for San Quirico d'Orcia; right over bridge. Follow road around town walls for 700m. Right again, signposted; 5.3km to Castello.

Pienza has a beautiful main square. You can walk along the town walls and enjoy the views over the Val d'Orcia.

Famiglia Aluffi Pentini Rossi
tel +39 0577 897376
fax +39 0577 898038
e-mail info@castelloripadorcia.com
web www.castelloripadorcia.com

B&B & Self-catering

La Locanda del Loggiato
Piazza del Moretto 30, 53027 Bagno Vignoni

You wouldn't know this existed. An inconspicuous door off the Piazza del Moretto leads to a delightful, unexpected room full of light, muted colours and fine furniture. Grandma's baby grand piano stands in one corner; she was obviously much loved for there are reminders of her everywhere. On one wall is the coat of arms, dated 1473, of the Chigi family – one of many discoveries made when this delectable house was renovated. A spiral staircase takes you up to a little, beamed mezzanine but the bedrooms all open off the main room. They are graceful and pretty, with big, antique beds, soft neutral fabrics and stencilled borders. Some look out to the square, others onto the old thermal bath – the house was once an inn for people who visited Bagno Vignoni for the *terme*. Breakfast is across the square and down a few steps to the little wine bar, Il Loggiato; a stable in the 14th century, then a refectory for the monks next door, it's a cool stone room with huge jars of mushrooms in oil and herbs, and olives bottled by Barbara and Sabrina. There are other good eating places in this tiny, beautiful village, too.

rooms	6: 1 double, 5 doubles/twins.
price	€ 130.
meals	Il Loggiato Wine Bar or other restaurants a few minutes away.
closed	Rarely.
directions	From North A1 exit Certosa. Superstrada for Firenze, exit Siena sud, take La Cassa for Roma. Through San Quirico D'Orcia, at crossroads to Bagno Vignoni; house in centre.

Barbara & Sabrina Marini

tel	+39 0577 888925
fax	+39 0577 888370
e-mail	locanda@loggiato.it
web	www.loggiato.it

The hot spring waters of Bagno Vignoni have been used in the treatment of arthritis and rheumatism since Roman times.

B&B

map 10   entry 184

www.thirdangle.com

umbria

Hotel Villa Ciconia

Via dei Tigli 69, Loc. Ciconia, 05019 Orvieto

A feeling of calm, refined elegance pervades this delightful small hotel – in the family for three generations. The elegant stone villa enjoys a fine position in one of Umbria's most beautiful hill towns, secreted away in its own park and gardens, with pool. It's hundreds of years old; staircases wind, cavernous rooms ramble and there's a fantastic feeling of space. The entrance is grand with tapestries and deep sofas, and two vast dining rooms occupy the rest of the ground floor; one has superb fireplace dating back to the 1400s (magically lit in winter) and a stunning wood-panelled ceiling and frieze. Breakfast is deluxe continental and dinner is superb, the regional food accompanied by the Petrangelis' own excellent wines. Service is attentive but discreet. Bedrooms are large – some huge – and quietly elegant, with lovely old floor tiles, white walls, a canopied wrought-iron bedstead here, a handsome old-fashioned wardrobe there, and jugs of fresh flowers. White bathrooms are functional; two have a jacuzzi bath. Such a warm, friendly, family-run hotel. We long to return.

The cathedral at Orvieto was described by Burckhardt as 'the greatest polychrome monument in the world'.

rooms	12: 10 doubles, 2 triples.
price	€ 130–€ 155. Singles € 108–€ 134.
meals	Lunch/dinner € 18.
closed	Rarely.
directions	Exit A1 at Orvieto. From roundabout SS71 for Arezzo. Villa Ciconia 1km on left.

Signor Valentino Petrangeli

tel	+39 0763 305582
fax	+39 0763 302077
e-mail	villaciconia@libero.it
web	www.bellaumbria.net/hotel-villaciconia

Hotel

Locanda Rosati
Loc. Buonviaggio 22, 05018 Orvieto

From the moment you turn off the road – whose proximity is quickly forgotten – the atmosphere is comfortable and relaxed. The house has been gently modernised but remains firmly a farmhouse; the summer-cool rooms on the ground floor – with open fires in winter – have been furnished with an eye for comfort rather than a desire to impress, and flowers, books and magazines are scattered everywhere. Dinner is the thing here; it's great fun and Giampiero and Paolo are natural hosts, full of stories and excellent advice on what to do and where to go. Tables are laid with simple cloths, glass tumblers and butter-coloured pottery, and the food is very good value. Bedrooms are simple, with pristine white bed linen and a splash of colour in the curtains. Much of the furniture comes from the famous Bottega di Michelangeli in Orvieto, whose rough-hewn pieces and jigsaw-like carved animal shapes characterise this region. The house is surrounded by gardens, from the highest point of which you can see the spiky skyline of Orvieto. A delightful place.

rooms	10: 4 doubles, 5 family, 1 single.
price	€103–€120. Singles €85–€100. Half-board available.
meals	Dinner €27.50.
closed	7 January-February.
directions	Exit A1 at Orvieto; for Viterbo, Bolsena & Montefiascone. After 10km Locanda on right.

	Signor Giampiero Rosati
tel	+39 0763 217314
fax	+39 0763 217314
e-mail	info@locandarosati.orvieto.tr.it
web	www.locandarosati.orvieto.tr.it

Maitani's reliefs on the façade of Orvieto Cathedral are the only rivals in Italian Renaissance art to Ghiberti's bronze doors in Florence.

Inn

map 11   entry 186

La Fontana

Strada di Palazzone 87, 05022 Amelia

Two golden retrievers, several cats and your English hostess, April, make these three small creeper-clad self-catering cottages feel like a home from home. An ideal hideaway for couples, they each fit at least two comfortably, each with its own private sitting and eating out area. Furnishings are an intriguing, jostling mix of styles, as are the pictures, *objets* and masses of books, many in English. One cottage, Limonaia, has both open fireplace and central heating: a winter break here would be extremely cosy. Set in seven acres of hillside, below the ancient town of Amelia, the mature garden flows through a small orchard and to olive groves beyond. The water, from a private source and pure enough to be bottled and sold, is yours for free, so there is no need to lug plastic bottles from the supermarket. April lives in the main house, and will leave you to your own devices; however, she is ready and only too willing to be of help. Ask her for advice on places to visit (here or, equally, in Rome – she lived there for 30 years) and where to shop and eat out. *Minimum stay one week.*

rooms	3 cottages: 2 for 2, 1 for 2–3.
price	€ 450–€ 550 per week.
meals	Self-catering.
closed	Rarely.
directions	Exit A1 for Orte; follow Terni; exit Amelia. In front of main walls follow Giove to 1st intersection. Left & immed. right. 1st left to Strada di Palazzone.

Amelia, one of the oldest towns in Italy, was founded by obscure Pelasgian tribes, precursors of the Etruscans.

April Davis
tel +39 0744 983465
e-mail aprilkathleen.davis@tin.it

Self-catering

Cesa Leonica

Via Cappuccini 36, 05022 Amelia

Daniela brought up her family here and it is a very good place for young children. The house is peaceful and secluded, standing in 10 hectares of woodland, olive trees and vines, with only the sound of birds to disturb you. There are lots of forest tracks and nature trails to explore and the lively, pretty town of Amelia is a short drive away. The pleasant, refreshingly ungroomed garden has an attractive swimming pool surrounded by shrubs and trees, and if the sun gets too hot, there's a covered terrace to retreat to. Step inside and back to your childhood, maybe... to bedrooms with floral wallpapers, candlewick bedspreads and antique pieces; immaculate, old-fashioned bathrooms; a gentle yellow sitting room and a spotless, blue-and-white tiled kitchen without microwave or dishwasher! It's comfortable, unpretentious and homely. Daniela lives here for three-quarters of the year and leaves everything as it is for her guests. When it's let, she has her own small apartment with a separate entrance, so she's on the spot. She is charming and full of energy – as is her amiable golden retriever, Johnny. *Minimum stay one week.*

rooms	Sleeps 6: 2 doubles, 2 singles.
price	€ 1,134–€ 1,340 per week.
meals	Self-catering.
closed	October–May.
directions	From Amelia for Orvieto. 1km over bridge, sign on right for Cappuccini; over small bridge & up hill. After 3km, Cesa Leonica sign on right. Follow through woods, 1km.

	Daniela Delille
tel	+39 0744 988274
fax	+39 0744 988274

Though Cato states that Amelia was founded in 1134 BC, recent archaeological findings suggest a much earlier date.

Self-catering

måp 11 entry 188

Antica Dimora alla Rocca
Piazza Rocca, 26039 Trevi

Perched at the top of the medieval hill town of Trevi, this is the only palazzo in Umbria that has become a hotel. Built in 1650, it was the family home of the Valenti. (Ask Livio Bordoni, the manager, about its intriguing history: he cares passionately about the place – and the town – and is hugely knowledgeable.) Four years were spent restoring the building before the hotel could open in 2002, and the work has been beautifully done. Original frescoes on the first floor represent the seasons, though Winter is unaccountably missing (perhaps theft, perhaps wishful thinking). The magnificent bedrooms have exquisitely painted wooden ceilings, rich fabrics and deliciously sybaritic bathrooms. Throughout, the interior is elegant and sophisticated – though not oppressively so: there's a lively, welcoming atmosphere and the staff are friendly and attentive. The vaulted dining room, once Trevi's olive press, has a glass viewing panel in the floor – gaze down on the press itself; the hooks in the ceiling were used for drying prosciutto. It's a memorable room to dine in and the food and wines are excellent.

rooms	34: 22 doubles, 2 suites. Annexe: 7 doubles, 3 suites for 2-4.
price	€ 104–€ 164. Annexe € 55–€ 80.
meals	Dinner from € 25, wine list.
closed	Monday.
directions	From Rome A1 for Orte, then Terni Spoleto-Trevi. At Foligno S3 to Trevi, signs.

The Trevi Flash Art Museum in the Palazzo Lucarini is a must for Modern Art enthusiasts.

	Livio Bordoni
tel	+39 074 238541
fax	+39 074 278925
e-mail	hotelallarocca@libero.it
web	www.hotelallarocca.it

Hotel

entry 189   map 11

Locanda di Colle dell'Oro
Strada di Palmetta 31, 05100 Terni

Candles flicker alongside the path, illuminating your way as you return from the garden restaurant. It's a thoughtful, imaginative touch, very much in keeping with the *locanda*'s ethos. Gioia delights in sharing her family's country home and takes quiet pleasure in watching guests unwind and relax – and you will, from the moment you step into the striking open-plan entrance hall and breathe in the heady scent of jasmine. Every corner of the restored 19th-century house is deliciously harmonious and calm. Large, lovely bedrooms, named after plants, have neutral colour schemes and bleached wooden furniture, hand-painted with flowers by Gioia. There are framed flower designs by her father, too. Sheets and towels are of the purest linen and the bathrooms are beautifully planned. The luxury is real and understated. French windows lead from the breakfast room to the terrace looking down over Terni. The garden is full of birdsong and geraniums, jasmine, roses and hydrangeas; a swimming pool is hidden on a lower terrace. Yoga classes happen three times a week, and cookery classes out of season. *Minimum stay two nights.*

rooms	12: 7 doubles, 4 triples, 1 suite.
price	€ 129. Triples € 159. Suites € 144.
meals	Dinner € 25.
closed	Rarely.
directions	From A1 exit 'Terni ovest'. Follow signs for Norcia Cascia until signs for Locanda.

	Gioia Iaculli
tel	+39 0744 432379
fax	+39 0744 437826
e-mail	locanda@colledelloro.it
web	www.colledelloro.it

Terni is on the confluence of the river Nera and Serra: the old name for the town was Interamna, meaning city between two rivers.

Inn

map 11   entry 190

Abbazia San Pietro in Valle

Via Case Sparse di Macenano 4, 05034 Ferentillo

Ancient, venerable, spectacular. Originally founded in the eighth century, the abbey sits tranquilly on the side of a wooded valley, well beyond reach of the industrial outskirts of Terni. The church is full of good things; look out for the lion rampant which you'll find carved on much of the abbey's furniture, the *stemma* of its first secular owners. These days Letizia Costanzi, daughter of the present owners, runs the place. Most of the plainly furnished rooms have views over the valley and nearly all open off a courtyard, so if it's raining you'll need an umbrella for that dash from room to reception or restaurant. The cloisters are lovely, the setting beautiful, and there are plenty of places where you can sit and watch the light changing round the towers and cypresses. Below is the river Nera, where in summer you can go rafting from Scheggino, and across the valley is the deserted village of Umbriano a Rocca di Protenzione, said to be the first human settlement in Umbria. You can truffle-hunt in autumn here (by request), then cook your spoils!

rooms	22: 19 doubles/twins, 3 suites.
price	€98–€125. Suites €130–€145.
meals	Restaurant à la carte, €30.
closed	3 November-March.
directions	A1 Florence-Rome exit Orte; SS206 to Terni. Exit for Terni East; take SS209 (Visso, Norcia, Cascia) after 20km follow sign to abbey.

The altar of the abbey's church, carved in lovely rose-coloured stone, is an important and rare example of Lombard sculpture.

Letizia & Chiara Costanzi

tel	+39 0744 780129
fax	+39 0744 435522
e-mail	abbazia@sanpietroinvalle.com
web	www.sanpietroinvalle.com

Hotel

La Fenice

Via dei Mercanti 26, Capitone, 05020 Narni

Deirdre is a vivacious English lady, who welcomes babies and children to her jewel of a village house. (Young families are usually accommodated on their own.) You can't miss the lovely pale peach façade and green shutters beside the church, and it is prettier still inside. Full of flowers and family photographs, books, toys, bits from India – the land of her birth – and the cat Chi Nu. Luxuriate in crisp, feminine bed linen, have a bottle of something well chilled brought to you on a private balcony, sip tea in bed in the morning. A hidden garden above the old village walls overlooks the countryside and sunsets. In the evening Deirdre will serve you her excellent home dishes – she once cooked professionally in Rome; discuss the menu over breakfast. If free, she will happily babysit should you want to go out, and even childmind during the day if she's not cooking your dinner that night. There's a maid who will wash and iron, and a library of English books and videos. The village is a delight. *Watch steep stairs with toddlers. Minimum three nights.*

rooms	3: 1 double. 1 double, 1 family sharing shower.
price	€ 60–€ 100. Rental of whole house € 1,000 for 8 per week.
meals	Dinner, 2 menus € 12–€ 28, on request.
closed	November-Easter.
directions	Exit Terni-Viterbo m'way at Narni Scalo for Capitone. There, follow one-way street to church. House beside bell tower.

	Signora Deirdre Galletti di Cadilhac
tel	+39 0744 730066
fax	+39 0744 730066
e-mail	deirdreg@tin.it
web	umbrianhols.interfree.it

Christian or New Age? The twelve-sided bell-tower of the 'Duomo' in Amelia may be a reference either to the Apostles or the signs of the Zodiac.

B&B & Self-catering

map 11   entry 192

Casa Regina

Via Regina Elena 22, 06010 Lippiano

Once there were three wealthy families in this medieval village. One built the castle, one the Villa Pia and one the 350-year-old Casa Regina. It was in the last – a sprawling, likeable village house – that Vincent settled when he left Scotland seven years ago. Lippiano is a quiet, sleepy village in the hills of the upper Tiber valley, surrounded by trees and a green and gold patchwork of fields. The air is deliciously pure and fresh and you can walk from the house into the woods and hills without meeting another soul. Vincent is a warm, friendly and unflappable host; his house is a relaxing and informal place to stay (and tremendously good value). A splendid stone staircase leads up to enormous bedrooms with vast, comfortable beds. The furniture – much antique – is on a grand scale, too, and each bedroom has an original old tiled floor, a wood-burning stove with a basket of chopped firewood and spectacular views. Immaculate white and terracotta-tiled shower rooms are bright and full of lovely white towels. Vincent organises cookery courses given by a neighbour – and stays to translate and wash up!

Piero della Francesca (1418-1492) lived and worked in San Sepolcro and his Madonna del Parto is in nearby Monterchi.

rooms	3: 2 doubles, 1 twin, sharing 2 showers.
price	€52–€58.
meals	Restaurant 5-minute drive.
closed	January-February.
directions	S221 for Arezzo as far as Monterchi. At entrance to Monterchi, left to Lippiano. Round side of castle, house no. 22 on right.

Vincent Baruffati
tel +39 075 8502126
e-mail vibaruf@tin.it

B&B

Pereto

Fraz. Carpini Sopra, 06014 Montone

All but hidden in the Carpina valley and surrounded by 900 hectares of private estate, these lovely buildings are far from any madding crowd yet only a couple of miles – and two possible fordings of the river – from the outside world. Televisions and telephones are delightfully absent – it's that sort of place. Sharing the same swathe of lawn as the *casa padronale*, where your delightful hosts live, these holiday homes are the quintessence of carefree country living. Generous, comfortable and stylish, each has a large fireplace and a free supply of wood for chilly days. In early May, when we visited, diaphanous curtains billowed at wide open windows and the sun beat down on the old terracotta roofs. Antique country furniture, painted wrought-iron beds, attractive rugs and prints combine harmoniously with bold coloured kitchen tiling and ancient rafters. Giulio has written a history of the della Porta family which has also been published in English: indispensable holiday reading, to be sure. A gem of a place.

rooms	2 apartments: 1 for 4, 1 for 6.
price	€ 450–€ 1,350 per week (Sat-Sat); weekends € 100–€ 125 per day. Maid service € 7 per hour.
meals	Restaurants nearby.
closed	Rarely.
directions	Exit E45 at Montone for Pietralunga. After 5km left to Pereto.

	Signor Giulio della Porta
tel	+39 075 9307009
fax	+39 075 9307009
e-mail	pereto@pereto.com
web	www.pereto.com

The church of San Francesco in Montone has a good collection of 15th-century paintings. Città di Castello has a festival of chamber music during August.

Self-catering

map 9   entry 194

Casale

S. Faustino, Montone, Pietralunga

Both house and setting are spectacular. Tim and Austin have a Special Place in the Yorkshire Dales; now, too, a house in the Umbrian hills. The old stones, tiles, rafters and shutters have been beautifully restored, giving you three cosy bedrooms, pristine bathrooms and a kitchen and living area worthy of an interiors' magazine. The country dining table seats eight, there are sofas and an open fire, a gleaming stainless steel oven, masses of workspace and a sink with a view. Preparing your *tartufi neri arrosto* – Umbrian black truffles wrapped in pancetta – or polenta cake stuffed with pine nuts and apples would be no hardship here. Nothing is busy or overdone, the views are amazing, and the saltwater pool, with terraces and wooden loungers, impossible to resist. You have Umbertide for provisions and hilltop Montone is a gem – narrow cobbled streets tumbling with geraniums, restaurants, bars and ancient-rampart views. For art and architecture there's Perugia, San Sepolcro, Cortona and Assisi, all under an hour's drive. And if you're more than eight, put your friends up at the *agriturismo* up the hill. *Minimum stay three nights.*

rooms	Sleeps 6: 3 doubles.
price	£140; £850–£1,800 per week.
meals	Self-catering.
closed	Rarely.
directions	From Carpini signs for Monte Valentino, right at third sign up to house.

Pietralunga was founded by ancient Umbrian peoples. This has been testified by the finding of an Etruscan flute made out of a human tibia, now in the Archaeological Museum of Perugia.

Austin Lynch & Tim Culkin
tel +44 (0)1748 823571
fax +44 (0)1748 850701
e-mail oztim@millgatehouse.demon.co.uk
web www.oztiminitaly.com

Self-catering

Le Cinciallegre
Fraz. Pisciano, 06020 Gubbio

This was once a tiny 13th-century hamlet on an ancient crossroads where local farmers met to buy and sell their produce. It's an incredibly peaceful spot, overlooking the valley, meadows and woods, and reached by a long, unmade road. Fabrizio used to be an architect and his conversion of these old houses has been inspired – it feels entirely authentic and delightful. In the cool, beamed living room, comfortable seats are gathered round a 200-year-old woodburning stove; there's a fine old dresser and lots of pleasantly rustic furniture. The simple, comfortable bedrooms, named after birds, have their own terrace areas and immaculate bathrooms. Cristina is a wonderful cook, serving real country foods and Umbrian wines. Afterwards, guests settle down to enjoy *rosolios* and *ratafias* (homemade liqueurs). Fabrizio and Cristina are warm, hospitable, interesting people, passionate about the environment, and their lovely, natural garden and the 10 hectares of land are full of wildlife. Fabrizio will be happy to tell you about some super walks – indeed, he'll be disappointed if you don't have time to explore.

rooms	8: 4 doubles, 2 triples, 1 family, 1 single.
price	€90. Half-board €60–€70 p.p.
meals	Half-board available.
closed	January-February.
directions	A1 exit Val di Chiana for Perugia & follow E45 to Cesena. Exit Umbertide Gubbio. Follow 219 for Gubbio. Signposted from Mocaiana.

Fabrizio & Cristina De Robertis

tel	+39 075 9255957
fax	+39 075 9255957
e-mail	cince@lecinciallegre.it
web	www.lecinciallegre.it

Just across the valley is the closed convent of Monastero di Betlemme.

B&B

map 9   entry 196

Locanda del Gallo

Loc. Santa Cristina, 06020 Gubbio

A restful, almost spiritual calm emanates from this wonderful home. In a medieval hamlet, the *locanda* has all the beams and antique tiles you could wish for. Light, airy rooms with pale limewashed walls are a perfect foil for the exquisite reclaimed doors and carved hardwood furniture from Bali and Indonesia; your charming hosts have picked up some fabulous pieces from far-flung places, and have given the house a colonial feel. Each bedroom is different, one almond with Italian country furniture, another white, with wicker armchairs and Provencale prints; some have carved four-poster beds. Bathrooms are gorgeous, with deep baths and walk-in, glass-doored showers. A stunning veranda wraps itself around the house: doze off in a wicker armchair, sip a drink at dusk as the sun melts into the valley. The pool is spectacular, like a mirage clinging to the side of the hill. Jimmy the cook conjures up food rich in genuine flavours, with aromatic herbs and vegetables from the garden; he and his wife are part of the extended family. As guests you will be made to feel every bit as much at home.

Gubbio is one of the most secluded and beautiful towns in Umbria. Look out for the gaunt 14th-century 'Palazzo dei Consoli'.

rooms	9: 6 doubles, 3 suites for 4.
price	€ 102-€ 112. Suites € 184-€ 204. Half-board € 70-€ 75 p.p.
meals	Dinner available on half-board basis € 22.
closed	December-March.
directions	Exit E45 at Ponte Pattoli for Casa del Diavolo; for S Cristina 8km. 1st left 100m after La Dolce Vita restaurant, continue to Locanda.

Signora Paola Moro

tel	+39 075 9229912
fax	+39 075 9229912
e-mail	info@locandadelgallo.it
web	www.locandadelgallo.it

Inn

Prato di Sotto

Santa Giuliana, 06015 Pietrantonio

The visitors' book glows with accounts of all too brief stays; some have called Prato di Sotto "heaven on earth". Penny and Harry have nurtured the hilltop farmhouse and its outbuildings resplendently back to life – French beams were imported for the ceilings, the doors leading to the library come from a monastery, some fireplaces are Sicilian. Sri Lankan armchairs live harmoniously alongside antique mirrors, deep sofas, cushions, kilims and deliciously comfortable beds, and no expense has been spared in the kitchens, designed with serious cooking in mind – one of Penny's passions. Casa Antica is deeply luxurious with many bedrooms and bathrooms, dining terrace and upstairs balcony/terrace with stupendous views; La Terrazza has a large terrace draped in wisteria and white roses; the ancient olive mill is a romantic studio with a huge veranda; the cottage, too, has a vibrant terrace and a glorious view. Borrow a labrador for your rambles across the hills, swim here, sail on Lake Trasimeno. Penny and Harry care for you as family friends and bring you fresh-laid eggs for breakfast.

rooms	Sleeps up to 16: 2 for 2, 1 for 4, 1 for 8.
price	Apartments € 655–€ 2,500 per week. Shorter breaks possible.
meals	Self-catering. Breakfast & dinner by arrangement.
closed	Rarely.
directions	Exit N3 (s) at Badia Monte Corona. Under bridge, left at junc. 3km after Badia left onto track. Follow for 4km veering left near S. Giuliana; 1st house on right. Phone to be met.

Santa Giuliana (St Juliana) was born in Florence in 1270. She formed a community of sisters in 1304 called the 'Mantellati'.

Penny & Harry Brazier
tel   +39 075 9417383
fax   +39 075 9412473
e-mail   pennyradford@libero.it
web   www.umbriaholidays.com

Self-catering

map 9   entry 198

Casa San Martino

San Martino 19, 06060 Lisciano Niccone

Perhaps this is the answer if you are finding it hard to choose between Tuscany and Umbria – a 250-year-old farmhouse that sits on the border. Sit with a glass of wine in your Umbrian garden, watch the sun set over the Tuscan hills. The lovely, rambling house is alive with Lois's personality and interests: she's a remarkable lady who has lived in Italy for many years and is a fluent linguist. Her big kitchen is very well equipped – Lois will find you a cook, if you like to be totally indulged – but has an air of charming, ordered chaos. An arch at one end leads to a comfortable family room, a door at the other to a pretty veranda with a stone barbecue. Up the narrow staircase is a large, light sitting room with flowery sofas, masses of books and an open fireplace, perfect for roasting chestnuts. The whitewashed bedrooms and bathrooms are cosy and attractive. Lois is there when you need her, and lives in the most stunningly converted pigsty next door! The big garden with its dreamy pool looks across the Niccone valley and there are a couple of villages with shops close by. *Central heating. Min. three nights. Self-catering May-Oct; B&B Nov-April.*

In 217BC Hannibal massacred the Roman army at nearby Tuoro. Ask Lois about The Hannibal tours.

rooms	4: 1 double, 1 twin; 1 double, 1 twin sharing bath.
price	€ 140. Whole house rental € 2,500-€ 3,000 per week.
meals	Dinner 4-5 courses with wine, € 30. Restaurants 3km.
closed	Rarely.
directions	A1 exit Valdichiana. Then 75 bis for Perugia, then for Tuoro & for Lisciano Niccone.

	Lois Martin
tel	+39 075 844 288
fax	+39 075 844 422
e-mail	casasm@tuscanyvacation.com
web	www.tuscanyvacation.com

Self-catering & B&B

Castello di Montegualandro

Montegualandro 1, 06069 Tuoro sul Trasimeno

The castle, perched on one of the highest hills overlooking Lake Trasimeno, feels ancient and remote, yet the 21st century lies minutes down the hill. What we see now was begun in the ninth century, and its first known owner was Charlemagne: the castle was a mini-estate then, with its own penal system and dungeons. It is a privilege to stay in such a unique place, and a pleasure too: the apartments are comfortable and your hosts attentive and delightful. (Do accept their offer to collect you from Tuoro when you first arrive: this is not an easy place to find.) Rooms in the apartments, once simple dwellings, are not large but they are peaceful and stylish, with whitewashed walls, stone or brick floors, beams, open fires and country antiques. Two have extra beds on a mezzanine reached by a stepladder – not ideal for the young or infirm. All have small kitchens with a well-stocked fridge and a complimentary bottle of the estate's own – exceptional – olive oil. You are well placed for Perugia, Assisi and Florence, and tempting food markets and restaurants are a 10-minute drive. *Minimum stay three nights.*

rooms	4 apartments: 3 for 3, 1 for 4.
price	€550–€660 per week.
meals	Self-catering. Wide range of restaurants 5km.
closed	Rarely.
directions	Exit Bettolle-Perugia m'way at Tuoro. Right for town, then left for Arezzo. After 2.2km right at *Vino Olio* sign, on to *castello*. Right before 'strada della caccia' sign, on to iron gate.

An enjoyable day trip is to Isola Maggiore on the lake. The Sauro, in the via Guglielmi, is a delightful restaurant serving mainly fresh fish dishes.

	Claudio & Franca Marti
tel	+39 075 8230267
fax	+39 075 8230267
e-mail	montegualandro@iol.it

Self-catering

map 9   entry 200

La Casa Colonica

Loc. Vernazzano, 06069 Tuoro sul Trasimeno

Stefania really seems to enjoy having families to stay here and it's certainly a super place for children. As well as the full-size pool, set in a long avenue of trees, there's a small round one for the very young to splash in, and a wonderful play area. Not to mention a shed full of mountain bikes for guests to use whenever they like... The closely-clustered buildings which make up La Casa Colonica are old and dignified. Beautifully restored, with mellow stone walls and faded terracotta roofs, they're surrounded by lush lawns and 20 hectares of olive trees and vines. (The estate's wines and olive oils can be bought at a small shop on the complex.) The attractive, well-equipped apartments come in a variety of sizes and room combinations. What they all have in common is plenty of space and country charm – whitewashed walls, massive golden beams and polished wooden or tiled floors with pretty rugs. The bathrooms and kitchens are good, too, but for those wanting a break from cooking, there's a restaurant serving good value local cuisine. Stefania is friendly, full of energy and always around to help or advise.

rooms	9 apartments for 2–6.
price	€ 400–€ 800 per week.
meals	Pizzeria 1km.
closed	Rarely.
directions	From A1 exit Valdichiana; superstrada Siena-Perugia for Perugia exit Tuoro sul Trasimeno. Signs for Passignano; 1km, signs for Vernazzano & La Casa Colonica.

'Not bound to swear allegiance to any master,
wherever the wind takes me, I travel as a visitor.'
Horace (65-8BC), Epistles, Bk 1.

Stefania Mezzetti

tel	+39 0575 674 51
fax	+39 0575 679 798
e-mail	smezzet@tin.it
web	www.lacasacolonica.com

Self-catering

Villa Giulia

Loc. Caselle 1, Borghetto di Tuoro, 06069 Tuoro sul Trasimeno

The gorgeous views from the house reappear as wall paintings in the beamed bedrooms – a hilltop castle, local scenes, the lake itself... Villa Giulia is at the foot of Mount Qualandro, surrounded by olive groves and looking out over the blue reaches of Lake Trasimeno. A small road runs in front of the house and the rose-filled garden has a delicious pool and – tucked discreetly away – a play area for children. Originally an 18th-century olive mill, the villa has been beautifully restored. In the main house, the ground floor is taken up by a farmhouse kitchen and a big uncluttered dining and living area. A sofabed here and another in the little reading room upstairs means there is scope to sleep an extra four. The two bedrooms on the first floor can also be reached by an outside staircase, and there are two more in the attic – one with a canopy bed and an antique writing desk. On each of the three floors is a bath/shower room, each a delight. The smaller villa is equally pleasing with simple, country-style interiors. Though the two are only let together during high season, they may be rented separately at other times of the year.

rooms	2 villas: 1 for 2, 1 for 8.
price	€ 1,500–€ 3,000 for 8 per week.
meals	Pizzeria within walking distance.
closed	Rarely.
directions	From North motorway A1 exit Valdichiana Bettole; highway Siena-Perugia for Perugia, exit Tuoro sul Trasimeno. Signposted after 1km.

	Stefania Mezzetti
tel	+39 0575 674 51
fax	+39 0575 679 798
e-mail	info@villa-giulia.it
web	www.villa-giulia.it

'Fortunate, too, is the man who has come to know the gods of the countryside.'
Virgil *(70-19 BC)*

Self-catering

map 9   entry 202

Villa Rosa

Voc. Docciolano 9, Montemelino, 06060 Magione

A beautifully restored farmhouse looking out over fields and farms to the villages of Solomeo and Corciano, with Perugia in the distance. Distant church bells, the hum of a tractor, the bray of a donkey… yet you are five kilometres from the superstrada. You couldn't find a better spot from which to discover Tuscany and Umbria. Megan (who is Australian) and Lino are the nicest of hosts, and will help you enjoy every aspect of your stay: hunt for truffles – or cashmere, in Solomeo! – have fun on a cookery class with a chef from Perugia. Megan and Lino used to dabble in antiques and the house is dotted with them, some inherited, some acquired; the B&B bedrooms, private and self-contained, are charming. For a family, the two-storey *casetta* at the end of the garden is perfect – a delightful mix of recycled beams and terracotta tiles, with brand-new dishwasher, air conditioning and jacuzzi. The flat on the ground floor of the farmhouse is similarly stunning. Breakfasts, served when you wish, are abundant and delicious, there's a saltwater pool to cool you down, and the views from every window are wonderful.

In 217 BC the Romans suffered one of their worst defeats on the shores of Lake Trasimeno, lured into a masterful ambush by the Carthaginian general, Hannibal.

rooms	2 + 2: 1 double, 1 twin. 1 cottage for 5; 1 flat for 2-4.
price	€80. Singles €45. Half-board from €60 p.p. Cottage €500–€900 per week. Flat €400–€600.
meals	Dinner with wine, from €20.
closed	Rarely.
directions	Exit Perugia-Bettolle at Corciano, for Castelvieto through village (via underpass & bridge) to shrine. Left & on to 2nd shrine; right uphill. House after a couple of bends.

	Megan & Lino Rialti
tel	+39 075 841814
fax	+39 075 841814
e-mail	meglino@libero.it

B&B & Self-catering

Villa Tre Archi

Strada Vicinale delle Spinale 6, 06077 Ponte Felcino

When they'd finished renovating the lovely Corbine di Sotto (entry 207), Frederik and Wendy found another challenge. Just down the valley was Villa Tre Archi, built in 1768 and slowly, sadly, crumbling away. No longer: they've restored it to all – and more – of its former glory. Décor and furnishing show assurance and style; the overall result is a big, gracious, comfortable house with real designer flair. It's in a fine position, too, with great views of distant mountains – Umbrian and Tuscan – and a garden (and super pool) to make the most of them. Recessed terraces either side of the house offer shade to the scorched and the inside of the house is cool and inviting. The walls are mellow stone and plaster, the floors terracotta and the ceilings beamed. Light, airy bedrooms have open fireplaces, comfortable beds and pretty blue and white bathrooms. The kitchen, with a superb long farmhouse table, is state-of-the-art and fantastically well equipped. Nothing has been forgotten. It's a house easily capable of absorbing a lot of people but, if all this space isn't enough, there is an extra apartment in the outbuildings as well.

rooms	Sleeps 10-12: 5 doubles. Also annexe for 2.
price	€ 2,750–€ 4,750 per week.
meals	Self-catering.
closed	Never.
directions	From Bologna A14 for Ancona, exit Cesena Nord; E45 exit Ponte Pattoli, through village & left for Ponte Felcino. Right on Strada Vicinale Dello Spinale, right through gates.

	Frederik & Wendy Meijer
tel	+39 075 5913060
fax	+39 075 5914182
e-mail	wenfri@libero.it
web	www.villatrearchi.com

Perugino was born in Città della Pieve. His Saint Augustin Polyptych (1470) is in the Galleria Nazionale dell'Umbria in Perugia.

Self-catering

map 9   entry 204

Castello dell'Oscano
Strada della Forcella 37, 06010 Cenerente

At the turn of the century Count Telfner visited England and was so taken by the opulent intimacy of its grand country houses that he couldn't wait to get back and do up his own place. Hence Oscano today – a glorious, lovable parody of England. There is a grand, balustraded central staircase (suitably creaky), huge landscapes on most of the walls, a grand piano in the drawing room and a proper library – for afternoon tea. The sitting room would not be out of place in Kent. Maurizio has nurtured the house almost since its rebirth as a hotel. He returned from Belgium with a *trompe l'œil*, commissioned ceramics from Deruta, and stocked the cellars with the best Umbrian wines. Bedrooms have a faded baronial elegance, somewhat in the National Trust spirit: they have floral wallpapers, period furnishings and large windows which look over the garden and park. Bathrooms are big and modern. The rooms in the Villa Ada, though less stylish, could be described as 'well-appointed', and hugely comfortable. The whole experience is of comfort, unpretentious refinement, and utter peace. The food is excellent, to boot.

rooms	30 + 13: 20 doubles, 10 suites. 13 apartments for 2-5.
price	€ 150–€ 230. Suites € 290–€ 310. Apartments € 325–€ 775 per week.
meals	Dinner € 35.
closed	Rarely.
directions	Exit E45 Perugia Madonna; from Perugia for San Marco. Take small road for Cenerente. Signposted.

The old centre of Perugia is centred on the Corso Vannucci, named after the local artist Piero Vannucci, better known as Perugino.

	Michele Ravano & Maurizio Bussolati
tel	+39 075 584371
fax	+39 075 690666
e-mail	info@oscano.com
web	www.oscano.com

Hotel & Self-catering

Castello di Petroia

Scritto di Gubbio, 06020 Perugia

Brave the loops of the Gubbio-Assisi road and arrive at the castle at dusk – you could be in a Gothic thriller. The front gate is locked, you ring to be let in; an eerie silence, then the gates creak open. Inside, lights are dim, furnishing austere. However, come morning, you will appreciate the stone-walled, vast-fireplaced magnificence of the place. With a full house, dinner is a sociable affair, graciously presided over – when he's at home – by the owner, Conte Carlo Sagrini. It takes place in one of two grand dining rooms and is rounded off by the house speciality, a liqueur made by Carlo's wife. Then up the stairs (some steep) to bed. Rooms have tiled floors, dark old furniture, flowery beds. A feeling of feudalism remains – this is a place where four staff serve 12 guests – and the landscape is similarly ancient. The castle is set on rising ground in beautiful, unpopulated countryside, with a marked footpath, the Sentiero Francescana della Pace, running through it: walk to Assisi – it takes a day – then taxi back. There's plenty of walking on the 900-acre estate, too. Beyond, endless, undulating hills fading into the Apennines.

rooms	6: 2 doubles, 4 suites (1 in tower).
price	€ 105–€ 125. Suites € 140–€ 180.
meals	Dinner with wine € 28–€ 34.
closed	January–March.
directions	S298 from Gubbio south for Assisi & Perugia. After Scritto, just before Biscina & Fratticiola, take stoney road signed to Castello.

	Conte Carlo Sagrini
tel	+39 075 920287
fax	+39 075 920108
web	www.castellodipetroia.com

Piero della Francesca's portrait of Federico, Duke of Montefeltro (who was born here) has one of the most famous noses in art history.

Hotel

map 9   entry 206

Corbine di Sotto

Strada Vicinale delle Spinale 6, 06077 Ponte Felcino

Mellow stone buildings cluster round a courtyard, overlooked by a handful of tall cypresses, enveloped by wooded hills. It's a entrancing place. Twelfth century in origin, it has been restored by Frederik and Wendy using local craftsmen and materials – they've done a wonderful job. Soft curves and arches, beams and old-style plastering give the apartments their restful, traditional character. Natural colours, flagged or terracotta floors, beautiful understated furniture and secluded terraces suggest a great sense of style and space. Each apartment is extremely well equipped and has an excellent kitchen – though, if you fancy a night off, catering can be arranged. Frederik has a good wine cellar, too, which he is proud of, and will happily organise wine-tasting evenings with fellow enthusiasts. The swimming pools are super: you can splash indoors under high, attractive brick arches or outside, surrounded by lavender. The imaginatively terraced gardens are as inspired as the interiors, with stone walls and huge terracotta urns, olive trees and pines. Come in early summer and you'll see the hillside above scarlet with poppies.

rooms	3 apartments: 1 for 2, 1 for 4, 1 for 6.
price	€750–€1,950 per week.
meals	Self-catering.
closed	15 October-15 March.
directions	From Bologna A14 for Ancona, exit Cesena Nord; E45 exit Ponte Pattoli, through village left for Ponte Felcino. Right on Strada Vicinale delle Spinale, right through gates.

Perugia, one of the 12 cities of Etruria,
surrendered to Rome in 309 BC.

Frederik & Wendy Meijer

tel	+39 075 5913060
fax	+39 075 5914182
e-mail	wenfri@libero.it
web	www.corbinedisotto.com

Self-catering

Brigolante Guest Apartments

Via Costa di Trex 31, 06081 Assisi

In the foothills of St Francis's beloved Mount Subasio, the 16th-century stone farmhouse has been thoughtfully restored by Stefano and Rebecca. She is American and came to Italy to study, he is an architectural land surveyor – here was the perfect project. The apartments feel very private but you can always chat over an *aperitivo* with the other guests in the garden. Rooms are light, airy and delightful, full of Grandmother's furniture and Rebecca's kind touches: a welcome basket of goodies from the farm (wine, eggs, cheese, honey, olive oil, homemade jam), handmade soap and sprigs of lavender by the bath. Pretty lace curtains flutter at the window, kitchens are well-equipped, and laundry facilities are available on request. This is a farm with animals, so ham, salami and sausages are produced as well as wine. Feel free to pluck whatever you like from the vegetable garden – red peppers, fat tomatoes, huge lettuces. A lovely, peaceful place for families and walkers; you are deep in the Mount Subasio National Park and there are dozens of trails to explore. *Minimum two nights.*

rooms	3 apartments: 1 for 2; 2 for 2-4.
price	€255-€440 per week. Shorter stays possible low-season.
meals	Self-catering.
closed	Rarely.
directions	Assisi ring road to Porta Perlici, then towards Gualdo Tadino, 6km. Right on gravel road signed Brigolante. Over 1st bridge, right, over 2nd narrow bridge, up hill 500m, right at 1st gravel road.

	Signora Rebecca Winke Bagnoli
tel	+39 075 802250
fax	+39 075 802250
e-mail	info@brigolante.com
web	www.brigolante.com

Augustus Hare describes the hermitage on Mount Subasio where St Francis retired to 'combat with his passions' as occupying the most picturesque position in the gorge.

Self-catering

map 11   entry 208

Hotel Le Silve

Loc. Armenzano, 06081 Assisi

Everything about Le Silve is gorgeous and the setting, deep in the heart of the Umbrian hills, takes your breath away. (It is so remote, in fact, that you should fill up with petrol before leaving Spello or Assisi.) The ancient, medieval buildings have been beautifully restored and the whole place breathes an air of tranquillity. Superb, generous-sized bedrooms are in the main building and in the annexe; they have stone walls, exquisite terracotta floors, beautiful furniture, old mirrors and (a rarity, this!) proper reading lights. Bathrooms with walk-in showers are similarly rustic with terracotta floors and delicious pampering extras. We loved the restaurant, too – it is intimate and inviting both indoors and out, and on summer nights you dine by candlelight under a huge canopy. Food is wonderful, mostly organic; the bread is homemade, the cheeses, hams and salami are delectable. There's tennis and table-tennis, a pool with a bar, a hydromassage and a sauna and hectares of hills and woods in which to walk or ride or walk. Such a happy, friendly place, and very popular – make sure you book well in advance.

rooms	15 doubles.
price	€83–€91. Half-board €112–€120 p.p.
meals	Dinner €30, on request.
closed	November-March.
directions	From Milan A1 exit Valdichiana for Perugia, then Assisi. Signs for Gualdo Tadino then Armenzano, km8, signs for hotel, 2km.

Cimabue's simple painting of St Francis (c.1228) captures the humility of the saint around whom the spiritual metropolis of Assisi was built.

	Signora Daniela Taddia
tel	+39 075 8019000
fax	+39 075 8019005
e-mail	hotellesilve@tin.it
web	www.lesilve.it

Hotel

Hotel Palazzo Bocci
Via Cavour 17, 06038 Spello

A beautiful townhouse in Spello's cobbled centre, whose pale yellow façade, with dove-grey shutters and little wooden door, barely hints at the grandeur inside. Enter a tranquil courtyard with a tiny, trickling fountain; then through to a series of glorious reception rooms, most with painted friezes. The most impressive is the richly-decorated drawing room, the *sala degli affreschi*; there is also a reading room filled with old books and travel magazines. The whole building is multi-levelled and fascinating with its alcoves, nooks and crannies. Guest bedrooms are immaculate, with serene cream walls, polished chestnut beams, big comfortable beds, simple drapes. The suites have frescoed ceilings, the bathrooms are a delight. Delicious breakfasts are served on the herringbone-tiled terrace in warm weather; it overlooks Spello's ancient rooftops and makes an exquisite spot for a sundowner. Step across the cobbled entrance to the restaurant, Il Molino – once the village olive mill – and dine under an ancient, brick-vaulted ceiling. A charming, quietly luxurious country hotel.

rooms	23: 15 doubles, 2 singles, 6 suites.
price	€ 130–€ 150. Singles € 70–€ 90. Suites € 180–€ 250.
meals	Lunch & dinner at 'Il Molino' restaurant, approx. € 30.
closed	Rarely.
directions	From Assisi for Foligno. After 10km, leave main road at Spello. Hotel opp. Church of Sant'Andrea in town centre. Private parking.

The frescoes in the palace are by Benevenuto Crispoldi. The restaurant (opposite) is much earlier (1300), and is built on the site of an olive press.

	Signor Fabrizio Buono
tel	+39 0742 301021
fax	+39 0742 301464
e-mail	bocci@bcsnet.it
web	www.palazzobocci.com

Hotel

map 11   entry 210

Villa Aureli

Via Luigi Cirenei 70, 06071 Castel del Piano

D rive up the avenue of ancient limes, imagine you have arrived by carriage. Little has changed since the Villa first became the country house of the Serègo Alighieri family in the 18th century, and the ornamental plasterwork, furniture and paintings remain largely intact. The house has its origins in the 16th century, and the grounds are suitably formal, overgrown here, tamed there, with lemon trees in amazing 18th-century pots and a swimming pool created from an irrigation tank. The apartments are big and beautiful. Floors have mellow old tiles, ceilings are high and raftered, and some are intricately panelled. Bedrooms are delightfully faded, one with an exquisite painted ceiling, aqua-blue bedsteads, raspberry covers and an antique painted wardrobe. The long drawing room in the centrally-heated upstairs apartment (available all year) has unusual yellow-panelled shutters, echoing the pattern of the terracotta floor. You are on the edge of the village, so can walk to the few shops and bar. A quietly impressive retreat – though not ideal for young children – and wonderfully peaceful.

rooms	2 apartments: 1 for 4, 1 for 4+2.
price	€950–€1,200 per week.
meals	Self-catering. Dinner in garden €36, on request.
closed	Rarely.
directions	From A1, exit Valdichiana for Perugia, exit Madonna Alta towards Città della Pieve. At square signs for Bagnaia. Villa on left after 200m.

The name 'di Serègo Alighieri' is of course well known through this family's famous ancestor, Dante. See also entry 35.

Flavia di Serègo Alighieri
tel   +39 075 5159186
fax   +39 075 5149408
e-mail   villa.aureli@libero.it

Self-catering

Villa di Monte Solare

Via Montali 7, Colle San Paolo, 06070 Fontignano

A hushed, stylish, country retreat in a perfect Umbrian setting. This noble villa, encircled by a formal walled garden and orangery, has been transformed into a small hotel with uniformed staff, elegant rooms and fine restaurant. The grounds, which include the little chapel of Santa Lucia, two pools, a tennis court and a small maze, envelop the hotel in an atmosphere of calm. The public rooms retain much of their original charm, with painted cornices and friezes, huge fireplaces, ancient terracotta floors, superb paintings and antiques; the sitting room has an exquisite, white-painted ceiling. The restaurant, a gorgeous beamed room with a roaring fire in winter, seats bedroom capacity, so non-residents may only book a table if guests are dining out. The mood is stylish and refined (jackets are usually worn, but not insisted upon, at dinner), and matched by the food and wines on offer; the cellar contains over 120 local wines. Drinks are sipped on the terrace, and there is a look-out point on the top floor with books and games for children. The view stretches out in all directions.

rooms	28: 21 doubles, 7 suites.
price	€ 148–€ 190. Suites € 182–€ 216.
meals	Lunch € 15-26. Dinner € 35-45.
closed	Rarely.
directions	Exit A1 at Chiusi-Chianciano. Right to Chiusi, then right for Città della Pieve. Through town, wall on right. Left for Perugia-Tavernelle (SS220). 1km after Tavernelle, left for Colle S. Paolo. Straight on 4km to villa.

	Rosemarie & Filippo Iannarone
tel	+39 075 832376
fax	+39 075 8355462
e-mail	info@villamontesolare.it
web	www.villamontesolare.it

Monte Solare, rising above Lake Trasimeno, has been associated from ancient times with Apollo, the sun god.

Hotel

map 11   entry 212

The Country House Montali

Via Montali 23, 06068 Tavernelle di Panicale

It's an irresistible combination – a gorgeous place *and* superb vegetarian food. Alberto's expertise in restoring historic buildings and his desire to give vegetarians something more inspired than brown rice have resulted in the creation of Montali. It stands on a plateau surrounded by woodland and reached by a long, bumpy track. From the gardens you can walk straight over the hills or down to Lake Trasimeno – spectacular. The guest rooms, in three separate, single-storey buildings, have verandas, wide views and a pleasantly colonial air. White walls show off hand-carved teak furniture and oil paintings by Alberto's talented brother; terracotta floors are strewn with Indian rugs. And not a TV in sight. As for the food – it's exquisite. Served with good local wines in the serene little restaurant, it's mainly mediterranean, with touches of nouvelle and haute cuisine. Malu, Alberto's wife, is the head chef and Montali is fast making an international name for itself. (Cookery courses available on request.) Alberto and Malu are both delightful; they are also keen musicians and sometimes organise evening concerts.

rooms	10 doubles.
price	Half-board only € 170–€ 200.
meals	Half-board.
closed	Rarely.
directions	A1 from Rome, exit Fabro, for Tavernelle. 2km after Tavernelle, left for 'Colle San Paolo'. Up hill 7km, following signs. Left at top of hill, hotel 800m on left.

The 16th-century church of San Gervasio in Città della Pieve is built on the site of a 4th-century Christian church and has some beautiful Renaissance paintings.

	Alberto Musacchio
tel	+39 075 8350680
fax	+39 075 8350144
e-mail	montali@montalionline.com
web	www.montalionline.com

Hotel

Madonna delle Grazie

Agriturismo Madonna delle Grazie 6, 06062 Città della Pieve

Children who love animals will be in heaven. Renato will pluck a cicada from an olive tree and show them how it 'sings'; they can pet the rabbits, dogs – even ducks and chickens – to their hearts' content. There's are horses here, too. This is a real farm, not a hotel with a few animals wandering around, so don't expect luxury; it's *agriturismo* at its best and you eat what they produce. The simple guest bedrooms in the 18th-century farmhouse are engagingly old-fashioned; all have their own terraces or balcony; bathrooms are spotless. The farm is now fully organic, and the the food in the restaurant delicious: make the most of Renato's own salami, chicken, fruit and vegetables, olive oil, grappa and wine. As if the animals weren't enough, there's also a big playground for children, and table-football in the house. Your youngest offspring, still free from the tyranny of taste, will adore the Disney gnomes incongruously dotted around the picnic area. For the grown-ups there's riding, archery, a discount at the San Casciano Terme spa... and views that stretch to Tuscany in one direction, Umbria in the other. A great little place.

rooms	7 doubles, 1 with balcony.
price	€ 104–€ 124.
meals	Dinner, € 25–€ 30.
closed	Rarely.
directions	From A1 exit Chiusi south for Città della Pieve. Just outside town, right for Ponticelli; downhill for 1km. House on left.

	Signor Renato Nannotti
tel	+39 0578 299822
fax	+39 0578 299822
e–mail	madgrazie@ftbcc.it
web	www.madonnadellegrazie.it

Città della Pieve is the birthplace of Perugino (1446-1523) and several local churches, including the 'Duomo', contain paintings by him.

Hotel

map 11   entry 214

Fattoria di Vibio

Loc. Doglio, 06057 Montecastello Vibio

Get away from it all at this farmhouse in a magical setting – you feel miles from anywhere. The collection of well-restored and equipped buildings is more 'residential complex' than *agriturismo*: there is a definite sense of the countryside being kept at a distance, with outside lighting and occasional late-night muzak doing their best to keep rude nature at bay! Bedrooms are comfortable, some of them really big, with room for additional beds, if needed, and superb views. There is a delightfully cosy sitting room with chunky beams, big lamps and open fire. You are promised some exceptional walking: ask to borrow one of the large-scale maps of the area, book a picnic and discover the virtually uninhabited valleys and hills. The brothers produce organic olive oil, honey and fruit which you can buy; their mother, Signora Moscati, runs cookery courses (take her cookbook *Entriamo in Cucina* away with you for inspiration at home). Limited English is reluctantly spoken, so translators are brought in for the courses and other themed happenings. *Minimum stay two nights, or one week in August.*

rooms	13 + 2: 13 doubles/twins. 2 apartments: 1 for 4-5, 1 for 6.
price	€90–€160. Apartment €800–€1,800 per week.
meals	Restaurant à la carte.
closed	10 January-28 February.
directions	From Florence Exit A1 at Orvieto. SS448 for Todi. Left for Prodo-Quadro (SS79); signposted.

Montecastello di Vibio has a tiny theatre, built by nine local families in 1808, which seats 99 and is purported to be the smallest in the world.

Filippo & Giuseppe Saladini
tel	+39 075 8749607
fax	+39 075 8780014
e-mail	info@fattoriadivibio.com
web	www.fattoriadivibio.com

Self-catering & B&B

entry 215   map 11

Tenuta di Canonica

Loc. Canonica m.75/76, 06059 Todi

The position is wonderful – on a green ridge with stunning views – and the house is equally exciting. It was a ruin (mostly 17th century, with medieval remnants and some Roman foundations) when Daniele and Maria bought it in 1998. Much thought and creative flair have gone into its resurrection. There's not a corridor in sight – instead, odd steps up and down, hidden doors, vaulted ceilings, enchanting corners.... Cool, beautiful reception rooms are decorated in mellow, muted colours and given a personal feel by family portraits, photos and books. The bedrooms are vast, intriguingly shaped and alluring, with lovely rugs on pale brick or wooden floors and gorgeous beds and fabrics. Lots of individual, exotic touches, too. All in all, it's a house which reflects its owners' personalities: Daniele and Maria are vivid, interesting people, well-travelled and good company. Meals are cooked by two teachers from the Cordon Bleu school in Perugia. The dining room opens on to a covered terrace surrounded by roses and shrubs and there are many good walks over the 24-hectare estate and the surrounding countryside. *Minimum stay 2 nights, 1 week in August.*

rooms	11 + 2: 11 doubles. 2 apartments for 2 + 2 children, or 3 adults.
price	€ 130–€ 190.
meals	Dinner € 30; wine-list.
closed	January–February.
directions	From A1 Florence-Rome exit Valdichiana, E45 Perugia-Terni exit Todi-Orvieto; SS448 for Prodo-Titignano; 2km, Bivio per Cordigliano; 1km, signs.

	Daniele Fano
tel	+39 075 8947545
fax	+39 075 8947581
e-mail	tenutadicanonica@tin.it
web	www.tenutadicanonica.com

The Piazza del Popolo in Todi was built in 1213 and is a perfect example of a medieval piazza.

Self-catering & B&B

map 11 entry 216

Relais Il Canalicchio

Via della Piazza 4, 06050 Canalicchio di Collazzone

Not only a pleasant detour between Perugia and Orvieto but a dreamlike retreat. Once known as the Castello di Poggio, the pretty 13th-century hamlet in the green Umbrian countryside is almost a principality in itself: 51 rooms, two pools, gym, tower and gardens with white roses, all within ancient fortress walls. The decoration is a surprisingly international mix, a quirk which is reflected in the various names of the guest bedrooms, such as Isabelle Rubens and The Countess of Oxford. Some are tucked under the white-painted beams of the roof; many open onto little balconies or terraces. The bathrooms are a treat. We loved the rooms in the new wing, with their sponged walls and hand-stencilled details (charming, not twee). Views from the tower rooms sweep in all directions over an endless valley of olive groves, vineyards and woods. Downstairs you can enjoy a frame of billiards and a glass of grappa – having eaten first at Il Pavone, blessed with views and good food. Others may prefer to retreat to the quiet of the library. There's character here, a great feeling of space, and Dorine masterminds her flurry of staff beautifully.

rooms	51: 34 doubles, 16 suites, 1 single.
price	€ 149–€ 179. Singles € 120–€ 143. Suites € 209–€ 239.
meals	Lunch/dinner in restaurant Il Pavone, set menu € 36, or à la carte.
closed	Rarely.
directions	From Rome A1 for Firenze, exit Orte. E45 Perugia-Cesena, exit Ripabianca & for Canalicchio.

The hill town of Montefalco has lovely things to see, particularly the church of San Francesco with its wonderful frescoes by Benozzo Gozzoli.

Dorine Kunst
tel	+39 075 8707325
fax	+39 075 8707296
e-mail	relais@relaisilcanalicchio.it
web	www.relaisilcanalicchio.it

Inn

I Mandorli

Loc. Fondaccio 6, 06039 Bovara di Trevi

I Mandorli is aptly named: there is at least one almond tree outside each apartment – although you will need to be here in February to see the blossom. Masses of greenery surrounds the old *casa padronale*, so there is plenty of shade at the height of summer. Once the centre of a 200-hectare estate, the buildings – the shepherd's house and the olive mill in particular – are a fascinating reminder of days gone by. Mama Wanda is passionate about the place and will show you around, embellishing everything you see with stories about its history. Widowed, with three daughters, she manages the remaining 47 hectares, apartments and rooms, *and* cooks we are told, for the small taverna. Bedrooms are sweet, simple affairs with new furniture and patchwork quilts; white bathrooms are excellent. Children will love the wooden slide and seesaw, and the old pathways and steps on this shallow hillside – magic to return to after cultural outings to Assisi and Spoleto. This is olive oil country so make sure you go home with a few bottles of the best. *Laundry facilities with small charge.*

rooms	3 + 3: 3 doubles/twins. 3 apartments: 1 for 2, 2 for 4.
price	€46–€72. Apartments €310–€619 per week.
meals	Dinner €18. Self-catering in apartments.
closed	Rarely.
directions	From Foligno, SS3 south for Spoleto; left to Bovara. Signposted from main road.

	Signora Maria di Zappelli Cardarelli
tel	+39 0742 78669
fax	+39 0742 78669
e-mail	mandorli@seeumbria.com
web	www.seeumbria.com/mandorli

'The first joy of the year being in its snowdrops, the second, and cardinal one, was in the almond blossom'. John Ruskin *Praeterita.*

Self-catering & B&B

map 11   entry 218

Le Logge di Silvignano
Frazione Silvignano 14, 06049 Spoleto

Wrought-iron gates swing open onto a shingled courtyard... and there is the house, in all its unruffled beauty. The views reach as far as Assisi. Set in well-kept gardens in the Spoleto hills, this is one of the most important medieval buildings in the area. The graceful open gallery with octagonal stone pillars dates from the early 15th century but the main building has its roots in the 12th. Much thought, care and talent have gone into its restoration. The suites have enormous, beautiful bedrooms, Amalfi-tiled bathrooms, pretty sitting rooms with open fireplaces, tiny kitchens for preparing snacks and drinks. Bedcovers and curtains made on antique looms in Montefalco look perfect against stone walls, arches and massive beams. The linen is crisp and cool, and the furniture antique – or fine, locally-crafted pieces. Diana and Alberto are delighted if you join them for a glass of wine before you go out to dine – or a nightcap on your return. They're warm, interesting people, who really seem to enjoy hearing about their guests' day and are happy to help with ideas for the next. *Minimum stay 2 nights. Children over 12 welcome.*

In Silvignano village there is a 14th-century votive chapel with original frescoes by the Maestro di Fossa.

rooms	5 suites, tiny kitchen available for guests.
price	€ 190-€ 220.
meals	Good restaurants 1.5-4km.
closed	10 January-20 February.
directions	A1 Florence-Bologna exit Bettolle-Sinalunga, then E45 for Perugia-Assisi-Foligno. SS3 Flaminia until Fonti del Clitunno then towards Campello-Pettino; 3km after Campello right for Silvignano, 1.5km.

Alberto Araimo

tel	+39 0743 274098
fax	+39 0743 270518
e-mail	mail@leloggedisilvignano.it
web	www.leloggedisilvignano.it

B&B

Castello di Poreta

Loc. Poreta, 06049 Spoleto

From a distance, it looks like a pink church enclosed in ruined walls. But the church and castle of this old fortified village were revived when a co-operative from Poreta won the right to transform the ancient stones and rafters into a country-house hotel. They've made a huge success of it, creating somewhere individual and attractive. Simple and comfortable bedrooms — two in the old priest's house, six in a new part off the terrace — reflect the pastel shades of the sun-bleached, olive-growing hills outside. The intimate, two-roomed restaurant (open to the public, so you need to book) serves excellent food. Donatella, the talented young chef, is enthusiastic and creative: the menu changes often and is seasonally aware. The restaurant walls are enlivened by exhibitions of work by modern artists and there are early-evening classical or jazz concerts once a month. As one visitor noted in the guest book: "the impossible dream. It's all here..." Birdsong, wild flowers, walks from the door, young and cheerful service — an unusual and delightful place to stay, well off the beaten track.

rooms	8 doubles/twins.
price	€ 85–€ 114.
meals	Restaurant à la carte.
closed	Rarely.
directions	Signposted on Via Flaminia between Spoleto & Foligno.

The best view of Spoleto to be had without going to Italy is in the background of Poussin's painting Landscape with St. Rita *in Dulwich Picture Gallery.*

	Luca Saint Amour di Chanaz
tel	+39 0743 275810
fax	+39 0743 270175
e-mail	castellodiporeta@seeumbria.com
web	www.seeumbria.com/poreta

Inn

map 11   entry 220

Photography by Michael Busselle

the marches & abruzzo molise

Country House Parco Ducale

Loc. Parco Ducale, 61049 Urbania

Definitely the right sort of address, with Barco, hunting lodge of the Dukes of Urbino, just next door! And, not surprisingly, a very pretty setting against a backdrop of wooded hills. The three-storeyed, 19th-century building has been entirely rebuilt using the original stone and brick. So, too, has the outhouse – once used for drying tobacco but now housing the largest of the suites. Attractive brick terraces and lawns with flowering shrubs merge into fields of wheat and sunflowers. Daniela, helped by Roberto (who also runs a language school in Urbania), manages the place with friendly efficiency. It has only been open since 2002, and the overall effect is pleasant and uncluttered, with cream walls, terracotta tiled floors and beamed ceilings. Comfortable, well-proportioned bedrooms have solid, reproduction country furniture, fridges disguised as cupboards, double-glazing to keep out noise from the nearby road, air conditioning to keep you cool, and well-equipped kitchenettes in the suites. There's fine walking country all around and the Renaissance delights of Urbania five minutes by car. *Minimum stay three nights.*

rooms	11: 6 doubles, 5 suites for 2-3.
price	€ 60–€ 80. Suite € 80–€ 105.
meals	Choice of trattoria & osteria, 1km.
closed	Rarely.
directions	SS73 bis from Urbania for San Angela in Vado. After 1km, you will see 'Barco' the grand villa, immediate right into Park gates. Next to Barco.

The Barco, summer residence of the Dukes of Urbino, was begun by Francesco di Giorgio and finished by Genga.

	Giovanni Carrara
tel	+39 0722 312872
fax	+39 0722 317022
e-mail	parcoducale@tiscali.it
web	www.ilparcoducale.it/

B&B & Self-catering

Le Querce

Loc. Calmugnano, 61020 Frontino

Take a break from Tuscany and come here! The countryside is as captivating as the house, and behind soars the Monte Carpegna. The rooms of this delightful, mellow, country-house B&B are in two buildings. White muslin flutters at the shuttered windows of the barn – the Locanda – where each of the six bedrooms is en suite. Everything is well-crafted and has a light and airy feel; there's a cosy sitting room with an open fire where you breakfast, and a kitchen where longer-staying guests can make their own. Rooms in the Casa Vecchia are bigger, ideal for families holidaying together: a two-room suite with homely kitchen on the first floor and above, three bedrooms and a bathroom. The beautiful Blue Room, a sitting/music room with a fireplace dated 1580, is full of lovely things found and acquired by Federica. For dinner, visit the country restaurant, a short, winding drive (or walk) away. This really is a great place for families: the Crocettas have cats and children, and summer activities. No fences break the view – just stroll out into the meadows, shaded by the 100-year-old oaks that give the house its name.

rooms	8 + 2: 6 doubles, kitchen available for groups; 2 apartments, 1 for 4–5, 1 for 6–8.
price	€ 62–€ 72. Apartments € 124–€ 186.
meals	Self-catering.
closed	Rarely.
directions	From Rome-Umbria exit A14 at Orte, E17 to S. Giustino; for Bocca Trabaria to S. Angelo in Vado; for Piandimeleto. Through Piandimeleto. After 10km, ignore left to Frontino; further 3km on, then signed left.

	Antonio Rosati & Federica Crocetta
tel	+39 0722 71370
e-mail	lequerce32@hotmail.com
web	www.locandalequerce.com

Carpegna is famous for its proscuitto crudo which is not to be missed – hard to miss if you go there, for the factory is a bit of a blot on the landscape.

B&B & Self-catering

map 9   entry 222

Locanda della Valle Nuova

La Cappella 14, 61033 Sagrata di Fermignano

An unusual, rural, unexpectedly modern place whose owner is an architect with a special interest in eco-friendly buildings and organic farming. His conversion has given La Locanda the understated elegance of a discreet modern hotel. Perfectly turned sheets lie on perfect beds in perfect bedrooms — as crisp and as clean as a new pin. In gentle hills surrounded by ancient, protected oaks and within sight of the World Heritage Site of Urbino, this 185-acre farm produces 100% organic meat, vegetables and wine. Signora Savini and daughter Giulia cook delicious meals served on white porcelain and local terracotta; bread, pasta and jams are homemade. Water is purified and de-chlorinated, heating is solar, truffles are gathered in autumn from the woods. There's a riding school here with two outdoor arenas, several horses for lessons or hacks and a three-legged cat! The swimming pool is delicious. If you arrive at the airport after dark, generous Giulia meets you to guide you back; in the morning, you catch your first mellow glimpses of Montefeltro, Monti Carpegna and Catria. *Children over 12 welcome. Min. stay three nights.*

rooms	6: 5 doubles, 1 twin.
price	€ 96. Half-board € 70 p.p.
meals	Dinner, set menu, € 25.
closed	November–June.
directions	Exit Fano-Rome motorway at Acqualagna & Piobbico. Head towards Piobbico as far as Pole; right for Castellaro; signs.

Urbania takes its name from Pope Urban VIII who dreamed up the notion of converting the medieval village of Castel Durante into a model Renaissance town.

Signor Augusto Savini

tel	+39 0722 330303
fax	+39 0722 330303
e-mail	info@vallenuova.it
web	www.vallenuova.it

B&B

Studio Apartment
Via Piave 7, 61029 Urbino

Open the gate in the wall of the tiny, brick-paved alley… and enter an enchanting terrazzo garden. A fabulous sun trap, even in the winter, it stands above the city ramparts with glorious views to the south. Double-shuttered French windows lead from the garden to the apartment, ingeniously created from an old chapel. The crisp lines of contemporary furniture and fittings harmonise well with the gentle curves of the apse; white walls and floors offset the odd colourful fabric and pretty picture. Storage units separate the living from the sleeping area; a perfect little kitchen and bathroom have been excavated out of the ground on either side. Make yourself at home and relish the fact that you are at the centre of things in this most delightful of university cities. The ducal palace is almost next door – a Renaissance gem housing the National Gallery of the Marches. You won't easily tire of Urbino, but should you do so, there are several Adriatic coastal towns nearby – always a pleasure to explore out of season. Stay as long as you can.

rooms	1 apartment for 2.
price	€550 per week; €950 per fortnight.
meals	Self-catering.
closed	June–15 November.
directions	Full directions when booking.

	Signora Adriana Negri
tel	+39 0722 2888
fax	+39 0722 2888
e–mail	gsavini@supereva.it

Urbino was one of Europe's most prestigious courts under Federico, Duke of Montefelto, whose 'Palazzo Ducale' is a monument to the ideals of the Renaissance.

Self-catering

map 9   entry 224

Locanda San Rocco

Fraz. Collaiello 2, 62020 Gagliole

Decent, honest and without a whiff of pretension, this inn calls itself an *agriturismo* (touristic farmhouse) – there are many now in Italy. Originally 18th century, the building has kept its purity of style with its old brick walls, exposed beams and expanses of quarry tiles remaining intact. The bedrooms are attractively and simply furnished, with some nice brickwork above the beams; beds are of wrought iron or handsome wood, the furniture is properly old-fashioned and the walls almost bare. The overall effect is most characterful and bathrooms are spotless. The house is part of a 55-hectare estate which supplies the San Rocco with fresh vegetables and fruit the whole year round, as well as wine, olive oil, cheese and free-range poultry; you eat well here. The countryside is wooded and rolling, lusher than Tuscany's and in an area less well-trodden. You can borrow mountain bikes for exploring, and there is stacks to see and do. Delicious food, lovely hosts, good, solid B&B. *Minimum stay two nights.*

rooms	6 + 1: 6 doubles. 1 apartment for 4.
price	€85. Apartment €490 per week.
meals	Dinner on request.
closed	October-mid June, excluding Easter.
directions	From SS361 left 1km after Castelraimondo for S. Severino Marche. In Gagliole signs for Collaiello & Locanda.

San Rocco was on pilgrimage to Rome when plague struck and he began healing people. He was himself struck down at Piacenza and nursed by a dog (his attribute in art).

Signora Gisla Pirri
tel +39 0737 642324
fax +39 0737 642324

B&B & Self-catering

entry 225   map 12

Azienda Agrituristica 'Il Quadrifoglio'

Strada Licini 22, Colle Marconi, 66100 Chieti

Il Quadrifoglio – The Four-Leaved Clover – is an auspicious place. Those in the know travel many miles to be looked after by Anna, who knows exactly how to make her guests feel comfortable and at ease. The house is modern, whitewashed and red-tiled – pleasant though undistinguished – in the middle of farmland just beyond Chieti. It sits on the family farm, detached from the other farm buildings but with chickens still; the hen house is the most luxurious we've ever seen! There are four newly furnished bedrooms, decorated with terracotta, cane and fabrics in simple prints, and a self-contained apartment with kitchen and log fire. Guests share a large sitting/dining area and a balcony. The garden, with its wooden summer house, swing and climbing frame, is just the thing for fidgety children who've been cooped up all day in the car. Anna used to cook for private families in the South of France and will cook dinner for guests if they ask her. She also runs gourmet cooking courses. Unbelievably good value. *Extra beds available for children.*

rooms	4 + 1: 4 doubles, 1 apartment for 2.
price	€45-€55. Apartment €70 per night, €400 per week.
meals	Breakfast €4. Lunch/dinner €13.
closed	Rarely.
directions	From A25 exit Chieti. Rght onto SS5 for Popoli 1.7km; further left for Chieti; 4km to Colle Marconi. Right onto Strada Licini; right again. Quadrifoglio 1st drive on right.

Signora Anna Maria D'Orazio

tel	+39 0871 63400
fax	+39 0871 63400
e-mail	annamaria@agriturismoilquadrifoglio.191.it or anndora@tin.it

The Roman name for Chieti, 'Theatinum', gave its name to the Theatine order whose schemes to help the poor included not-for-profit pawnshops.

B&B & Self-catering

map 12   entry 226

Dimora del Prete di Belmonte
Via Cristo 49, 86079 Venafro

The old palace is found among the cobbled streets of the medieval centre – unremarkable from the outside but an absolute gem once you step inside. Venafro, a Roman town, lies in the lovely valley of Monte Santa Croce, ringed by mountains. The first thrill is the enchanting internal garden with its lush palms, where a miscellany of Roman artefacts and stone olive presses lie scattered among tables and chairs. Next, discover the frescoed neo-classical interior in an astonishing state of preservation; painted birds, family crests, and lovely *grotteschi* adorn the walls of the state rooms and entrance hall. Bedrooms on the upper floor are furnished in simple good taste, one huge, with big fireplace and sleigh bed, another with chestnut-wood country furniture. Dorothy is a wonderful hostess, friendly and talkative and with fantastic local knowledge; she is a natural for B&B. She also runs an organic farm with 3,000 olive trees (many of them over 400 years old), vines, walnuts and sheep. An area and a palace rich in content – and the dinners do full justice to the setting.

rooms	5 doubles.
price	€ 105.
meals	Lunch/dinner with wine, € 25, on request.
closed	Rarely.
directions	Exit Rome-Naples m'way at S. Vittore for Venafro, Isernia & Campobasso. Palace signposted from Venafro centre.

The Abbey of Montecassino, founded on one of Italy's best natural fortresses, was utterly destroyed in 1943; its Renaissance cloisters are reconstructions.

Dorothy Volpe

tel	+39 0865 900159
fax	+39 0865 900159
e-mail	info.dimora@tin.it
web	www.dimoradelprete.it

B&B

HOW TO USE THIS BOOK

explanations

❶ rooms

Assume all rooms are 'en suite' unless we say otherwise.

If a room is not 'en suite' we say **with separate,** or **with shared bathroom**: the former you will have to yourself, the latter may be shared with other guests or family member. Where an entry reads 4+2 this means 4 rooms and 2 self-catering apartments or similar.

❷ room price

The price shown is for one night for two sharing a room. A price range incorporates room/seasonal differences. We say when the price is per week for self-catering.

❸ meals

Prices are per person. Meals in B&B must be booked in advance.

❹ closed

When given in months, this means for the whole of the named months and the time in between.

❺ directions

Use as a guide; the owner can give more details.

❻ map & entry numbers

Map page number; entry number.

❼ type of place

❽ vignette

❾ symbols

sample entry

PUGLIA

Acquarossa
C. de Acquarossa 2, 72014 Casalini, Brindisi

It's like a fairytale. You're high in the hills above the quiet Itria valley, looking out over olive groves and orchards. Suddenly the *strada bianca* peters out among scrubby juniper bushes and there, in front of you… an extraordinary cluster of round buildings, their conical roofs topped by stone balls. Acquarossa is a 19th-century *trulli* settlement and some of the foundations go back 500 years. Timeless and disarming, the restored, white-painted stone buildings stand in courtyards and terraces lavishly planted with clumps of lavender and herbs, surrounded by arches and drystone walls. Their immensely thick walls and pointed roofs make them beautifully cool in summer, and the little rooms have been delightfully, rustically decorated. Delicious country antiques, niches bright with flowers, voile curtains over small, deep windows and arched doorways, flagged floors and wood-burning stoves – an imaginative mix of style and tradition. The bathrooms are simple and pretty; the kitchens tiny and minimalist. And if you have the urge to cook something ambitious, there's an oven in the courtyard.

rooms	6: 3 doubles, 3 family rooms.	❶
price	€78–€91. Family rooms€88–€103.	❷
meals	Choice of restaurants nearby. Self-catering in family rooms.	❸
closed	Rarely.	❹
directions	SS379 for Bari; exit Ostuni-Villanova for Ostuni. At Agip station, left up road to r'bout, signed 'Strada dei Colli'. Left after '200m fine strada' sign. Uphill for 1km & left at end of road. Track ends at Acquarossa.	❺

 *Puglia produces some distinctive food and dishes and holds various food festivals every year. The Sagra della puccia celebrates the small bread shapes that are filled with olives and grapes.*

	Luca Montinaro
tel	+39 080 4444 093
fax	+39 0831 524826
e-mail	lucamontinaro@libero.it
web	www.acqua-rossa.com

❼ B&B & Self-catering

❻ entry 272 map 19

❾

See the last page of the book for fuller explanation:

- wheelchair facilities
- step-free access to bathroom/bedroom
- all children welcome
- no smoking anywhere
- smoking restrictions
- credit cards accepted
- English-speaking hosts
- vegetarians catered for with advance warning

- pets can sleep in your bedroom
- this house has pets
- working farm
- swimming pool
- bike hire
- walking nearby
- And for self-catering properties…
- shop within 5km

Photography by Philippa Rogers

lazio

B&B Vatican Museums

Via Sebastiano Veniero 78, 00192 Rome

Just three minutes' walk from the Vatican… hence the name! This apartment makes a relaxing change from staying in a hotel and is perfect for families. It is a large apartment in an attractive, russet-coloured townhouse, built in 1927 just off a busy road but approached through an verdant communal courtyard dominated by a massive palm. This is a real home from home, unpretentious, informal. Though not always in town, Erminia is friendly, easy-going and speaks English well; she is a graphic artist and out most of the day but gives you the run of the kitchen leaving cereals, bread, pastries and jams for you to help yourself to. The three bedrooms are simple but attractive with brightly coloured bedspreads, whitewashed walls with framed posters and marbled tiled floors; two share a bathroom. There are overhead ceiling fans too – a boon when it's hot. The views are not particularly exciting but no matter; there is so much to see and do in Rome. *Minimum stay four nights.*

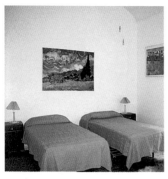

Rome was not built in a day. Proverb

rooms	3: 1 double; 1 twin, 1 double, sharing bath.
price	€ 70–€ 80.
meals	Great choice of restaurants nearby.
closed	Rarely.
directions	From ring road take Via Aurelia towards Citta del Vaticano. On Via Candia right into Via Sebastiano Veniero.

Signora Erminia Pascucci

tel	+39 06 68210776
fax	+39 06 68210776
e-mail	bbcenter@tin.it
web	www.bbroma.com/vening.htm

B&B

Hotel Modigliani

Via della Purificazione 42, 00187 Rome

There's a sense of anticipation the moment you enter the marble hall, with its deep, pale sofas and fresh flowers. Marco's wide smile and infectious enthusiasm reinforce the feeling and a glance round the hotel confirms your pleasure. This is an unusual, delightful place, hidden down a side street just five minutes' walk from the Spanish Steps and Via Veneto. The house belonged to Marco's father, and Marco and Giulia (he a writer, she a musician) decided two years ago to turn it into a hotel. It has a minimalist and immensely stylish air, yet is still friendly and intimate. Marble floors and white walls are a dramatic setting for poster-sized, black-and-white photos, their starkness softened by luxuriant plants. The dining room – it was a bread oven in the 1700s – has vaulted ceilings, whitewashed walls, cherry-wood tables and more fabulous photos taken by Marco. Grey and white bedrooms are restful, fresh and elegant. Some have balconies and wonderful views; they all have small, perfect bathrooms. It's amazingly quiet for the centre of Rome and there's a patio rich with shrubs and the smell of jasmine.

rooms	24: 22 doubles/twins, 1 suite. 1 family suite for 5.
price	€ 195–€ 270. Suite € 250–€ 340. Family suite € 430–€ 618.
meals	Choice of restaurants nearby.
closed	Rarely.
directions	5-minute taxi ride from Stazione Termine. 5-minute walk from Spanish Steps.

	Giulia & Marco di Tillo
tel	+39 06 42815226
fax	+39 06 42814791
e-mail	info@hotelmodigliani.com
web	www.hotelmodigliani.com

The Bocca della Verità, in which Gregory Peck forced Audrey Hepburn to put her hand in the film Roman Holiday *is in the church of Santa Maria in Cosmedin.*

Hotel

map 11 entry 229

Aventino Sant'Anselmo

Piazza Sant'Anselmo, 2, 00153 Rome

You really can walk anywhere in Rome from the Sant'Anselmo: through the *giardini degli aranci* and down the steep slope to Santa Maria in Cosmedin is a good place to start. The Aventino is quietly residential, an oasis of pink plaster and huge cloud-like umbrella pines like those in a Claude Lorraine landscape – for those wanting peace and quiet this hotel could hardly be bettered. The bedrooms are all different, and in the process of being refurbished. The best are at the top, up three floors with no lift – worth it for the Roman views. Two of them have terraces and all are a generous size, with air-conditioning. The bathrooms vary, from large with hydromassage baths to shower rooms with no window (worth noting by those who like a long hot soak in a tub). The garden is a wonderful, scented surprise, with a stone pergola, table and chairs and a happy profusion of jasmine, orange, lemon, wisteria and fern; escape here with a book and a drink after a hard day's sightseeing. Staff are on the formal side and the hotel is a touch jaded, but this is a haven in a city where peace is at a premium.

rooms	45: 26 doubles, 9 singles, 10 family.
price	€ 166. Singles € 109. Family € 192.
meals	Restaurant Il Giardino degli Aranci nearby.
closed	Rarely.
directions	From Viale Aventino to Piazza Albania; Via di S. Anselmo uphill to Piazza Sant' Anselmo.

Round the corner is Piranesi's Piazza dei Cavalieri di Malta. Peep through the huge keyhole in the bronze door of the Priory for a wonderful surprise.

Signora Roberta Piroli

tel	+39 06 5783214/5743547
fax	+39 06 5783604
e-mail	info@aventinohotels.com
web	www.aventinohotels.com

Hotel

Domus Tiber

Lungotevere De' Mellini 35, 00197 Rome

Imagine you are living in Rome. Free to come and go as you like, you can wander out into the city – the Piazza del Popolo is five minutes' walk away – or simply relax indoors listening to the music of your choice and watching the Tiber flow by. It's an informal, pleasant apartment on the fourth floor of an 18th-century block, reached by stairs and an open lift. The big, high-ceilinged sitting/dining room makes an attractive, airy living space; long, white-shuttered windows overlook the main road (which, up here at least, is surprisingly un-noisy) and the river. Pale, plain walls emphasise the mosaic patterns of the tiled floor and there are tall green plants dotted around. Two colourful sofabeds, heaped with bold cushions, make a good place to lounge, and the gaily painted bedroom at the back of the apartment is also light and roomy, comfortable and minimally furnished. Bathroom and kitchen are narrow, adequate and functional, not luxurious. This is a superb city-centre spot and most of Rome's main attractions are within walking distance to the south and east. *Minimum stay two nights.*

rooms	Sleeps 2-6: 1 double, 2 sofabeds in lounge.
price	€140 for 2, €160 for 3, €180 for 4.
meals	Good restaurants nearby.
closed	Rarely.
directions	From Piazza del Popolo (metro Flaminio) cross Ponte Marguerita. Left onto Lungotevere De' Mellini. Apartment 300m along overlooking Tiber.

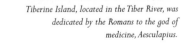

	Paolo Serpone
tel	+39 081 19565835
fax	+39 081 289780
e-mail	myhomeyourhome@virgilio.it
web	www.myhomeyourhome.it

Tiberine Island, located in the Tiber River, was dedicated by the Romans to the god of medicine, Aesculapius.

Self-catering

map 11   entry 231

Casa Trevi

Via in Arcione 98, 00187 Rome

A hop, skip and a jump from Rome's most famous fountain, the Casa Trevi is a hidden treasure. Find yourself in an astonishingly peaceful courtyard, with olive trees and scented oranges and a fountain inhabited by small turtles. Though you're in Rome's most vibrant heart, not a sound penetrates from outside. The apartments are on the ground floor of one of the old buildings and open directly off the courtyard. Interiors are minimalist in the nicest possible way, with white walls and terracotta floors, modern posters and furniture a mixture of white IKEA and flea-market finds. There are no windows as such but the double glass-paned doors let in plenty of light. Hobs and fridges are provided in the airy, spotless kitchens, though serious cooking is not catered for (who wants to eat in in Rome?). Bathrooms are excellent. On three sides are 17th-century buildings in yellows, ochres and reds; on the fourth, a modern monstrosity. Marta could not be nicer, and the security is excellent, with a porter and security camera in the main entrance – a big plus. Great value for central Rome. *Minimum stay four nights.*

The Trevi Fountain is well-loved, not least as the setting for Anita Ekburg's frolic in Felline's film, La Dolce Vita.

rooms	2 apartments: 1 for 2-3, 1 for 4.
price	€ 105-€ 130 per night for 2-3; € 155 per night for 4.
meals	Self-catering.
closed	Rarely.
directions	Details on booking but no parking provided & surrounding streets are pedestrianised. 10-minute taxi ride from central railway station. Nearest metro stop: Piazza di Spagna.

	Signora Marta Nicolini
tel	+39 06 69787084 (& fax)
mobile	+39 335 6205768
e-mail	info@casaintrastevere.it

Self-catering

Hotel Villa del Parco

Via Nomentana 110, 00161 Rome

The frenzy of Rome can wear down even the most enthusiastic of explorers, so here is a quiet, dignified place to which you can retreat: a 19th-century villa in a residential area, surrounded by shrubs and trees. Inside the mood is relaxed, charming and friendly – the Bernardinis are quietly proud of the hotel that has been in the family for over 40 years. Good-sized bedrooms are cosy and fresh; in some, a hint of Laura Ashley, in others, colour-washed walls and wrought-iron beds. All have good lighting, crisp cotton, double-glazing and carpets (unusual so far south). Shower rooms are being modernized and the newest are tiled from top to toe – beautifully. The remnants of frescoes on the stairs are a comforting reminder of Italy's past, though the house is fin de siècle in spirit. A pretty terrace with white-painted, wrought-iron tables and big parasols is the setting for summer breakfasts; the bread basket is full of delights and the cappuccino delicious. The vaulted dining room makes an intimate setting for dinner, and there's a delightful reading room, too. *Special weekend rates.*

rooms	30: 10 doubles, 14 singles, 6 triples.
price	€135–€175.
meals	Restaurants 200m.
closed	Rarely.
directions	From Termini train station right into Via XX Settembre; past Piazza di Porta Pia into Via Nomentana. 1km from station. Bus: In square in front of station, take bus no.36 or 84; get off at 2nd stop after Villa Torlonia.

Signora Elisabetta Bernardini

tel	+39 06 44237773
fax	+39 06 44237572
e-mail	info@hotelvilladelparco.it
web	www.hotelvilladelparco.it

On your walk into Rome, you could look at the British Embassy building by Sir Basil Spence – but as the Porta Pia by Michelangelo Buonarotti is next to it...

Hotel

map 11　entry 233

Hotel Santa Maria

Vicolo del Piede 2, 00153 Rome

All around are cobbled streets, ancient houses and the captivating chaos of cafés, bars and tiny shops that is Trastevere. And, just behind the lovely Piazza Santa Maria, a pair of green iron gates that open to sudden, sweet peace and the fragrance of honeysuckle. On the site of what was once a 17th-century convent lies this secluded single-storey hotel, its courtyards bright with young orange trees. The layout is a tribute to all those earlier cloisters: rooms open onto covered, brick-pillared terraces that surround a central, gravelled courtyard – and you can sit out here in summer. Authentic materials have been used throughout – Peperino marble for the floors, new walnut and chestnut for the ceilings – while the breakfast room has the original terracotta floor. Bedrooms, decorated in soft yellows, have high ceilings and big, floral beds. It's an unexpected find in Rome's heart and what makes it even more special is the service. Stefano runs a delightful staff (the ratio of staff to guest is unusually high) and you are looked after wonderfully well. He's a qualified guide, too, and will organise private tours of the ancient city.

rooms	18: 13 doubles, 3 triples, 1 quadruple, 1 suite for 6.
price	€ 145–€ 207. Triple € 166–€ 233. Quadruple € 181–€ 259. Suite for 6 € 240–€ 300.
meals	Wide choice of restaurants nearby.
closed	Never.
directions	Take a taxi from the Termini train station, approx 10 mins.

'These apartments are generally commodious and well furnished ... and the lodgers are well supplied with provisions and all the necessaries of life.' Tobias Smollett, Rome, 1766

Stefano Donghi

tel	+39 06 5894626
fax	+39 06 5894815
e-mail	hotelsantamaria@libero.it
web	www.htlsantamaria.com

Hotel

Hotel Villa San Pio

Via Santa Melania 19, 00153 Rome

Sister to the Sant'Anselmo, the Hotel San Pio is newly renovated and in pristine condition. It was a private villa, one of the many that gives the Aventine hill its air of serene calm and makes an evening stroll up here – past the Church of Santa Sabina to the orange gardens, or Giardini degli Aranci – such a joy after sightseeing below. This large hotel congregates around a central garden crammed with bougainvillea, camellias and palms. An elegant, modern, verdigris conservatory is where you breakfast, buffet-style, sometimes to the accompaniment of a minuet or sonata; you may also eat in your room. Bedrooms have pretty painted furniture, brocade bedcovers and frescoed or stencilled walls – all freshly applied, all gorgeous. There's much comfort, bathrooms are immaculate, and the larger rooms have balconies filled with flowers. The family rooms are really special (529 and 530 have the best views). The conveniences of the modern city hotel are all here – minibar, air conditioning, parking... best of all, a short walk to the metro whisks you into *centro storico*. Yet you wake to birdsong and the scent of the orange blossom.

rooms	78: 3 singles, 61 doubles, 14 family.
price	€ 197. Singles € 130–€ 181. Family € 217.
meals	Restaurants nearby.
closed	Rarely.
directions	Take Rome metro, Piramide stop.

The only claim to fame of the wealthy praetor Caius Cestius is his huge pyramidal tomb near the Porta San Paolo.

	Signora Roberta Piroli
tel	+39 06 5783214/06 5745174
fax	+39 06 5741112
e-mail	info@aventinohotels.com
web	www.aventinohotels.com

Hotel

map 11   entry 235

Casa in Trastevere

Vicolo della Penitenza 19, 00165 Rome

If you are feeling independent and are lucky enough to be planning more than a fleeting trip to Rome, this apartment is a great base, deep in the fascinating old quarter of Trastevere. The area, though residential, has a happy buzz at night and the shops, bars and restaurants are a treat to discover; you are also a short walk from St Peter's. Signora Nicolini has furnished the sunny first-floor townhouse flat as if it were her own home. She has kept the original 19th-century brown and black terrazzo floor but has added many contemporary touches: a cream sofa, an all-white kitchen, kilims, modern art. You have a big open-plan living/dining room with screened kitchen, a double and a twin bedroom, each with a white bathroom, and an extra sofabed. All is fresh and spotless, and the big bedroom is particularly inviting with its beautiful hand-quilted bedspread. Marta is a delight and does her best to ensure you go home with great memories. Put your feet up after a long day, read a book, browse TV… then out again to explore this magical city. *Minimum stay four nights.*

rooms	1 apartment for 2-6.
price	From € 130 for 2; from € 155 for 4; from € 175 for 6.
meals	Self-catering.
closed	Rarely.
directions	From Ponte Sisto cross Piazza Trilussa. Right into Via della Lungara, right into Via dei Riari; right into Vicolo della Penitenza.

So close it musn't be missed is the Villa Farnesina, with frescoes by Rapheal and Peruzzi, on the Via della Lungara.

Signora Marta Nicolini

tel	+39 06 69924722
fax	+39 06 69787084
e-mail	info@casaintrastevere.it
web	www.casaintrastevere.it

Self-catering

Casa Plazzi

Via Olivetello 23, 00069 Trevignano Romano

The immensely sociable Gianni treats guests as friends, and gives you free run of the house. The building is modern, wonderfully set on a terraced olive grove high up above the Lago di Bracciano. Bedrooms are clean and comfortable, some with lake views, and all are individual: Margherita's and Mimma's are gently floral with matching bedcovers and drapes, Marco's has a plain, wrought-iron bed. The suite is luxurious, with CD player, bathroom of Peperino marble, jacuzzi and private rooftop terrace. There are two sitting rooms, one with a fireplace and a grand piano, and a kitchen sometimes open for cookery lessons so you can watch Gianni in action. The terraces have fabulous lake views, and the pool has a kitchen area so you can prepare a salad for lunch and chill a bottle of wine. Like any good host, Gianni gets the measure of your needs and provides accordingly. Book in advance if you want dinner – or cook it yourself under your host's expert guidance! He'll start by introducing you to the vegetable garden, then scour the local market for the best buys. *Unsuitable for young children.*

rooms	8 + 1: 4 doubles, 1 single, 2 triples, 1 suite for 2, 1 apartment for 2-3.
price	€100, suite €136, triple €140. Apartment €775 per week
meals	Dinner €35, wine list.
closed	Rarely.
directions	Main road west through Trevignano Romano, before IP service station, right into Strada Olivetello (steep with sharp bends). Plazzi almost at end of road, on left.

View the Lago di Bracciano from the ramparts of the Castello Orsini-Odelscalchi in Bracciano town. Good places to swim between Trevignano and Anguillara.

	Signor Gianni Plazzi
tel	+39 06 9997597
fax	+39 06 99910196
e-mail	casaplazzi@tin.it
web	www.casaplazzi.com

B&B & Self-catering

map 11   entry 237

La Chiocciola

Seripola, 01028 Orte

Perhaps the name has something to do with the pace of life here. *Chiocciola* means 'snail' and certainly this is the most unhurried, serene place imaginable. Maria Cristina and Roberto have turned a 15th-century stone farmhouse and outbuildings in the Tevere valley into an entrancing small hotel and restaurant. Gardens full of flowering shrubs and peaceful walkways are set in 25 hectares of woods, olive groves and orchards. Indoors, things are just as restful. You're greeted by mellow, gleaming floors and furniture – and the intoxicating smell of beeswax polish. A beautiful staircase sweeps up to the bedrooms, each of which has its name painted on the door: Mimosa, Coccinella, Ciclamine… They are absolutely delightful rooms – big, uncluttered and arrestingly individual. Terracotta tiles contrast with pale walls and lovely fabrics, family antiques with elegant modern furniture or pieces that Maria Cristina and Roberto have collected on their travels. They're a charming, gentle young couple, very proud of what they have created here, and their 'Before and After Renovation' albums show the full extent of that achievement.

rooms	8: 5 doubles, 1 family, 2 suites.
price	€95–€115. Half-board €140–€150.
meals	Half-board only.
closed	November-February.
directions	Exit autostrada at Orte for Orte Town. After 3km, right for Amelia. Left for Pennadi Teverina after 300m. After 2.5km, sign for La Chiocciola on left.

Cristina and Roberto discovered an old Roman port on the river Tiber at the edge of their property, which you can visit.

Inn

	Roberto & Maria Cristina de Fonseca Pimentel
tel	+39 0761 402734
fax	+39 0761 490254
e-mail	info@lachiocciola.net
web	www.lachiocciola.net

La Meridiana

Strada Cimina 17, 01100 Viterbo

Sometimes called Meridiana Strana, on account of the sundial's erroneous habit of recording sun at 11pm, this old farm crouches above the gently sloping hills around Viterbo, facing eastward towards the sea. Its 25 hectares of woodland yield honey and chestnuts – and delightful botanical trails in summer. This is an activity-orientated place, where courses are organised most weekends from June. The nearby stables and riding school are the pride and joy of Salvatore Ranucci, a showjumper himself. His father, Giuseppe (often to be seen about the place sporting the flat cap of the English country gent), knows a lot about family geneology – if your Italian is up to it! The family love La Meridiana, whose stones and rafters go back some three hundred years, and work hard to keep farm and *agriturismo* ticking over. Bedrooms are unmodernised but the best are charming and furnished with old family pieces; bathrooms are new and make simple use of Peperino marble; living rooms are cosy with fireplaces in winter. Fish, walk, mountain-bike-ride, play golf; 'photographic trekking' is yet another option here.

rooms	5 + 3: 5 doubles. 3 apartments: 1 for 2, 1 for 4, 1 for 5.
price	€70. Singles €40.
meals	Self-catering in apartments. Restaurants 4km.
closed	Rarely.
directions	5km from Viterbo centre. Take Strada Cimina; pass Fina petrol station; pass 3 bends. Sign opposite ISAL Industria Salumi.

In the Palazzo Papale in Viterbo, Cardinals were locked up for the first time 'con chiave' (with a key) to encourage them to get on with choosing a new Pope.

	Signor Salvatore Ranucci
tel	+39 0761 344917
fax	+39 0761 306230
e-mail	b.b@lameridianastrana.com
web	www.lameridianastrana.com

Self-catering & B&B

map 11   entry 239

L'Ombricolo
01020 Civitella d'Agliano

Eighteen years ago it was a ruin. Now it's a mellow stone house with a warmth and character all of its own. Dawne has used local materials and craftspeople to restore the vaulted ceilings and flagged floors, and her own considerable insight and flair to create arrestingly attractive rooms. Where cattle once slept – you can see the marks where they rubbed against the stone arches – is now an inviting sitting room with a beautiful fireplace, cream sofas and lots of books and music. The pretty bedrooms are all very individual, with steps here and there, odd corners and turns, beamed, sloping ceilings. But the glorious heart of the house, created from an old, dismantled grocery store in Rome, is Dawne's kitchen. She'll be here, unhurriedly preparing a meal when you return from a day out, ready with a glass of wine so you can sit down, chat and take it all in. She's a great person to talk to, having lived in Italy for 40 years, worked in the film industry in Rome and travelled widely. Her garden is as relaxed and unfussy as her home, with climbing plants swarming over the veranda, shady trees and dogs and cats galore.

Viterbo has been a renowned spa centre since medieval times. Hot sulphur baths can be found about 3km out of town.

rooms	5 doubles.
price	€ 130.
meals	Dinner € 45.
closed	Rarely.
directions	From A1 to Orvieto, exit Baschi. Right for Castiglione in Teverina. After 2km left at fork for Bomarzo. Right in front of Battisti Cereali gates; house first on right.

	Dawne Alstrom
tel	+39 0761 914735
fax	+39 0761 914735
e-mail	lombricolo@virgilio.it

B&B

La Tana dell'Istrice

Piazza Unita 12, 01020 Civitella D'Agliano

The area known as Tuscia may be less famous than Tuscany and Umbria, but it is rich in natural beauty and culture. The local tourist board produces a leaflet giving seven good reasons for coming here: archaeology, art, architecture, nature, lakes, food and wine. Add to that a special place to stay... The small, family-run hotel was once a palace and sits on the central square opposite a medieval castle in a state of photogenic decay. The old house has been thoroughly renovated without sacrificing the character of the original, and is unusual and delightful. A big drawing room has sofas, antiques and stacks of books; bedrooms are all different – an olive bedcover here, red and white floral drapes there – with wrought-iron beds and the occasional desk, armchair or armoire. Bathrooms are modern. Red tables glow in the yellow restaurant – food and wine are taken seriously here, and cookery mornings are an option, with some well-known chefs presiding. Most of the produce used is organic. A visit to the ancient cellars where Mottura's sparkling wines are locked away is a must. *Minimum stay two nights.*

rooms	12: 9 doubles, 3 suites.
price	€ 135. Half-board € 113–€ 159 p.p. Suites € 226.
meals	Dinner with wine € 47. Vineyard tour, wine-tasting & dinner € 70.
closed	10-26 December; 7 January-21 March; 1-15 August.
directions	From A1 exit Orvieto for Todi. After 1km, right under bridge for Castiglione in Teverina. Towards Civitella; signs after 21km.

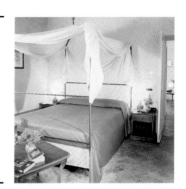

	Signora Alessandra Falsetti
tel	+39 0761 914501
fax	+39 0761 914815
e-mail	mottura@isa.it
web	www.motturasergio.it

'One barrel of wine can work more miracles than a church full of saints.' Italian Proverb

B&B

map 11   entry 241

La Torretta

Via G. Mazzini 7, 08400 Casperia

Casperia is a beautiful, car-free maze of medieval streets in the still relatively unknown Sabine hills. La Torretta has the dreamiest views from its terrace, and interior spaces that have been beautifully designed by architect Roberto. A huge, ground-floor sitting room with partially-exposed frescoes around the cornice welcomes you with fireplace, modern sofas and chairs, books, paintings and piano. The upper room, where meals are taken, opens onto the terrace; it is a gorgeous, vaulted, contemporary space with open stainless-steel kitchen and views through skylights to the church tower and valley. Maureen is warm and hospitable and runs courses on cookery and Italian language. She will cook dinner on request using whatever is in season; mushrooms, truffles, wild boar and olive oil are specialities of the region. Whitewashed, high-ceilinged bedrooms are charming in their simplicity; beds are made and towels changed daily, and bathrooms are fabulous. Don't worry about having to leave your car in the square below the town: Roberto has a buggy for your luggage.

There are four Franciscan Shrines in Sabina, at Rieti, Bustone, Fonte Colombo and Greccio. Combine a cultural pilgrimage with a gastronomic one.

B&B & Self-catering

rooms	7 + 1: 5 doubles, 1 single, 1 family room for 4. 1 apartment for 4.
price	€92. Singles €75. Family room €150. Apartment €92.
meals	Dinner €34, on request.
closed	Rarely.
directions	From North, A1, exit Ponzano Soratte towards Poggio Mirteto. Continue on SS657 for 5km to T-junction. Left on SS313 to Cantalupo towards Casperia.

Roberto & Maureen Scheda

tel	+39 0765 63202
fax	+39 0765 63202
e-mail	latorretta@tiscalinet.it
web	www.latorrettabandb.com

Sant'Ilario sul Farfa

Loc. Colle, 02030 Poggio Nativo

Straightforward good value, and only an hour from Rome by car. The approach, along a steep, unmade track, is marked by that wonderfully Italian juxtaposition of the electric security gates and an olive tree of staggering antiquity. This little farm sits on one of the steeply terraced hills above the river Farfa, with views from its terrace to the Sabine hills. Susanna Serafini is a chatty and energetic hostess whose dinners — rustled up on request, and using farm produce — are amazingly good value. The aspect of the place is rather ranch-like, with bedrooms in two separate single-storey farm buildings, painted white with wooden shutters. Bedrooms are snug and wood-panelled with some fine antique bedheads, white walls and showers. There are also two apartments in the main house with small kitchens (perfect for preparing a simple meal). A pleasing tangle of trellises extends across the garden — more farmyard than formal. Children will love it. Take a dip in the pool or the river, spin off on a mountain bike, participate in an olive- or grape-harvesting weekend. There are cookery and craft classes for children, too.

rooms	6 + 2: 2 doubles, 4 family. 2 apartments: 1 for 3, 1 for 5.
price	€ 62. Half-board € 47. Apartment € 516–€ 723 per week.
meals	Dinner & Sunday lunch with wine, € 15.
closed	January–March.
directions	From SS4 Rome-Rieti exit to Poggio Nativo & Monte S. Maria. Just before Monte S. Maria sharp left onto track signed to S. Ilario sul Farfa.

The Abbey of Santa Maria di Farfa founded, allegedly, by San Lorenzo in the 6th century was for centuries the most powerful monastic centre in central Italy.

	Signora Susanna Serafini
tel	+39 0765 872410
fax	+39 0765 872410
e-mail	santilario@tiscalinet.it
web	www.santilariosulfarfa.it

B&B & Self-catering

map 11   entry 243

Villa Sanguigni
Bagnolo di Amatrice, 02012 Rieti

The snow-capped Laga mountains, glimpsed from some windows and seen as full-blown panoramas from others, are a constant reminder of how close you are to some of Italy's most spectacular scenery. Yet, even though this tiny mountain village stands like Horatius at the gates of Umbria, the Marches and the Abruzzi, the temptation to stay indoors at Villa Sanguigni is strong. The delightful owners, the Orlandi Sanguigni, have restored their ancestral home with unusual sensitivity and care. The five good-sized double bedrooms are beautifully furnished with 18th- and 19th-century bedheads, old washstands, chests, rugs and pictures, and the main rooms are even more delightful: the grand *sala* with huge fireplace, rafters and cream sofas; the elegant dining room, reminiscent of a banqueting hall, with long table and lovely pale stone walls. Best of all, perhaps, is the library, which guests are free to use: curl up with a book, or choose from Signor Sanguigni's vast collection of classical music CDs. *Minimum stay two nights.*

rooms	3 doubles.
price	€80. Singles €52.
meals	Restaurants by lake, 3km.
closed	Rarely.
directions	Take SS4 (Via Salaria) for Ascoli Piceno to Bagnolo. At km129.400 before lake turn for Bagnolo. Villa on right just inside village.

When in Rome, do as the Romans do. And when in Amatrice , no gastronomic experience is complete without sampling Spaghetti all' Amatriciana.

	Anna Maria Orlandi Sanguigni
tel	+39 0746 821075
fax	+39 0746 821075
e-mail	sanguigni1@libero.it
web	www.primitaly.it/bb/villasanguigni

B&B

TYPE OF PROPERTIES

Each entry is labelled eg B&B or Hotel to guide you but these pages reveal a plethora of different terms to describe the various hostelries. We include no star ratings in our guides; we feel they are limiting and often misleading; let our descriptions inform you. This list serves as a rough guide to what you might expect to find behind each name.

Locanda Literally means 'inn' but is sometimes used to describe a restaurant only.

Agriturismo Farm with rooms or apartments.

Azienda Agraria / Agricola Farm company.

Country House A new concept in Italian hospitality, usually family run and akin to a villa.

Podere Farm, smallholding.

Cascina Originally a farmhouse.

Corte Literally, court.

Albergo The Italian word for 'hotel' but perhaps smaller and more personal than its larger sister.

Palazzo Palace or mansion

Cà / Casa (Cà in Venetian dialect) or *casa*, means, simply, house.

Villa Privately owned, usually but not always a country residence.

Relais An imported French term meaning 'inn'.

Residenza An apartment or house with rooms for guests (not manned 24 hours, but usually 8am-8pm) guests have a key to come and go as they please and use of communal areas.

Photography by Il Cortile, Cicciano, entry no 247

campania

Azienda Mustilli

Via dei Fiori 20, 82019 S. Agata dei Goti

Since ancient times, Benevento and the surrounding area has been famous for the quality of its wines; here is a chance to stay on an estate steeped in the history and art of viticulture. The Mustilli Wine Company, run by Leonardo and Marilì Mustilli, is housed in a 16th-century palace, one wing of which has been restored and converted for guests' use. Bang in the centre of town, on a quiet piazza, this makes a fine base from which to explore the upper reaches of Campania. Comfortable bedrooms up under the roof have tiled floors, antique beds and cosy floral wallpapers. The restaurant below is huge, often used for weddings and other events; local dishes are prepared by Marilì herself, washed down with some of their delicious wines. The family knows a lot about the history of the area, and will help you organise your time. Their programme of cultural activities includes a tour of the vineyards and of the historic centre of the town. They will also tell you where to buy local produce and ceramics – bring a large suitcase so you can carry it all home! A deeply civilised place.

rooms	5: 4 twins, 1 suite for 4.
price	€ 67.50–€ 70. Half-board € 55 p.p. Suite € 114–€ 128.
meals	Lunch/dinner € 18; festive lunch € 26.
closed	Rarely.
directions	Leave Rome-Napoli Autostrada at Caianello towards Beneveneto & then Incrocio & S. Agata dei Goti. Azienda Mustilli signposted from *centro storico*.

Sicily's St Agatha was allegedly martyred by having her breasts cut off. In art, she carries them on a dish and became patron saint of bell-founders because of their shape.

	Leonardo & Marilì Mustilli
tel	+39 0823 717433
fax	+39 0823 717619
e-mail	info@mustilli.com
web	www.mustilli.com

B&B

Casa Lerario

Contrada Laura 6, 82030 Melizzano

It's hard to believe that this big, traditional yellow *casa* was only built 12 years ago, so naturally has it merged into the hillside below little Monte Taburno. Surrounded by olive groves, fruit trees and vineyards, it already has an ageless feel. It was designed by Pietro, his mother and Sonia, with stone staircases inside and out and balconies, loggias and terraces galore. Fresh flowers, plump cushions and a kitchen full of delicious things give a welcoming air. Generously-sized rooms are furnished with country antiques and curved ceilings are decorated with hand-painted stencils. One suite has a vast double bedroom with windows on three walls and a huge terrace; another is very private, with its own entrance and sitting room. Guests eat in the entrance hall, where light streams in through arched windows, or out on the mosaic-paved terrace where dinner is cooked in a huge stone oven. An antique fair is held here on the last weekend of every month. The only nightlife is watching the fireflies but if you put your foot down – and don't lose your way – you can be in Naples in 45 minutes. *Minimum stay two nights.*

rooms	4: 2 suites for 2, 2 suites for 4.
price	€ 110.
meals	Dinner € 15–€ 25.
closed	Rarely, but book ahead.
directions	From Caserta SS265 for Telese. 5km, for Melizzano, right over level crossing. Right by methane plant; after 1.5km right by 'mirror', 1.5km on 2nd lane on left.

	Paolo Serpone
tel	+39 081 19565835
fax	+39 081 289 780
e-mail	myhomeyourhome@virgilio.it
web	www.myhomeyourhome.it

Tomatoes from Campania are exported all over the world, but trying them here is a unique experience, particularly the San Marzano sweet plum variety.

B&B

map 13   entry 246

Il Cortile

Via Roma 43, 80033 Cicciano

Arriving here is one of those special moments. If you have spent a day being jostled and hooted at in Naples, or you've arrived hot and tired from the train station you'll love it here... The anonymous black door in the suburban Neapolitan street opens onto a beautiful white-walled courtyard rich in bougainvillea, jasmine and lemon trees. The villa was built as a summer retreat for Arturo's forebears, and now has accommodation in two large, self-contained units with their own secluded entrances – perfect for families with children. Delicious meals are served in the main part of the house or in the courtyard, and there is guest sitting room/library filled with family antiques, comfortable sofas and pictures. Bedrooms are cool, with pale washed walls, tiled floors and some nice antique furniture. Sijtsken (who is Dutch) is a charming and thoughtful hostess, bringing you little vases of flowers from her lovely garden beyond the courtyard. She is also a fantastic cook, and has been known to give lessons on request.

Nearby Cimitile, orginally an Early Christian graveyard as the name suggests, contains a group of Early Christian basilicas.

rooms	2: 1 suite for 2-3, 1 suite for 4-5.
price	€ 60–€ 70.
meals	Dinner with wine, € 24.
closed	Rarely.
directions	From Rome or Naples highway to Bari; exit Nola for Cimitile & Cicciano. House 10-minute drive from highway.

Arturo & Sijtsken Nucci

tel	+39 081 824 8897
fax	+39 081 826 4851
e-mail	dupon@libero.it

B&B

Albergo Sansevero d'Angri
Piazza VII Settembre 28, 80138 Naples

Naples Yellow – that elusive colour somewhere between ochre and primrose, known to painters and visitors to Naples but hard to describe – is the colour of this palace. The huge column-flanked entrance does little to inform you of the existence of the comfortable Albergo Sansevero on the upper floors; ring one of a number of buzzers to enter. Once inside, bright white corridors are interspersed with sitting areas furnished with wicker and antique furniture and Persian rugs. High-ceilinged bedrooms, with elegantly tall windows, are white, with a splash of colour from sunflower-yellow bedcovers; all are air-conditioned and have TVs. You may come and go as you please, and breakfast is laid on at the Bar Fiorillo next door – just tell them where you're staying. The Piazza Bellini round the corner is an oasis of calm in this hooting, vrooming city; in its centre stands the statue Vincenzo Bellini liberally splattered with graffiti, and, behind, the Poesia Moenia, an internet-cafe/bookshop that lends a bohemian tone. Book, music and antique shops line the fascinating Via Costantinopoli.

rooms	11: 3 doubles, 8 doubles/suites for 2-6, 2 sharing wc.
price	€88–€110.
meals	Half-board available.
closed	Rarely.
directions	On the corner of Via Roma & Via S. Anna dei Lombardi.

Nearby is the Spaccanapoli district, with dozens of churches, built on a network of underground passages (they say Naples has even more catacombs than Rome).

Signora Auriemma Armida
tel	+39 081 790 1000
fax	+39 081 211 698
e-mail	albergo.sansevero@libero.it
web	www.albergosansevero.it

Hotel

map 13   entry 248

Albergo Sansevero Degas

Calata Trinità Maggiore 53, 80134 Naples

So called because the French painter Degas and his family once lived here. The Piazza del Gesù Nuovo is one of the most famous in Naples, the ornate obelisk at its centre built to mark the end of a time of plague and disease, and the Gesù Nuovo is memorable for its lava façade and its wildly extravagant baroque interior (in which the Spanish painter Ribera had a hand). Across the piazza, the Albergo Sansevero Degas is marked by a hugely grand entrance – gaze up at the capitals of the columns as you pass through. You will be greeted at the modern, elegant reception with a warm smile. Bedrooms have white floor tiles, even whiter walls, new beds, deep orange curtains from ceiling to floor; some rooms are vast, all are air-conditioned. A compactly furnished tea and coffee room, with a view across the square, makes a relaxing spot after a day's sightseeing. And all around are the vibrant bars and cafés, teeming alleyways, dark passages and souk-like shops of the fascinating Spaccanapoli district.

rooms	7 rooms for 2-6.
price	€ 88–€ 110.
meals	Dinner € 15.
closed	Rarely.
directions	From station or airport, hotel easily reached by taxi, bus or metro. Hotel 100m from National Archeological Museum in Old Town.

Facing the Gesù is the church of Santa Chiara – sadly gutted during the last war. The attached convent has a cloister that is one of the gems of the city.

	Signora Auriemma Armida
tel	+39 081 790 1000
fax	+39 081 211 698
e-mail	albergo.sansevero@libero.it
web	www.albergosansevero.it

Hotel

B&B Terrazza Pignatelli
Via Ascensione 8, 80100 Naples

A few paces from the waterfront and within walking distance of the old town, a reassuring place to stay in a frenetic, fascinating city. And Ottavio is a warm, amusing young host, keen to share his love of Naples. A law graduate and keen ocean sailor, he has come back home to continue his studies. The apartment, in a late-19th-century building, is in a narrow, paved street in a smart part of town. Behind are the lush gardens of the Museo Pignatelli. As the lift only goes to the third floor, you will have to lug your cases up the last flight of stairs. The reception/sitting area has a comfortable, friendly air, with interesting pictures and framed ecclesiastical embroidery panels (Ottavio's family business has specialised in such things since 1820). WP access and a range of books on Naples add a pleasantly studious touch. The traditional bedrooms each have a private terrace (though not all with direct access) and good bathrooms. There's a big, tranquil roof terrace, too, bright with flowers and herbs. It looks west over the museum gardens and is just the place to sit back with a glass of wine as you watch the sun set. *Minimum stay two nights.*

rooms	3: 2 doubles, 1 triple.
price	€ 160–€ 180.
meals	Good restaurants nearby.
closed	August.
directions	From Riviera di Chiaia walk north on Via Ascensione; house on left.

	Ottavio Serpone
tel	+39 081 19565835
fax	+39 081 289 780
e-mail	myhomeyourhome@virgilio.it
web	www.myhomeyourhome.it

'The whole city is mad with joy. The Neapolitans have written up "Vittoria" and "Viva Nelson" at every corner of the street.'
Miss E C Knight, *on Nelson's 40th birthday celebrations*

B&B

map 13   entry 250

B&B Portalba

Port Alba 33, 80100 Naples

How about something eye-catchingly, audaciously different? You wouldn't guess it from the discreet 19th-century exterior but this second- and third-floor apartment is like a Hollywood set inside. The three bedrooms have gleaming wooden floors, big beds, lovely linen. So far, so conventional – but then the fun starts. Camera Africa, brown, white and gold, has fur rugs and tiger-patterned valances on its two double beds. The bed hangings are lavish and cream, and there's a little balcony from which you can gaze at the Neapolitan night sky. Camera Almovada is bewitchingly demure, with sky-blue walls, a white cotton-draped ceiling and bed, and scarlet rugs and lampshades. Camera Napoli has orange and gold cushions and curtains that blaze against pale green walls; gauzy bedhangings swoop from a dark beamed ceiling. Bathrooms, reception and sitting rooms are similarly striking, there's an exercise area with formidable machines and a delightful, multi-striped hammock. Gorgeous, high quality theatricality just off Piazza Dante, right in the middle of Naples. *Minimum stay two nights.*

'Redeth the grete poete of Ytaille / That highte Dant...' Chaucer The Monk's Tale

rooms	3: 1 double; 2 doubles, both with separate bath.
price	€ 140–€ 160.
meals	Restaurants within walking distance.
closed	Rarely.
directions	Port Alba runs off north east corner of Piazza Dante. Number 33 is first gate on right.

Gabriella Chitis & Francesca Pacifico

tel	+39 081 19565835
fax	+39 081 549 3251
e-mail	info@portalba33.it
web	www.portalba33.it

B&B

Soggiorno Sansevero

Piazza San Domenico Maggiore 9, 80134 Naples

Once a prince's palace. This refreshing little hotel is owned by that same efficient Signora Armida who presides over the Albergo Sansevero and the Sansevero Degas. Like its sisters, it is in a prime position in the historic centre, mercifully free of traffic yet in a piazza vibrant with cafés, bars and stalls. A rather forbidding, massive doorway in dark grey stone with huge rusticated columns (note the bizarre Ionic capitals) marks the entrance – unmissable. Then a lift whisks you up a few floors to the discreet little hotel of six rooms, whose bedrooms, though simply furnished, are vast – most could fit five or six with ease. Walls are white, ceilings are arched, floors gleam; all have air conditioning and TVs. Along the corridors are prints of Vesuvius in various stages of eruption – an understandably popular Neapolitan theme. This is an area pulsating with things to see: the sculptures by Donatello and Michelozzo in the church of Sant'Angelo a Nilo; the Largo di Corpo di Nilo, where a Roman statue of a reclining old man (a representation of the Nile) is said to whisper to women as they walk by.

rooms	6 rooms for 2-6.
price	€ 88–€ 110. Half-board also available.
meals	Restaurants nearby.
closed	Rarely.
directions	From the station or airport, hotel easily reached by taxi, bus or metro. Hotel 100m from National Archeological Museum in historic centre.

The Capella Sansevero is a bizarre monument. A family tomb upstairs; while downstairs are the ghoulish results of the alchemist Prince Raimondo's experiments.

	Signora Auriemma Armida
tel	+39 081 790 1000
fax	+39 081 211 698
e-mail	albergo.sansevero@libero.it
web	www.albergosansevero.it

Hotel

map 13   entry 252

B&B L'Appartamento Spagnolo

Via Nuova S. Maria Ognibene 30, 80100 Naples

The balconies offer glimpses of Neapolitan life across the narrow street. Washing flutters, cats preen by bright pots of geraniums. From a nearby school comes the sound of children singing. You're in the old Spanish quarter, with tortuous streets (don't even think of bringing your car to the door) and a glorious bustle. The apartment is on the second floor (no lift) of a 19th-century block. Each of the big, high-ceilinged bedrooms has French windows, tiny balconies and a quirky little shower room. The floors are cool, polished, speckled stone and the furnishings simple and pleasing. Heavy shutters help keep out the street noise at night. Breakfast is prepared by Anita, who arrives bearing fresh croissants, cakes and fruit, and is served in the *salone* at an American drugstore table with jaunty red seats. There are masses of restaurants outside the door, but you may also arrange to use the little 1950s-style kitchen to prepare your own food. It even has views of the Bay of Naples. Paolo plans to use the apartment as a gallery for contemporary artists and it does have great individuality and style. *Minimum stay two nights.*

rooms	3 doubles.
price	€ 85–€ 100.
meals	Restaurants on your doorstep.
closed	Rarely.
directions	Street east off, & parallel to, Via Croci S. Lucia al Monte. Steps lead from Via Nuove S. Maria Ognibene, up to Via Croci SL al Monte; up to Corso V Emanuel; brings you out at Hotel San Francesco, no. 328, Corso V Emanuel.

Naples has some of the Baroque period's grandest architecture, for example, in the Chiesa dei Girolamini and the Piazza del Gesù.

Paolo Serpone

tel	+39 081 19565835
fax	+39 081 289 780
e-mail	myhomeyourhome@virgilio.it
web	www.myhomeyourhome.it

B&B

Villa Giusso

Via Camaldoli 25, Astapiana, 80069 Vico Equense

This is where Napoleon's brother-in-law spent his last days before his exile from Naples – it has barely changed. Once a monastery, the villa stands high on a promontory overlooking the Bay of Naples. There are at least five sitting rooms including a wonderful salon (wisely roped-off) full of collapsing 19th-century sofas and silk-covered chairs. Bedrooms have original 17th-century furnishings, somewhat worn, and huge paintings; most overlook the ramshackle courtyard where dogs roam. The big gardens and terrace are wonderful for children. You breakfast on figs (in season), fresh ricotta and homemade cakes in the vaulted kitchen, magnificent with fireplace and old Vetri tiles, at tables that seat at least 20. Giovanna has her hands full – she looks after the estate and a young son – but always finds time for guests. She organises Saturday cookery classes, too, and tours of the monastery. Roam the surrounding vineyards and olive groves, drink in the views of the Sorrento coast. It's an adventure to be here and an adventure to arrive – bring a small car with plenty of ground clearance! *Minimum stay two nights.*

rooms	5: 2 doubles, 1 suite for 4; 2 doubles sharing bathroom.
price	€78–€95.
meals	Dinner, €18.
closed	November–Palm Sunday
directions	Exit Napoli-Salerno m'way for Castellammare di Stabia; follow Sorrento. At Seiano, after Moon Valley Hotel, left for M. Faito for 4.6km. Right at x-roads for 'Passeggiate Vicane'; Villa after 1.2km.

Astapiana was built in 1600 by Matteo di Capua, Lord of Vico Equense. Luigi Giusso, Duke of Galdo, the present owners' ancestor, bought it in 1822.

	Famiglia Giusso Rispoli
tel	+39 081 802 4392
fax	+39 081 403 797
e-mail	astapiana@tin.it
web	www.astapiana.com

B&B

map 13   entry 254

Agriturismo La Ginestra

Via Tessa 2, Santa Maria del Castello, 80060 Moiano di Vico Equense

There is a delightfully fresh, rustic feel to this farmhouse, and its position, 680m above sea level, is truly special. From the flower-rich terraces stunning sea views stretch in two directions: the Bay of Naples and the Bay of Salerno. The hills behind hold much delight for serious walkers: the 'Sentieri degli Dei' and other CAI-signed routes are a stone's throw away, and some of the paths, especially those down to Positano, are vertiginous and tough. The landlord can organise guided nature walks or trips to nearby tourist spots if you are interested. Some of the farm's organic produce – nuts, honey, vegetables, olive oil – is sold from a little cottage; it's also served in the restaurant (converted from the old stables), where the traditional Sorrento cooking is immensely popular with Italians, especially for Sunday lunch. This is quite a tribute to La Ginestra as it is not the most easily accessible of places. But not so inaccessible that the local bus can't make it up the hill. *Minimum stay three nights.*

Vico Equense is named after the Roman town of Aequana (Vicus Aequanensis), famous for its wines.

rooms	8: 2 doubles, 3 triples, 3 family.
price	Half-board €80–€90, triples €110–€125, family €145–€165. Full-board €98–€110, triples €138–€155, family €170–€195.
meals	Dinner €19.
closed	Rarely.
directions	From A3 exit Castellamare di Stabia; SS145 coast road to Vico Equense; SS269 to Raffaele Bosco; at Moiano-Ticciano for Santa Maria del Castello.

tel	+39 081 802 3211
fax	+39 081 802 3211
e-mail	info@laginestra.org
web	www.laginestra.org

Inn

Le Tore

Via Pontone 43, Sant'Agata sui due Golfi, 80064 Massa Lubrense

Vittoria is a vibrant presence and knows almost every inch of this wonderful coastline – its paths, its flora, its hill-perched villages, its secret corners. She sells olive oil, vinegar, preserves, nuts and lemons on her organically-cultivated, terraced five hectares. The cocks crow at dawn and distant dogs bark in the early hours... it's rural, the sort of place where you want to get up while there's still dew on the vegetables. The names of the guest bedrooms reflect their conversion from old farm buildings – Stalla, Fienile, Balcone; they are simply but solidly furnished. The excellent food is home-cooked and served to guests together; breakfast is taken at your own table under the pergola, and may include raspberries, apple tart and fresh fruit juices. You must descend to coast level to buy your postcards, but this is a great spot from which to explore, and to walk – the CAI Alta via di Lattari footpath is nearby. There's no pool but Vittoria has arranged a special price with a private swimming club five kilometres away. A haven to return to after a day's sightseeing; you can see the sea, and fireflies glimmer at night in the lemon groves.

rooms	6 + 1: 6 doubles. 1 apartment for 5.
price	€ 82–€ 110. Half-board € 120. Apartment € 700–€ 1,000 per week.
meals	Dinner € 22–€ 40, book ahead.
closed	November-Palm Sunday. Open 26 December-7 January.
directions	A3 Naples-Palermo, exit Castellamare di Stabia for Positano. At x-roads for Positano, by restaurant Teresinella, follow sign for Sant'Agata. 7km on, left on Via Pontone, 1km to Le Tore.

	Signora Vittoria Brancaccio
tel	+39 081 808 0637
fax	+39 081 533 0819
e-mail	letore@iol.it
web	www.letore.com

The Emporer Tiberius retired to Capri where he 'succumbed to all the vicious passions which he had for a long time tried, not very successfully, to disguise.' Suetonius

Self-catering & B&B

map 13   entry 256

Albergo Punta Regina

Via Pasitea 224, 84017 Positano

Catch the sea breezes as you sit on the terrace and drink in the views. The superb, rocky coastline disappears into a distant, shimmering haze yet, just across the bay, you can pick out the enchanted island of Li Galli. Beside you, flowers romp over pergolas and tumble out of pots. This typical, white-painted, late-19th-century building – just a short walk from the town centre and approached by steps – clings steeply to the hillside, with terraces and balconies on its upper three floors. Once a *pensione* and more recently a dressmaker's workshop, it has been transformed by a local family into a small, good hotel. Though they already own a number of larger hotels in the area, they wanted to offer somewhere quiet and welcoming, where guests could simply have B&B, then go off to explore. The bedrooms are roomy, traditional and comfortable. Some have pretty vaulted ceilings, others beds set into arched recesses; all except those at street level have glorious views. Immediately off the cool, attractive reception area is a big shower room, so guests who have checked out but spent the day on the beach below can shower before moving on.

rooms	18: 16 doubles, 2 suites.
price	€ 170–€ 255. Singles € 180–€ 195. Suite € 335–€ 365.
meals	Choice of restaurants nearby.
closed	November-March.
directions	Leave coast road, 163, drive right down into Positano. Ask for full directions on booking.

Legend has it that it was on the islands of Li Galli that the sirens tried to cast a spell over Ulysses — and were turned to stone for their failure.

Benedetta Russo

tel	+39 089 812020
fax	+39 089 8123161
e-mail	info@puntaregina.com
web	www.puntaregina.com

B&B

Casa Albertina
Via della Tavolezza 3, 84017 Positano

Positano is a honeycomb of houses clinging to the hillside between beach and high coast road – the famous Amalfitana, often seen in film footage. Among the marzipan facades you cannot miss the chocolate-coloured Casa Albertina. Mere minutes from the thronged one-way road system, you walk to get here – but not far – and leave car and luggage in the able hands of the hotel staff. (There is a charge for this and you need to pre-book, or ring as you approach.) Here is the one-time refuge of the playwright Pirandello – a wonderfully quiet, historic *casa* with stupendous views. Air-conditioned bedrooms are comfortable and hotel-smart, many with terraces. The stylish restaurant serves regional food, including the local *azzurro* (blue) fish, and there's a comprehensive, though expensive, wine list. Lorenzo, whose family owns the hotel, combines impeccable manners and relaxed charm with good English and his staff are cheerful and hardworking. A great spot from which to visit Amalfi, Sorrento, Pompeii or Paestum. Or take the boat to magical Capri, with its cobblestone streets, chic shops and stunning vistas.

rooms	20 doubles/twins, all with balcony.
price	Half-board €210–€250 for 2.
meals	Breakfast & dinner included. Lunch available on request.
closed	Rarely.
directions	From motorway, exit Castellamare di Stabia towards Sorrento & then Positano. Hotel on only street in village.

	Lorenzo Cinque
tel	+39 089 875143
fax	+39 089 811540
e-mail	info@casalbertina.it
web	www.casalbertina.it

You can ask for the room which used to be taken regularly by Luigi Pirandello, the poet and playwright, who used to come here several times a year.

Hotel

map 13   entry 258

Villa en Rose

Via Torretta a Marmorata 22, 84010 Ravello

You really get a feel here of what life must have been like before roads and motorised transport came to these steep hillsides. The position is stunning, halfway between Minori and Ravello on a marked footpath which was once a mule trail. In fact, the only way to get here is on foot, with about 15 minutes' worth of steps down from the closest road. Getting your provisions up here might be something of a challenge in bad weather! The apartment itself is modern-functional not aesthetic and the bedroom has no window, but the views are wonderful and the house is set amid lemon groves. (The locals are still squeezing a living out of lemons, which *limoncello* has done much to boost.) You are miles from the crowds clustering around the coast, and the pool means you don't have to venture down to the beach. If you don't feel like cooking, the walk up to the main square in ravishing Ravello would certainly earn you a cappuccino and a brioche. And don't miss the glorious gardens of the Villas Rufolo and Cimbrone. *Minimum stay three nights.*

The Limunciel shop at Corso Vittorio Emanuele 9 in Minori is a veritable temple to limoncello, a liqueur made from an infusion of the hand-peeled rinds of the greenest of lemons in first flower.
Self-catering & B&B

rooms	1 apartment for 2.
price	From € 104.
meals	Self-catering. Breakfast € 6 on request. Choice of restaurants nearby.
closed	Rarely.
directions	Directions at time of booking.

Signora Valeria Civale
tel +39 089 857661
e-mail valeriacivale@yahoo.it

Azienda Agrituristica Seliano

Via Seliano, 84063 Paestum

The *masseria* – the converted farm and stables – is about a mile from Seliano where the warm-hearted Baroness Cecilia Baratta lives. She and her sons keep a 600-strong buffalo herd; the milk makes delicious butter and mozzarella. The five bedrooms in the old stone barn and pigeon loft are furnished in country style; there are more rooms in the villa, where Cecilia cooks for her family and many guests. (It can be hugely busy at weekends.) You eat – authentically, generously and very well – in the dining room, or under pergolas in the scented gardens. There's also a long sitting room to share, charmingly furnished with sofas and well-polished country pieces. When he has a spare moment, Ettore is happy to give farm tours; children love to see the buffalo – not far from the *masseria* – sitting up to their necks in their pool of black mud. Cecilia holds cookery courses in the big, well-equipped kitchen below your rooms, and there's a lovely pool at the main house. The beach is a bike or horse ride away (experienced equestrians only), and the Greek temples at Paestum are not to be missed. Wonderful. *Minimum stay two nights.*

rooms	5 doubles.
price	€72–€112. Half-board €104–€144.
meals	Dinner at sister house Seliano, €18–€26 with wine.
closed	Mid-January–mid-February.
directions	From A3 to Battibaglia, right onto SS18 to Cappacioscalo (20km). Signs to Seliano on right.

Baroness Cecilia Bellelli Baratta

tel	+39 0828 724544
fax	+39 0828 723634
e-mail	seliano@agriturismoseliano.it
web	www.agriturismoseliano.it

The Bellelli family appear in Degas' most famous group portrait of 1821. The Baroness Bellelli Baratta, who runs this estate with her two sons, is a descendant.

Inn

map 14   entry 260

Hotel Villa Sirio

Via Lungomare de Simone 15, 84072 Santa Maria di Castellabate

Look down and you will see clear green water splashing against the rocks below the terrace. The hotel is in a prime position at the end of the promenade, with glorious views of the bay and the hills. From the outside, it still looks like the late-19th-century gentleman's summer residence it probably once was; inside, it has been converted into a bright and pretty small hotel. Alfonso and Rosalinda have gone to much trouble to make it comfortable and cheerful. The white-walled bedrooms, with their vivid, marine-coloured curtains and bedcovers, look out to sea or to the 12th-century castle on the hill behind. Andrea, the owners' son, has come home to take charge of the kitchen after training in Montreux, and you dine on specially commissioned Venetian glass, silver and china. Below, the vaulted lower-ground-floor (where the bar is and where a buffet breakfast is served) still has the thick walls and tufa arches of earlier foundations. Rather more modern is the generous sundeck jutting out over the water; the hotel also has a private piece of beach a few minutes' walk away. *Minimum stay three nights.*

'The kingly brilliance of Sirius pierced the eye with a steely glitter.' Thomas Hardy

rooms	14 doubles/twins.
price	€ 115–€ 210.
	Half-board € 166–€ 260.
	Full-board € 206–€ 300.
meals	Dinner € 25.
closed	15 November-27 December ;
	5 January-20 March.
directions	Hotel last of houses on sea front; at southern end of esplanade of Lungomare de Simone.

Rosalinda & Alfonso Tortora

tel	+39 0974 960162
fax	+39 0974 960507
e-mail	villa.sirio@costacilento.it
web	www.villasirio.it

Hotel

La Mola
Via Adolfo Cilento 2, 84048 Castellabate

You'll catch your breath at the views as you step onto your balcony. La Mola is perched high up in the old town, way above the tourists who congregate down the hill in Santa Maria. It is a grand old 17th-century palace and incorporates a 12th-century tower – an interesting building in its own right. The huge round stone olive press found in the cellars during restoration gives the hotel its name; now it forms the base of a vast, glass-topped drinks table. The sea is everywhere: your room looks onto it, as do the communal sitting areas, and the terrace where you take your meals. Furnishings are pristine; bedrooms have tiled floors, wrought-iron bedsteads with crisp linen and the odd antique. La Mola is the ancestral home of Signor Favilla, who spends every summer here with his wife, running the hotel with admirable – and amiable – efficiency. Away from the seafront resorts the countryside up here is lovely, and Paestum, Agropoli and Velia are a short drive away.

rooms	5 doubles.
price	€ 103–€ 114. Singles € 77.
meals	Dinner with wine, € 31–€ 39; book ahead.
closed	November–March.
directions	From Naples A30 south to Battipaglia, then Agropoli - Castellabate. La Mola is in *centro storico*.

Castellabate looks out over the Tyrrhenian Sea, named after the Tyrrheni or Etruscans.

	Francesco & Loredana Favilla
tel	+39 0974 967053
fax	+39 0974 967714
e-mail	lamola@lamola-it.com
web	www.lamola-it.com

B&B

map 14   entry 262

Il Tower Enormo
Roman Road, 00000

The retreating army of Charles V passed by on the other side, so awe-inspiring was the reputation for ferocity that the tower had in those days. Most of the base is of solid stone and therefore impregnable – and there is nothing there to pregn. The top half has always been virtually beyond reach, inhabited by a very strange family of recluses. It is their surviving female member who has opened the tower for guests – a breakthrough for the local tourist board. Few would have imagined it, and we have to admit that your reception is likely to be, at first, austere. Note how you are watched upon arrival, in a rather stiff sort of way. But the stiffness soon gives way to cultured ease and this will be a wonderful experience, isolated and lofty, unrepeatable. You are well-catered for in winter, with a blaze of fireplaces and a fine cellar of wines to lubricate your soirees. By the time you have emerged from the place you will want to spend the whole day out – and there is a lot to do: walks in those hills are inspiring.

It is said (in hushed voices by local folks) that the Romans once passed through here – in a cart.

rooms	1: ceiling too high by half. Would have been much better as two floors...
price	Money is not valued here, but a ladder would be appreciated.
meals	None: this place provides nourishment just for the soul.
closed	Only until you can force the door.
directions	Follow Roman Road past Rome (this one forgot where it was leading to) and take fifty-fourth left.

Principessa Niente Particularia

tel	0102030405
e-mail	look@thestateof.it
web	vvv.tall-isnt.it/?

Il Tufiello

SS. 399 Km 6, 83045 Calitri

Sunflowers alternate with wheat and oats in the rolling acres that surround the farm. Tomatoes dry in wicker baskets in the sun, others are bottled with basil; there are chestnuts and honey and vegetables in abundance – all organic. The Zampaglione family have farmed here for generations; wholly committed to ecological principles, they are proud to show guests around the place, and delighted if you help out in the vegetable garden! A white house standing four-square in the fields is the family home, but it is the old, single-storey farmhouse, and Grandfather's House, that have been made over to house guests. The old stable, with its huge fireplace, high rafters, excellent sofas and little library full of local information, serves as a general gathering place. Borrow a bike and set off for a nearby farm to buy fresh ricotta and pecorino, book in for a cookery course, bake bread in a wood oven. This is a fascinating area, where Campania, Basilicata and Puglia meet... don't miss the castle of Frederico II di Swebia, or Calitri, with its sensational, steeply terraced houses, and its pottery. *Minimum stay two nights.*

rooms	4 + 2: 4 doubles. 2 apartments: 1 for 2-4, 1 for 4.
price	€ 50. Apartment € 65–€ 105 per night.
meals	Breakfast € 3. Packed lunch € 6. Restaurants nearby, 6km.
closed	16 November-Easter, except Christmas.
directions	A16 Naples-Bari exit Lacedonia towards Calitri. Il Tufiello between Bisaccia & Calitri.

The character and hardships of life in the south were vividly captured by Carlo Levi in his novel Christ stopped at Eboli.

Pierluigi & Nerina Zampaglione

tel	+39 081 5757604 (& fax)
fax	+39 0827 38851 (& tel)
e-mail	info@iltufiello.it
web	www.iltufiello.it

B&B & Self-catering

map 14　entry 264

Photography by Masseria Il Frontoio, Puglia, entry no 270

calabria, basilicata, puglia

Il Giardino di Iti

Contrada Amica, 87068 Rossano

The farm, a five-minute drive from the Ionian sea, has been in the same family for three centuries. A massive arched doorway leads to a courtyard and vast enclosed garden; meals are served here, and at night the citrus and olive trees glow magically from lights hidden in their branches. The rooms have been simply and prettily decorated by the owner, Baroness Francesca Cherubini. Ask for one that opens directly off the courtyard, its original fireplace and terracotta tiles intact. Each room has a wall painting of one of the farm's crops, and is correspondingly named: Lemon, Peach, Aubergine, Cucumber. Why not extend your repertoire of recipes here and take one of their courses on regional cookery? If you've always wanted to learn how to weave, there's a course on that, too. If neither appeals, revel in the atmosphere and the gastronomic delights of the restaurant... *lagane e ciceri, elisir di limonettie piretti* – and atone for the calories later. There's a host of activities on offer in the area, and, of course, heaps of history.

Nearby lie the ruins of the ancient city of Sibaris, famous for its high living, from which we get the word 'sybaritic'.

rooms	12 + 2: 10 family rooms; 2 doubles sharing bath. 2 apartments for 3-4.
price	Half-board € 40–€ 50 p.p. Full-board € 41-59 p.p.
meals	Self-catering possible in apartments.
closed	Rarely.
directions	A3 Salerno-Reggio Calabria exit Sibari. Rossano road (SS106) to Contrada Amica & then towards Paludi.

Baroness Francesca Cherubini

tel	+39 0983 64508
fax	+39 0983 64508
e-mail	info@giardinoiti.it
web	www.giardinoiti.it

B&B & Self-catering

entry 265   map 18

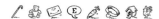

Villa Cheta Elite

Via Nazionale, 85941 Acquafredda di Maratea

Villa Cheta Elite is a godsend in an area with few really nice hotels. It is a gracious Art Nouveau villa set back from the coast road, with a terraced garden of winding paths, tropical trees, scented plants and exotics in amphora-style pots... and views, which will keep you rooted to the spot. Relax in the shade of the gardens, or cross the road and plunge down 165 steps for a swim in the clear green waters below. (Then trek up again!). Bedrooms are comfortable, with good, slightly maiden-auntish furniture, large windows and plenty of light; some are being redecorated in Art Nouveau style. The public rooms, with ornate cornices and mouldings, are more elaborately furnished with antiques, good paintings and a number of portraits of previous occupants. There's also a small sitting room, and a library where you can bone up on the history of the region. Five chefs conjure up delicious food, served on the upper terrace in summer with views of the sea – and moon. It's a hugely romantic spot; you may even hear nightingales sing. Stefania and Piero are lovely hosts and everyone who works here is courteous and kind.

rooms	20 doubles.
price	€ 120–€ 250.
	Half-board € 144–€ 300.
meals	Breakfast € 10. Lunch/dinner € 30.
closed	November–Palm Sunday.
directions	From A3 exit Lagonegro-Maratea; 10km, SS104 right to Sapri. In Sapri left onto coast road for Maratea. Villa 9km along coast, above road on left.

The Acquafredda of the place name refers to a freshwater spring which appears in the sea just off the rocky headland.

	Signora Stefania Aquadro
tel	+39 0973 878 134
fax	+39 0973 878 135
e-mail	info@villacheta.it
web	www.villacheta.it

Hotel

map 17 entry 266

San Teodoro Nuovo

Loc. Marconia, 75020 Marconia di Pisticci

A haven in a green sea of citrus and olive groves. Flowering creepers disguise the lower half of the 200-year-old, rose-tinted mansion but design is apparent in the symmetry of the upper shuttered windows. Rent a self-catering apartment, furnished with family antiques, in a wing of the house or choose one of three beautifully converted apartments in the same building as the restaurant, a five-minute walk away. The rooms are large and light, with marvellous vaulted ceilings; elegantly and simply furnished, they also have air conditioning. Small parterre gardens, and a whitewashed chapel alongside, lend a Mexican feel. The full range of Basilicata cuisine is here – breakfasts and dinners are unusually good. The whole place is beautifully maintained, with capable Antonio, with the family for 25 years, at the helm. You are three miles from the Ionian Sea with its white sands; golf is not much further, and archaeological sites abound: follow the routes taken by 18th-century trophy-hunting travellers, or visit workshops devoted to reproducing classical antiques. *Minimum stay two nights.*

The Italian south is known as the Mezzogiorno, the 'land of the midday sun'.

rooms	9 apartments for 2, 4 or 6.
price	€90–€110, incl. breakfast.
meals	Dinner €20–€25.
closed	Rarely.
directions	From Bari E843 south to exit Palagiano. South to SS106 for Metaponto & Policoro. About 4-5km after Metaponto right at milestone 442km; left at T-junction. San Teodoro on right.

Marchesa Maria Xenia D'Oria

tel	+39 0835 470042
fax	+39 0835 470223
e-mail	info@santeodoronuovo.com
web	www.santeodoronuovo.com

B&B & Self-catering

Masseria Agriturismo Il Cardinale

Contrada Capoposto, 70020 Poggiorsini

There's been a hostelry here since 1197. Now it is a relaxed *agriturismo* run by Anna – serious, wry, intelligent and kind. She married Leonardo 20 years ago, a dashing national event rider who introduced her to these deep, wild hills. The main house forms a square with the guest rooms, which resemble a row of stables on each side; the farm workers' dwellings, and the stables housing the 30 thoroughbreds, lie beyond. The feel is of a slightly shabby South American hacienda: there's a dusty rose garden in the centre and the simple guest rooms, though spotless, are outdated. The *grande sala* is vast and vaulted and 700 years old, used for dining when large parties are present, and there's a big sitting room filled with interesting family portraits and numerous pictures of horses, rosettes and silver cups. There's masses of space for children to explore, a good swimming pool, a big fish pond, tennis and billiards. Come for the atmosphere, for Anna and her cooking – the food is excellent and generous – and, above all, for the horses. If you time it right you could be galloping across the hills with Leonardo at full moon.

rooms	17: 2 doubles, 10 suites, 5 family apartments.
price	€56–€60.
meals	Dinner €30.
closed	Rarely, but book in advance.
directions	From Pioggiorsini 2km to Il Cardinale. Ring for exact directions.

The town name is derived from the Orsini family, who were the masters and land owners during feudalism, 1609 to 1810.

Leonardo & Anna Terribile

tel	+39 080 323 7279
fax	+39 080 323 7279
e-mail	info@ilcardinale.it
web	www.ilcardinale.it

Inn & Self-catering

map 14   entry 268

Masseria San Domenico
Savelletri di Fasano, 72010 Brindisi

It looks magical in the evening light, this white, 15th-century *masseria*, still with the bell-tower and cross of its founders, the Knights of Malta. Between the trees and shrubs – tall palms, ancient olives, oleanders, jasmine, roses – are tantalising glimpses of the sea, just 500m away. Dazzling white walls and a bunch of tall palm trees lend a Moorish air, arches and vaulted ceilings give a sense of light and space. Bedrooms have an Italian country-house feel, with walnut furniture, wrought-iron beds and polished stone tiles. The food is excellent – Puglian with an emphasis on fresh fish – and the wines equally good. You are served by young, charming staff in the dramatic, vaulted dining room or out on the terrace overlooking the seawater pool. Landscaped to look like a cove, an entrancing place to swim... San Domenico has its own small, sandy beach, too, with stripey umbrellas, sunbeds and a friendly attendant. Or you can indulge yourself in the hotel's superb Thalassotherapy Spa, or try out the new 18-hole golf course (and the amenities of the club) which abuts the Roman ruins of Egnathia. Unadulterated indulgence.

rooms	45: 40 doubles, 5 suites.
price	€ 240-€ 484. Singles € 209-€ 297. Suites € 412-€ 935.
meals	Lunch & dinner € 60. Dinner € 40. Good wine list. Restaurant closed on Tuesdays.
closed	Rarely.
directions	From the motorway Bari-Brindisi, exit Savalletri. From Savalletri, south along coast on 379 for Torre Canne. Masseria after 2km. Train station 5km.

This masseria is an ancient watchtower guarding the road between Bari and Brindisi. Here the Knights of Malta defended themselves against the Ottoman attack.

Signor Antonio Polesel
tel +39 080 4827769
fax +39 080 4827978
e-mail info@masseriasandomenico.com
web www.masseriasandomenico.com

Hotel

Masseria Il Frantoio

Strada St. 16 KM. 874 , 72017 Ostuni

So many ravishing things! An old, white house clear-cut against a blue sky, mysterious gardens, the scent of jasmine – and a private beach five kilometres away. Armando and Rosalba spent a year restoring this 17th-century house (built over a sixth-century oil press) after abandoning city life. Inside – sheer delight. A series of beautiful rooms, ranging from the fairy-tale (a froth of lace and toile) to the endearingly simple (madras bedcovers and old desks) and the formal (antique armoires and doughty, gilt-framed ladies) – a gloriously eclectic mix. Dinner is equally marvellous – if you're lucky enough to be there on the right night and have put your name down. Rosalba specialises in wonderful Puglian dishes washed down with good local wines; Armando rings the courtyard bell at 8.30 and the feast begins, either in the arched dining room or outside in the candlelit courtyard. It will stay in your memory – as will other details: an exterior white stone stair climbing to a bedroom, a tiny, faded green window peeping out over a deep sill, an arched doorway swathed in wisteria. *Minimum stay two nights.*

rooms	8 + 1: 3 doubles, 2 triples, 3 family rooms. 1 apartment for 2-4.
price	€ 176–€ 208; € 54–€ 61 for children. Apartment € 290–€ 365.
meals	Dinner € 48–€ 51; book ahead. Also local restaurants.
closed	Rarely.
directions	From Bari airport superstrada E55 exit for Pezze di Greco towards Ostuni. On SS16, watch for Ostuni until km sign 874. Right into drive.

Masserias were the houses of the land agents who managed estates for absentee landlords.

	Armando Balestrazzi
tel	+39 0831 330 276
fax	+39 0831 330 276
e-mail	armando@trecolline.it
web	www.trecolline.it

B&B & Self-catering

map 15   entry 270

Caelia

Contrada S. Anna, Ceglie Messapica

Conical stone houses peculiar to this area – *trulli* – make a deliciously eccentric contribution to this remote, beautiful landscape. You'll spot their distinctive round shape and pointed roofs cropping up among the more traditional farm buildings. At Caelia you get the chance to sleep in one. Davide has converted part of some old farm dwellings into an apartment for himself (he works in Milan) and a separate B&B. The outside, all different levels, is painted dazzling white, with terraces bright with flowers. Both bedrooms are small and vibrant, with well-designed shower rooms. The *trullo* room has narrow ledges running round its curved walls, lit by ceramic lights, and a double bed directly under the cone of the roof. A vase of flowers glows in a deep alcove and a blue stable door leads outside via three stone steps. The arched *lamia* room, opening on the terrace, has a small window set into its thick wall and a painted stone fireplace. The living room is new, with a flagged floor and windows and doors on both sides to allow a through draught. Works by Davide's grandmother, a well known naïf artist, add charm and colour.

rooms	2 doubles.
price	€ 70-€ 90.
meals	Self-catering; restaurants nearby.
closed	October-Easter.
directions	Ceglie Messapica to Fedele Grande, after 5km right (sign Padre Pio). After 1km, blue gate on left; house 50m on right.

The lovely baroque town of Martina Franca has its roots in the 10th century when people sought refuge on Monte di San Martino from the cruelty of the Saracens.

Davide Vincenzi

tel	+39 333 25 74 101 (Mobile)
e-mail	info@caelia.it vincenzidavide@hotmail.cc emails)
web	www.caelia.it

B&B & Self-catering

Acquarossa

C. de Acquarossa 2, 72014 Casalini

It's like a fairytale. You're high in the hills above the quiet Itria valley, looking out over olive groves and orchards. Suddenly the *strada bianca* peters out among scrubby juniper bushes and there, in front of you… an extraordinary cluster of round buildings, their conical roofs topped by stone balls. Acquarossa is a 19th-century *trulli* settlement and some of the foundations go back 500 years. Timeless and disarming, the restored, white-painted stone buildings stand in courtyards and terraces lavishly planted with clumps of lavender and herbs, surrounded by arches and drystone walls. Their immensely thick walls and pointed roofs make them beautifully cool in summer, and the little rooms have been delightfully, rustically decorated. Delicious country antiques, niches bright with flowers, voile curtains over small, deep windows and arched doorways, flagged floors and wood-burning stoves – an imaginative mix of style and tradition. The bathrooms are simple and pretty; the kitchens tiny and minimalist. And if you have the urge to cook something ambitious, there's an oven in the courtyard.

rooms	3 + 3: 3 doubles. 3 family rooms.
price	€78–€91. Family rooms €88–€103.
meals	Choice of restaurants nearby. Self-catering in family rooms.
closed	Rarely.
directions	SS379 for Bari; exit Ostuni-Villanova for Ostuni. At Agip station, left up road to r'bout, signed 'Strada dei Colli'. Left after '200m fine strada' sign. Uphill 1km, left at end of road. Track ends at Acquarossa.

Puglia produces some distinctive food and dishes and holds various food festivals every year. The Sagra della Puccia celebrates the small bread shapes that are filled with olives and grapes.

	Luca Montinaro
tel	+39 080 4444 093
fax	+39 0831 524826
e-mail	lucamontinaro@libero.it
web	www.acqua-rossa.com

B&B & Self-catering

map 15   entry 272

Hotel Palazzo del Corso

Corso Roma 145, 73014 Gallipoli

A fascinating maze of narrow streets, hidden entrances, baroque facades and balconies bright with washing and geraniums make up the old part of Gallipoli. Dott. de Donno is a native of the town and loves it all. In 2000, despite also running an organic farm, he decided to buy the 18th-century Palazzo del Corso, near the old quarter, and turn it into a small hotel. It's an elegant, stucco-fronted house close to the waterfront. A small sitting room runs from front to back, with a fine vaulted ceiling, panelling and oriental rugs. The suites, too, have vaulted ceilings and parquet or marble floors. If there's a slight flavour of the gentlemen's club about the brown leather sofas in the sitting rooms, it's redeemed elsewhere by soft colours, pretty bedheads and beautiful linen. Up on the roof is a terrace looking over moored yachts to the harbour and the Gulf of Taranto, and if you don't feel like going down to the private beach, you can bask under big cream cotton umbrellas — or in the hydrotherapy/hydromassage pool. In summer, dinner is served up here by candlelight. *Minimum stay one week, 15 June-14 September.*

'Upon the margin of a rugged shore there is a spot now barren, desolate...' John William Street, *Gallipoli*

Hotel

rooms	7: 2 doubles, 2 doubles with sofa beds, 3 suites.
price	€ 155-€ 205. Suites € 180-€ 310.
meals	Dinner € 50. Choice of restaurants nearby.
closed	Rarely.
directions	From Lecce superstrada for Santa Maria di Leuca, exit Gallipoli centro. Hotel on left side of Corso Roma, a one-way street, parallel to harbour.

Dottor Pasquale de Donno

tel	+39 0833 264 040
fax	+39 0833 265 052
e-mail	info@hotelpalazzodelcorso.it
web	www.hotelpalazzodelcorso.it

Relais Corte Palmieri

Corte Palmieri 3, 73014 Gallipoli

Brilliant, whitewashed walls, square outlines and stone staircases... There's a distinctly Greek flavour to this arresting 17th-century building with charmingly haphazard levels and unexpected views. It's in the old fishing quarter of Gallipoli, surrounded by narrow, colourful streets where fisher families have lived for generations. Each cool, pretty, newly renovated room is different – some have high, arched ceilings, others are lower and beamed. Soft, glazed cotton curtains on iron poles and painted, hand-stencilled furniture give a subdued, country feel – so restful. Most of the rooms open on to their own terrace, where you can breakfast in seclusion among potted palms and flowering shrubs should you decide not to go down to the bar. There's a pretty beach nearby, and dinner is a walk along the waterfront to the elegant Palazzo del Corso, Dott. Pasquale de Donno's first hotel. Corte Palmieri is his new venture and very different in style; however, his enthusiastic commitment to ensuring that his guests are comfortable and well looked after is unwavering. *Minimum stay one week in August.*

rooms	9 doubles.
price	€ 100–€ 180.
meals	Dinner € 50 at Hotel Palazzo del Corso, 10-minute walk.
closed	November-Easter.
directions	From Riviera Colombo south on Via Roncella & Corte Palmieri, third street on right.

Dottor Pasquale de Donno

tel	+39 0833 265 318
fax	+39 0833 265 052
e-mail	info@hotelpalazzodelcorso.it
web	www.hotelpalazzodelcorso.it

'For we are lovers of the beautiful, yet simple in our tastes.' Thucydides, *471BC*.

B&B

map 16   entry 274

Photography by Il Limoneto, Catania, entry no 281

sicily

Hotel Signum

Via Scalo 15, Malfa, 98050 Salina, Isola Eolie

Leave your car and the bustle of Sicily behind. Lush Salina isn't as famous as some of her glamorous Aeolian neighbours (even though *Il Postino* was filmed here) but is all the more peaceful for that. The friendly, unassuming hotel sits so quietly at the end of a narrow lane, that you'd hardly guess it was there. Dine on the shaded terracotta terrace with its chunky tile-topped tables, colourful iron and wicker chairs; gaze out over lemon trees to the glistening sea. Traditional dishes and local ingredients are the norm. Then wind along the labyrinth of paths, where plants flow and tumble, to your simple and striking bedroom: cool pale walls, pretty antiques, wrought-iron beds and good linen; starched lace flutters at the windows. The island architecture is typically low and unobtrusive and Clara and Michele have let their hotel grow organically as they've bought and converted nearby farm buildings. The result is a beautiful, relaxing space where even at busy times you feel as if you are one of only a handful of guests. Snooze on a shady veranda, take a dip in the infinity pool – that view again – or clamber down the path to a quiet pebbly cove. Bliss.

During La Sagra dei Capperi (The Caper Festival) in June the people of Salina prepare an enormous table full of dishes using capers.

rooms	30: 28 doubles, 2 singles.
price	€ 100–€ 200.
meals	Dinner € 25–€ 30.
closed	1 November–13 March.
directions	By boat or hydrofoil from Naples, Palermo, Messina and Reggio Calabria. If you want to leave your car there are garages in Milazzo.

Clara Rametta & Michele Caruso

tel	+39 090 9844222
fax	+39 090 9844102
e-mail	salina@hotelsignum.it
web	www.hotelsignum.it

Hotel

L'Appartamento

Via Scalo 15, Malfa , 98050 Salina, Isola Eolie

The volcanic archipelago seduces all who visit. Brilliant light, black pebble beaches, clear waters teeming with fish, sea breezes... the islands are named after the Greek god of winds who kept all the earth's breezes stuffed in an Aeolian cave. Come here to learn the art of *dolce far niente*, the idle life, to sample Malvasia, the sweet golden wine, and *granitas*, iced fruit (or coffee) pureés, the best in the world. Here in your fisherman's cottage you have all the advantages of the Hotel Signum just up the road – restaurant, bar, pool, Clara and her staff's gentle attention – yet you are wonderfully private. You have a living room, two smallish bedrooms, a rustic kitchen with pretty tiles, a microwave and a hob. Rent a boat from the local fishermen and explore the coves, take the bus (or electric car) to the best scuba-diving spot, book the ferry and island hop. On still-steaming Stromboli see the red lava flow, on Alicudi ride a donkey up the hill (what views!). Salina, with its vineyards and lemon groves, is perhaps the most beautiful of all the islands; its restaurants and bars are delectable, its twin peaks happily extinct.

rooms	Sleeps 4: 2 doubles.
price	€ 600–€ 1,400 per week.
meals	Self-catering; dinner € 25 in Hotel Signum
closed	Rarely.
directions	By boat or hydrofoil from Naples, Palermo, Messina and Reggio Calabria.

Clara & Michele Rametta

tel	+39 090 9844222
fax	+39 090 9844102
e-mail	salina@hotelsignum.it
web	www.hotelsignum.it

The Æolian Islands are a group of volcanic islands, inhabited since the Neolithic era. The Greeks made them home of King Æolus, the god of winds.

Self-catering

map 17   entry 276

Green Manors

Borgo Porticato, 98053 Castroreale

Your hosts spotted the dilapidated 1600s manor house years ago but its restoration began more recently and is a huge success. Flower-filled bedrooms, some with their own terrace, are elegant with a touch of rustic: tiled floors, heavy drapes, Sicilian patchwork counterpanes, lace-edged linen, family antiques, tapestries and paintings, all lit by chandeliers and finely tapered candles in silver candelabra. Bathrooms have huge baths or showers, delicately scented homemade soap and waffle towels. Chris, Paolo and Pierangela have also been busy establishing their bio-dynamic orchard and you reap the rewards at breakfast – a stylish affair with silver cutlery, antique napkins and linen. The homemade jams are divine – cherry, apricot, ginger, and the freshly squeezed lemon juice alone is worth getting up for. Dinners are delicious served outside behind a curtain of shimmering plants or by the huge fireplace when the weather is cooler. There's a charming wooden cabin in the olive groves, with an outside kitchen and bathroom; a lush tropical park with peacocks and ponies; and occasional summer concerts beneath the mulberry tree…

rooms	10 + 2 : 5 doubles, 3 suites, 2 singles. 2 houses for 2.
price	€80–€180; houses €60 for 2.
meals	Dinner €20–€25, good wine list.
closed	Rarely. Houses only open in summer.
directions	From Milazzo for Palermo exit Barcelona; immediately before Terme bridge sharp left. Signs.

Come in late spring when the valley is filled with oleanders.

Paolo & Pierangela Verzera & Chris Christiaens

tel	+39 090 9746515
fax	+39 090 9746507
e–mail	greenmanors@interfree.it
web	www.greenmanors.it

Hotel

entry 277   map 19

Hotel Villa Schuler

Via Roma 2, 98039 Taormina

Late in the 19th century, Signor Schuler's great grandfather travelled by coach from Germany and built his house here, high above the Ionian Sea. He chose the site well: the views of the Bay of Naxos and Mount Etna are spellbinding. And he built on a grand scale. When he died in 1905, Great Grandma decided to let out some rooms and the villa has been a hotel ever since. Though restored and brought up to date, it still has an old, elegant charm and a cool, quiet atmosphere. Lavish breakfasts are served on an antique buffet with Sicilian lace in the chandeliered breakfast room or out on the lovely terrace. Bedrooms vary from older rooms with beautifully tiled floors, antique furniture and stone balconies to more modern ones at the top of the hotel with new bathrooms and large terraces. All look out to sea or over the garden, which is a delight – vast, sub tropical and scented with jasmine – and magical when lit up at night. Hidden away behind a stone arch is a delightful, very private little apartment. A path leads through the gardens and out into Taormina's famous, traffic-free Corso Umberto.

rooms	25 + 1: 21 doubles, 4 triples. 1 garden apartment for 2-4.
price	€ 116-€ 168. Apt € 220-€ 374.
meals	Restaurants nearby.
closed	December-February.
directions	A18 Catania-Messina exit Taormina. There, follow white hotel signs. Right at city gate Porta Messina, up Via Circonvallazione. Left at Mediterannée Hotel; at Porta Catania take road down from post office, signs.

	Gerado Schuler
tel	+39 0942 23481
fax	+39 0942 23522
e-mail	schuler@tao.it
web	www.villaschuler.com

'You never enjoy the world aright, till the sea itself floweth in your veins.' Thomas Traherne, *Centuries of Meditation.*

Hotel & Self-catering

map 19   entry 278

Hotel Villa Belvedere
Via Bagnoli Croci 79, 98039 Taormina

It is aptly named – stunning views sweep down over the botanical gardens to the azure sea. Each front room has a balcony or bougainvillea-draped terrace, and tantalizing glimpses of the sea can be caught from every angle – even from the public rooms downstairs. The five rooms on the first floor have beautiful big private terraces (no. 25 is particularly lovely, with arched windows and alcoves), those on the second floor have pretty little French balconies, and the bright-white 'attic' rooms on the top floor, with smaller terraces, are delightful. The family rooms are at the back with views to the hills. The hotel has been in the family since 1902. Monsieur Pécaut, great-grandson of the founder, is French, his wife Italian, and they are a friendly, helpful and constant presence. There is no restaurant but light lunches of pasta, sandwiches and snacks can be taken by the pool – a cool, delicious oasis shaded by sub-tropical vegetation and dotted with waving, century-old palms. A short walk away is a cable car that takes you down to the sea; medieval Taormina, where Lawrence wrote *Lady Chatterly's Lover*, is enchanting by day and night.

rooms	52: 20 doubles, 23 doubles with terrace, 9 family rooms.
price	€ 100–€ 200. Singles € 65–€ 134. Family room € 130–€ 260 for 3.
meals	Light lunches only. Good trattoria 800m.
closed	20 November–10 March.
directions	Follow town centre, then ringroad. At Hotel Méditerranée, left into Via Dionisio. At Piazza S. Antonio take Via Pietro Rizzo left of chapel, then Via Roma. Right into Bagnoli Croci.

'Sicily is the schoolroom model of Italy for beginners, with every Italian quality and defect magnified, exasperated and brightly coloured.'
Luigi Barzini

	Signor Christian Pécaut
tel	+39 0942 23791
fax	+39 0942 625830
e-mail	info@villabelvedere.it
web	www.villabelvedere.it

Hotel

Romantik Hotel Villa Ducale

Via L da Vinci 60, 98039 Taormina

The ebullient Dottor Quartucci and his family have restored this fine old village house with panache, re-using lovely old terracotta tiles on the floors and in the bathrooms, and mixing family antiques with brightly painted Sicilian-naive wardrobes and chests. Taormina, with its fabulous bays and lively clientele, is the most fashionable resort in Sicily – rich in archeological and architectural sites, too – and from the flower-filled terrace of Villa Ducale, high on the hill, distance lends enchantment to the view. You can see the sweep of five bays and the looming presence of Mount Etna as you breakfast on Sicilian specialities until late in the morning. Flowers are the keynote of this eccentric little hotel: there are fresh ones in every room, pots, placed like punctuation marks on the steps and terraces, romp with geranium and bougainvillea, and every bedroom features a cornucopia of painted produce – flowers, lemons, pomegranates. The style is antique-Sicilian; the extras – air conditioning, minibar, extra-terrestrial television – entirely modern.

rooms	13 doubles.
price	€ 140–€ 240.
meals	Wide choice of restaurants in centre, 10 minutes by car.
closed	5 December–21 February.
directions	From Taormina centre towards Castelmola. Hotel signposted.

Ancient navigators believed Etna to be the highest point on earth. The Arabs called it Jebel, hence its other name, Mongibello, the 'mountain of mountains'.

	Dottor Andrea Quartucci
tel	+39 0942 28153
fax	+39 0942 28710
e-mail	villaducale@tao.it
web	www.villaducale.com

Hotel

map 19   entry 280

Limoneto

Via del Platano 3, 96100 Siracuse

Dogs doze in the deep shade of the veranda. In the lemon grove, ladders disappear into trees and occasionally shake as another full basket is lowered down. This is 'rustic simplicity' at its best. The main house is modern and white, with as many openings as it has walls, through which chairs, tables and plants burst out on all sides. Lemon and olive trees (buy their olive oil and *limoncello*) stop short of the terrace where meals are eaten throughout the summer. The bedrooms are simple, cabin-like arrangements with unapologetically straightforward furniture. Those in the main house look out across the garden to a play area. Three larger rooms in the pale pink *casa* across the courtyard sleep five, with twin beds on an upper mezzanine level. The jovial Adelina and husband Alceste want to keep alive the traditions of the region and are full of ideas for you: visit Noto, Palazzolo and the soft sands of Siracusa. Tennis, golf and swimming are a short drive. Those who like to get up early (or those whose children oblige them to) can watch the goats being milked nearby, and see how Sicilian cheeses are made. *Air conditioning.*

rooms	8: 2 doubles, 3 triples, 3 family.
price	€ 70–€ 76. Singles € 40-55. Family rooms from € 125.
meals	Sunday lunch (except July & August) € 18. Dinner € 18, on request.
closed	15 November–15 December.
directions	From Catania towards Siracusa, when road becomes motorway, take exit for Palazzolo & follow signs for 'Limoneto'.

'So many lemons! Think of all the lemonade crystals they will be reduced to! Think of America drinking them up next summer.'
D H Lawrence, *Sea & Sardinia*

	Signora Adelina Norcia
tel	+39 0931 717352
fax	+39 0931 717728
e-mail	limoneto@tin.it
web	www.emmeti.it/Limoneto

B&B

Hotel Lady Lusya

96100 Feudo Spinagallo

Over the door of this fine Bourbon house is the coat of arms of the family who first owned it. By the time Lusya's grandfather acquired it, it was in ruins. Now, restored and painted a traditional rusty pink, it has recently opened as a hotel – a new venture for Lusya and her family and the only way they could save the place. It looks very lovely lit up at night and the position and sea views are wonderful. All around are lemon groves and ancient olives, and from the roof terrace you can see a cave where the remains of a dwarf mammoth were found. The oldest part of the house is the breakfast room, which has 16th-century floor tiles, a dovecote and stone basins once used in wine-making. Limestone stairs lead to the bedrooms, which have been simply but very stylishly done. High ceilings give them an air of grandeur and keep them cool and airy. Some are in a separate building and have their own terrace. The suites are splendid, with four-posters and rich fabrics. One has a small fresco found during the renovation work. Lusya and her husband make charming, elegant hosts; they have lived in the US and speak excellent English.

rooms	17 doubles.
price	€ 90–€ 120.
meals	Lunch € 20. Dinner € 25.
closed	Rarely.
directions	SS114, motorway Siracusa-Gela exit Cassibile, after 2km right, signs.

The Armistice between Italy and the Allies was signed in Cassibile on 3rd September 1943.

	Lusya Giardina
tel	+39 0931 710277
fax	+39 0931 710274
e-mail	info@ladylusya.it
web	www.ladylusya.it

Hotel

map 19   entry 282

Bed & Breakfast Villa Sara

Contrada Senna, 97014 Ispica

Once the Caruso family's summer house, Villa Sara is now a relaxed and friendly place to stay thanks to Enrico's gentle manner; he has also worked in city hotels. His parents live nearby; Signora Caruso bakes fabulous cakes and tarts for breakfast and it was Signor Caurso who shaped these surroundings, his architect's eye searching out pleasing angles and his careful attention to detail making the whole place feel simple and uncluttered. Cupboards hide flush to the walls, stylish shutters soften the harsh Sicilian light and low round windows are designed to let moonlight fill the corridor. Bedrooms are minimalist with white, bright walls and bold bedcovers. Upstairs rooms share a long terrace shaded by a huge carob tree. (Families can use a couple of rooms together.) Tiled bathrooms – some huge and with sea views – sparkle and come with solar-heated water. A tree was planted to mark the birth of each of the three children and the garden is now luscious and filled with all kinds of tree: banana, orange, lemon, almond… you can read in their shade, work up a steam on the tennis court, then cool off in the stripey pool.

rooms	7: 5 doubles; 2 doubles with separate bath.
price	€ 50–€ 80.
meals	Restaurants 1.5–4km.
closed	Rarely.
directions	From Siracusa to Ispica; SP46 Ispica-Pozzallo for Pozzallo, house 4km. Signposted.

'Well, Suracusian; say in brief the cause Why thou departest from thy native home, And for what cause thou cam'st to Ephsus.' Shakespeare

	Enrico Caruso
tel	+39 0932 956575
fax	+39 0932 956575
e-mail	villasara@villasara.it
web	www.villasara.it

B&B

Fattoria Mose

Via M. Pascal 4, 92100 Villaggio Mosé

When this area was the hunting ground of Sicilian princes, Fattoria Mose was a mere hunting lodge. Today it still sits proudly on top of its hill but surveys the family's olive groves and the steadily encroaching town beyond. The imposing exterior belies a less austere feel inside – lovely antiques, superb floor tiles and Sicilian candelabra along with family photos and a general informality. The B&B room is here in the main house and has a charming, idiosyncratic bathroom with olive-grove views. Breakfast is in a huge, shutter-shaded dining room, or out on the terrace if it's not too hot. The lazy-Susan is laden with all sorts of jams: lemon, orange, grapefruit, apricot, served on silver. Chiara's family used to escape from the summer heat of Palermo here – there's often a blessedly cooling breeze. An ex-architect, she has converted the stables for guests and the apartments created are big and modern with high, pine-clad ceilings and floral bedspreads, plain white walls and paper lantern lampshades. Most have their own terrace and all spill out onto the lovely plant-packed courtyard (with guests' barbecue).

rooms	1 + 6 apartments: 1 double. 6 apartments (sleep 6, 4 & 2).
price	€80. Apartments €434 for 2, €869 for 4, €1,092 for 6 per week.
meals	Restaurants short drive.
closed	November-22 December, 7 January-March.
directions	From Agrigento SS115 for Gela-Siracusa. At end of Villaggio Mosé road (past supermarkets, houses) left at sign for Fattoria Mosé; signs.

Visit the Valley of the Temples in the early morning light, floodlit by night or when the valley is in full bloom from thousands of almond trees in February.

	Chiara Agnello
tel	+39 092 260 6115
fax	+39 092 260 6115
e-mail	fattoriamose@libero.it
web	www.fattoriamose.com

B&B & Self-catering

map 19 entry 284

Villa Mimosa

La Rocchetta, Selinunte, 91022 Castelvetrano

Not far away are the breathtakingly beautiful Greek temples of the ancient city of Selinunte. They overlook the sea, just a short drive along the main road which passes quite close to Villa Mimosa. The house was a ruin when Jackie found it crumbling among umbrella pines and olive groves six years ago; she has restored and rebuilt it as traditionally as possible. The apartments (self-catering or B&B) stretch along the back of the house and open on to a long, pergola-shaded terrace and a pretty, practical garden full of vines, olives and orange trees. In the spring it's ablaze with poppies. Each apartment is one big room, with a little shower room in one corner and a kitchen area. They are homely, cosy spaces, traditionally furnished with chunky, carved Sicilian armchairs, high antique beds, fine linen and lots of pictures. If you dine with Jackie, you'll eat out on the terrace on her side of the house – or in her *salotto* if the weather isn't good. She's lived in Sicily for over 25 years and is gentle, considerate and very knowledgeable about the island. There are some wonderful beaches and nature reserves nearby.

rooms	3 apartments for 2.
price	€ 50; € 300 per week.
meals	Dinner with wine, € 24; book ahead. Choice of restaurants in Selinunte, 6km.
closed	Rarely.
directions	From Agrigento SS115 to very end, exit Castelvetrano. At end of slip-road sharp right; 2nd entrance on left.

Selinunte gets its name from the wild celery (selinon) which still grows at the mouth of the river.

	Jackie Sirimanne
tel	+39 0924 44583
fax	+39 0924 44583
e-mail	j.sirimanne@virgilio.it
web	www.aboutsicily.net

B&B & Self-catering

Zarbo di Mare

Contrada Zarbo di Mare 37, 91010 San Vito Lo Capo

A simple stone-built house, slap on the sea, on a beautiful stretch of coast to the north-west tip of the island, designed to catch the sun. Sun-worshippers can follow, sunflower-like, the progress of the rays by moving from terrace to terrace through the day; those who seek the shade will be just as happy. A vine-clad courtyard behind the house is a lovely place to take breakfast; you might move to the large shady terrace with a barbecue at the side of the house for lunch... later dine on the front terrace looking out to sea. There are two bedrooms, each with two beds, and the open-plan sitting-room with pine-and-white kitchen has space for a further two to sleep. Below the house are steps down to a private swimming platform – the sea is deep here, and perfect for snorkelling. (Families with small children may prefer to swim from the beach nearby at San Vito, where the water is shallow.) There are some lovely things to see in this part of Sicily, like the extraordinary Greek temple at Segesta, which stands grave and quiet at the head of the valley as it has done for centuries. *Contact numbers are in Belgium.*

rooms	House for 2-4: 2 doubles/twins with bath & shower, sitting room with kitchen area.
price	€ 600–€ 650 per week.
meals	Self-catering.
closed	7 July–20 August.
directions	Approx. 120km from Palermo airport. Motorway to Trapani, exit Castellammare del Golfo. Coast road SS187 to Trapani. San Vito clearly signed. House 3km after village.

	Barbara Yates
tel	+32 25 12 45 26
fax	+32 25 12 45 26
e-mail	barbara.yates@belgacom.net

Beyond 'Monte Cofano' is the 'Grotta Mangiapane'. Inside is an abandoned village, the poignant setting for a yearly enactment of the Christmas story.

Self-catering

map 19 entry 286

Photography by Nick Thomas

sardinia

Hotel Villa Las Tronas

Lungomare Valencia 1, 07041 Alghero

It could be the setting for an Agatha Christie whodunnit (the Hercule Poirot, not Miss Marple variety): a crenellated, late-19th-century hotel dramatically set on a rocky spit of land jutting into the sea. The outer walls, gate and entry phone give the requisite aloof, cut-off feeling and the atmosphere within is hushed and stately. Originally owned by a Piedmontese count, it was bought by the present owners in the 1950s and they take huge pride in the place. The big reception rooms and bedrooms – formal, ornate, immaculate – have a curiously muted, old-fashioned air. Only the high-ceilinged bathrooms are brand new – vibrant with modern fittings and green and blue mosaic tiles. On all sides, windows look down at accusatory fingers of rock pointing into the blue Sardinian waters. There's a little lawned garden, and a swimming pool poised immediately above the rocks – hear the waves crashing below as you bathe. Close by is the pretty, interesting town of Alghero and there are fabulous beaches and good restaurants up and down the coast. An imposing place in a matchless setting.

rooms	26: 22 doubles, 4 suites.
price	€200–€330. Suites €380–€490.
meals	Dinner €50.
closed	Never.
directions	Leave Alghero, signs for Bosa/Lungmare. Hotel on right.

There are thirty-six sandstone tombs, three of which are decorated with stylised bulls' heads, in the necropolis of Anghelu Ruju in Alghero.

Signora Masia

tel	+39 079 981818
fax	+39 079 981044
e-mail	info@hvlt.com
web	www.hvlt.com

Hotel

Hotel Cala di Volpe

Costa Smeralda, 07020 Porto Cervo

Stranded on the north-east Sardinian coast during a yachting holiday in the 1950s, the Aga Khan was bewitched by its barren beauty, crystal waters and magical light. So he bought up a chunk of the coastline and developed a resort with luxury hotels to allow other, well-heeled folk to share his discovery. Hotel Cala di Volpe is like an impossibly perfect village, the vernacular transmuted into a rustic paradise. As well as white rough-plastered walls, wide arches and twisted beams, there are all sorts of unusual features – tree stumps, metal sculptures, coloured bottles set in walls. Big, airy bedrooms are charmingly, self-consciously naïf. But, in case painted murals, rush-seated chairs and Sardinian embroidery don't suffice, you also have the hi-tech accessories so essential to the jet-setting life. Outside, immaculate gardens slope to the sea. There's a gorgeous saltwater pool, but if you prefer the real thing, take the private launch to the hotel beach. Or, if you've over-indulged on Cala di Volpe's fabulous food, walk instead. If you fancy hob-nobbing with the rich and famous, this is the place.

rooms	125: 99 doubles, 18 suites, 8 singles.
price	Half-board only €475–€875 p.p. per night, plus 10% tax.
meals	Restaurant in hotel. Choice of restaurants in Porto Cervo.
closed	November–March.
directions	Fom Olbia follow signs to Costa Smeralda.

	Marco Milocco
tel	+39 0789 976111
fax	+39 0789 976617
e-mail	caladivolpe@luxurycollection.com
web	www.luxurycollection.com/caladivolpe

'Pleasure's a sin, and sometimes sin's a pleasure.' Lord Byron, *Don Juan*

Hotel

map 20   entry 288

Hotel Su Gologone

Loc. Su Gologone, 08025 Oliena

Lavender, myrtle and rosemary scent the valley. The dazzling white buildings of Hotel Su Gologone stand among ancient vineyards and olive groves at the foot of the towering mountains of the Supramonte. The hotel takes its name from a nearby spring and began life in the 1960s as a simple restaurant serving traditional Sardinian dishes – roast suckling pig, wild boar sausages, *dolci sardi* – and the local, potent red wine. It has gradually grown; now the restaurant is famous throughout Europe. Run by the founders' daughter, Giovanna, it employs only local chefs and some of the loveliest waitresses in Italy. (Oliena is as famous for the beauty of its women as for being the home of Gianfranco Zola.) It's an elegant, restrained, magical place in this wilderness region of the island, 30 minutes' drive from the sea. Juniper-beamed bedrooms have intriguing arches and alcoves and make much of local crafts: embroidered cushions, traditional Sardinian fabrics, handmade towels. In the grounds, the enormous pool is fed by cold spring water, and there's an outdoor jacuzzi, too. *Advisable to book in advance between May and September.*

rooms	69: 54 twins/doubles, 15 suites.
price	€91–€119.
meals	Restaurant in hotel.
closed	Rarely.
directions	From Oliena towards Dorgali. Right at sign for Su Gologone; hotel on right.

The first inhabitants of Sardinia were the Nuraghic people, who arrived in 2000BC. The conical stone towers Nuraghi crop up all over Sardinia.

tel	+39 0784 287512
fax	+39 0784 287668
e-mail	gologone@tin.it
web	www.sugologone.it

Hotel

Li Licci

Loc. Valentino Stazzo, La Gruci, 07023 Calangianus

Twenty years ago this tranquil, lovely place was overgrown and inaccessible. Deserted for many years after the death of Gianmichele's grandfather, it was rescued by Jane and Gianmichele in 1985. Once they had moved in, the almost nightly entertaining of friends began. Buckinghamshire-born Jane is an inspired cook of Sardinian food and the entertaining grew into the opening of a delightful restaurant – mentioned in the Michelin guide – using much of their own, organic produce. Now they have added four simple, white-walled guest bedrooms, with basic en suite shower rooms. Jane's approach as a hostess is to look after guests as she would like to be looked after herself; it works wonderfully well. Staying here is like being in the home of a relaxed and hospitable friend. Li Licci has its own wells, producing the most delicious clear water, and a 2,000-year-old olive tree. Breakfast is outside in summer, overlooking the oak woods and hills of Gallura, or by the fire in the converted stables in winter: the perfect start to a day's walking, climbing or sailing... or lazing on the north coast beaches. *Minimum stay two nights.*

rooms	4: 1 double, 2 twins, 1 family for 4.
price	€60–€80. Half-board €65–€75p.p.
meals	Dinner €30–€35.
closed	Rarely.
directions	Through S. Antonio until r'bout, then towards Olbia. After 3.5km right at sign; left through gates, house on right.

	Francesca Abeltino
tel	+39 079 665114
fax	+39 079 665029
e-mail	info@lilicci.com
web	www.lilicci.com

The 1977 film, Padre Padrone, based on Gavino Ledda's autobiography, was filmed in Sardinia.

B&B

map 20 entry 290

Ca' La Somara

Loc. Sarra Balestra, 07020 Arzachena

Only 15 minutes' drive from the coast, but a far cry from the flesh-pots of Costa Smeralda, Ca' La Somara's white buildings stand out against the peaceful wooded hills and jutting limestone crags of Gallura. As you'd expect from the name, donkeys feature here – both in reality (in the ranch-fenced paddocks) or as a painted silhouette (on the main building). They're one of Laura's passions. She's an ex-architect who gave up city life over a decade ago and has used her skill and flair to convert the stables; once used to shelter sheep, they now provide simple, stylish rooms. Bedrooms are traditional with whitewashed plaster walls, locally carved beds and tiled shower rooms. There's also a striking, galleried living/dining room, its stone walls decorated with harnesses and lanterns, farm implements and baskets. And the odd amphora. Dinner is mainly Mediterranean in style, served with Sardinian wines. Outside, scattered benches in the informal garden and hammocks in the paddock give you a chance to lie and gaze over the valley and windswept cork oaks. It's all deliciously restful and undemanding. *Relaxation therapy available.*

rooms	8 doubles.
price	€ 52–€ 84.
meals	Dinner € 17.
closed	Rarely.
directions	From Arzachena towards San Pantaleo. Left at T-junction for S. Pantaleo, signs.

There are over 60 Romanesque churches on Sardinia – all quite small and simple because of the poverty of the islanders.

Alberto & Laura Lagattolla

tel	+39 0789 98969
fax	+39 0789 98969
e-mail	calasomara@libero.it
web	www.italiaagriturismo.net/calasomara

B&B

Is Morus Relais

Santa Margherita di Pula, 09010 Pula

Quiet, understated luxury in a magical spot – the hacienda-style hotel sits scattered among the eucalyptus and the pines on its own perfect piece of the Mediterranean. The pale sands of its beach are lapped by turquoise waters – crystal clear apart from the seaweedy fronds – and the scent of the pines is all-pervading. The resort dates from the Fifties and has grown organically; bedrooms are divided between those in the main building and those in the villas. Interiors are elegant with white walls, tiled floors, wrought-iron bedsteads, silk drapes. Loll by the curvaceous pool – the deep blue loungers perfectly match the water – and when you're done with lolling, step inside for a massage or a manicure. Colourful local dishes are served on the terrace restaurant, and there's a snack bar on the beach for lunch. When you decide a little diversion or excursion might be in order, you'll find you're a shuttle-ride away from golf, 100m from horse-riding on the ranch, and an easy drive from the Punic-Roman charms of Nora, once Sardinia's most important city.

rooms	85: 69 doubles, 16 single. Some rooms in main building (ask for view), others in villas.
price	Half-board € 200–€ 560.
meals	Half-board only.
closed	November–Easter.
directions	From Cagliari airport for Pula & Teulada, road no. 195. After 40km Relais signposted.

Maurizio Maffei

tel	+39 070 921 171
fax	+39 070 921 596
e-mail	ismorusrelais@tin.it
web	www.ismorusrelais.it

Grazia Deledda (born in Nuoro 1871)
Sardinian novelist and writer was awarded the
Nobel Prize for Literature in 1926, one of only
nine women to have received the prize.

Hotel

map 20   entry 292

WHAT'S IN THE BACK OF THE BOOK?

GLOSSARY

Italian words which appear in our descriptions

affresco	a wall painting (the pigment being applied while the plaster is still wet)
all'aria aperta	in the open air
all'antica	in the old or antique style
belvedere	a gazebo or open-sided room, often on the roof
borgo	village
cantina	cellar or winery
cantucci	almond biscuits
casa	house
casa padronale	manor house
casa colonica	farm house
cascina	originally a farm
casetta	little house
centro storico	historic centre, the old part of town
Cinquecento	sixteenth century
Coraggio!	Take courage!
digestivo	digestive (usually a drink after dinner)
dipendenza	annexe
di lusso	luxury
duomo	cathedral
enoteca	a stock of vintage wines
giallo	yellow
grotteschi	fanciful ornament in paint or stucco
loggia	gallery open on one or more sides, often with columns
masseria	originally a farm
palazzo	palace/mansion
pecorino	cheese made from sheep's milk
piazzetta	little square
pietra serena	a grey-green type of stone used decoratively in architecture
podere	farm, estate
Quattrocento	fifteenth century
sala	hall, room
salone / salotto	sitting room
Siete quasi arrivati	You are almost there
stemma	coat-of-arms
stube	bar (German)
Vin Santo	Tuscan sweet wine
villetta	little villa

USEFUL VOCABULARY

Making the booking	Do you speak English?	*Parla inglese?*
	Do you have a	*Avete una camera*
	single/double	*singola/matrimoniale*
	Twin/triple room available?	*doppia/tripla (disponibile)?*
	For this evening/tomorrow	*Per questa sera/domani sera*
	With private bathroom	*Con bagno (privato)*
	Shower/bathtub	*Doccia/vasca*
	Balcony	*Balcone*
	Is breakfast included?	*La colazione è compresa?*
	Half-board	*Mezza pensione*
	Full-board	*Pensione completa*
	How much does it cost?	*Quanto costa?*
	We will arrive at 6pm	*Arriveremo verso le sei*
	We would like to have dinner	*Vorremmo cenare qui*
	What is the charge?	*Quanto costa, per favore?*
	Left/right	*Sinistra/destra*
	Excuse me	*Mi scusi*
Getting There	We're lost	*Ci siamo persi*
	Where is....?	*Dov'è....?*
	Could you show us on the map	*Mi può indicare sulla cartina*
	Where are we?	*Dove siamo?*
	We are in Florence	*Siamo a Firenze*
	We will be late	*Arriveremo tardi*
On Arrival	Hello	*Buon giorno* (am-mid-pm)
		Buona sera (mid-pm-evening)
	May I see a room?	*Posso vedere una camera?*
	I would like to book a room	*Vorrei prenotare una camera*
	We will stay three nights	*Ci fermeremo tre notti*
While you are there	A light bulb needs replacing	*C'è una lampadina fulminata*
	The room is too cold/hot	*La camera è troppo fredda/calda*
	Do you have a fan?	*Ha un ventilatore?*
	There is no hot water	*Non c'è acqua calda*
	What time is...	*A che ora c'è...*
	breakfast/lunch/dinner?	*la colazione/il pranzo/la cena?*
On Leaving	We would like to pay the bill	*Vorremmo pagare il conto*
	Do you take credit cards?	*Accetta la carta di credito?*
	Are you looking for a new	*Cercate altro personale per*
	employee by any chance?	*caso?*
	Goodbye!	*Arrivederci!*

CITTÀSLOW - SLOW CITY MOVEMENT

They are considered jewels of modern Italian living: cobblestoned Orvieto in Umbria, vineyard-wrapped Greve in Tuscany and perfect Positano, perched above the Amalfi coast.

These small towns are also at the forefront of a young but growing movement, Cittàslow. All over the country, councils are queuing up to climb on this very Italian bandwagon, and so far, fifty or more (maximum population 50,000) have made the committment to resist Americanisation and to "go slow". No car alarms, no neon signs, no McDonald's

It's a spin-off of the anti-fast-food movement, Slow Food, founded in 1986: Italy's way of thumbing its nose at multi-national fast foods, hot dogs and fat-friendly meals. Today the organisation spans 50 countries and has a membership of over 70,000. Ludlow in Shropshire has been selected to pilot the scheme in Britain, and in parts of the US Americans are waking up to "the delicious revolution". Fast times call for slow food, and food tastes best when it is grown organically, harvested locally and eaten in season. Slow Food believers celebrate meals prepared with love and consumed at leisure — as in Italy, where life grinds to a magnificent halt in the middle of the day. The logo — a snail inching past two buildings, one modern, one ancient — says it all.

Cittàslow not only resists the globalisation of food and culture but positively applauds the values of diversity. It is not a reactionary movement but a forward-looking one, both cherishing and preserving local traditions and at the same time encouraging the best of new technology. "Orvieto is a slow city, not a backward one," says its mayor. Low-energy transport systems are being introduced and street lighting systems are being redesigned... with a bit of luck, we'll soon be able to see the stars.

Radical in its quiet way, Cittàslow provides a counter-balance to our culture of haste — to cities besieged by car, noise and air pollution, to skipped lunches and the 50-hour week. Manhattan and Rome throb to a different beat... but how right it seems that cars are banned during the day in medieval Montefalco, and scooters after 10pm. Pedestrian areas are being enlarged, parking removed from historic centres, eco-friendly architecture sponsored. The fruit in Bra's schools is 100% organic, every council speaks up for recycling, every town square rejoices in its farmers'

CITTÀSLOW - SLOW CITY MOVEMENT

market, and there is a real effort to boost the rural economy. Tourism is profiting too, as wealthy globe-trotters are happy to pay good money to escape life in the fast lane and relearn the slow.

Towns with Cittàslow status at the time of going to press

Asti
Bra
Canale
Castelnuovo Berardenga
Castelnuovo di Garfagnana
Castiglione del Lago
Chiavenna
Città di Castello
Civitella in Val di Chiana
Francavilla al Mare
Greve in Chianti
Loreto
Martinafranca
Massa Marittima
Medea
Orvieto
Palestrina
Penne
Positano
Rivello
San Daniele del Friul
San Miniato
San Vincenzo
Sangemini
Satriano
Teglio
Todi
Trani
Trevi
Urbino
Verteneglio
Viareggio
Zibello

www.cittaslow.stratos.it

FAI - FONDO PER L'AMBIENTE ITALIANO

For over 25 years FAI, the Italian Artistic Environment Foundation, has been contributing to the protection and care of Italy's cultural and environmental heritage. It has over 30,000 members, 59 regional offices and 1,500 volunteers. Today FAI protects and cares for 30 fabulous fragments of the Italian heritage, among them historic houses, castles, gardens, parks and beautiful natural sites.

The ongoing work of FAI includes plans for the restoration of the ancient paths around Ieranto Bay on the Amalfi coast, replanting olive trees and opening this beautiful stretch of coast to the public.

The garden at Kolymbetra in the Valley of the Temples at Agrigento, Sicily, is another project, restoring the garden to its former glory, replanting orange trees and opening it to the public.

The properties below, which are owned by FAI, are open to the public. The opening times given may vary and check with the individual property, or consult the FAI web site before setting out.

Villa Della Porta Bozzolo – Casalzuigno (Varese)
October-December 10am-1pm & 2pm-5pm
February-September 10am-1pm & 2pm-6pm
Closed Mondays (except public holidays), January and last two weeks December. Tel: 0332 624136

Villa Menafoglio Litta Panza – Varese
Tuesday-Sunday 10am-6pm; closed Mondays (except public holidays), Christmas Day and New Year's Day. Tel: 0332 239669

Villa del Balbianello – Lenno (Como)
April-October 10am-12.30am & 3.30pm-6.30pm every day except Mondays and Wednesdays. Tel: 0344 56110

Monastero di Torba – Gornate Olona (Varese)
October-December 10am-1pm & 2pm-5pm
February-September 10am-1pm & 2pm-6pm
Closed Mondays (except public holidays), January and last two weeks December. Tel: 0331 820301

San Fruttuoso Abbey – Camogli (Genoa)
December, January, February public holidays only 10am-4pm; March, April 10am-4am; May 10-6; June-Sept 10-6; Oct 10-4 open every day (except public holidays). Closed November . Tel: 0185 772703

FAI - FONDO PER L'AMBIENTE ITALIANO

Castello di Avio – Avio (Trento)
October-December 10am-1pm & 2pm-5pm
February-September 10am-1pm & 2pm-6pm
Closed Mondays (except public holidays), January and last two weeks December. Tel: 0464 684453

Castello della Manta – Manta (Cuneo)
October-December 10am-1pm & 2pm-5pm
February-September 10am-1pm & 2pm-6pm
Closed Mondays (except public holidays), January and last two weeks December. Tel: 0175 87822

Castel Grumello – Montagna in Valtellina (Sondrio)
October-February Saturdays & Sundays 10am-5pm;
March-September Saturdays & Sundays 10am-6pm.
Tuesday-Friday by appointment. Closed Mondays
(except public holidays) and January.

Teatrino di Vetriano – Pescaglia (Lucca)
Visits by appointment only. Closed Mondays (except public holidays), January and last two weeks December.
Tel: +39 0583 358118

Giardino della Kolymbetra – Valley of the Temples (Agrigento, Sicily)
November-March 10am-5.30pm; April-October 10am-7pm
Closed Mondays (except public holidays) and 7-31 Jan.

Baia di Ieranto – Massa Lubrense (Naples)
Open from dawn to one hour before sunset.
Guided visit by appointment.

Edicola per giornali – Mantova

Collezione De'Micheli – Milan

Bottega di Barbiere – Genoa
Vicolo Caprettari 14/rosso. Open 8.30am-4.30pm

New places to visit
Parco "Villa Gregoriana" – Tivoli (Rome)
Casa Necchi Campiglio – Milan
Casa Carbone – Lavagna (Genoa)

FAI Head office
Viale Coni Zugna 5, 20144 Milan
tel: 02 4676151 fax: 02 48193631
e-mail: info@fondoambiente.it web: www.fondoambiente.it

EUROPE - COURSES & ACTIVITIES

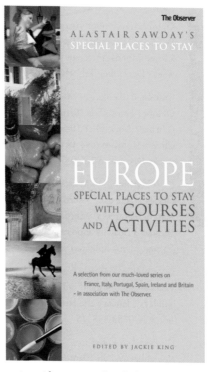

The properties with entry numbers below also appear in our
Europe: Special Places to Stay with Courses & Activities guide
(£12.99).

Art & Culture • 124 • 129 • Arts & Crafts • 119 • 135 • 175 •
210 • 217 • 226 • 247 • 265 • Cities • 28 • 122 • 124 •
Cookery • 4 • 68 • 69 • 97 • 106 • 110 • 114 • 122 • 124 •
129 • 135 • 157 • 165 • 170 • 186 • 191 • 197 • 203 • 210 •
217 • 226 • 241 • 247 • 260 • 262 • 265 • Drawing, Painting &
Sculpture • 60 • 97 • 110 • 114 • 129 • 135 • 170 • Flora &
Fauna • 34 • 68 • 114 • 191 • Food & Wine • 28 • 60 • 68 • 69
• 110 • 114 • 119 • 122 • 124 • 135 • 165 • 170 • 191 • 203 •
210 • 217 • 241 • Gardens & Gardening • 106 • 157 • History
• 79 • 129 • 185 • 247 • 260 • Landscape • 124 • Languages &
Creative Writing • 28 • 34 • 110 • 122 • 185 • 186 • 191 • 232
• Mind, Body & Spirit • 28 • 60 • 197 • 241 • 266 • Music &
Dance • 135 • 197 • Photography & Video • 34 • Sports &
Outdoor Pursuits • 34 • 69 • 79 • 94 • 97 • 106 • 185 • 186 •
197 • 217 • 262 • 266

WHAT IS ALASTAIR SAWDAY PUBLISHING?

Twenty or so of us work in converted barns on a farm near Bristol, close enough to the city for a bicycle ride and far enough for a silence broken only by horses and the occasional passage of a tractor. Some editors work in the countries they write about, e.g. France; others work from the UK but are based outside the office. We enjoy each other's company, celebrate every event possible, and work in an easy-going but committed environment.

These books owe their style and mood to Alastair's miscellaneous career and his interest in the community and the environment

These books owe their style and mood to Alastair's miscellaneous career and his interest in the community and the environment. He has taught overseas, worked with refugees, run development projects abroad, founded a travel company and several environmental organisations. There has been a slightly unconventional streak throughout, not least in his driving of a waste-paper-collection lorry, the manning of stalls at jumble sales and the pursuit of causes long before they were considered sane.

Back to the travel company: trying to take his clients to eat and sleep in places that were not owned by corporations and assorted bandits he found dozens of very special places in France – farms, châteaux etc – a list that grew into the first book, *French Bed and Breakfast*. It was a celebration of 'real' places to stay and the remarkable people who run them.

The publishing company grew from that first and rather whimsical French book. It started as a mild crusade, and there it stays – full of 'attitude', and the more appealing for it. For we still celebrate the unusual, the beautiful, the individual. We are passionate about rejecting the banal, the ugly, the pompous and the indifferent and we are passionate, too, about 'real' food. Alastair is a trustee of the Soil Association and keen to promote organic growing and consuming by owners and visitors.

It is a source of deep pleasure to us to know that there are many thousands of people who share our views. We are by no means alone in trumpeting the virtues of resisting the destruction and uniformity of so much of our culture – and the cultures of other nations, too.

We run a company in which people and values matter. We love to hear of new friendships between those in the book and those using it, and to know that there are many people – among them farmers – who have been enabled to pursue their decent lives thanks to the extra income our books bring them.

WWW.SPECIALPLACESTOSTAY.COM

Britain

France

Ireland

Italy

Portugal

Spain

Morocco

India...

all in one place!

On the unfathomable and often unnavigable sea of online accommodation pages, those who have discovered **www.specialplacestostay.com** have found it to be an island of reliability. Not only will you find a database full of trustworthy, up-to-date information about all the Special Places to Stay across Europe, but also:

· Links to the web sites of all of the places in the series

· Colourful, clickable, interactive maps to help you find the right place

· The opportunity to make most bookings by e-mail – even if you don't have e-mail yourself

· Online purchasing of our books, securely and cheaply

· Regular, exclusive special offers on books

· The latest news about future editions and future titles

The site is constantly evolving and is frequently updated with news and special features that won't appear anywhere else but in our window on the worldwide web.

Russell Wilkinson, Web Producer
website@specialplacestostay.com

If you'd like to receive news and updates about our books by e-mail, send a message to newsletter@specialplacestostay.com

FRAGILE EARTH SERIES

The Little Earth Book
Now in its third edition and
as engrossing and
provocative as ever,
it continues to highlight
the perilously fragile
state of our planet.
£6.99

The Little Food Book
Makes for a wonderfully
stimulating read – one that
may change your
attitude to the
food choices you
make daily.
£6.99

The Little Money Book
Could make you look
at everything financial –
from your bank statements
to the coins in
your pocket –
in a whole new way.
Available November 2003
£6.99

This fascinating series has been praised by politicians,
academics, environmentalists, civil servants – and 'general'
readers. It has come as a blast of fresh air, blowing away
confusion and incomprehension.

www.fragile-earth.com

SIX DAYS

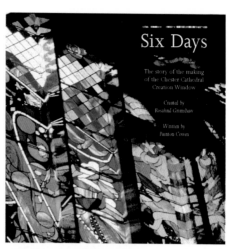

Celebrating the triumph of creativity over adversity

An inspiring and moving story of the making of the stained glass Creation window at Chester Cathedral by a woman battling with Parkinson's disease.

"Within a few seconds, the tears were running down my cheeks. The window was one of the most beautiful things I had ever seen. It is a tour-de-force, playing with light like no other window ..."

Anthropologist Hugh Brody

In 1983, Ros Grimshaw, a distinguished designer, artist and creator of stained-glass windows, was diagnosed with Parkinson's disease. Refusing to allow her illness to prevent her from working, Ros became even more adept at her craft, and in 2000 won the commission to design and make the Creation Stained Glass Window for Chester Cathedral.

Six Days traces the evolution of the window from the first sketches to its final, glorious completion as a rare and wonderful tribute to Life itself: for each of the six 'days' of creation recounted in Genesis, there is a scene below that is relevant to the world of today and tomorrow.

Extracts from Ros's diary capture the personal struggle involved. Superb photography captures the luminescence of the stunning stained glass, while the story weaves together essays, poems, and moving contributions from Ros's partner, Patrick Costeloe.

Available from Alastair Sawday Publishing £12.99

ORDER FORM UK

All these books are available in major bookshops or you may order them direct. **Post and packaging are FREE within the UK.**

		Price	No. copies
French Bed & Breakfast	Edition 8	£15.99	
French Hotels, Châteaux & Inns (Nov 03)	Edition 3	£13.99	
French Holiday Homes (Jan 04)	Edition 2	£11.99	
Paris Hotels	Edition 4	£9.99	
British Bed & Breakfast	Edition 8	£14.99	
British Hotels, Inns & Other Places (Nov 03)	Edition 5	£13.99	
Bed & Breakfast for Garden Lovers	Edition 2	£14.99	
British Holiday Homes	Edition 1	£9.99	
London	Edition 1	£9.99	
Ireland	Edition 4	£12.99	
Spain	Edition 5	£13.99	
Portugal	Edition 2	£8.99	
Italy	Edition 3	£12.99	
Europe with courses & activities	Edition 1	£12.99	
India (Oct 03)	Edition 1	£10.99	
Morocco (Dec 03)	Edition 1	£10.99	
The Little Earth Book	Edition 3	£6.99	
The Little Food Book	Edition 1	£6.99	
The Little Money Book (Nov 03)	Edition 1	£6.99	
Six Days		£12.99	

Please make cheques payable to Alastair Sawday Publishing   Total £ _____ _____

Please send cheques to: Alastair Sawday Publishing,
The Home Farm Stables, Barrow Gurney, Bristol BS48 3R N.
For credit card orders call 01275 464891 or order directly
from our web site **www.specialplacestostay.com**

Title   First name   Surname

Address

Postcode   Tel

If you do not wish to receive mail from other like-minded companies,
please tick here ☐

If you would prefer not to receive information about special offers on our books,
please tick here ☐

ORDER FORM USA

All these books are available at your local bookstore, or you may order direct. Allow two to three weeks for delivery.

		Price	No. copies
Europe (Spring 04)	Edition 1	$19.99	
Morocco (Dec 03)	Edition 1	$15.95	
Spain	Edition 5	$19.95	
Ireland	Edition 4	$17.95	
French Bed & Breakfast	Edition 8	$19.95	
Paris Hotels	Edition 4	$14.95	
British Bed & Breakfast	Edition 8	$19.95	
British Holiday Homes	Edition 1	$14.95	
British Hotels, Inns and other places (Jan 04)	Edition 5	$17.95	
French Hotels, Châteaux and Inns (Jan 04)	Edition 3	$19.95	
Portugal	Edition 2	$14.95	
London	Edition 1	$12.95	
French Holiday Homes (Mar 04)	Edition 2	$17.95	

Total $ _____ _____

Shipping in the continental USA: $3.95 for one book,
$4.95 for two books, $5.95 for three or more books.   _____ _____
Outside continental USA, call (800) 243-0495 for prices.
For delivery to AK, CA, CO, CT, FL, GA, IL, IN, KS, MI, MN, MO, NE,
NM, NC, OK, SC, TN, TX, VA, and WA, please add appropriate sales tax.

Please make checks payable to: **Total $** _____ _____
The Globe Pequot Press

To order by phone with MasterCard or Visa: (800) 243-0495,
9am to 5pm EST; by fax: (800) 820-2329, 24 hours;
through our web site: **www.GlobePequot.com**; or by mail:
The Globe Pequot Press, P.O. Box 480, Guilford, CT 06437

Date

Name

Address

Town

State

Zip code

Tel

Fax

REPORT FORM

If you have any comments on entries in this guide, please let us have them. If you have a favourite house, hotel, inn or other new discovery, anywhere, please let us know about it.

Existing Entry:

Name of property: _____

Entry no: _____ Edition no: _____

New recommendation:

Name of property: _____

Address: _____

_____

_____

_____

Tel: _____

Comments:

_____

_____

_____

_____

_____

_____

_____

_____

_____

Your name: _____

Address: _____

_____

Tel & e-mail: _____

Please send the completed form to:

Alastair Sawday Publishing, The Home Farm Stables, Barrow Gurney, Bristol BS48 3RW
or go to www.specialplacestostay.com and click on 'contact'.

Thank you.

BOOKING FORM

All'attenzione di:
To:
_____
Date:
_____

Egregio Signor, Gentile Signora,

Vorrei fare una prenotazione in nome di:
Please could you make us a reservation in the name of:
_____

Per	*notte/notti*	*Arrivo: giorno*	*mese*	*anno*
For	night(s)	Arriving: day	month	year
		Partenza: giorno	*mese*	*anno*
		Leaving: day	month	year

Si richiede :   *camera/e sistemazione in:*
We would like   room/s, arranged as follows:

Doppia/e	*Due letti*
Double bed	Twin beds
Tripla/e	*Singola/e*
Triple	Single
Suite	*Appartamento*
Suite	Apartment

Si richiede anche la cena per . ... persone il ....
We will also be requiring dinner for ...... person on .... (date)

Per cortesia inviarmi una conferma della mia prenotazione al mio indirizzo in fondo pagina.
Please could you send us confirmation of our reservation to the address below.

Nome: Name:
_____
Indirizzo: Address:
_____
_____
Tel No: E-mail:
_____
Fax No:
_____

Scheda di Prenotazione — Special Places to Stay: Italy

QUICK REFERENCE INDICES

Organic   Owners of these places tell us that they grow and/or use organic produce. Many are certified organic.
Piedmont • 5 • 7 • Valle D'Aosta • 15 • Emilia-Romagna • 67 • Liguria 89 • 91 • 96 • Tuscany • 173 • Umbria • 214 • Marches • 223 • Campania • 255 • 256 • 264 • Puglia • 273 • Sicily • 277

Wine   These owners have vineyards or are small wine producers.
Piedmont • 5 • 6 • 10 • Veneto • 38 • Friuli-Venezia Giulia • 60 • Emilia-Romangna • 76 • 77 • 78 • Liguria • 93 • Tuscany • 115 • 130 • 131 • 132 • 135 • 136 • 140 • 141 • 145 • 173 • 183 • Umbria • 185 • 201 • 208 • 214 • Marches • 223 • 225 • Campania • 245 •

Olive oil   These places produce their own olive oil.
Lombardy • 27 • Veneto • 35 • 38 • Emilia-Romangna • 77 • 78 Liguria • 93 • Tuscany • 127 • 131 • 132 • 135 • 140 • 141 • 153 • 154 • 171 • 173• Umbria • 200 • 201 • 208 • 214 • 215 • Marches • 225 • Campania • 255 • 256 • Sicily • 281

Horses   These places offer, or can organise, horse-riding.
Piedmont • 9 • Lombardy • 22 • 29 • Emilia-Romagna • 64 • 69 • Liguria • 91 • Tuscany • 133 • 141 • 143 • 156 • Umbria • 214 • Marches • 223 • Lazio • 239 • Campania • 260

Gardens   These places have exceptional gardens.
Piedmont • 2 • 3 • 8 • Lombardy • 27 • 28 • Veneto • 35 • 37 • 39 • 41 • 54 • Liguria • 81 • 87 • 95 • Tuscany • 108 • 115 • 117 • 126 • 132 • 134 • 144 • 148 • 154 • 157 • 165 • 170 • 176 • 178 • 179 • Umbria • 187 • 190 • 207 • Marches • 224 • Lazio • 230 • 237 • 238 • Campania • 247 • 250 • Calabria • 265 • Basilicata • 266 • Sicily • 278 • 279

Public Transport   You can easily reach these places by public transport.
Lombardy • 20 • 23 • 24 • Veneto • 41 • 42 • 43 • 44 • 45 • 46 • 47 • 48 • 49 • 50 • 51 • 52 • 53 • Emilia-Romagna • 70 • 71 • 72 • 73 • 74 • 75 • Liguria • 81 • Tuscany • 116 • 118 • 119 • 120 • 121 • 122 • 172 • Lazio • 228 • 229 • 230 • 231 • 232 • 233 • 234 • 235 • 236 • Campania • 248 • 249 • 250 • 251 • 252 • 253 • Puglia • 269 • Sicily • 278 • 279

QUICK REFERENCE INDICES

Self-catering These places have self-catering accommodation.
Piedmont • 2 • 3 • 5 • 7 • 8 • 11 • 12 • Valle D'Aosta • 16 •
Lombardy • 18 • 23 • 29 • 30 • Veneto • 35 • 38 • 39 • 41 • 42
• 46 • 49 • 50 • 54 • Friuli-Venezia Giulia • 60 • Emilia-
Romangna • 65 • 76 • Liguria • 79 • 80 • 88 • 89 • 93 • 94 •
95 • Tuscany • 99 • 100 • 101 • 103 • 105 • 106 • 107 • 108 •
109 • 111 • 112 • 113 • 114 • 115 • 124 • 125 • 126 • 127 •
128 • 129 • 131 • 132 • 135 • 136 • 137 • 139 • 140 • 144 •
145 • 147 • 148 • 152 • 154 • 155 • 156 • 157 • 158 • 159 •
160 • 161 • 162 • 170 • 173 • 176 • 177 • 179 • 180 •183 •
Umbria • 187 • 188 • 192 • 194 • 195 • 198 • 199 • 200 • 201
• 202 • 203 • 204 • 205 • 207 • 208 • 211 • 215 • 216 • 218 •
Marches • 221 • 222 • 224 • 225 • Abruzzo-Molise • 226 •
Lazio • 231 • 232 • 236 • 237 • 239 • 242 • 243 • Campania •
256 • 259 • 264 • Calabria • 265 • Basilicata • 267 • Puglia •
268 • 270 • 271 • 272 • Sicily • 278 • 284 • 285 • 286

Good value These places have rooms for two for under € 100 per night.
Piedmont • 2 • 3 • 4 • 5 • 6 • 7 • 8 • 9 • 10 • 11 • 12 • Valle
D'Aosta • 14 • 15 • 16 • Lombardy • 17 • 19 • 21 • 22 • 23 • 26 •
27 • 28 • 29 • Trentino-Alto Adige • 33 • 34 • Veneto • 36 • 40 •
44 • 45 • 46 • 51 • 52 • 53 • 54 • 55 • 56 • 57 • Friuli-Venezia
Giulia • 59 • 62 • Emilia-Romangna • 64 • 65 • 67 • 68 • 69 • 72 •
73 • 76 • Liguria • 82 • 84 • 88 • 91 • 94 • 96 • Tuscany • 97 • 98 •
100 • 104 • 105 • 120 • 121 • 123 • 128 • 129 • 132 • 133 • 136 •
138 • 141 • 142 • 146 • 156 • 159 • 161 • 162 • 166 • 171 • 174 •
175 • 182 • Umbria • 191 • 192 • 193 • 196 • 203 • 209 • 215 •
218 • 220 • Marches • 221 • 223 • 225 • Abruzzo-Molise • 226 •
Lazio • 228 • 237 • 238 • 239 • 242 • 243 • 244 • Campania • 245
• 247 • 248 • 249 • 252 • 253 • 254 • 255 • 256 • 260 • 264 •
Calabria • 265 • Basilicata • 267 • Puglia • 268 • 271 • 272 • Sicily
• 277 • 281 • 282 • 283 • 284 • 285 • Sardinia • 289 • 290 • 291

Wheelchair These owners have told us they have facilities for people in
wheelchairs. Do confirm what is available when booking.
Piedmont • 7 • Valle D'Aosta • 13 • Lombardy • 22 • 29 •
Trentino-Alto Adige • 31 • Veneto • 39 • 54 • Friuli-Venezia Giulia
60 • Emilia-Romangna • 76 • Liguria • 83 • 86 • 91 • Tuscany •
102 • 115 • 127 • 141 • 142 • 143 • 149 • 157 • 161 • 167 • 168 •
Umbria • 186 • 189 • 190 • 210 • 217 • Marches • 225 • Lazio •
234 • 235 •243 • Campania • 261 • Puglia • 269 • Sicily • 277 •
282 • 284

INDEX - TOWN

INDEX - TOWN

INDEX - TOWN

INDEX - TOWN

INDEX - PROPERTY NAME

INDEX - PROPERTY NAME

INDEX - PROPERTY NAME

INDEX - PROPERTY NAME

INDEX - PROPERTY NAME

HOW TO USE THIS BOOK

explanations

❶ rooms

Assume all rooms are 'en suite' unless we say otherwise.

If a room is not 'en suite' we say **with separate,** or **with shared bathroom**: the former you will have to yourself, the latter may be shared with other guests or family member. Where an entry reads 4+2 this means 4 rooms and 2 self-catering apartments or similar.

❷ room price

The price shown is for one night for two sharing a room. A price range incorporates room/seasonal differences. We say when the price is per week for self-catering.

❸ meals

Prices are per person. Meals in B&B must be booked in advance.

❹ closed

When given in months, this means for the whole of the named months and the time in between.

❺ directions

Use as a guide; the owner can give more details.

❻ map & entry numbers

Map page number; entry number.

❼ type of place

❽ vignette

❾ symbols

See the last page of the book for fuller explanation:

sample entry

PUGLIA

Acquarossa

C. de Acquarossa 2, 72014 Casalini, Brindisi

It's like a fairytale. You're high in the hills above the quiet Itria valley, looking out over olive groves and orchards. Suddenly the *strada bianca* peters out among scrubby juniper bushes and there, in front of you… an extraordinary cluster of round buildings, their conical roofs topped by stone balls. Acquarossa is a 19th-century *trulli* settlement and some of the foundations go back 500 years. Timeless and disarming, the restored, white-painted stone buildings stand in courtyards and terraces lavishly planted with clumps of lavender and herbs, surrounded by arches and drystone walls. Their immensely thick walls and pointed roofs make them beautifully cool in summer, and the little rooms have been delightfully, rustically decorated. Delicious country antiques, niches bright with flowers, voile curtains over small, deep windows and arched doorways, flagged floors and wood-burning stoves – an imaginative mix of style and tradition. The bathrooms are simple and pretty; the kitchens tiny and minimalist. And if you have the urge to cook something ambitious, there's an oven in the courtyard.

rooms	6: 3 doubles, 3 family rooms.
price	€78–€91. Family rooms €88–€103.
meals	Choice of restaurants nearby. Self-catering in family rooms.
closed	Rarely.
directions	SS379 for Bari; exit Ostuni-Villanova for Ostuni. At Agip station, left up road to r'bout, signed 'Strada dei Colli'. Left after '200m fine strada' sign. Uphill for 1km & left at end of road. Track ends at Acquarossa.

Puglia produces some distinctive food and dishes and holds various food festivals every year. The Sagna della puccia celebrates the small bread shapes that are filled with olives and grapes.

	Luca Montinaro
tel	+39 080 4444 093
fax	+39 0831 524826
e-mail	lucamontinaro@libero.it
web	www.acqua-rossa.com

❼ B&B & Self-catering

❻ entry 272 map 19

❶
❷
❸
❹
❺

❾

---

wheelchair facilities

step-free access to bathroom/bedroom

all children welcome

no smoking anywhere

smoking restrictions

credit cards accepted

English-speaking hosts

vegetarians catered for with advance warning

pets can sleep in your bedroom

this house has pets

working farm

swimming pool

bike hire

walking nearby

And for self-catering properties…

shop within 5km